The Promise of Lutheran Ethics

KAREN L. BLOOMQUIST and JOHN R. STUMME, Editors

Fortress Press

Minneapolis

THE PROMISE OF LUTHERAN ETHICS

Published in cooperation with and with funding from the Division for Church in Society of the Evangelical Lutheran Church in America.

Cover design: Marti Naughton
Interior design: Julie Odland Smith

ISBN 0-8006-3132-3

Manufactured in the U.S.A.   AF 1-3132

02   01   00   99   98   1   2   3   4   5   6   7   8   9   10

Contents

Contributors

Robert Benne is Jordan-Trexler Professor of Religion, Roanoke College, Salem, Virginia.

Karen L. Bloomquist is Director for Studies, Division for Church in Society, Evangelical Lutheran Church in America, Chicago, Illinois, and Associate Professor of Theological Ethics, Wartburg Theological Seminary, Dubuque, Iowa.

James M. Childs Jr. is Dean of Academic Affairs and Joseph A. Sittler Professor of Theology and Ethics, Trinity Lutheran Seminary, Columbus, Ohio.

David E. Fredrickson is Associate Professor of New Testament, Luther Seminary, St. Paul, Minnesota.

Reinhard Hütter is Associate Professor of Christian Ethics and Theology, Lutheran School of Theology at Chicago, Illinois.

Cynthia D. Moe-Lobeda is a doctoral student, Union Theological Seminary, New York, New York.

Richard J. Perry Jr. is Assistant Professor of Church and Society, Urban Ministry, Lutheran School of Theology at Chicago, Illinois.

Larry L. Rasmussen is Reinhold Niebuhr Professor of Social Ethics, Union Theological Seminary, New York, New York.

Martha Ellen Stortz is Professor of Historical Theology and Ethics, Pacific Lutheran Theological Seminary, Berkeley, California.

John R. Stumme is Associate Director for Studies, Division for Church in Society, Evangelical Lutheran Church in America, Chicago, Illinois.

Introduction

A Tradition of Christian Ethics

John R. Stumme

Christian ethics thinks and talks about the moral life from within the life of faith. This book brings a Lutheran accent to this venerable, ongoing ecumenical conversation. It arises out of the life of one church body that confesses to be part of the "one, holy, catholic and apostolic church." It stands within a distinctive tradition that shares with other traditions faith in the God of Scriptures and the church's historic creeds and the challenges that the church and world face in our turbulent times.

The authors of the essays in this book are "on assignment" to help members of the Evangelical Lutheran Church in America to think through the nature of Christian ethics today. These teachers of the Church bring the uniqueness of their own experience, interests, and gifts to a common project: to clarify, deepen, and enliven a contemporary Lutheran understanding of the moral life. The authors do not, of course, resolve all the questions, perennial and new, about Lutheran ethics nor produce a single harmonious treatise. They all, however, illumine basic dimensions of the moral life from within the life of faith, and together their essays comprise a significant contribution to the Lutheran church and the ecumenical conversation.

A Lutheran accent in Christian ethics is marked inevitably by the Reformation's witness to Jesus Christ, God's savior of sinners. "We receive forgiveness of sin and become righteous before God by grace, for Christ's sake, through faith."[1] The witness takes on a critical edge (not "by our own merits, works, or satisfactions") when we trust our moral activity to achieve what comes only as God's gift in faith. This no, however, is in service of affirming the moral life, for love is the fruit of faith. The faith that trusts God's saving love in Jesus Christ binds us to do freely "the good works . . . God has commanded."[2]

If the authors have a Lutheran accent, it is because they stand in the confessional tradition initiated by the Reformation and passed on now for nearly five centuries. They are shaped by the practices of the Lutheran church, remember its tradition, speak its language, and hold themselves accountable to its public witness to the truth of Jesus Christ as attested to in Scripture, creed, and confession. They are indebted to earlier generations of Lutherans who passed their faith, example, and insight on to a new generation. The authors are appreciative and critical of their tradition, committed to contributing to its staying power in a time when traditions easily erode and fragment.

Their approach to ethics is strongly theological, which is as it should be in a tradition that believes all life is lived in the presence of God. They concern themselves with communities of the baptized gathered by the Holy Spirit through the gospel, and with the way and form of life that flows from and corresponds to God's promise in Jesus Christ. They readily draw upon themes in the scriptural narrative and explore the meaning of the church's beliefs and practices for the moral life. Tested and fresh perspectives on God, creation, the human being, Christ, the church, and the kingdom of God fill these pages. Explicitly and implicitly, they enter into discussion with the distinctions and relations Lutherans have drawn, for example, between law and gospel, creation and redemption, church and world, faith and good works.

In developing their own accounts of what it means to stand within the Lutheran tradition, the authors may draw on different themes or strands and recall different sources. They may interpret the significance of the Reformation differently, and their perceptions and evaluations of what is good and true in the Lutheran tradition may vary. They may read the present situation of the Lutheran church differently and make different proposals for the future. Some of the differences are complementary, while others point to genuine disagreements.

The Lutheran tradition of theological ethics, it should be recalled, is a changing, diverse, and contentious one, and this book, even with its civil tone, fits well in that tradition. Martin Luther and Philip Melanchthon differed in their theological approaches, interests, and emphases. The Lutheran "concord" in the sixteenth century came through conflict and controversy. This tradition through the centuries has incorporated a broad array of ethical approaches (both to its benefit as well as its detriment), as the Bibliography in this book illustrates. The memory of profound struggles, such as the one involving both Lutheran acquiesce and resistance to the Nazis, continues to influence its present. Readers of these essays are invited to take part in a continuing argument over what is enduring and timely in a living tradition embodied in the history of the Lutheran church.

The Lutheran tradition is not interchangeable with other Christian traditions, and neither is it self-contained and closed off from other traditions and its social setting. Both by conviction and necessity, its borders are quite permeable, with movement going both ways. The authors of these essays are conditioned—in different ways—by the dynamics of the society they are addressing. Their essays show how much they have learned from the teachers, theologians, and ethicists of other traditions as well as from commentators on our cultural context. As we will see, they also show how deeply immersed the authors are in the trials and hopes of people today.

While some authors give more extensive accounts of the context than do others, they all recognize that their perception of and attitude toward the present is an integral part of their ethical reflections. Their distinct interpretations, which are often mutually enriching and at times are at odds, place the book in the midst of the change, complexity, conflicts, and challenges of our society.

There is a clear interdependence between what the authors see happening in society and what they remember in their tradition. A perception of a culture of rampant individualism fits with drawing a comprehensive picture of basic themes in the ethics of a living tradition (Robert Benne). An interpretation of modern society in terms of individual freedom without God is tied to exploring the relation of Christian freedom and God's commandments (Reinhard Hütter). A recognition of the essential but today fragile role of formative practices for the moral life forms a backdrop for recalling Luther's instruction on prayer (Martha Ellen Stortz). Experience with racism corresponds with enlarging the tradition by learning about moral agency from forgotten Lutheran voices in the struggle for African American liberation (Richard Perry). Awareness that church and society are deeply divided over ethical questions goes hand-in-hand with considering the church's authority to deliberate and speak on ethical issues in an ambiguous world (James M. Childs) and with examining how Paul dealt with conflict in his congregations (David Fredrickson). A conviction that present patterns of human activity threaten nature and society connects in the spirit of a reforming tradition with a critical retrieval of Luther's theology of creation and the sacraments (Larry Rasmussen with Cynthia Moe-Lobeda).

In working through this interdependence the authors test the foundations and the vitality of the Lutheran ethical tradition. They offer direction for the Christian life, shed light on difficult and contested questions in Christian ethics, identify future tasks, and affirm the promise of Lutheran ethics. Their essays bear the marks of a common endeavor. They determined the approach and content of their essays in mutual conversation, and twice they discussed together drafts of one another's essays. They carry on dialogue among themselves in their texts and explicitly in some of their endnotes (indicated by asterisks). In their conversation or "Table Talk" on the contemporary nature of Lutheran ethics (see chapter 9), the authors demonstrate what they hold in common, clarify where and why they differ, and draw out the significance of their views for the life of the church and its witness in the world.

Fifty years ago, in 1948, an agency of another Lutheran body, the United Lutheran Church in America, commissioned the development of "a scholarly study . . . of the Lutheran approach to Christian social responsibility." The result nine years later was a three-volume set, *Christian Social Responsibility*.[3] This endeavor remains a landmark in the development of Lutheran ethics in the United States. Its authors, including Joseph Sittler and William Lazareth, and others writing at the same time, such as George Forell, Conrad Bergendoff, and Edgar Carlson, worked out a Lutheran theology that understands social responsibility to be integral to the life of the church and the Christian. Their enduring contribution is to have provided a theological basis for critical participation in contemporary society through a new reading of Martin Luther and the Lutheran Confessions.

The ground-breaking work of theologians in the years following World War II opened up the most fruitful period in the history of Lutheran ethics in the United States. The growing corporate social witness of Lutheran church bodies during the last half-century as well as to the expanding company of Lutheran scholars working in ethics testify to this flourishing (see the Bibliography). Many of these scholars now gather annually to discuss the problems, fault-lines, identity, and possibilities of Lutheran ethics. In this time of ferment, the authors of these essays seek to chart future directions for Lutheran ethics. The recent history of Lutheran ethics expressed in church documents, individual writings, and ongoing discussion makes such a forward-looking task possible and requires that it be done.

This book, too, was commissioned by a Lutheran church body, acting through its Church Council and its Division for Church in Society. A church-wide discussion of human sexuality in the early 1990s revealed some significant differences on what the church should teach on aspects of sexuality. Behind these differences there often existed different understandings of Lutheran ethics. It became apparent that in order to further discussion on this and other controversial moral issues, there was need for teachers in our church to examine in a fundamental way the nature of Lutheran ethics today. The authors in this book take up this daunting challenge. With their Lutheran accents, they think and talk about the moral life from within the life of faith with the hope of building up the church and equipping the saints in the time and place God has given us. They write with the confidence that the promise of Lutheran ethics, like all Christian ethics, is given finally in the life, death, and resurrection of Jesus Christ.

In Today's Context

Karen L. Bloomquist

The authors in this book respond in complementary and contrasting ways to social and intellectual currents of the late twentieth century. In doing so, they indicate some distinctive contributions that Lutheran understandings and dynamics might make to the church catholic and to our increasingly pluralistic society as we move into the twenty-first century.

Intellectual ferment today is marked by ongoing critiques of what has transpired due to Enlightenment-based influences and developments. Some of these influences have been positive, such as enhanced freedom and human rights; other developments have been negative, such as unbridled individualism and exploitation of human beings and the rest of creation. Still other effects are ambiguously mixed. There are commonalities in how these authors view this contemporary milieu, as well as important differences in their analyses and strategic responses.

Some of the earlier idealism associated with the Enlightenment legacy in the United States, as exemplified in social movements of the 1960s, has waned or even lapsed into cynicism. During the Cold War our national identity, values, and actions tended to be viewed over and against a clear foreign "enemy." By the 1990s the focus had shifted to "culture wars" over domestic social issues that pit groups of people and the issues themselves against one another, often to the detriment of those who are the least powerful. Subjective values and assertions loom in ways that overshadow moral truths. Moral authority, including the church's, has been pervasively questioned, making so formidable the challenge that Childs addresses here: How can the church today speak with courage and confidence? Rather than moral consensus drawing people together for the sake of concerted address of injustices, moral fragmentation and an anxious obsession with private ("I want mine!") to the exclusion of public concerns now constitutes the prevailing ethos. Many today deplore what has happened to the substance of a guiding moral vision, to the formation of character and dispositions previously taken for granted, and to the sense of a common good for which people are willing to sacrifice. Individualism run rampant is how the overall situation is often characterized. These chapters have been written against the backdrop of these uneasy stirrings.

One reaction to these trends is to reassert or make a new case for moral absolutes that are universal and unchanging through history. This can provide an anchor of stability and reassurance amid what seems like a sea of moral relativism. In face of this challenge, Benne here makes a case for an unchanging moral core. With a somewhat different emphasis, Hütter views God's commandments not as abstract universals but as "the shape and form of believers'

lives with God . . . in concrete historical practices and activities" (44). A number of the authors point to Lutheran benchmarks—particularly the
Decalogue—as providing structure and substance for the moral life. At the
same time, Rasmussen and Moe-Lobeda remind us of Luther's sense that the
search for a fixed order can lead to idolatrous propensities to "close the circle
and fix the universe" (145). They, as well as Childs, point out the danger of
static "orders of creation" thinking that accommodates dominant culture as
normative and does not challenge unjust relationships.

The recent turn in philosophical and theological ethics that retrieves earlier Aristotelian emphases on virtue, character, and habits (dispositions) has
been stimulated especially by writers such as Alasdair MacIntyre and Stanley
Hauerwas. Although in the past Lutherans have tended to view such emphases
with caution, considerable appreciation of such a turn is reflected in much of
what is written here. Attention is given to what forms us as moral agents and
how this occurs—through distinct beliefs and practices of the faith, as well as
through stories, histories, and communities that shape us. This moral formation is most explicitly evident in the attention Stortz gives to the practice of
prayer. Instead of focusing on the moral formation of persons, Fredrickson
highlights the ethical character of the faith communities themselves and especially the need to rectify internal power inequities. Similar emphases emerge
in the "Table Talk."

What is evident today is that who we are, our world, our relationships, our
seeing, our values, our desires, our actions, even our bodies are deeply and pervasively embedded in history and culture. As an extension of this, one of the
most trenchant critiques is of abstract, universal categories regarding human
beings, reason, and what is morally normative, especially when these are
asserted as if they are "above" history. Universal generalizations tend to
abstract persons from the specificities of their lives, which is where actual
moral dilemmas arise. Hütter calls for a concrete community of remembrance
and interpretation of God's commandments in order "to overcome the abstract
universalism of modern ethics" (45).

The particular cries, social forces, and relationships affecting human
beings evoke the ethical questions that matter to people. This is where a pas-
torally engaged ethical method begins. The heart of what we as Christians
profess is that God became incarnate not in an abstract sense but in the historical particularities of Jesus of Nazareth. As Lutheran ethicist Gene Outka
has stated, "awareness of the historical and social dimensions of moral thought
can aid and abet attention to Christianity's historic particularity."[4] A Christian
ethic in a Lutheran vein needs to take seriously the particularities that profoundly shape persons, their situations, and their moral agency in the world.

Since the 1970s, considerable attention has been given to the histories, cultures, and experiences of those who are "other" than relatively privileged European-American men, who thus far have been the predominant shapers of normative theological and ethical traditions. This means taking seriously the specificities of those who are of Latin American, African, or Asian origin, and the differences that gender, class, and other social locations make, as points of engagement with understandings assumed to be "universal." In this book, for example, Perry probes for historical roots of moral agency among African American Lutherans. The many types of liberation theologies seek to remedy modernity's distortions of rationality and moral judgment by emphasizing praxis, by questioning massive suffering, and by pursuing social transformation. An epistemology of the cross enables us to see and hear those who have been overlooked. Globally this has been a significant factor in the evolution of Lutheran theology and ethics, especially through the *communio* focus of the Lutheran World Federation. In this country, these voices and perspectives have generally not been taken that seriously in the authoritative shaping of the Lutheran tradition in the past, but there are signs that this may be changing. Those articulating the Lutheran tradition in the twenty-first century are likely to sound and look more hetergeneous.

In the case of women, for example, this increasing focus on particularity began with a pivotal article in 1960, which called into question the adequacy of applying to women the universal descriptions of the human situation as described especially in neo-orthodox theology.[5] The considerable and diverse writings in Christian feminist ethics of the past twenty-five years have taken seriously the full humanity, equality, and experiences of women. On this basis, they have challenged many assumptions and categories that have prevailed in ethics—such as separating personal from social ethics, reason from passion, love from justice, and the many ways in which dualisms of body vs. spirit and nature vs. culture are perpetuated.

To the extent that these essays have been affected by such discussions, they sound and feel different than they might have a generation ago. Today moral knowing and acting are increasingly seen as shaped and influenced by a full range of human experiences. Many voices have insisted that human beings are embodied creatures, connected with rather than set over and against the rest of nature. This embodied human connection with nature, and thus the call to move beyond an anthropocentric ethic, is highlighted in Rasmussen and Moe-Lobeda's prophetic appeal for a more sustainable world. Furthermore practices are constitutive of who we are. Beginning here, as Stortz does, suggests an approach to ethics that is intentionally empirical, descriptive, concrete, and inductive rather than abstract and speculative.

In contrast to the philosophical ideal of autonomy, recent ethical approaches that emphasize how human beings are embedded in a whole web of personal, social, economic, political, and ecological relationships resonate with biblical and Lutheran understandings. For example, Lutheran ethicist Elizabeth Bettenhausen has connected Luther's view of "becoming the neighbor" with this relational constitution of the self.[6] Rationality and moral freedom are not posited above history but are problems to be faced within structures or relationships. Here power becomes an ethically crucial matter. Differences are multifaceted, making it untenable to generalize for any one identifiable group (such as all women or men). Rasmussen and Moe-Lobeda point to the sinful tendency of using "our" inward-focused standards of normativity to objectify and judge those who are "other" from us. Faith, they suggest, does not confuse "our truths" with reality. Thus, we need to hear the distinct voices, stories, and perspectives of those who have been assumed to be "like us," such as those whose race, ethnicity, class, or lifestyle differs from "ours," and shapes their distinctive moral life in the world. This is why projects such as Perry's are so strategic.

At the same time, these differences present formidable challenges for those who take seriously what ethics in its usual sense implies, namely, making normative judgments that go beyond particularity. As Benne here suggests, the Lutheran tradition or moral core may be at risk. If particularities and differences are so accentuated that they preclude the possibility of any shared basis for moral judgments or cooperative justice-seeking across these differences, what happens to ethics or to moral authority? Are there no objective ethical standards that transcend our differences? In the face of this dilemma, Benne raises up "places of responsibility" as those given relationships where the ethical mandate to love the neighbor takes shape and substance. Hütter makes a strong case for the embodiment of God's law, which gives form to the freedom of the Christian life. Through the law we are enabled to see things rightly rather than only through what we desire or take for granted.

Although affected by some of the above postmodern developments, writers in this volume root themselves and their ethics in fundamental faith claims that are trinitarian and focused eschatologically on God's promises. Childs shifts the locus of what is morally authoritative to a radical hope in the fulfillment of what God promises. The ethical significance of bodies, creation, and nature, of the holy calling of daily life and its practices, of structures as the moral context in which we live, of the Spirit's power working through our many relationships, and of our hope in the justice that God will bring about— these are some of the faith claims in this volume that can speak persuasively to the current malaise. God is not removed from actual suffering and death but, as a theology of the cross reminds us, enters fully into these concrete experiences, there to bring new life.

Writers beyond this book have suggested that the differences themselves, in communication with one another, can give rise to a moral outlook, a common moral substance that emerges through interactions in which our perspectives are enlarged and we ourselves are transformed. What is shared in common is reached in and through particularities that create "practical bonds of connection without which moral reasoning is cold. . . . [c]ommon footing can be found on which moral communication, and eventually judgment and action, can take place."[7] As the concluding "Table Talk" indicates, this is akin to what occurred as these writers listened to and engaged with one another.

This process of engaging and deliberating diverse perspectives reminds us of important Lutheran themes and dynamics. Because of the limits and fallibility of human knowing, Lutherans have reason to be cautious about moral generalizations. Central in our ethical tradition is the call for neighbor love, which entails "putting on the neighbor," seeking to understand the other in all of her or his concreteness—and difference—from ourselves. The "heart-turned-in-on-itself is shattered open" (Rasmussen/Moe-Lobeda, 143). Agape love "summons the Christian to widen and deepen the 'reach' of covenantal existence" (Benne, 16).

In reading key Pauline texts, Fredrickson shifts the focus away from what guidance Paul provides on ethical matters to the dynamics of how congregations arrive at moral decisions and especially the importance of the participation of all members. These dynamics themselves become a theological matter: We are transformed into how Christ himself extended participation (and empowerment) to others, by becoming a "slave" to them. This reading of Paul challenges the tendency to apply pre-existing moral codes of a tradition and challenges how private and public distinctions have functioned in modern society and in much of Lutheran ethics.

The local congregation's key role in forming and nurturing moral character or disposition is implied throughout these chapters. Teaching and practicing the faith as a way of life are foundational and crucial for Lutheran ethics. Overall these writers seem to give less attention to the role of contemporary knowledge or to principles or norms held in common with those outside of the church than have some Lutheran writers in the recent past. This shift does not imply that common address of social issues is less important today but that an internal or ecclesial deficit needs to be addressed now that was less evident in earlier periods.

Renewed attention is given here to the importance in ethics of the First Article of the Creed, as well the Second Article. Focusing on what occurs in ecclesial settings suggests that there also are significant Third Article implications for Lutheran ethics. The work of the Holy Spirit is what undergirds the church as a community of moral deliberation and action. The Spirit's activity has important implications for how faith becomes active, for how power operates in this community, for how diversity is dealt with, and for how the church lives out its witness in the world. Through the power of the Spirit, the church becomes more "public": As a relational power that is the very nature of the triune God, the Spirit connects us in new ways not only with one another but also with the rest of creation.

What these combined writings clearly convey is how dynamic and vital the Lutheran ethos as a way of life can be in the kind of disturbing, unpredictable world we face at the turn of the millennium. The tradition with which these writers identify is not static. The current context and challenges pose ever-new questions that need to be faced. In some cases, they call for retrieving traditional themes or resources in the Lutheran tradition that can counter disturbing developments. In other cases, Lutheran themes or emphases are nuanced or reworked, provoked at least implicitly by these influences and challenges. Still others set aside certain characteristically Lutheran conceptualizations that are highly problematic in light of these critiques while reconstructing other aspects of the tradition that can more helpfully engage the challenges we face. Together these different approaches are part of a common conversation, or at times argument, in which shared theological understandings and dynamics make it possible to converse together, in quest of what is "good and acceptable and perfect" (Rom. 12:2).

Lutheran Ethics
Perennial Themes and Contemporary Challenges

Robert Benne

Introduction

A living tradition, writes Alasdair MacIntyre, is "an historically extended, socially embodied argument, and an argument precisely in part about the goods which constitute that tradition. Within a tradition the pursuit of goods extends through generations, sometimes through many generations."[1] Lutheranism if it is anything is such a tradition. It is an ethos, a way of life shaped by a vision of God's activities and purposes. It is constituted and sustained by practices of many sorts: liturgical, religious, moral, and intellectual. One of these practices is ethics—the disciplined reflection on Christian moral life, Lutheranly construed. Lutheran ethics is critical and constructive reflection on Christian moral practice. As such it is both descriptive and normative.[2]*

My chief purpose in the following is to identify the basic themes of Lutheran ethics that are discernible within the larger tradition of Lutheran theological and ethical writing. This project will not be primarily historical in a technical sense, nor will it be a survey of Lutheran writers and how they have employed these themes. Rather I see this chapter as a task of discernment, of recognizing and apprehending what is common and recurrent in Lutheran ethical reflection.[3]

My second purpose is to reflect critically about the points at which the modern world challenges the tradition of Lutheran ethical reflection. These challenges sometimes reveal the weaknesses and lacunae of Lutheran ethics but at other times disclose unrecognized strengths. The final section will identify such challenges.

I take up these tasks with some sense of urgency because I believe Lutheranism as a living tradition is at risk. In another generation or two the

Lutheran church itself may be merged into a generic amalgam of declining American Protestant groups. This may occur because of their inability to transmit particular Protestant traditions to new generations, especially in the face of the rampant individualism of postmodern American culture. Mergers may disguise for a historical moment the underlying decay of the traditions. In the coming century there may be little or no distinctive Lutheran ethos for ethicists to describe. Ethicists, however, may compound the problem by doing their share to dissolve the ethos. They may so strongly exercise various "hermenuetics of suspicion" on the moral and ethical tradition that has been handed down that there will be neither enough interest nor confidence in it to sustain it. So I pursue these tasks with the heightened awareness that the Lutheran tradition may be at risk.

I begin with themes in personal ethics and then move on to social ethics. This distinction continues to be useful because there is an irreducible personal dimension to moral agency that cannot be exhausted by institutional analysis or action.

The Christian's Calling in the World

The central principle of Lutheran ethics is identical with its central theological principle: justification by grace through faith on account of Christ. As George Forell so succintly put it:

> [Martin] Luther said that justification is the basis for all Christian ethics. There is no Christian ethics apart from Christian people; and only people justified by faith are Christian people. It was Luther who insisted that the person precedes the act, that ethics is always the ethics of people, and that one cannot have moral acts apart from moral people.[4]

Or to quote another master of Lutheran ethics, Einar Billing:

> Whoever knows Luther, knows that his various thoughts do not lie alongside each other, like pearls in a string, held together only by common authority or perchance by a line of logical argument, but that they all, as tightly as petals of a rosebud, adhere to a common center, and radiate out like the rays of the sun from one glowing core, namely, the gospel of the forgiveness of sins.[5]

Christian morality then is response to the Christian gospel. God in Christ offers the grace and mercy that justifies us mortal and sinful beings. We need not climb up some ladder of increasing righteousness to make ourselves worthy before God. Such a path is fruitless because none can stand on their own before God's demand. Attempts to do so lead only to frustration and a destructive spiritual pride. Rather we are justified before God on account of Christ.

We become saints before God not on account of any extraordinary obedience or even faith that we might offer but because of the extraordinary grace of God in Christ. We are called by God to be his own in Christ.

Such a powerful event, however, has a history; it is not a point in time suspended above and beyond a prior and succeeding history. God has long dealings with Israel and the church; God has long dealings with us.

This is another way of saying that Lutheran ethics is not simply Christomonist. The gospel is preceded by the law—by the workings of God as creator, lawgiver, sustainer, and judge. The God of the Old Testament is active in world history as well as in our own personal history before we meet the Christ of the gospel.

We meet God in our creation in his image. We are given the capability of entering into covenantal relationships with God and with each other. We are given both an eternal and temporal destiny. We are given a meaningful story in which to fit our obedient lives. We are meant for covenantal existence.

We do not construct this covenantal existence *de novo*. It is already present in the structures of life in which we are embedded. Lutherans have called such structures "orders of creation" or "mandates" (Dietrich Bonhoeffer)[6] or "natural orders" (Forell)[7] or "places of responsibility" (Benne).[8] God works through these structures to provide moral contexts within which we can live.

God gives these structures moral direction, using many means to sustain their moral character. The standards for them are derived at times directly from the Decalogue, sometimes from a rational appropriation of the moral law, and sometimes from human practical experience or engagement with the world. Externally they are guided by positive law, but at deeper levels that law is often shaped by moral reason. This moral reason is finally a reflection of the law "written on the heart" (Rom. 2:15) that God has placed in every human soul. Thus non-Christians also have God-given capacities to discern the moral ordering of our common life.

Modern Lutheran ethics have recognized that these "natural orders" are not static. God's "Law of Creation,"[9] to use Gustaf Wingren's phrase, is dynamic. Older structures are reshaped in accordance with God's will, which both Christians and non-Christians try to discern in their own ways. These structures are shaped not only by God; they are subject to the individual and corporate sins of humans, who can bend them away from God's intentions. They are battlefields upon which both God and Satan contend. They are arenas of blessing, conflict, and judgment. God's hidden hand works through them in mysterious and unrecognized ways.

Discerning God's law in these structures is thus a great challenge for Christian ethics. We are called to reject those guidelines and practices that are directly contrary to God's will and to affirm and work toward those that more adequately represent the divine purposes. This task is fraught with ambiguity. This, however, does not excuse us from making clear judgments when possible and maintaining a humble uncertainty when necessary.

The law of God not only orders our common life (its political use); it also serves as a teacher that convinces us of our sin and drives us to the gospel of grace and mercy. In Lutheran terms this is the "theological" use of the law.

Lutherans have a very realistic estimate of our life under the law in relation to other humans as well as in relation to God. Both relationships lead inexorably to a crisis of conscience that opens the way for the gospel. In our common life we are buffeted by claims and obligations—behind which is God's law—that divest us of our proud self-sufficiency or complacency. We know we are up against a great Demand. This Demand often comes to us through other human beings, but the sensitive conscience also examines itself before God. In the court of God we know, as Luther confessed, "that we are all beggars."

Driven by life under the law, Christians finally open their repentant hearts to the gospel that offers affirmation and forgiveness. We are back at the center of the Christian life: justification by grace through faith on account of Christ. From this glowing core of God's extravagant love in Christ, we move outward and forward in the Christian life.

Faith fastens in trust to the God who has offered such grace in Christ. It allows the love of God in Christ to permeate the soul and to bend the will outward to the neighbor. Indeed in the "happy exchange" with Christ, our faithful hearts receive the righteousness of Christ. Our faith becomes active in love. This love expresses itself in deeds that follow spontaneously from faith and no longer from the compulsion of the law. Such love is creative and dynamic. It goes beyond the limits and structures of the law but does not violate them. It "grasps the kind of hand that need holds out," to use the words of Joseph Sittler.[10] It is a love shaped by the engendering deed of God's love in Christ. It is self-giving and neighbor-regarding.

This agape love that moves from God-in-Christ through the Christian is initiatory; it does not wait on formal signs of distress to grasp the hand that need holds out. It is disinterested; it does not demand a return before it acts. It is extravagant; it does not parcel its efforts out in a quid pro quo. It is universal; it does not observe the limits that human love sets around its own in-group. It is biased toward the lost, the last, and the least, much like parents who lavish love on the needy child even while loving all their children equally. It invites mutuality; it does not keep the other dependent. It risks forgiveness; it is not bound to a strict reciprocity.

This heightened sense of both divine and human agape seems to differentiate Lutheran ethics from others. Without affirming the exaggerated separation drawn by Anders Nygren between eros and agape,[11] Lutherans seem to have such a high estimate of human agape because they have such an acute sense of God's agape in Christ. Reinhold Niebuhr in a back-handed compliment confirmed this observation when he remarked that Lutheran ethics are so unworldly because they have such a profound notion of agape love.[12]

This emphasis on the transcendent character of agape love leads Lutheran ethics to a paradoxical view of agape's relation to mutual loves. The denial and affirmation of these loves reflect their denial and affirmation in the cross of Christ. Agape love can never be domesticated into principles and rules, however important these are for the moral life.

This whole dynamic of faith that fastens to the gospel and love that is activated by this faith is illustrated in Luther's well-known formulation of the Christian life in "Treatise on Christian Liberty": "A Christian is a perfectly free lord of all, subject to none. A Christian is a perfectly dutiful servant of all, subject to all."[13] The Christian is freed by the gospel from all striving for salvation even as he or she is sent to love the neighbor. The Christian life is seen as the response of obedient and grateful love to the gospel.

It is important to note that Lutherans see the whole of salvation, including the ensuing sanctification, as the work of the Holy Spirit in their lives.[14] There is no room for boasting. The whole of the Christian life is a work of the Spirit.

I return now to the "places of responsibility" in which all humans are located. It is in these places that we are called by God to exercise our obedient love to the neighbor in response to the gospel. If we are called by God through the gospel to be eternally his, we are also called by God to help the neighbor in and through the places of responsibility we have been given. We are given both an eternal and a temporal destiny by God.

Luther enumerated three "orders" to which the Christian is called: family, state, and church. This number reflects a medieval context in which family and economy were not differentiated.[15] Later Lutheran ethics recognize four: marriage and family life, work, public life (citizenship and voluntary associations), and church.[16]

As mentioned above, these places of responsibility are guided and sanctioned by positive law, cultural expectations, and finally by moral claims that are sometimes in tension with both positive law and cultural expectations. These places are also ambiguous in that they can be both gifts—covenantal structures—sustained by God and curses twisted by sin and evil. Lutheran ethics maintains that these are the places in which all humans are given the obligation to live responsible lives. Christians moreover are to see them as divinely given callings in which to exercise their particular gifts for the sake of the neighbor.

Lutheran ethics thereby affirms that faith not only fastens to Christ for salvation but also discerns a deeper meaning in the ordinary structures of life.

They are, in spite of all, blessings of God to be accepted with gratitude and joy. Further they are the places in which we discern our special missions in life, our callings. They provide roles for Christians to play in the drama that God is unfolding. They are the location for Christians to play out their temporal destinies.

Yet these structures and their demands are very worldly. Some of the demands are clearly helpful, but some are highly ambiguous. Some occupations and roles are even "out of bounds" for Christians. Those that are legitimate according to the law press certain demands on the Christian. For example, we are obligated to a specific family and a specific occupation with all the prescribed roles that these places of responsibility demand. These demands are the way the world under the law must come to terms with both finitude and sin. They are the work of the hidden God but also the work of sinful human beings under the sway of Satan.

While beholden to their particular responsibilities, Christians do not simply live up to the worldly demands of the callings; they also go beyond them. This is the dynamic work of love. The agape love that flows through the Christian creates a lively tension with worldly demands. Some demands are simply accepted and obeyed with a joyful heart. Others are stretched intensively and extensively. The radical force of agape love leads to a restlessness about the world as it is. It summons the Christian to widen and deepen the "reach" of covenantal existence.[17] It awakens the Christian to the call of Christ to love others as he has loved us.

In attempting to state concretely what this lively obedience might look like, Lutherans have often turned to the Decalogue. Following Luther, they exposit the Decalogue not only in its negative formulation but also in its indeterminately positive thrust.[18] The call of love therefore does not lead to antinomianism; there is structure and form to the Christian life. Love is the leaven and salt that enriches these structures and forms without violating them. For the mainstream Lutheran ethical tradition, however, there is no third use of the law that stipulates a specifically Christian form of existence replete with distinctive patterns of obedience. The dynamic and indeterminate command of God in the Decalogue is quite enough.

When Christians "stretch" the worldly expectations of their roles in their places of responsibility, they often run into difficulties and/or resistance. There can be an excruciating gap between what the world demands or allows and the summons of Christian love. In these instances the Christian is conformed to the crucified Christ.[19] As Luther said, if Christians take their callings seriously, they will not have to seek the cross; it will find them. Love does not simply triumph in this world. Worldly success is not a guaranteed product of the Christian life; bearing the cross is more likely.

The theology of the cross permeates Christian existence in the world. It disallows an optimism that suggests Christians can build the kingdom of God by their energy and will or even that they can discern clearly and confidently what "God is doing in the world." Such confidence is more Reformed than Lutheran.[20] Yet Christian obedience makes a difference in the world. It sustains and renews as God wills. To the eyes of faith, agape love is the scarlet thread that holds together the fabric of covenantal existence; without it the world would indeed unravel.

The theology of the cross likewise prevents undue optimism about our own sanctification. Even though the Spirit imputes to us and indwells in us the righteousness of Christ, the old Adam in us never dies. We are sinners and saints all the days of our life on earth. We regress as well as progress. The struggle goes on.

This struggle throws us back onto the mercy of Christ, which is new every morning. We are reminded again and again that our status before God depends on his grace in Christ and not on our own works. We are driven back to the promises of our baptism and to the Table of the Lord for sustenance for our daily lives. Our hope in the steadfastness of God's mercy enables us to move forward into the future, confident that the paralyzing obstacles of our sinful existence can be overcome by a power beyond us.

Taken as a whole, our lives in the Spirit can show growth. In one of his more surprising sayings, Luther remarks:

> This life, therefore, is not godliness but the process of becoming godly, not health but getting well, not being but becoming, not rest but exercise. We are not now what we shall be, but we are on the way. The process is not yet finished, but it is actively going on. This is not the goal but it is the right road. At present, everything does not gleam and sparkle, but everything is being cleansed.[21]

This exposition of Christian life applies to all callings whether they operate in the private or public spheres. The personal and social are inextricably related. Husbands and wives in marriage, teachers in school, politicians in office, and pastors in the church are all summoned by God to work out their callings in those places. In so doing they transform ordinary places of responsibility into Christian callings.

The Church's Calling in Public Life

If the above applies to the individual Christian's calling in his or her places of responsibility, the following pertains to social or institutional relationships. The church as an institution has a calling in a world of institutions. As a corporate body it is called to relate to the corporate structures of the world. The church is and has a social ethic.

Clearly the Lutheran tradition has a particular way of construing the relation of the church to public life. Some scholars, such as Ernst Troeltsch,[22] and, following his lead, Reinhold Niebuhr,[23] have condemned this particular way as cynical and defeatist, leading to a pallid quietism. But such a posture has not been true of the Lutheran tradition in America, especially as it has developed in this century. Lutheranism in America, surrounded by a heavily Calvinist ethos and fed by the Luther research of the Scandinavians, has not been so passive. Yet, due mainly to theological themes that have shaped its tradition, it has related to the public world differently than have the Reformed and Catholic traditions. A number of scholars have called for a stronger Lutheran voice in the ongoing discussion of religion's role in public life.[24]

I contend that Lutheran social ethics does not lead in a specific ideological direction, if that is taken to mean a fairly detailed blueprint for public policy. Rather Lutheran ethics provides a framework for doing social ethics or public theology. It elaborates a set of theological assumptions that stipulate how the church and public life ought to be related. It does so not only for the sake of politics and society but also for the sake of the church's fidelity to its own biblically warranted mission in the world. What is legally permitted in our society—the direct and aggressive intervention of the church in political affairs—may well not be good for the church and its mission. Undue entanglement in politics can be the ruination of the church.

The Lutheran ethical tradition does, however, set a general direction for public policy. It tends toward "Christian realism," a general tendency that can be refracted in a number of different policy directions. Lutherans of various political persuasions share commitment to this framework.[25]

Four main themes constitute the Lutheran ethical tradition as it applies to public life. They are: (1) a sharp distinction between salvation offered by God in Christ and all human efforts, (2) a focused and austere doctrine of the church and its mission that follows from the first theme, (3) the twofold rule of God through law and gospel, and (4) a paradoxical view of human nature and history.[26]

Salvation versus Human Effort. I have stated a distinction as a contradiction, but overstatement often has a point. Particularly in the political sphere, humans are prone to claim salvific significance for their efforts at social or political transformation. The twentieth century, perhaps the bloodiest of all centuries, has been crammed with these attempts. When the God-man Jesus Christ is refused as Savior, the man-god in many different guises rushes in.

The good news of the gospel is that God saves us through his gift of grace in Christ alone. We need do nothing but accept the sheer gift of salvation with repentant hearts. This Lutheran insistence on a radical doctrine of grace puts all human efforts into proper perspective. They deal with penultimate attempts to improve the human condition, with relative goods and bads, not with salvation. This means that politics is desacralized and relativized, as are education and therapy. Salvation is through Christ, not through human political schemes or educational or psychological efforts. Lutherans might appropriately speak of liberation ethics but never of liberation theology in the sense that revolutionary praxis is synonymous with salvation. This understanding of the gospel provides a critical shield against the constant attempts in American Christianity to give redemptive significance to movements of social transformation.

The world has had enough experience of revolutionary change to obviate any claims that political or social "transformation" leads to anything remotely resembling human fulfillment. Such a negative verdict is supported by human observation and experience. But for religious people to make those claims is especially baffling. The Lutheran vision cuts off such claims for the sake of the radicality and universality of the gospel. If we do not recognize that salvation is a pure gift of God, we dishonor God, who gave his Son in the unique and decisive saving act. When we claim an active part in the drama of salvation, we are implying that God's action in Christ is not good enough. Something else, presumably our virtuous action, must be added.

The universality of the gospel is compromised if we fail to distinguish sharply between God's saving act in Christ and all human efforts at improving the world. In any overt or covert claim for human effort as a constitutive part of our salvation, there are always those on the right side of the struggle and those on the wrong. Some are saved and some are damned, not because of their faith or lack of faith in God's work in Christ, but because they either are or are not participants in the group or process that claims to be bringing redemption. Their salvation is made dependent on which side they find themselves.

The picture is clear: The claims of the man-god always exclude; the gospel, however, does not. All humans, regardless of their location along the world's fault lines, are equidistant from and equally near the grace of God in Christ.

The New Testament gospel of the suffering God who abjured all worldly power and all worldly group identification rules out schemes that compromise the radicality and universality of the gospel. The cross of Christ freed the gospel from enmeshment in all human efforts to save the world. No one was with Christ on the cross to die for our sins. Or viewed differently, everyone was with Christ on the cross but only as passive inhabitants of his righteous and suffering person.

When we are freed from the need to look for salvation in human schemes, our eyes should be clearer to make the very important distinctions between the relatively good and the relatively bad in the realm of human action. Liberated from the worry about our salvation, we can turn unobsessively to the task of building a better world, not by prideful claims of transformation, but by determined yet humble attempts to take firm steps for the better.

The Purpose of the Church. If the most important event that ever happened in human history is the event of Christ, particularly his cross and resurrection, then the essential and unique mission of the church is its calling by God to proclaim the gospel in Word and Sacrament. In the Lutheran vision, the gospel of Christ is the church's treasure. The church is the earthen vessel whose sacred obligation is to take the gospel to every nook and cranny of the world. Its calling is to proclaim and gather a people around the gospel, forming them through the Spirit into the body of Christ.

No other community has that calling; no other will promote the gospel if the church fails in its task. So the church must take with utmost seriousness the terrible simplicity of its task. Of course it must be engaged in deeds of charity, and it must be concerned with justice. Of course it must involve itself in many other activities—financial, administrative, liturgical, and educational. Of course it must witness in the public sphere. But the church is not primarily a political actor, a social transformer, or an aggressive interest group. If it acts primarily as one of these, it is identified and treated as one more contentious worldly group. Furthermore it loses its own integrity or reason for being.

The church must attend to its own core vision by proclaiming it and attempting to be faithful to it through its practices. (Stanley Hauerwas is at least partially correct when he argues that the church does not have a social ethic; it is a social ethic.[27]) The church cannot assure that its gospel vision will prevail in human hearts; only the Holy Spirit can capture these hearts for the gospel.

At the very center of this core vision is the event of Jesus as the Christ. Surrounding it is the biblical and early church's witness to the events of Jesus' life, death, and resurrection. This apostolic witness is both a record and inter- pretation of that revelatory event. It incorporates not only the "glowing core" of God's justification of sinners on account of Christ but also the key teach- ings without which the gospel makes little or no sense. The Old Testament background, the doctrine of the Trinity, the eschatological tension between the Christ event and the coming kingdom, and the calling of the church and individual Christians to their mission in the world are all essential elements in this core vision. These are well summarized in the ecumenical creeds.

This core vision should be held with clarity and confidence by the church. Its main elements are stable through time, though they must be interpreted afresh for each new generation. This core makes up the great tradition that can be traced from the time of the apostles to the present day. Its main tenets are not negotiable if the Christian faith is to remain the Christian faith.

Closely related to this central religious core is the central moral vision of the Christian faith. The Decalogue, the calling of all Christians to faith active in love and justice, the preciousness of all created life redeemed by Christ, and the covenantal structure of God's creation (which includes the special covenant of man and woman in marriage) constitute the moral core of the Christian vision. They too are constant through time, though they must be applied creatively to each new historical situation. It is difficult to imagine authentic Christian identity without them.

The next concentric circle away from this inner orb includes the more speculative theological reflections of the church, including its social teachings. This band represents the efforts of the church to apply its religious and moral vision to the dynamic world around it. These efforts entail significant steps in moving from the core vision to its application to specific problems. Each step means an increasing chance for disagreement among Christians who hold their core vision in common. Theological reflection on society, the arts, science, and so on, and social teachings on economics, politics, and society are examples of this extension of Christian meaning. Ventures in this direction are important in the life of the church but unanimity on them is highly unlikely. The church needs to allow a good deal of latitude for disagreement and plurality of opinions. These extensions should not conflict with the core vision itself.

Finally there is a concentric circle that represents the church's posture on specific public policy issues. Such specific commitments on the part of the church should generally be quite infrequent. In special times with regard to special issues, the church may have to stand for or against particular policies. In normal times, however, it is important for the church not to commit to particular policies since there are many other agencies through which Christians can exert their influence. Further there is much difference of opinion among intelligent Christians of good will on such specific policies.

It is essential that the church be able to distinguish these different circles or levels of discourse. It must hold their contents with differing degrees of authority and commitment. The central religious and moral core ought to be held with clarity, confidence, and steadfastness. It has the highest degree of authority and consensus in the church. The outer circles are much more susceptible to genuine and permissible disagreement. In moving toward the outer circles, the church has less and less warrant and knowledge for pronouncing or acting upon its judgments. (Again there are exceptions. If a social practice is glaringly in opposition to the Christian religious and moral core, the church must speak and act, even though there would yet be room for discussion of how it must speak and act.)

The American Lutheran tradition has been quite admirable in distinguishing these levels of authority. It has been a refreshing alternative to the American churches on both the left and the right that conflate the levels into one or collapse the periphery into the core. The liberal churches are often confused or permissive about the core but dogmatic about the periphery. Denial of the decisiveness and uniqueness of Jesus as the Christ creates little alarm while dissent on "inclusive language" can bring ostracism. Current secular ideologies play the functional equivalent of the core. No longer clear or confident about their central reason for being, such religious groups turn to secular sources for their identity.

Activist conservative churches are more likely to elevate their conservative political commitments to the level of dogma. They often engage in "straight-line" thinking. They hold their religious and political commitments with equal intensity and are thus as likely as their liberal compatriots to exclude persons from the "circle of faith" on the basis of their political persuasion. In either case, the integrity of the church and its mission is threatened along with the radicality and universality of the gospel.

The Twofold Rule of God. Perhaps the most difficult element in Lutheran social ethics, yet one of the most important, is the doctrine of the twofold rule of God, sometimes called the "two-kingdoms" doctrine. This doctrine has also been the most vulnerable to distortion. Karl Barth was the first to call this Lutheran teaching "the two-kingdoms doctrine," and he was not paying a compliment to the Lutheran tradition. Rather he was sharply criticizing those Lutherans in the 1930s who had used Lutheranism's doctrine of the twofold rule of God to justify Adolph Hitler and National Socialism.[28] Actually Barth was criticizing the misuse of the teaching.

This teaching is misused when it is interpreted dualistically instead of being seen as a highly dialectical and paradoxical view of God's twofold rule. In a dualistic model, which is a Lutheran heresy, there are two completely separate spheres, one having to do with earthly society and the other having to do with the salvation of our souls. Moreover this dualism is often spatial: The secular world and the world of the church are seen as two separate realities. The secular world becomes autonomous, running according to its own principles and rules, and the Christian must simply submit to them. The church preaches the gospel, which then affects only the inner souls of Christians and perhaps their intimate relationships. As one Lutheran jurist put it, the issues of public life "should remain untouched by the proclamation of the Gospel, completely untouched."[29]

Such a dualistic approach was used to argue that Christians as Christians had no grounds for resisting tyrannical governments, be they of Hitler, Joseph Stalin, Auguste Pinochet, or John Vorster. This led to the infamous political quietism that Lutherans have sometimes fostered. As with all heresies, this dualistic approach has an element of truth in it, but it is so magnified that it pushes out the other elements that make it a genuinely useful doctrine.

The doctrine of the twofold rule of God is more than useful, however. It is deeply biblical and Christian and not a Lutheran oddity. In Romans 5 Paul writes of the two aeons: the new era that Christ is bringing into the world and the old aeon that is under the rule of law and sin. The same eschatological tension is present in other biblical sources. The new order of Christ is in tension with the old order, yet Christians must live in both. Jesus said we must give Caesar what is his and God what is God's (Matt. 22:21). There is a duality but not a dualism at the heart of the Christian vision. It cannot be flattened into one dimension. We are caught in two realities that must be taken seriously. Carl Braaten puts the essence of the doctrine succinctly:

> This doctrine of the two kingdoms marks out the identity of the church within the global horizon of the politics of God and the divine governance of the world. This doctrine draws a distinction between the two ways of God's working in the world, two strategies that God uses to deal with the powers of evil and the reality of sin, two approaches to human beings, to mobilize them for active cooperation in two distinctly different kinds of institutions. One is created as an instrument of governance seeking justice through the administration of law and the preservation of order, and the other as an instrument of the Gospel and its sacraments announcing and mediating an ultimate and everlasting salvation which only Christ can give in an act of unconditional love and personal sacrifice.[30]

This biblical and Christian perspective arose when the kingdom expected by the followers of Jesus did not come. The kingdom had come in Jesus—the preacher had become the preached—but the full realization of what was announced and experienced in the Christ event did not take place. Nevertheless Christians believed that the world they were given to live in and to follow Christ in was not abandoned by God. The Old Testament witness to God's creating, sustaining, and judging activities was not discarded. Instead it was affirmed in the face of heresies that tried to split the creator from the redeemer God.

Surely the God who in Jesus suffered on a cross and died for all and who rose again approaches humans differently in the gospel than in their worldly life in society. There is a twofoldness in God's action in the world, a twofoldness that both generates and reflects a real tension in the individual and corporate lives of Christians. All major Christian religious traditions recognize in some fashion this tension between Christ and the ongoing societal necessities of the world. They are aware that following Christ and living in the world is no easy task. Those who are unaware of that understand neither Christ nor the world.

Christian traditions, however, handle this tension in very different ways. H. Richard Niebuhr's *Christ and Culture* is a classic analysis of these differences. The "Christ against culture" (sectarian) tradition escapes the tension by withdrawing from the world. The classic "Christ above culture" (Roman Catholic) tradition aims to manage the tension by forging Christ and culture into a grand synthesis presided over by the church. The "Christ transforming culture" (Reformed) tradition seeks to convert the culture toward the will of God as it is discerned by the church and carried out by its members. "The Christ of culture" (liberal religion) tradition escapes the tension by absorbing Christ into the enlightened culture of the day.[31]

The "Christ and culture in paradox" (Lutheran) tradition handles the tension in a paradoxical way through its teaching on the twofold rule of God. It is not the tension of Christ and culture that is contentious but how that tension is handled. Of the five possible ways of managing it suggested by Niebuhr, the Lutheran way comes closest to living with an unresolved tension. The others move more vigorously toward resolution, which can often be problematic and perhaps unbiblical.

In the Lutheran ethical view, Christians live in two realities at the same time. Each reality is under the governance of God but in sharply different ways. God governs the "kingdom on the left" with the law and the "kingdom on the right" with the gospel. God's aim in both modes of rule is the same—to overcome evil and recall disobedient creation to himself—but God uses very different means in each "kingdom."

The twofold rule of God is closely related to a Lutheran understanding of law and gospel. If the law and gospel are not accorded their proper meaning and functions, either the law is made into the gospel or the gospel made into the law. In the former, the demands and operation of the law are viewed as redemptive, which makes Christ unnecessary. In the latter, the extravagant love revealed in the gospel becomes a guiding principle for ordering life in the rough and tumble of this world. In this case little account is taken of the power of sin and evil in the world, and society becomes vulnerable to the most willful agencies of evil. Such an approach dishonors God the creator.

Both pitfalls are common in American Christianity. Human efforts are often made de facto substitutes for the liberating power of the gospel (making the law into the gospel), and the radical love revealed in the gospel is often used as a direct principle for commending public policy (making the gospel into the law.) The former secularizes the gospel while the latter sentimentalizes it.

While the two ways that God rules the world must be clearly distinguished (for sake of both the gospel and the law), they are not finally separated. God the creator and God the redeemer are not separate deities. Likewise the two ways that God reigns are not separate spatially or existentially; they interact in creative ways. A tentative duality does not lead to a final dualism. There are three ways in which the twofold rule of God comes together creatively in this world.

The first way is in the calling of each Christian person as elaborated above. As faith, love, and hope are kindled by the Spirit in the hearts of Christians, they will practice those virtues within and through the worldly callings they have been given. These Spirit-driven virtues will affect the responsible roles Christians have as family members, workers, citizens, and church members. They will transform these worldly responsibilities into authentic Christian callings. God's creative love enters the world through the exercise of Christian vocation.

Christian virtue will be a leaven that works creatively on the hard demands of worldly life. It is the creative task of each Christian to find the fitting deed between an adventureless acceptance of the world as it is and an irresponsible desire to replace it with some utopian scheme. Insofar as that deed is truly fitting, it will cooperate with God's dynamic law of creation.

Second, in corresponding fashion, the church is a place where the twofold rule of God is conjoined. It is called to proclaim the whole Word of God—both gospel and law. The church's proper work, of course, is to proclaim the gospel, but the church is also responsible for addressing the world according to God's law. Since the church operates in society only with the power of the word, the powers it claims are thoroughly in the realm of persuasion, not coercion.

The church is called to apply the dynamic law of God to all the structures of social life. The radical love expressed in the gospel is relevant, at least indirectly, to the affairs of the world, just as Christian virtues are relevant to the lives of individual Christians in their callings. These insights are to be applied vigorously and realistically, avoiding both cynicism and sentimentalism. The gospel is relevant to the world's affairs in a paradoxical fashion. It constantly judges whatever is achieved in the world and is a constant lure to higher achievement. It is always "out in front," as is God's eschatological future, and cannot be captured or legislated in the present. The person who fully expressed this radical gospel love was crucified; the gospel ethic does not fit smoothly into the world.

Finally it is within God's total action in the world that we confess the conjoining of the two ways he reigns. The actions of God the creator and God the redeemer cannot finally be separate. Yet in this world even the eyes of faith cannot perceive how this is so. Short of the eschaton, God's rule is of a twofold nature. We affirm this with humility and openness, for our human constructs cannot hold God hostage. Signs of God's ongoing redemption may indeed erupt spontaneously in the midst of this world. While they may not fully manifest the final kingdom of God, they may be anticipations of the eternal *shalom* for which the whole world strains. Yet they must be consistent with the only clear anticipation we have of that kingdom, Jesus as the Christ.[32]*

The Paradox of Human Nature and History. "Whatever your heart fastens to, that is your god," said Luther. From the viewpoint of Lutheran theological ethics, humans are irretrievably committed to finding something other than God on which to fasten their hearts. This inescapable sin, however, is not so simple. We do not fasten to the unalluring and worthless things of the world but to what really tempts us. The highest temptation is devotion to ourselves. Obsessed with ourselves, we make ourselves the center of the universe. This crowds out everything else except what will feed the image of ourselves we have concocted. Whether our obsession be that of willful assertion or self-pitying negation, it mocks the divine command "to love the Lord your God with all your heart, mind, and soul." We love ourselves or what gives us importance and immortality.

None are good. All human actions are tainted with the effect of our sin. Christians can never be completely free of the old Adam in this life. This Augustininan view of human nature extends to human action in society. Human sin is particularly magnified and unrestrained in the life and collective action of groups.

Yet humans are not dirt. Even in their fallen state they possess qualities of being created in the image of God. The created self longs for wholeness and completion, though it cannot heal or complete itself. The created self has capacities for moral reason, which Luther called "civil righteousness." Humans have capacities for justice.

Moreover humans never lose their dignity in God's eyes. They are beloved for what God has made them to be, not for what they have made of themselves. They are infinitely valuable because they have been given a destiny in their creation and have been redeemed by the work of Christ. They can refuse that destiny and that redemption, but they can never lose the "alien dignity" that creation and redemption bestow on them.

Humans find themselves in a paradoxical predicament. Created and redeemed by God, they are "exalted individuals."[33] They have a capacity for freedom, love, and justice. Yet they use their freedom to fasten to lesser things, creating a hell for themselves, other human beings, and the world around them. They are a paradox of good and evil, manufacturing idols of the good things they are given. They cannot solve this predicament on their own.

This paradox of human nature creates the paradox of human history. "History cumulates, rather than solves, the essential problems of human existence," wrote Niebuhr.[34] The fulfillment and perfection of history are not ours to grasp; we cannot be gods in history. Great evil is done by those who try to complete history by their own powers.

Rather it is up to God to bring history to an end (its *finis*) and to fulfill its purpose (its *telos*). God has given us an anticipation of the kingdom in Christ and will bring it to fullness in God's own time and by his own will. We live in an interim time of struggle between Christ's first and second coming.

Given this scenario, we are freed from trying to manage history according to great schemes. Instead we must strive for relative gains and wait on God. We must work for reform without cynicism's paralysis or idealism's false hope. The Lutheran vision leads to a non-utopian view of history that is not cynical. It expects neither too much nor too little of history.

The "Lutheran attitude" reflected in these four main themes provides a wholesome corrective to an American Christianity that is all-too prone to identify promising human achievements as the salvation of God, to make the church into anything but the proclaimer of the gospel, to apply directly the "gospel ethic" to the power struggles of the world, and to hope for the intractibilities of individual and corporate sin to be completely overcome by some sanctified human effort.

Contemporary Challenges

The perennial themes I have elaborated provide Lutheranism with a coherent and persuasive account of Christian ethics in both its personal and social dimensions. As these themes engage the modern world, they meet challenges that demand serious reflection and in some cases reconstruction. By way of conclusion I examine three clusters of challenges: theological, ecclesiological, and epistemological. I will only sketch the outlines of what are enormous, complex challenges.

Theological. A persisting tendency in Lutheran ethics is to reduce the whole of ethical life to the motivation touched off by justification. Dazzled as they are by the wonder and profundity of God's justifying grace in Christ, Lutherans are tempted to think that the only really interesting ethical question is the motivational one. After being affirmed and reconciled in Christ, Christians are powerfully motivated to live the life of love.

The theological problem revealed here is a kind of a soteriological reductionism that downplays the role of the First and Third persons of the Trinity. The ethical weakness that ensues is one of lack of ethical substance. The gospel forgives and motivates, but from what and to do what? Lutherans have shied away from contemporary explications of the Decalogue that would give Old Testament content to the ethical life. Love becomes both a permissive affirmation of any behavior and a rather amorphous serving of the neighbor. Without a richer notion of life in community (covenantal existence) that comes from our Jewish roots, Lutheran ethics does not really know what is "good for the neighbor."[35]* We tend to beg the question. Likewise without a richer doctrine of creation, we do not know what is "good for the creation." A more fulsome theological explication of the First Article will aid in giving more content to an ecological ethic.[36]*

We Lutherans also tend to have an undeveloped doctrine of the Spirit in the Christian life on the other side of justification. We seem to be uninterested in the holiness or righteousness that is given to us in the Spirit. Recent Finnish Luther research[37] has argued that Luther had a strong notion of the actual living Christ being infused by the Spirit into the Christian, leading to some notion of divinization. Such a line of argument has ethical implications. Perhaps more can be said about such "sanctification" than Lutherans have been willing to say. Certainly there is a powerful challenge to say more about the nature of the Christian life, whether shaped by the Decalogue and/or the Spirit.

Like other mainstream Protestants, Lutherans have relied on the general culture to do their work for them. The general Protestant Ethic had established notions of marriage and sexual ethics, the calling, and humane values of justice and civility. But that established culture has been fractured by the new world that surrounds us. Lutherans need a more specific notion of the Christian life if they are to respond to this chaotic world. They cannot do that by relying solely on justification. Lutheran ethics will have to be more trinitarian.

Ecclesiological. Lutherans are debating whether the church is a constitutive dimension of the gospel. Traditionally the word is proclaimed from "outside us" and "over against the church." While this emphasis on the transcendence of the word over all institutional forms is salutory in many ways, it also leads to an undeveloped notion of the church.

Thus Lutherans have been weak in developing a notion of the church as "a community of character." We have left that to our sectarian and Catholic comrades. But we need to get serious about this issue. Can Lutherans talk about the church as a living tradition that forms moral virtues, or does such talk threaten the spontaneous love that flows "unmotivated" from justification? What is the relation between agape and virtue? Are they antithetical? If they are, can Lutheranism ever talk persuasively about Christian virtue?[38]*

Further can Lutheran ethics really talk about a decision-making process without questioning the "ecstatic" notion of motivation with which they have operated for so long? Will such attention to weighing relative goods and bads clash with the spontaneity of love with which we have been enamored? Will we be able to give ethical dignity to anguished decisions? How does a community of faith sustain and support such ethical necessities?[39]

This eccesiological underdevelopment also relates to social ethics. Does Lutheranism have any received body of social teachings? I have argued above that Lutheranism provides an important framework for social ethics and that it leads toward a form of "Christian realism." But can we be more specific about this "Christian realism"?

It has often been remarked that Lutheran social teachings are very thin compared with Catholic social doctrine. We simply do not have much of an inheritance. A good deal of this has to do with confusion about authority within the Lutheran churches. The sixteenth century confessions have little authoritative social doctrine. Our contemporary Lutheran churches claim little authority for their social teaching. Indeed with each new church merger what little authority achieved in the past is jettisoned as the church tries again to re-invent social doctrine. Even when it is able to make social statements, it is unclear how much authority such documents indeed carry.[40]* This confusion about the authority of Lutheran social teaching simply reflects the larger problem of authority for the Lutheran churches.

A more robust trinitarian ethic as well as a more developed ecclesiology may together help to address this problem of authority. Further such an approach may strengthen the motivation for Christians in the body of Christ to become a "people," a counter-culture that implants in its members a comprehensive vision of life out of which they live their whole lives.[41]

Epistemological. This challenge emerges globally with the severe questioning directed at Enlightenment claims for autonomous reason, reason with a capital "R." The Enlightenment project lifted up universal, autonomous reason as the way to Goodness, Truth, and Beauty. But as Western people have become more and more aware of the historical conditionedness of all epistemological claims, such an elevated notion of reason has been dramatically diminished. Indeed autonomous reason claims less and less substantive meaning for itself and has become more and more procedural in character. The earlier claims of autonomous reason have also been challenged by the masters of suspicion—Sigmund Freud, Karl Marx and Friedrich Nietzsche—and by their intellectual descendants—some feminists and multiculturalists.

This dethroning of reason has interesting consequences for Lutheran ethics, which have always had a high regard for reason when it comes to ascertaining the secular values of truth and justice. Luther had a good deal of confidence in practical moral reason. Immanuel Kant took him one further and made reason the only trustworthy source of moral guidance. But were the guiding norms attributed to moral reason more an unrecognized vestige of the surrounding Christian culture than the products of that reason itself? Can reason play such a constructive role in the Lutheran ethics of the future? Or are the historicist postliberals right in their claim that reason is simply an instrument that operates within traditions?

But reason has not been the only target of the various forms of the "hermeneutic of suspicion." The Lutheran tradition itself has become an object of critical scrutiny, as have other religious traditions. Feminists, liberationists, and multiculturalists have all discerned the biases of the "oppressor" in the theological and ethical formulations of these traditions. How far do these suspicions reach? Into the institutional forms that are the external accoutrements of the tradition? Into the traditional social and moral teachings of the church? Into the core itself? How far can these suspicions be taken before the tradition itself is either dissolved or divided? Can those who bear the suspicions also be constructive? Is there a yes to go with the no? Or are we left with a limp maybe, an attitude upon which it is difficult to preserve or renew a tradition?

I end where I began. Lutheran ethics needs a Lutheran ethos upon which to reflect. A Lutheran ethos needs a living tradition to form it. A living Lutheran tradition needs the Holy Spirit to keep it living. The promise of Lutheran ethics depends on how the above challenges are met, but it depends far more on whether the Spirit continues to bless the Lutheran church with life and power.

3

The Twofold Center of Lutheran Ethics
Christian Freedom and God's Commandments

Reinhard Hütter

Introduction

Protestant ethics has been a complex and contested field from its inception. Every history of Protestant ethics has included a justification of the author's own position. In making historical claims, I do the same and as a Lutheran "boldly" so. Furthermore the topic involves highly contested questions: What is "Lutheran" ethics? How does it differ or coincide with "Protestant" ethics in general? In what ways does it agree and disagree with Roman Catholic moral theology? What is its indebtedness to moral philosophy? Renowned Lutheran theologians in the last two centuries have given remarkably differing answers to these questions.[1]

In addition my contribution is both untimely and timely. It is untimely since I do not write as a "professional ethicist," a recently emerged species of specialists who like to present themselves as part of a new expert-culture trained to solve complex moral problems and quandaries.[2*] In this form of quasi-technical expertise, ethics claims a central place of relevance in modern high-risk societies.[3] Instead I write simply as a theologian who happens to teach "Christian ethics" at a Lutheran school of theology. What could be more untimely!

Nevertheless I hope my chapter proves to be timely in three respects: First it revisits the supposedly originating moment of "Protestant ethics": the (re-) discovery of "Christian freedom."

Second, it is timely in regard to the current cultural and intellectual situation of the "Western world," that is, the habitat and ambiance of relative material affluence, legal security, and domestic peace that most people in

Europe, Canada, and the United States enjoy. The idol of this culture—its golden calf—is "individual freedom." This freedom is bound up with the idol of individual or private "happiness" understood as the fulfillment of whatever personal desires we might have.[4]

Third, it is timely as a Lutheran response to an event with ecumenical implications: the promulgation of the papal encyclical *The Splendor of Truth (Veritatis Splendor)* in 1993.[5] The importance of this encyclical for Protestantism in general and Lutheranism in particular is that it could awaken our ethical reflections from their theological and conceptual slumber caused by the canonization of Enlightenment convictions in the center of our moral matrix. *Veritatis Splendor* can catalyze Protestant ethics to return to and to recapture its own theological foundations in order to overcome the remarkable theological and conceptual impoverishment in significant strands of modern Protestantism.[6] The encyclical's core challenge for which Protestant ethics is completely unprepared is its focus on God's law, both natural and revealed. *Veritatis Splendor* relates God's law to a rich and complex notion of human freedom, although not without some highly questionable moves. It thus attempts to overcome the recent dichotomy between law (understood primarily as legislation instead of an external principle of action) and freedom (understood primarily as the license of autarky).[7]

In the first section I entertain the following thesis: *There is no way to ask what "Lutheran ethics" might be like in the contemporary matrix of the Western world without addressing and correcting the deeply problematic opposition that many allege exists between "freedom" and "law."* Because freedom is most often seen as the license of autarky, any concept of "law" has to be understood as random legislative imposition. But if freedom is understood as the movement of the human toward any good, especially toward God, "law" can be seen as an external principle of action that gives shape and form to this freedom by directing it toward both God and created goods. I will show where we have come from and flesh out what is entailed in overcoming the opposition between freedom and law.

In the six sections of this chapter, I attempt to recover the twofold center of Christian ethics in the Augsburg Confession's catholic tradition:[8*] Christian freedom and God's commandments. First I address the modern theological impoverishment of Protestant ethics. Second I identify three twentieth-century movements that aim to overcome this impoverishment. Third I remember Luther's theology of Christian freedom. In a fourth part I sketch out five aspects of how God's commandments should be understood as the very path of Christian freedom. On this ground, in a fifth section, I develop a notion of "rediscovering" the "natural law" under pluralistic conditions. Finally I return to the underlying theme of "law" and "gospel."

The Modern Theological Impoverishment
of Protestant Ethics

Christian freedom is the embodiment of practicing God's commandments as a way of life. It is necessary to reintroduce this positive and substantive notion of Christian freedom because in modern Protestant ethics "freedom" has come to be understood primarily as "negative" freedom. It is seen as a freedom "from" and not a freedom "for." Two complex developments have led to a deeply problematic dichotomy between a purely "negative" freedom and its arch-enemy, the law, which is seen to have a purely legislative and enforcing character.

The first development is an outgrowth of the "Luther renaissance" that has dominated the Luther-research for most of this century. Besides rediscovering the centrality of the doctrine of justification by faith alone, this significant movement construed "Protestantism" generically as an alternative in principle to "Roman Catholicism," both theologically and ethically. This misguided enterprise eventually overstretched itself and misapplied the doctrine of justification by faith alone by making it into the formal principle of Protestantism.[9]

The second development is associated with the overarching influence Immanuel Kant's philosophy—especially his concepts of "freedom" and "law"—had on modern Protestant ethics. Consequently modern Protestant ethics understands "freedom" primarily negatively as freedom "from" and views "law" either as heteronomous and thus as a threat to autonomy or as mediated through autonomy and thus as purely formal.

(1) The decisive core fallacy of modern Protestant ethics is a broadly shared assumption about justification: What makes Christian ethics "Protestant" is the conviction that everything must ultimately be framed by and derived from the one and only central article of Protestantism, namely, justification by grace through faith alone.[10] I am not challenging the central-ity of the doctrine of justification by faith alone; instead I am seeking to safe-guard it from the misuse of applying it beyond and against the Reformation's intention. The fallacy of modern Protestant ethics is not that it insists on the centrality of the doctrine of justification by faith alone but that it regards this doctrine as a ceiling that has to cover everything instead of the very floor on which we stand.

The doctrine of justification describes simply and precisely what God has done and still does for us through Christ's incarnation, death, and resurrection. Protestant ethics turned this doctrine into a systematic principle to govern and control every other element of the Christian faith. It understood the doctrine of justification exclusively in forensic terms, which eclipsed Luther's other emphasis, namely, the very presence of Christ in faith.[11] The first unintended consequence was that "justification" became a purely external, formal, and juridical transaction whose only immediately tangible effect was to be in faith free "from" the law's unmasking and convicting force. The second unintended consequence was an exclusive focus on the "theological use" of the law (its unmasking and convicting effect through which it prepares us for the gospel's word of forgiveness). This "use" of God's law became the only relevant one to the extent that God's law was simply identified with this use. Consequently it was forgotten that God's law was not the essential problem but human life under the condition of sin. God's law thereby received a pervasively negative connotation. While it clearly kept a "negative" (albeit a constructive) purpose theologically, it could not possibly matter ethically. If God's law was to be seen only in terms of its unmasking and convicting use, it had to be kept by all means from becoming ethically relevant. Otherwise it would once again endanger the newly-won freedom "from."

The focus on an exclusively forensic understanding of justification fostered the assumption that the gospel had only a negative relationship to God's law. This primarily negative relationship, of course, had to have inherently antinomian consequences.[12] If the gospel is interpreted as radically opposed to the law, the freedom that results in the gospel's acceptance can only be construed as a "negative freedom," as the freedom from all alienating, authenticity-inhibiting restrictions. The "law"—and not humanity under the condition of sin faced by God's law!—becomes the central problem.[13]

(2) Modern Protestantism inscribed its own agenda into Kant's framework. In this framework God matters in the realm of reason only as a transcendental idea maintained to account for human moral agency. The idea of God safeguards the agent's freedom and thereby moral responsibility. Kant's framework had two effects: First any externally encountered law would undercut the self-legislative nature of human freedom and thus had to be rejected as "heteronomous." Second, the only place left for the gospel was its "effect" on the agent, namely, making the freedom of the moral agent possible by redefining the agent and by liberating her or him from all heteronomy. This tendency later encouraged the exclusively forensic understanding of the doctrine of justification in the Luther renaissance. By becoming an abstract condition of the believer's constitution as moral agent, the gospel thus shrinks down to its forensic message that we are radically and unavoidably accepted by God. The "life in faith" that brings forth good works and is directed toward the neighbor's service is now inscribed into the logic of "motivation" and "effect." Yet this "service" has to remain completely formal in its description because the gospel-based "freedom" is caught in its purely negative relationship to the law (heteronomously understood). Any definite shape and form in which the end of this acceptance (communion with the triune God) is embodied must be

rejected because of the allegedly ever-present dangers of "works-righteous-ness" and "legalism."[14]*

On the one hand, both developments converge and radically eclipse the "first use of the law," that is, the human encounter with a moral order that is not self-legislatively grounded in human autonomy but represents the ordinance of a divine law-giver. According to the first development, this ordinance is in danger of being seen only as convicting and unmasking and irrelevant for the moral conduct of humanity *post lapsum*. According to the second development, the "first use of the law" is unavoidably heteronomous and therefore endangers human "autonomy" since in the external encounter with God's law, the self-legislative nature of practical reason seems to be eclipsed. Yet due precisely to human estrangement from God, God's law has a deeply heteronomous quality. These two developments lose the insight that it is not God's law but human life under the condition of sin that is the archenemy of genuine human freedom (*libertas*).[15]

On the other hand, both developments converge in a primarily "negative" understanding of human freedom. Freedom is not allowed to have a substantive *gestalt* or form, an orderedness through distinct practices that draw it ultimately into communion with God, the only giver of human freedom. For both developments but for different reasons, "freedom" remains essentially without *gestalt*. Due to its focus on justification as purely forensic, the first development sees this *gestalt* as a new, but only more sophisticated form of works-righteousness. The second development sees it as contradicting the self-legislative nature of human freedom. There is no place for a *gestalt* because there is no substantive place for Christ in the very concept of freedom. In the first case, justification works only by imputation and not also by Christ becoming the form of faith and thus allowing for a substantive *gestalt* of the very freedom that constitutes the life of faith. In the second case, faith is reduced to the "gnosis" of radical acceptance living only from its effect on the agency of the believer. While Christ is the medium of acceptance, he remains essentially to be "known" but not to be grasped by faith as the very *gestalt* of a particular way of life.[16]

In the framework of this "negative freedom," the gospel becomes the impetus for a "utilitarianism of love" directed to an abstract neighbor. Again the problem is the formalization of both "love" and "neighbor" that results from the eclipse of the "first use of the law." The law in its first use could give substance both to the love that is asked for in particular settings and to the neighbor we encounter in moral relationships. Such particular determinations and questions, however, are replaced by an abstract calculation needed to tell what kinds of acts best serve my neighbor in the sense of the agape-love that the gospel motivates.[17] This explains the strong need for analyses of political, social, and economic life that give these utilitarian calculations their necessary framework.[18] These analyses all too often depend on the ethicist's personal political preferences and identification with "progressive" or "conservative" ideological poles, a divide that is in and of itself constitutive of modernity.

A significant segment of contemporary Protestant ethics that wants to be intentionally "Protestant" travels with this light baggage: a motivating, gnostically understood gospel of radical acceptance, a broadly conceived tendency of utilitarian thinking oriented to "enhance" or "enrich" the neighbor's life, and some loosely knit set of framing analyses of political, social, and economic life. Compared to the rich, dense, and complex tradition and discourse of Roman Catholic moral theology and social teaching,[19] this kind of Protestant ethics looks like an emaciated enterprise. Yet according to our Protestant fallacy, this ethic is one of the supposedly crucial points of the Reformation's rediscovery of "Christian liberty." Christians act freely, spontaneously, and lovingly out of the gospel in light of the challenges they face.

The core assumption of this "radically Protestant," that is, "radically modern" reading of Luther and the Reformation is that the gospel makes possible this new moral subject. We are set free to do what we want, as long as we have a "good will" (are motivated by the "gospel") and thereby intend "something good" in what we do. Insofar as our doing is sinful—which it inevitably is—it is already forgiven by that radical acceptance that constitutes our existence as believers. With this worry out of the way, we are radically set free as moral agents to act on behalf of the gospel in the service of the neighbor and therefore "to sin boldly." We do not let ourselves be inhibited by moralistic scruples. As long as our intentions are well-meaning, we do what is necessary and anticipate God's forgiveness for our moral failures.

All additional baggage, such as concrete commandments, binding and even exceptionless norms, orienting and ordering goods, and formative virtues can only serve to infringe upon the precious freedom to which we are called. These only tempt us to the one unforgivable double sin in Protestantism: legalism and works-righteousness. If there is one thing modern Protestant ethics is dogmatic about—with a very good conscience—it is the protection of human freedom from the dangers of legalism and works-righteousness.

In our increasingly post-Christian environment in the Western world, this form of "Protestantism lite" turns out to be fatal. In our late modern sentiment, freedom and law, freedom and binding obligation, freedom and the encounter of an unambiguous commandment, have become mutually exclusive. From the once original heroism of Kantian autonomy in which freedom ultimately consists in giving oneself the law,[20] freedom now means doing one's own thing without being accountable to anyone but oneself. The result is that the moral law has been replaced by the law of our unexamined desires. Because "Protestantism lite" has given up a substantive notion of freedom in which the

relationship to God's commandments is constitutive, it has lost all critical perspective on the inflated notion of freedom, which is mistaken as genuine
"Christian freedom." While in traditional Protestant ethics "freedom and law"
or the "Christian life and God's commandments" were regarded as mutually
dependent on and presupposing each other, they have increasingly become
mutually exclusive in modern Protestant ethics because of the fallacy
described above. The result is that modern Protestant ethics has become
antinomian and at the same time very legalistic about particular "correctnesses"
that are reflective of distinct social and political agendas.

What has happened? Instead of Luther's "happy exchange" between the
person's sin and Christ's righteousness, during the last two hundred years there
has been quite an "unhappy exchange" between God and the self-sufficient
subject. God is no longer the defining horizon of the human good, the end of
all things, and present in our conscience. The eschatological horizon of a life
with God, God's utter proximity, the utter closeness of God's commandments,
slowly but increasingly have turned into a mode of life according to the
methodological procedure of modern science: *etsi Deus non daretur*, as if God did
not exist. Thus the thinking and judging individual subject has become the
central focus in theories of ethics and in the practical ways people go about
their lives morally.

Yet for Martin Luther, John Calvin, and the other Reformers—together
with the whole Catholic tradition—the Christian life (and any theological
reflection upon it) hinges first and foremost on God's future for and with us,
the resurrection of the dead, the last judgment, and the everlasting enjoyment
of the triune God. Second, it hinges on God's past for and with us, the creation of the contingent world we know, God's election of Israel, and the life,
death, and resurrection of Jesus of Nazareth, God incarnate in human flesh.
Third, Christian life hinges on God's presence with and for us, in God's word
proclaimed, in baptism and Holy Communion, in the ongoing presence of
Israel and in the tangible body of Christ, the church, and in God's ongoing
and sustaining care for God's creation and all of God's creatures, human and
nonhuman. Three times God, and each time irreplaceably constitutive of the
Christian life.[21]

When God's past sustaining and redeeming deeds, their proclamation and
remembrance, became less and less crucial for the Christian life, why should
God's presence and future still matter? When it became less and less sure that
we have a future with God and that God has a future for and with us, why
should God's presence matter for the Christian life? When God ceased to be
the Present One in the Christian life, we obviously needed a substitute for
God's absence. And, of course, a good substitute was ready to move in: we ourselves.[22]* As a result, the past and the future were reconstituted through the

human agent. In historicism and utopianism both past and future become human constructs. They are no longer received through remembrance and expectation.[23]

Modernity is constituted by a Copernican revolution in the moral universe. It moves from theocentricity, still characteristic for the Reformation, to a new, radical anthropocentricity. God first became a transcendental idea necessary to secure the inner stability of the moral agent.[24] While Kant was still quite serious about God as transcendental idea, this is not the case among Kant's most popular contemporary disciples, the school of discourse ethics. Presupposing the radical critique of Karl Marx, Friedrich Nietzsche, and Sigmund Freud, this neo-Kantian school fully operates as if God did not exist.[25] The human agent might need to be extended intersubjectively but God does not matter at all for most of contemporary ethics.[26] And a significant stream of Protestant ethics in the nineteenth and twentieth centuries has claimed the Kantian tradition as the best of Protestantism, a Protestantism without the outgrown baggage of metaphysics, moving on the upward road of seemingly inevitable moral, political, and scientific progress.

Yet the killing fields of World War I and II, the Holocaust, the Vietnam war, the collapse of the colonial empires (including the Soviet Union), and a sustained and sharp critique of all forms of Eurocentrism have shattered the self-confidence of modern Protestantism in the line of Kant and the neo-Kantians. Beginning earlier in the twentieth century, three movements in Protestant ethics have challenged the Kantian paradigm in modern ethics and have overcome some of the Protestant fallacy.

Three Twentieth-Century Movements in Protestant Ethics: Overcoming the Protestant Fallacy by Deconstructing the Modern Concept of Ethics

First "dialectical theology" and later the "theology of the Word of God" decentered the moral subject. One of the early battlecries of this movement after World War I was Karl Barth's claim that "the general concept of ethics interestingly coincides exactly with the concept of sin."[27] With this widely misunderstood statement, Barth was not arguing against "ethics" but was attacking all forms of Kantian ethics in which human agents and their practical reason constitute the center of the moral universe. It was not much of a step then for Nietzsche to advance the human agent from being the center to being the measure of the law of practical reason, of good and evil. His was the step from moral autonomy to moral sovereignty. In identifying this ethics with original sin, Barth was attempting to decenter the human being as the ethical subject, to remeasure the moral agent as a finite creature mortally wounded by sin.

God, the only good one, the only free one, again became the center of Christian ethics. This often had a strongly christological emphasis, as in the later Barth and in Dietrich Bonhoeffer's ethics.[28] Not surprisingly God's commandments reemerge as a theme in close connection with Christian freedom.

A second important movement in Protestant ethics differentiated the moral agent. It showed that moral agents are much more complex realities than the mathematical points to which they had shrunk in the wake of Kantian ethics. This movement recovered the concepts of "character" and the "virtues" for Protestant ethics. The Protestant rediscovery of Aristotle and of Thomas Aquinas helped significantly. This movement originated in the 1970s and 1980s in the United States and has made significant inroads into rethinking the moral agent in the context of Protestant ethics.[29] Introducing concepts of character-formation and virtues shows how particular goods and practices can direct and form the agent's character in a significant way, positively and negatively. "Freedom" is concretely enabled by particular virtues, such as prudence, justice, or courage, and hindered by particular vices, such as greed, pride, or impatience. Character and virtue ethics put flesh and bones back on the Kantian moral agent, who had shriveled down to the "punctual self" of reason.[30]

A third broad movement in recent Protestant ethics focused on overcoming the abstract universalism of modern ethics by recontextualizing the moral agent. This occurred through two theological foci: creation and God's economy of salvation.

In regard to creation, liberation theology reemphasized the sociopolitical location of agents as a crucial aspect of their identity and struggle.[31] Feminist theology sharpened our eyes to see gender-differentiation as crucial for an embodied moral agent,[32] and the emerging eco-ethics and animal ethics strongly push the embeddedness of the human agent into an intricate network of natural habitats on earth, of which the human is only one.[33]*

The second focus is God's economy of salvation as concretely embodied in Israel and the church. This movement in recent Protestant ethics emphasizes the communal existence of Christians and the ecclesial character of Christian ethics. It reflects on the morals, practices, and activity of a certain people, namely, God's people as a particular community of moral discourse and witness.[34]

One might ask whether it is helpful to lump liberation ethics and ecclesial ethics together as two modes of recontextualization. At first glance this grouping might seem to be heuristically helpful to describe their common opposition to abstract universalism. There is, however, a deep tension between the way "context" is understood and framed by the two movements. It is a significant tension, and I will argue that it can only be settled in light of the constructive interrelationship of "freedom and law."

All three movements are of great significance if Protestant ethics is to overcome its colonization by the Kantian paradigm and its confusion caused by the Protestant fallacy. Yet I claim a fourth movement is necessary, one that challenges head-on the widespread antinomianism of contemporary Protestant ethics. This antinomianism is its sheer indifference toward and even open rejection of the notion that God's commandments are of central, unnegotiable importance for Christian ethics, and more importantly that they are crucial for a substantive notion of Christian freedom. In other words Christian freedom, the true freedom of the Christian moral agent, and thereby genuine human freedom, is fatally misconstrued in the absence of a serious consideration of God's commandments. In this regard Martin Luther himself posed the initial challenge. His thought on Christian existence and the moral life represents an anticipatory critique of modernity's misconstruals of both "freedom" and "law."[35] This anticipatory critique points us toward a "decentered self" that understands itself as essentially gifted and its freedom as inherently relational. This decentered self is shaped by a way of life whose end is "good works" and whose shape is God's commandments.

Christian Freedom and God's Commandment: Remembering Luther's Theology of Christian Freedom

How do theology and ethics rooted in the Reformation tradition respond to this challenge? Does Lutheranism promote a "freedom without the law"? Are we as "catholics of the Augsburg Confession" responsible for the flat notion of autonomy characteristic of late modernity in which the autocratic self defines its own value-sets so long as the majority-defined rules are not breached? What is authentic human freedom? Is it in principle a freedom without the law so that we have the license to avoid serious and sustained attention to God's law? How are Christian freedom and God's commandments related? Does the first need to exclude any reference to the latter in order to avoid even the slightest danger of works-righteousness or legalism? Does any reference to the latter irretrievably destroy the precious good of freedom? In addressing these questions head on, I turn to a treatise of Luther. It is the one to which the Protestant fallacy most often refers rhetorically without fully taking into account all aspects of this rich text.

The Freedom of a Christian. Luther's *magna carta* of the Christian life, "The Freedom of a Christian" (1520), remains one of the most decisive and foundational texts for Christian ethics in the Reformation tradition. The text opens with a sharp and unforgettable dialectic: "A Christian is a perfectly free lord of all, subject to none. A Christian is a perfectly dutiful servant of all, subject to all."[36] The sad story of this formula is, however, that the dialectic has not been maintained. The first half was emphasized and its second half forgotten, which led to the late-modern notion of the moral autocracy of the independent self. Or its second half was emphasized and its first half forgotten, which led to the notorious Lutheran subservience to all kinds of political authorities based on a very problematic notion of Christian obedience. A third error was to dichotomize the two statements: freedom for the "inner" spiritual life and uncritical acceptance of all that constitutes "outer" political and economic life.[37]*

Anything less than the whole radical dialectic is a fatal mistake. What Luther says in two consecutive sentences—which cannot be said in one—is the one dynamic of the Christian life in faith, a life in union with Christ as part of his body. Insofar as we become one with Christ in faith, this dialectic of freedom in faith and service in love expresses God's own freedom in love.

After laying out the dynamic of salvation (with the image of the "happy exchange" of attributes between Christ and the sinner),[38] Luther focuses on the telos of it all, namely, the Christian life in which faith is embodied in love. How is this life of evangelical freedom in Christ to be understood and grasped? At this point Luther makes two very telling biblical references.

One is Phil. 2:4-11, the christological hymn.[39] Luther with St. Paul points to Christ's and in the most radical sense to God's own humility in the economy of salvation. This humility is the embodiment of God's freedom in love, which we are called to emulate in our own life in faith. This is the evangelical paradigm, the over arching model of our Christian freedom. God's self-giving love is the effective and the final cause of the shape of freedom in humility.

Christians are perfectly free lords over all things in creation. Because we are justified by faith, all created goods and powers through which we tend to justify ourselves along with our self-justifying deeds have been unmasked as false gods. Only insofar as these goods and powers serve God's sustaining and redeeming activity do they have authority over us. Their authority is limited by and completely derived from the One who authorizes them. Yet "in faith," in union with Christ, the Christian participates in God's own freedom, the inner dynamic of God's triune love. Through Christ and the Spirit's mission, this dynamic aims to draw all of creation into communion with the triune God. Christian freedom is our participation in this mission through our loving service to the neighbor.

But does not all this sound like the very "Protestantism lite" that I chastised earlier? The Christian life seems to come out of the free spontaneity of Christian faith and love. Otherwise it is guided by the needs of the neighbor and the concrete situation, in other words, by that utilitarianism of love for which modern Protestant ethics is so notorious. It seems as if the person in faith is in no need of God's commandments.[40]*

At this point, however, we need to recall another of Luther's frequent biblical references, one he made before turning to Phil. 2:

> We should think of the works of a Christian who is justified and saved by faith because of the pure and free mercy of God, just as we would think of the works which Adam and Eve did in Paradise, and all their children would have done if they had not sinned. . . . The works of a believer are like this. Through his faith he has been restored to Paradise and created anew, has no need of works that he may become righteous; but that he may not be idle and may provide for and keep his body, he must do such works freely only to please God.[41]

Luther is claiming that "in faith," that is, "in union with Christ," the Christian is restored to the original state of prelapsarian life with God. There is a way of life proper to that state of being. To understand fully what Luther has in mind with his theological claim that "in faith" we are back "in paradise," we need to turn to the second chapter of his *Lectures on Genesis*, written during the last ten years of his life.

Luther's "Lectures on Genesis": God's Command as Way of Life for Adam and Eve. In interpreting Genesis 2, Luther states:

> And so when Adam had been created in such a way that he was, as it were, intoxicated with rejoicing toward God and was delighted also with all the other creatures, there is now created a new tree for the distinguishing of good and evil, so that Adam might have a definite way to express his worship and reverence toward God. After everything had been entrusted to him to make use of it according to his will, whether he wished to do so for necessity or for pleasure, God finally demands from Adam that at this tree of the knowledge of good and evil he demonstrate his reverence and obedience toward God and that he maintain this practice, as it were, of worshipping God by not eating anything from it.[42]

David Yeago rightly draws the following consequence:

> The commandment is not given to Adam so that he might *become* a lover of God by keeping it; Adam already *is* a lover of God, "drunk with joy towards God," by virtue of his creation in the image of God, by the grace of original righteousness. The commandment is given, rather, in order to allow Adam's love for God to take form in a historically concrete way of life. Through the commandment, Adam's joy takes form in history as *cultus Dei*, the concrete social practice of worship. . . . The importance of this cannot be overstated, particularly in view of conventional Lutheran assumptions: here Luther is describing a function of divine law, divine commandment, which is neither

correlative with sin nor antithetical to grace; indeed, it presupposes the presence of grace and not sin. This function of the divine commandment is, moreover, its original and proper function. The fundamental significance of the law is thus neither to enable human beings to attain righteousness nor to accuse their sin, but to give concrete, historical form to the "divine life" of the human creature deified by grace. . . . The commandment is given originally to a subject deified by the grace of original righteousness, a subject living as the image of God; it calls for specific behaviors as the concrete historical realization of the spiritual life of the deified, God-drunken human being. What happens after sin comes on the scene is simply that this subject presupposed by the commandment is no longer there; the commandment no longer finds an Adam living an "entirely divine life," "drunk with joy towards God," but rather an Adam who has withdrawn from God, who believes the devil's lies about God and therefore flees and avoids God. It is precisely the anomaly of this situation that causes the commandment to become, in Luther's terms, "a different law" (alia lex).[43]

God's commandment is nothing else than the concrete guidance, the concrete social practice that allows us as believers to embody our communion with God in concrete creaturely ways. This always includes God's other creatures. God's commandment enables and guides that way of life for which human beings, created in God's image, are destined.[44]

Now we can understand the radical perspective behind Luther's rather innocently sounding claim that "in faith" we are "back in paradise." We are back in communion with God, sola gratia and sola fide, back in that righteousness that God's commandment presupposes and to which God's commandment gives creaturely form and shape! This is precisely why for Luther the "Freedom of a Christian" never contradicts God's commandments and never comes without them. Christian freedom rejoices in God's commandments and welcomes them as creaturely ways of embodying our love of God and neighbor. Sinful humanity typically receives the law as an external code. According to Luther, both the law of Moses and natural law are subject to this distortion under the condition of sin, where we have lost the original grace of humanity created in the image of God. God's grace received in faith rectifies this distortion by restoring believers to the state of being in paradise, drunk with joy for God. The original, spiritual understanding of the law is again accessible. As Yeago rightly puts it:

This means that one who understands the law spiritually remembers that all God's commandments presuppose a subject deified by grace, a human being who is drunk with joy toward God and rejoices in all God's creatures. This is, after all, precisely what Jesus teaches: the law and the prophets hang on the double commandment of love, the commandment to love God with all our heart, soul, mind, and strength and our neighbor as ourselves.[45]

Thus according to Luther's eschatological understanding of faith, when Christ himself, the new Adam, is present in the believer, there is no difference anymore between God's gospel—God's forgiving, restoring, and sanctifying activity in Christ—and God's commandments as the gospel's creaturely form of freedom. Christ's law, Luther says,

> is faith, that is, that living and spiritual flame inscribed by the Spirit in human hearts, which wills, does, and indeed is that which the law of Moses commands and requires verbally. . . . And so the law of Christ is properly not teaching but living, not word but reality, not sign but fulfillment. And it is the word of the gospel which is the ministry of this life, reality, and fulfillment and the means by which it is brought to our hearts.[46]

In fulfilling God's commandments, which are summarized in the double-love commandment, the freedom of the Christian finds its concrete fulfillment. While letter and spirit are never to be severed from each other, they need to be distinguished lest God's commandment be received again as a purely external code and not be spiritually understood as that which gives Christian freedom its concrete creaturely form.[47]

Christian Freedom: On the Path of God's Commandments

How does this reading of Luther's "Freedom of the Christian" connect with our first part, with the Protestant fallacy and the modern notion of freedom without the law? I will sketch five points on the importance of God's commandments for Christian ethics—not only in the Reformation tradition. I draw on Luther's catechisms in order to show that Christian freedom finds its appropriate *gestalt* in being continuously addressed by the Decalogue.[48]

(1) God's commandments are the shape and form of believers' lives with God. God's commandments allow us to embody our obedience to God and our service to humanity in concrete historical practices and activities. God's commandments are a welcome help to form the freedom of the Christian life. The remembrance of God's commandments, their interpretation and application, and the discernment of reality in light of them are worthy and important themes for Christian ethics. This is especially true for a Lutheran ethic that seeks to overcome contemporary impoverishments and to continue the fulness of the Reformation tradition. Most crucially the First Commandment undercuts modernity's operative axiom: as if God did not exist. It invites us to the life-long practical training of learning how to embody the First Commandment, that is, how to be a creature, how to trust completely in God as our ultimate good, and how to sustain our vulnerable dependence upon God's gift of sustenance and communion. Luther puts it the following way:

Thus you can easily understand the nature and scope of this commandment. It requires that man's whole heart and confidence be placed on God alone, and in no one else. To have God, you see, does not mean to lay hands upon him, to put him into a purse, or shut him into a chest. We lay hold of him when our heart embraces him and clings to him. To cling to him with all our heart is nothing else than to entrust ourselves to him completely. He wishes to turn us away from everything else, and to draw us to himself, because he is the one, eternal good.[49]

Christian freedom finds its *gestalt* most fundamentally in learning how to embody this most simple and therefore most difficult fact of our human lives. According to Luther it is wrong to assume that this simplicity is "at hand." Our radical estrangement from God, our bondage to sin, keeps this simplicity hidden from our gaze. We need to be liberated through God's grace from the force of sin in order to learn the radical simplicity of fulfilling the First Commandment by faith alone. Stanley Hauerwas calls this "learning to be a sinner";[50] Luther would have called it "learning Christ's Lordship." He explains it in a way offensive to our modern sensibilities: "What is it 'to become a Lord'? It means that he has redeemed me from sin, from the devil, from death, and from all evil. Before this I had no Lord and King but was captive under the power of the devil. I was condemned to death and entangled in sin and blindness."[51]

(2) To overcome the abstract universalism of modern ethics and the Protestant complicity in it, God's commandments are in need of a concrete community of remembrance and interpretation. We do not encounter God's commandments in an abstract way and an empty space but in a concrete ecclesial context, a dense web of relationships, and in light of particular challenges. God's commandments are not encountered solitarily via introspection but via an ecclesial hermeneutics in which God's commandments are constantly remembered, interpreted, and enacted in faithful service.[52]* Ecclesial hermeneutics must not mean that the church becomes the "master" of God's commandments, that we bend them to our purposes, that we streamline them according to the requirements of the Zeitgeist, or that we curtail them according to our small visions and our great anxieties.[53]* Instead ecclesial hermeneutics means that through the faithful remembrance of God's commandments in concrete ecclesial contexts we are stretched, challenged, and kept accountable by God's commandments.[54] They are breathtaking, exciting, and exhilarating. When received as a naked, external code, they are terrifying and deadly but nevertheless true. Yet one thing they surely are not, namely, something "at hand" for the relaxed and leisurely examination of a sovereign moral subject in need of some orientation, something to be checked out purely for information. Luther's urgent invitation in regard to the First Commandment extends to all of them:

> Let everyone, then, take care to magnify and exalt this commandment above all things and not make light of it. Search and examine your own heart thoroughly and you will find whether or not it clings to God alone. Do you have the kind of heart that expects from him nothing but good, especially in distress and want, and renounces and forsakes all that is not God? Then you have the one true God. On the contrary, does your heart cling to something else, from which it hopes to receive more good and help than from God, and does it flee not to him but from him when things go wrong? Then you have an idol, another god.[55]

Christian freedom is embodied in this ongoing ecclesial hermeneutics of remembering God's commandments. Otherwise it is not Christian freedom. Embodied in this ecclesial hermeneutics, Christian freedom becomes concrete as a spiritual discipline[56*] in practices such as meditation on Scripture, ongoing exegesis and scrutinization of God's commandments, and the continuing explication and application of the Decalogue.[57*]

(3) Part of this spiritual discipline of remembering God's commandments is to learn how to perceive rightly.[58*] The first question of Christian ethics should not be, "What ought I now to do?" but, "What does the world really look like?" Situations are not just "out there" for us to "bump" into. Rather the description of a situation is everything; it is the situation itself. In describing a "situation" the morally decisive choices and moves are already made. To be shaped by the spiritual practice of ceaselessly remembering God's commandments means being faced with God's constant critical intervention into our construals of "reality." God's commandments thus help us avoid getting trapped by false necessities and givens. They free us from becoming victimized by the power of facticity that continually presses in on us in order to submit us to its supposed necessities. God's commandments represent the creator's and redeemer's counterfactual, wholesome claim on us. This claim keeps in check those powers and principalities that would control our ways of seeing how things are. In the kabbalistic tradition, the Hebrew word for evil, *rah*, is interpreted as "to see, to perceive badly." Thus the double-love-commandment and the Decalogue, the one positively and the other negatively, teach us how to be a neighbor to others, to pay attention, and to care. By helping us to see rightly, God's commandments protect and concretely enable Christian freedom to fulfill its calling to be free from our self-absorption for the worship of God and the service of God's creation. The basic commandment that points to that practice through which we learn "to see rightly" is the Third Commandment, the sanctification of the holy day. This is not surprising if we understand that "seeing rightly" presupposes having a character formed by the ongoing encounter with God's Word. To learn how to be a creature and a neighbor happens precisely through those practices by which we sanctify the holy day, beginning with common worship. Through Word and Sacrament we

are being "neighbored to" by God in Christ and thereby "re-created" through the Spirit. Luther reminds us that this happens not only through weekly worship: "Indeed, we Christians should make every day a holy day and give ourselves only to holy activities—that is, occupy ourselves daily with God's Word and carry it in our hearts and on our lips. . . . Thus we may regulate our whole life and being according to God's Word. Where this practice is in force, a holy day is truly kept."[59]

(4) One of the most serious blind spots in contemporary ethics is the absence of any critical and constructive treatment of human desires. If there is one force that drives the relentless growth and dynamic of the modern market economy and technology, it is unexamined and unchecked human desire. Human desires are so fatally dangerous because they tacitly occupy and claim human freedom for their insatiable purposes. In the context of late modernity, freedom means happiness, and happiness is sadly defined as the fulfillment of desires. Coveting—the endless, limitless, ceaseless desiring of "things," of pleasures, of experiences—is the fuel that runs the motor of our consumer-oriented, supposedly "free" global market economy. Yet each thing acquired and each pleasure fulfilled only produce the thirst, the desire for more.

In this context the relevance of God's commandments becomes starkly clear: They stubbornly keep our desires directed toward God.[60]* To be clear: Desire as such is not the problem; it is not "bad." Indeed we are created as creatures with desires; to be human is to be desiring. All of our desires, however, are created to come to a rest in their one ultimate good, communion with God. Augustine's famous sentence from the *Confessions*—"You have made us and drawn us to yourself, and our heart is unquiet until it rests in you"[61]*— expresses how our desires find rest and fulfillment only in God. If other created things are elevated to the position of the ultimate good in ceaseless exchange, coveting is the unavoidable result, since none of these created things will ultimately bring our desiring to a rest. Without desire we would cease to be human; without God as desire's ultimate end, we become inhumane. Therefore Christian freedom has to be understood as true *askesis*[62] or chastity: to let all our desires be ordered by and fulfilled in the communion with God that begins in grasping Christ in faith. Instead of being governed by the unsatiability of our desires seeking fulfillment in finite goods, we become free to desire our ultimate good. In communion with God we receive the finite goods of creation that we also desire.

Positively the Decalogue can and should be summarized in the double-love-commandment; negatively it is summarized in the commandment "Thou shalt not covet." Do not submit yourself to the insatiable thirst of your desires directed toward the world—wealth, power, ownership of truth, and control of the neighbor and all the goods of the world.[63] Misdirected, our desires become insatiable and completely distort any serious notion of authentic freedom by subtly redefining it as the potentiality to fulfill whatever one desires. Freedom as slavery to one's desires is the result of living without God's commandment against coveting. That commandment directs our desire to the First Commandment, the one source that can give all our desires their rest and fulfillment. The fulfillment of the First Commandment through faith opens us for the presence and the need of the neighbor.[64]

(5) Life according to God's commandments with their center in the First Commandment is Christian freedom. In this life with God, we are drawn into the freedom of God's own inner trinitarian life of love. Participating in God's freedom, we walk the walk that God has already walked for us. "We are God's work, created in Jesus Christ for good works, which God has prepared beforehand, so that we may walk in them" (Eph. 2:10). Good works according to the Reformers are nothing else than the shape of Christian freedom as it is informed by God's commandments, thereby participating in the freedom of the one who already has prepared in triune love all of these good works. To put it differently, by showing the *gestalt* of Christian freedom, God's commandments are in their deepest sense "transmoral": They are actually "beyond good and evil." They do not thrive on the distinction of "good" and "evil" *post lapsum* by offering a map on which we can inscribe "good and "evil" according to our knowledge.[65] Instead they point to those "intrinsically good acts" through which we exercise Christian freedom.

God's Commandments and the "Natural Law"

This account is not yet sufficient for two important reasons that lead us back to the tension between a creation-centered ethics and an ecclesially-centered ethics.

First, as Bonhoeffer reminds us, the church occupies concrete space in the world. This means that the *gestalt* of Christian freedom encounters and relates to other ways of living and thinking about morality. The church has done so from its inception. Since it knows and confesses God as the creator of the universe, the church has expected to find traces of a knowledge of God's will in its encounter with non-Christians. Therefore my account of how the commandments guide us on the path of freedom is not a "sectarian" way of life of a ghettoized community. In our highly pluralistic context, it becomes a particular witness with universal implications. It is a particular embodied argument with universal intent rather than one of abstractly universalized principles.[66]

Second, a deep-seated assumption of modernity is that human practical reason is unimpaired and can come to certain results through the transparency of its own reflection.[67]* This seems to be possible to a certain degree. The phenomenon of the human conscience suggests this possibility. Thomas Aquinas classically expressed the view that still dominates Roman Catholic understanding. Humans are aware of basic moral principles; conscience is the judgment of practical reason as it brings these principles to bear on particular moral issues.[68] The broad acceptance of this experience is reflected in the Roman Catholic Church's traditional teaching that one must always obey one's conscience. In contrast to this notion of conscience that does not pay explicit attention to the human condition *post lapsum*, Luther distinguished sharply between a "conscience before people" and "conscience" in a theologically substantive and transmoral way. For Luther the conscience is where we are always already most radically addressed and questioned by God's word and exposed to God's judgment.[69] Faith, the very acceptance of God's judgment in Christ's cross and resurrection, is the good conscience. "Only Christ belongs in the conscience. The person God intends is the person of faith who is one person, 'one cake,' with Christ."[70] Without faith conscience remains anxious, exposed to the pressing onslaught of the law's continuous unmasking of our radical estrangement from God.[71] In an anticipatory critique of modernity, Luther identified the theological quality of conscience, the "blind spot" concealed by its primarily moral character.

The Enlightenment assumption of an unimpaired practical reason thus conceals the reality that due to their estrangement from God humans are battlefields of conflicting forces and desires. The claim of moral sovereignty and autocracy leads only to enslavement by our unexamined wishes, desires, and anxieties. Equally problematic is the assumption of modernity's self-critical turn, namely, that this "blind spot" can be gazed at and thus mastered by reason itself, be it through psychoanalysis, a phenomenology of existence, a hermeneutics of suspicion, or deconstruction. But the soteriological offense remains: The law's second use is intact; in its encounter with us, the law constantly convicts us as curved in on ourselves. This holds equally for Christians since the struggle between our renewal through the Spirit of Christ and our sinful habits, involvements, and practices is not yet over (Gal. 5:17).

Therefore there is no "upward" path from a stable, unimpaired, practical rationality toward the theological horizon that this rationality always presupposes and on which it already depends. Rather "natural law" constantly needs to be "discovered" and "recovered."

Interiorization and Memorization: Shaping the Intentionality. The Decalogue is the "foundationless" beginning of our practical thinking. It is the "efficient cause" from which practical thinking always begins anew. The Sermon on the Mount is its "final cause," the promise of the embodied ultimate good circumscribed by the practices toward which the Decalogue directs us. This beginning takes concrete form in continually new meditations on the

Decalogue. This inward "training" in God's commandments, starting from the Decalogue and moving toward the Sermon on the Mount, shapes the way a person's intentionality gives *gestalt* to Christian freedom.

Remembering: "Natural Law" as Particular Discourse Tradition Summarized in an Interpretation of the Decalogue.[72]* From antiquity there has been a tradition of basic axioms, "a natural law discourse." It was appropriated by the patristic writers and is part of the Christian tradition's consensus.[73] It constitutes much of the concrete substance of the "universal" ethics of the Enlightenment.[74] This particular tradition of a natural law discourse needs to be understood as part of the ongoing remembering and recovering of the natural law submerged and forgotten under the conditions of sin. A constructive awareness of historical change, experience, and growth in the tradition of the natural law discourse has its place here. This is not an awareness in the sense of a historicist critique; it is an *anamnesis* and a growth of insight into both the nature of the natural law axioms and the breadth of their application. This remembrance and recovery of the natural law in the form of an ongoing discourse is not, however, to be divorced from the church's way of life embodied in its practices. When it was turned into an "independent" secular enterprise, into a discourse of "nature" and "law" divorced from a substantively Christian theology, this tradition eventually became open to historicist, genealogical, and ideological criticisms from which the modern secular "natural law discourse" has never fully recovered.

Witnessing to and Arguing for the Decalogue as Summary of the Natural Law. Christians individually and the church corporately do not have any privileged knowledge in detailed practical moral matters. They, however, find themselves bound by the perspectives and insights of a path that God has willed for all humanity. The commandments as the way of human freedom in communion with God are the basis for re(dis)covering the "natural law." In a time of rampant individualism in so-called private moral matters and of an equally rampant commodification of humans on a global scale, the church witnesses to and argues for "natural law." It does so when it reminds humans of those limits to power and license that demarcate the path of God's commandments. There are no simple, fixed answers, but there are unquestionable limitations to which all humans are bound; that is the double-edged nature of God's commandments. On the one hand, they point out freedom's *gestalt* in communion with God, the intrinsically good works of faith. On the other hand, they identify the threshold of "intrinsically evil acts." The commandments do so by circumscribing essential moral notions like dishonoring one's indebtedness, unjust killing (that is, murdering), stealing, lying, coveting what is not one's own, and most fundamentally, failing to acknowledge the very source of our being as creatures.[75]

Re(dis)covering the "Natural Law" Concretely under the Conditions of Pluralism. This task is not a "theory" to be applied but a particular practice involving both theoretical and practical reasoning. It is bound to a way of theological thinking that presupposes (a) God the creator and redeemer who unmasks and judges human estrangement from the divine origin, from each other, and from creation and who calls humans into the communion of the divine life; (b) a created order and a "way of life" willed for all humans; and (c) a practical reason that is neither unimpaired nor fully transparent to itself but rather wounded and obscured by sinful desires, habits, and practices.[76]* Natural law is not "something out there" that we eventually "bump" into if we search long enough. Neither is it to be found "written" in our genes or in the stars. It does not mean that we have a priori access to the moral universal. While some principles of practical reason are accessible to all of us, the natural law in its fullness is not simply inscribed in our minds. Instead diverse practices and traditions that structure human society display a matrix of contingent and unpredictable resonances with God's purpose for humankind as articulated in the narratives of Israel and Jesus. In particular structures of responsibility (their vocations),[77]* Christians have to discern and judge the resonances and dissonances in light of God's commandments. Where we recognize a significant and broadly based correspondence between God's law and traditions and patterns of human society, there "natural law" has been re(dis)covered.

There are a variety of ways this re(dis)covery might happen. Particular "heroes"[78] and their distinct activities might make us "see" something that we otherwise would not have seen. We might think of Martin Luther King Jr., Mahatma Ghandi, Mother Teresa, and countless local figures who are less well known.[79]* It might also occur through extensive public discussions of particularly pressing questions that may lead to an extension or change of positive laws. Examples are the civil rights and environmental movements. It can also occur through symbolic witness and protest against existing laws that contradict both the Decalogue and the natural law tradition. Examples are nonviolent protests against laws legalizing abortion without specific qualifications and serious restrictions, laws legalizing euthanasia, or laws legalizing distinct forms of discrimination. It also occurs through ongoing discernment and discourse about complex social and cultural phenomena that need to be sorted out. An obvious example pervasive in Western societies today is the broad insecurity over the various options and issues related to human sexuality outside the vocations of marriage and celibate singleness.

Yet we must not assume that this approach might "work" as a "method" to be "applied" irrespective of and independent from the church's faithful witness to and teaching of God's law. Modernity's project of accessing the "natural law" as something "at hand" to human reason in isolation from a theology of the natural law produced its own most radical critique in Friedrich Nietzsche's deconstruction of these assumptions. That critique created the basis for post-modernity's celebration of the ultimately plural, pragmatic, and political nature of any kind of "law" and "morality."

Law and Gospel—
or Redeemed Life "Already and Not Yet"

In discussing "recontextualizing the moral agent," I pointed to a significant tension between creation-focused ethics (liberation and feminist ethics) and ecclesially-focused ethics. I asked if it is helpful or appropriate to group these two quite distinct approaches together and whether this might not conceal the significant differences in how each understands and uses "context." I also claimed that one can deal with this tension in light of the constructive inter-relationship between "freedom" and "law." God's commandments encompass both sides: They presuppose the ecclesial context of particular practices in and through which God's economy of salvation is communicated and embodied, above all, in Word and Sacrament. Through these distinct ecclesial practices, the Decalogue points us to those intrinsically good acts (the "good works" of faith) in which Christian freedom has its *gestalt*. While rooted in the primary context of ecclesial practices, this *gestalt* is by no means limited to this context. Rather it is co-extensive with our scope as human agents and is primarily directed to the concrete creaturely contexts in which we find ourselves.

Here we share a whole range of determinations, qualifications, and con-ditions with people who do not share our ecclesial vocation. In these contexts in which we share inklings of the natural law, the Decalogue helps us to "re-member" the natural law more fully. Particular creaturely contexts frame the way in which our moral imagination is challenged by God's commandments. In light of hunger and poverty, the Fourth, Fifth and Seventh Commandments imply a radical social and economic critique. They demand just economic structures that enable if not the complete fulfillment of these commandments at least that all people be genuinely challenged by them. In light of the eco-logical crisis, a radical questioning of the unexamined ways of life intrinsic in an excessive and destructive consumer culture follows when we let ourselves be challenged by God's commandments. Yet these contexts that Christians share with all humans *post lapsum* are in tension with the context in which the *gestalt* of Christian freedom takes shape in accordance with the command-ments. As long as the church takes up space in the world, this tension will remain. Attempting to overcome it from the one side results in the eclipse of Christian freedom and its unique *gestalt*—the negation of the difference that the church's unique vocation creates. From the other side, it results in another form of Constantinianism—the church's succumbing to the temptation to make history come out right. As Stanley Hauerwas recently put it:

> A true and proper understanding of nature cannot be had apart from a true and proper understanding of the politics of God's rule. Any discussion of natural law which excludes or omits its ecclesial dimension is therefore bound to be distorted. The converse is also true: any understanding of ecclesiology which occludes its "natural" dimension is likewise skewed. In short, because the God who exercises "grace-full" dominion over creation (nature/human nature) is the same God who revealed himself in Jesus Christ, it follows that such a self-disclosure entails the eschatological necessity (though perhaps not the temporal permanence) of the church.[80]

The First Commandment lays bare the inner dialectic of our condition. We are created toward God, desiring God, yet we have lost the original communion with God. We nevertheless are commanded to attend before and above all other things—especially before ourselves—to God and to fulfill this commandment only through the gift of faith. This tension of our condition is held in suspense. To put it differently, this tension is the substance of the "law" and "gospel" dialectic, the final suspension for which we pray in the Lord's Prayer petition, "Thy kingdom come."

The End

Christian ethics in the tradition of the Reformation serves the remembrance of God's commandments and the interpretation of the innumerable challenges, complexities, and perplexities that we encounter in our world in the critical and wholesome light of God's commandments. Christian ethics in the Reformation tradition should, of course, always end with praise of God's commandments. Luther, the teacher of Christian freedom, wished that every student of theology—and what Christian is not always a student of theology?— would read, meditate, and scrutinize Psalm 119, the praise of God's commandments, on a daily basis.[81]

I began my reflections with the assumption that the themes of "commandment" and "law" are not popular topics today. They are neither "in" nor "cool." Yet, following the advice of Martin Luther, I end with the words of the psalmist, who believed that there could hardly be anything more exciting than to be graciously addressed by God's commandments:

> Thy testimonies are wonderful; therefore my soul keeps them. The unfolding of thy words gives light; it imparts understanding to the simple. With open mouths I pant, because I long for thy commandments. Turn to me and be gracious to me, as is thy wont towards those who love thy name. Keep steady

my steps according to thy promise; and let no iniquity get dominion over me. Redeem me from human oppression, that I may keep thy precepts. Make thy face shine upon thy servant, and teach me thy statutes. My eyes shed streams of tears, because they do not keep thy law (Ps. 119:129-136).[82]

4

Practicing Christians
Prayer as Formation

Martha Ellen Stortz

Introduction

In the midst of a locker-room discussion of religion, a woman asked me, "Are you a practicing Christian?" The word "practicing" caught my attention. "No, I got it right the first time," I said, and we both laughed. Then more soberly I continued, "But the truth is that I need all the practice I can get."

As I reflected more on the exchange, I realized how little in fact I had "gotten it right" and how much this tradition had "gotten" me, placing me in a community of people who, like myself, need all the practice they can get.[1]* In this chapter I will describe Lutheran ethics as a ethics of formation shaped by certain practices.[2] Then I will focus on one of the practices central to that community of faith, personal prayer, and investigate how this practice shapes the people who use it.

Practices of "Practicing Christians"

In the book *Practicing Our Faith*, Craig Dykstra and Dorothy Bass define "practices" as activities that compose a way of life. They identify four distinctive features:

(1) Practices address fundamental human needs and conditions through concrete human acts; they respond ritually to human need. For example, the liturgy of the funeral service contains and choreographs raw emotions of grief, sorrow, and fear.

(2) Practices are done together and over time; they presume community and tradition. We do not need to walk into Holy Week wondering, "What

shall we do this year?" The services follow a flexible pattern that Christians have observed for centuries.

(3) Practices possess standards of excellence that are internal to the practice itself. Prayer is an end in itself. When used as a means to an end and then judged in terms of whether it achieves that end, prayer is no longer a practice but a technique. Practices cultivate virtues; techniques require skills. Building a house is a technique, demanding many and various skills such as masonry, carpentry, and plumbing. The workmanship can be judged by the quality of the house produced. Making a home, on the other hand, is a practice that nurtures virtues of forgiveness, compassion, and fidelity and is possessed of goods internal to the activity of home-making.[3*]

(4) Practices foster perception; they create a distinctive horizon for action. A poet attends to her surroundings differently than a painter: one listens for language; the other watches form, textures, and colors. Christian practices name that horizon as the kingdom of God and train Christians to see God in all things. "Forgive us our trespasses, as we forgive those who trespass against us"; the effect of praying for our enemies is that we see them differently. They too live within the horizon of God's kingdom. A shift in perception fuels a shift in behavior. We treat the enemy differently, perhaps with distance but no longer with censure.[4]

A practice is both related to and distinct from praxis, or action. Praxis, often understood as "practice" and distinguished from theory, stands as a call to action and a complement to reflection. Always qualified by a definite or indefinite article, always described concretely as "a practice" of some habitual activity, a practice shapes action. A practice of prayer certainly forms, informs, and transforms action, discerning what actions to take, how to engage in them, and how to assess their consequences for the kingdom.

As activities that compose a way of life, practices frame a way of being in the world. Christian practices respond to God's initiating act of grace in Jesus Christ in ritual actions that have been transmitted by particular faith communities over space and time. They configure a certain ethos or way of life that is a main concern of ethics.

Traditionally Lutheran ethicists have turned to the doctrines of the faith and not its practices for their foundational insights into Lutheran ethics. Luther's rich theological writings offer many important doctrinal touchstones for the moral life: justification, law and gospel, orders of creation, two kingdoms, Christian freedom, and theology of the cross.[5] Grounding a Lutheran ethic on any one of these doctrines makes two common assumptions: Ethics flows from doctrine, and ethics is then applied deductively to concrete situations. Indeed much of the debate surrounding recent Lutheran social statements deals with questions about the most appropriate doctrinal starting point. Should a social statement on human sexuality begin from the doctrine of law and gospel or the doctrine of Christian freedom? Depending on the starting point, the resultant statement could be quite different.

But how might practices that compose a distinctive way of life inform a Lutheran sexual ethic?[6] This raises the issue of the relationship between practices and doctrines in a tradition that began essentially as a reformation of practices in the late medieval church. Luther found in the practices of the medieval penitential system a righteousness of works antithetical to the righteousness of Christ. He then reformed the practices to enact better the message of the gospel. The doctrine of justification normed the practices of penance, while the practices of penance enacted the doctrine of justification. This reflexive relationship between doctrine and practice suggests that practices embody doctrines and that doctrines norm practices.[7] In a very real way doctrines furnish the aforementioned standards of excellence for evaluating practices. Doctrine that is not enacted in practices is disembodied; practices that are not normed by doctrine are empty.

Linked with the Lutheran doctrinal touchstones listed above are central practices that define Christian communities. Luther called them the "marks" of the church. They are the means by which the church can be "externally recognized" as church.[8] Reflecting on the public character of the church embedded in these practices, Reinhard Hütter regards practices "as the other side of dogma."[9]* He then proceeds to distinguish an inner and outer circle of practices by which the church is publicly identified as church. Actions habitual in the life of any Christian community occupy the inner circle: the proclamation and reception of the Word; baptism; Eucharist; the office of the keys; ordination/offices; prayer/doxology/catechesis; and discipleship. Practices on the outer circle exist as challenges and calling to the church as a public witness: the remembrance of the saints and martyrs and an ongoing procedure of identifying exemplary lives and witnesses; the public stance of theology as ecclesial discourse; pacifism or a way of discerning just and unjust wars; Christian life as our primary vocation; a regular practice of church visitations; base Christian communities as challenge for all Christians; and mutual recognition and fellowship among all Christian communions.[10] These practices enact the doctrines, just as the doctrines inform the practices.

Similarly practices provide the soil for cultivating insight into the stuff of what we believe. The notions of divine mercy and judgment remain abstract until one takes seriously the response in the "Brief Order for Confession and Forgiveness": "We confess we are in bondage to sin and cannot free ourselves. We have sinned against you in thought, word, and deed, by what we have done and by what we have left undone." Reflecting on these words in relationship to self, community, and society and acknowledging the evident brokenness as sin yield insight into God's judgment and sorrow over a creation run amok. Because we confess daily our faults, because we experience daily the grace of forgiveness, we gain some insight into a God whose judgment is tempered with mercy.

In beginning with practices distinctive to Lutheran communities, I propose a starting point that is empirical, not theoretical; that is concrete, not abstract; and that is inductive, not deductive. It is empirical in beginning with the practices of the faith and looking at the kind of life they compose rather than beginning with a theory about ethics and applying it to the everyday. It is concrete in attending to these actual activities and asking how these shape moral agency rather than focusing on abstract principles and examining how they dictate action. Finally it is inductive in moving from actions to the principles that direct them rather than deducing actions from prescribed principles. I am concerned with how the concrete practices of the Christian life describe a certain way of life as "Christian" and define the people in it as "moral agents." These practices shape experience and train people in a certain way of life and a certain way of viewing relationships to God and the neighbor. My concern is with Christian nurture or formation.

Formation

Any talk of "formation" in Lutheran circles immediately meets the formidable challenge that this reintroduces "works-righteousness" into the Reformation. Identifying certain practices as "formational" risks prescribing a series of "self-chosen works" by which one might advance in holiness. These "works" habituate one into a certain way of life; one becomes a Christian by doing them. Being follows from doing.

Luther, it is argued, rejected such an Aristotelian understanding of practice and habituation whereby "one becomes a lutenist by often playing the lute."[11] While this understanding may work for "civil life," one becomes a Christian by grasping and being grasped by Christ in faith. Works follow naturally in response to this new identity. Organic metaphors describe this response: Works follow from faith as fruit from a tree. Thus doing follows from being, and both proceed organically from baptismal faith.

Theologians exploring a distinctively Lutheran understanding of "formation" underscore divine initiative again and again. Leif Grane forbids all talk of formation that does not begin with baptism and daily return to it. Moreover he describes this return as something that Christians do not do but rather undergo. To elaborate beyond this, Grane is convinced, would be to invite another "masterstroke of the devil."[12] Yet at some point do Christian communities not need to be more concrete about what this "daily return to baptism" looks like? What are the practices that sustain it? Grane says nothing about this, doubtless maneuvering around the devil himself.

Robert Jenson distinguishes between "formation," a horticultural metaphor that involves actively shaping something, and "nurture," an agricultural metaphor that suggests that one provides the objective conditions for something that has already begun. He prefers the latter term because it underscores divine initiative. Jenson charges congregations to provide the objective conditions in which the divine initiative can flourish: "a curriculum of theology study and reflection based upon the inherent curriculum of the congregation. . . ."[13] What might this "curriculum" actually look like? Jenson fails to specify.

Gilbert Meilander investigates the problems and possibilities of virtue ethics for Lutheranism in a chapter entitled "The Examined Life is Not Worth Living: Learning from Luther."[14] Meilander allows a limited place for formation so long as one recognizes God as the primary and originating agent. But the question remains: How might Christians respond deliberately to God's initiating action?

Each of these theologians expresses caution regarding any Lutheran appropriation of "formation." They capitalize on the organic language Luther so often uses to explain the relationship between faith and works. Yet they miss another dimension of Luther's language that speaks of practices and formation. In his catechetical material Luther trades organic metaphors for direct instruction. People are not plants; they both need and desire concrete ways of responding to divine initiative. In his pastoral counsel he exhorts pastors in their instruction to "lay the greatest weight on those commandments or other parts which seem to require special attention among the people where you are."[15] Instruction and exhortation replace organic necessity.

Baptism and a life of discipleship intersect in a series of practices that give a rough outline of what it might mean to live out of baptism. If Christian discipleship is the living out of baptism, baptism is the sacramental enactment of discipleship. In baptism the Christian receives both a name and a call. She is named "child of God;" she is invited to "Follow me." Simultaneously the Christian becomes "child of God" and "disciple" of Christ. Christian practices evolve as communities struggle to enact baptism in a life of discipleship. Far from being "self-chosen works," Christian practices allow the baptized to respond to their calling and to offer in lives of praise and service what baptism has conferred. Formation is nothing more and nothing less than initiation into those practices of discipleship. Understanding formation as initiation in the practices of discipleship has important implications for configuring Christian ethics in general and Lutheran ethics in particular.

Formation Shapes Moral Agency. On the first day of an introductory course in ethics, I ask students to define what they think they are there to study. For the most part, they define "ethics" as "doing the right thing." They are not alone. Most people turn to ethics for answers to the question, "What should I do?" They seek insight into action. An exclusive focus on actions, however, obscures other aspects of the moral life such as agency, consequences of actions, context of actions, and recipients.

Formation focuses on the moral agent and frames the question of ethics differently: "Who am I called to be?"[16]* Moral agency describes certain kinds of people or communities whose peculiar attitudes and values express themselves as certain ways of seeing the world and being in it. To a community of pickpockets, all the world is a pocket. More soberly, to a community of Lutherans, all the world is filled with neighbors.

Agency is not an alien emphasis for Lutherans. Exegeting the Sermon on the Mount, a text that for centuries had provided believers with acts of holiness, Luther moves from action to identity: "If you want to be a Christian, then be one."[17] Significantly he does not say: "If you want to be a Christian, do this, this, and that." Rather he focuses on questions of identity, "the kind of people" Christians should be. The heart, not the will, directs the moral life; throughout his exposition Luther exhorts his hearers to "keep a Christian heart."

Luther further sharpens the question of formation. The question "Who am I called to be?" becomes the question "Whose are we?" Justification rectifies the relationship between creator and creatures through Christ, and the moral life evolves out of the new relationship signed and sealed in baptism. Normed and informed by the Decalogue, which tells us "all that God wishes us to do or not to do,"[18] works or actions follow as a cheerful, joyful response to the conviction that in Christ God has acted to reclaim us as creatures of a loving creator. Christian practices choreograph that response. To focus ethics on actions misses the initiating shape of the Christian life: faith in the promises of God.

Formation Requires Community. The legacy of individualism that Robert Bellah and his colleagues documented so carefully in *Habits of the Heart* fashions people as solitary moral agents and makes moral debate a matter of conflicting opinions: my ethics versus your ethics.[19] "A decent respect for the opinions of mankind," language from the Declaration of Independence, relegates moral difference to mere clash of opinion, and the individual remains the locus of moral agency. Moral deliberation, discernment, and formation lose any input from a community.

Formation, in contrast, regards the self as relational. "I" am not an essence waiting to be excavated by the proper spiritual practices or enlightening therapeutic techniques. Rather "I" am quite literally the company I keep. Composing his portrait of "the responsible self," H. Richard Niebuhr delineates the contours of such a self embedded in relationships to God, to society, to time and history.[20] Formation focuses on the shaped and shaping role of individuals and communities.

Luther is deeply aware of how relationships constitute both the individual and the community. His explanation of the Fourth Commandment creates a taxonomy of reciprocal relationships between parents and children, church and believers, citizen and state, servant and master. Moreover the Christian's primary relationship to God orients all of these other relationships and organizes them toward fulfilling God's purposes in the creation.[21]

Formation Tackles the Ordinary. Many people turn to ethics for counsel in hard times and tough situations. Should the United States of America grant "most favored nation" status to a country alleged to sanction human rights abuses? Should you buy clothes that may have been made in sweatshops? How should a pastor respond to a pregnant youth-group member who feels she cannot talk to her parents? The questions reflect real and difficult situations. Yet if the moral life is construed as a series of tough cases, then ethics must accordingly solve problems, answer questions, and resolve quandaries.[22] Moreover unless one is engaged in a problem, question, or quandary, one is assumed to be morally disengaged or ethically in neutral gear. Finally ethics becomes a form of decisionmaking, disregarding who it is that is making the decisions and the arena in which they are deciding.

In contrast formation develops perceptual skills that are then focused on tough situations. Novelist and occasional philosopher Iris Murdoch cautions: "I can only choose within the world I can *see*," suggesting that the work of ethics is ongoing as we struggle to see more accurately the world, the people around us, and the God in whom "we live and move and have our being" (Acts 17:28).[23] Formation urges people to attend to details, identify which details are morally relevant, and make judgments informed by a certain way of seeing. Anyone who has meditated on the Psalms will not fail to notice the poor, because, as the Psalmist writes, "The needy shall not always be forgotten, and the hope of the poor shall not perish forever" (Ps. 9:18).

Writing about the Sermon on the Mount, Luther presents a moral optic. He uses the metaphor of vision to clarify moral orientation. The appropriate conduct, actions, and decision follow from true vision. "'Now, if your eye is sound,' Christ says, 'your whole body is light.' That is, all your activity and life, your outward conduct in your office and social station, is all upright."[24] True vision focuses on God and neighbor; false vision focuses only on the self, casting everything and everyone else in its dark shadow.

Christian Formation Is Essentially Ecclesial and Unabashedly Theological. Joseph Kotva criticizes a tendency in too much of what passes as Christian ethics "to declare Jesus irrelevant for ethics." His message was primarily spiritual, his way of life too deeply contexted in a world vastly different from the contemporary world, and his ethics decidedly interim and apocalyptic, unusable for those who must hunker down for the long haul.[25] To be credible in the public realm and in conversation with people of other faith traditions, Kotva fears, Christian ethics abandons what makes it distinctive in the first place.

Formation challenges this by presenting ethics as inculcation into a certain way of life. Novices encounter years of formation upon their entrance into a particular religious order as they study scripture, absorb the unique tradition they have entered, and learn its charisms. Luther had been so formed upon entrance into the Augustinian Eremites at Erfurt in 1505. Yet he razed the medieval two-story morality, which dictated a minimalist morality for the laity and demanded perfection of those in religious life.[26] He applied the commandments of God with equal rigor to everyone. Dietrich Bonhoeffer gives formation explicitly christological content:

> Formation is not an independent process or condition which can in some way or other be detached from this form. The only formation is formation by and into the form of Jesus Christ. The point of departure for Christian ethics is the body of Christ, the form of Christ in the form of the Church, and the formation of the Church in conformity with the form of Christ.[27]*

For Bonhoeffer as for Luther, ethics as formation can only be understood theologically and must be configured ecclesially.

I have argued for the importance of practices, as well as doctrines, for a Lutheran ethic. Accordingly I have presented formation as initiation into the practices of discipleship. In what follows I examine one such practice, exploring how it contributes to composing a distinctive way of life.

Practices of Formation: Luther's Three-Legged Stool

Practices of the medieval church—specifically the penitential system—provided the impetus for reform, but practices also figured into the mechanisms of reform. Formation was foremost on Luther's mind as he returned in despair from his congregational visitations of 1527 and 1528, stunned to find Christians ignorant of the rudiments of the faith and pastors unable to help them.[28]* The situation prompted publication of the Large and Small Catechisms. In them Luther raged about pastorates "declining and going to ruin" and about a world "now more wicked than it has ever been: there is no government, no obedience, no fidelity, no faith; only presumptuous, ungovernable people, whom no teaching or reproof can help."[29]

The compass of Luther's approach to formation extended beyond catechesis. His "German Mass" of 1526 marked another important catechetical effort because Luther clearly saw worship as opportunity for instruction as well as occasion for praise. "What we most need in our German worship, is a plain, simple, clear and succinct catechism."[30] When it was published in 1529, the Large Catechism circulated with a companion copy of the German Mass.

Finally individual prayer emerges as an aspect of formation. Luther's barber, Peter Beskendorf, asked his client for "a simple way to pray," and Luther responded by outlining "what I do personally when I pray."[31] What follows reads like the Small Catechism, as Luther instructed his friend in praying the Lord's Prayer, the Ten Commandments, and the Creed. Yet Luther prescribed a fourfold format, praying the various petitions and commandments first as instruction, then as thanksgiving, then as confession, and finally as prayer. The spirit of these texts changes as one hears in them "a school text, song book, penitential book, and prayer book." In such a hearing, the "heart comes to itself."[32]

Worship, catechesis, and individual prayer are practices dedicated to formation. They comprise a three-legged stool on which Luther's approach to formation rests. Because space does not permit extensive investigation of each of these, I will examine Luther's counsel on individual prayer for three reasons. First, the material is less well known than Luther's liturgical and catechetical writings. Second, late twentieth-century Christians express great interest in spirituality and the practices of prayer. If Lutherans find nothing in their own tradition, they will turn to other traditions for information and formation.[33] Finally, Luther incorporates worship and catechesis into his recommendations for individual prayer. In many ways the three discrete practices come together in individual prayer.

Luther on Individual Prayer: Instruction on a Practice

It is Luther the pastor and catechist rather than Luther the theological controversialist who offers counsel in Christian practices. Arguing that pastor and catechist were Luther's governing concerns, George Lindbeck observes that "Luther offered his theological ideas only in the context of his recommendations for practice."[34] Historian Marc Lienhard labels Luther's reformation as a "reformation of prayer," because Luther describes a practice that challenged medieval ways of praying.[35] Before examining his counsel on when and what to pray, it is important to situate it. Luther's counsel on prayer is direct, biblically based, tough-mindedly realistic, and crowded.

Context. *Direct.* Luther spoke to people who were not used to praying for themselves. They had been accustomed to an array of intercessors, living and dead, who would pray for them. The words *ora pro nobis*, "pray for us," were always addressed to someone else: Mary, the saints, priests, nuns, and other men and women.

In the face of these intercessory habits, Luther responds sharply: Pray for yourselves and for your neighbor. He chides John Frederick, Duke of Saxony, "Why, your Grace should not leave prayer to the cowls or to the chalices, [putting] . . . one's trust in other men's prayers, without praying oneself."[36] Not only dukes but also barbers! There is an entirely appropriate audacity in a barber asking Luther how he might pray and how he might himself be a pray-er for the neighbor.

Biblically based. The invention of the printing press in 1450 created a profusion of prayerbooks, which were regarded as indispensable to the devout layperson. A small volume functioned as the "yellow pages" of prayer, offering in rapid succession a catalogue of sins for use in confession, lists of ways to gain forgiveness, prayers for the festivals, acrostic prayers to the Virgin, prayers for the hour of death, prayers on the passion of the Lord, prayers guaranteeing a generous number of indulgences from the pains of purgatory if used in certain ways, prayers that guaranteed protection in childbirth or in the hour of death, catalogues of the virtues, lists of works of mercy, lists of the gifts of the Holy Spirit, morning and evening prayers, prayers to various saints and martyrs, the penitential psalms, and the highly regarded prayers of St. Bridget. These prayers covered every malady of the soul. Printers vied to produce the most beautiful, most edifying, and best-selling prayerbook.

In his personal prayerbook of 1522 Luther responds with "plain, ordinary Christian prayer."[37] In his ethical counsel Luther rages against "self-chosen works," and in his devotional counsel he rages against self-chosen prayers, prescribing instead prayers based on Scripture. Scripture was important because Luther deeply believed that through Scripture God addresses God's people in surprising and unexpected ways, even and especially in words that they had heard before.

Luther's prayerbook treats in succession the Ten Commandments, the Creed, the Lord's Prayer, the Hail Mary, and several psalms (12, 67, 51, 103, 20, 79, 25, 10), Paul's epistle to Titus, and woodcuttings of key Bible verses with the full text of the verse included. Medieval Christians, even those who could not read and could not afford prayerbooks, had already memorized the Ten Commandments, the Creed, the Lord's Prayer, and the Hail Mary. They had in their hearts everything they needed to pray.

Tough-mindedly realistic. Contemplative prayer throughout the Middle Ages followed a distinctive pattern: reading of Scripture, prayer, meditation, and contemplation (*lectio, oratio, meditatio, contemplatio*). Reading of Scripture or *lectio* initiated prayer or *oratio*, which was direct speech with God. This second stage of prayer should be pure, brief, and frequent (*pura, frequens, brevis*). Meditation focused on the appropriation and repetition of a word or words of Scripture. Contemplation brought all the activities together in a sustained attitude of attentiveness to God, "as a result of which everything became prayer and longing."[38] The goal of contemplative prayer was communion with God.

Luther, the former monk, broke with the pattern of prayer in which he had been instructed. His 1539 preface to the Wittenberg edition of his work changes and rearranges this order completely: prayer, reading of Scripture, and finally, suffering (*oratio, meditatio, tentatio*). Where traditionally the reading of Scripture prepared one for prayer, Luther suggests that prayer (*oratio*) prepares one for the reading of Scripture. Meditation (*meditatio*) follows, described as a reading of Scripture that engages the heart. Luther eliminates contemplation entirely, supplanting it with suffering (*tentatio*). He warns his readers that once the Word of God takes root and begins to grow, "The devil will harry you, and will make a real doctor of you, and by his assaults will teach you to seek and to love God's word."[39] In contrast to the medieval pattern of contemplative prayer, where everything became "prayer and longing," here everything becomes suffering and temptation. Only the Word sustains one in suffering, and the Christian returns to the beginning: prayer as preparation for the reading of Scripture. Engagement with the Word sustains one in the world.

Crowded. Resisting the Calvinist impulse to turn the city into a monastery by organizing it around quasi-monastic regulations, Luther turned the monastery into a city, placing the housewife and blacksmith alongside the theologian and inviting all to a common life of Christian discipleship. Prayer is a foundational part of that common life. Luther acknowledges days on which he is so busy "I cannot get on without spending three hours daily in prayer."[40] Perhaps it took him that long to drain the day's anxieties away so that he could concentrate on being with God. But it is also clear that Luther's considerable responsibilities took him not away from prayer but into it. The three hours Luther spent in prayer were far from solitary. He brought his concerns, his enemies and friends, his joys and frustrations before God.

Luther gives a rather unglamorous and stolid alternative to medieval prayerbooks: prayer that is direct, biblically based, tough-mindedly realistic, and crowded. Examining his context suggests a similarity to our own as we survey a marketplace of spiritualities that promise self-realization, problem-solving, and happiness. Perhaps Luther confronted demons in his time that have only scrambled through the centuries to lodge in our own. His specific instructions on when and what one prays suggest contours for contemporary formation into a Lutheran ethos.

When One Should Pray. For Luther prayer is a daily matter. He recommends praying first thing in the morning and last thing at night. Ever the realist, he cautions the Christian against putting off prayer: "Guard yourself carefully against those false, deluding ideas which tell you, 'Wait a little while. I will pray in an hour; first I must attend to this or that.' Such thoughts get you away from prayer into other affairs which so hold your attention and involve you that nothing comes of prayer for that day."[41] Count this as advice from a man who clearly worked too much but needed to pray more the more he had to do.

This may be chastening counsel for busy people, but with prayer the view alters. Murdoch observes that our horizons of vision can be expansive or truncated. She notes that we organize our moral universe in accord with what we see on that horizon of vision.[42] Prayer expands the horizon of vision from the landscape of a solitary life, family, or country to the geography of God. An event in one scenario suddenly gains the perspective of a larger terrain. Prayer orients one daily to a larger landscape and a divine terrain. In his chapter in this book, Richard Perry suggests that Sister Emma Francis' public practice of prayer, morning and evening devotions, and regular participation in church sustained her expansive vision of service.

Prescribing prayer every morning and evening suggests that Luther wants prayer to become a habit so that Christians would not have to worry about whether it happened, when it happened, and what would be said. Such a habit allows for an openness to other things, and in its very routine forces one deeper and deeper into the mystery of God. If prayer becomes routine, Christians' illusions about God will hopefully fade. They learn to see God more sharply; they learn to perceive the world through God's eyes. Hopefully conversations with God come to resemble the conversations one has with a husband or wife of forty years, a friend of long-standing. They may not be elegant, but they are real. The sheer routine of prayer dispels all illusions and banishes all formalities—something Luther doubtless knew when he counseled daily prayer.

What One Should Pray. Luther wants to routinize when one prays but also what one prays. He suggests a standard format for daily prayer, much like the stretches a runner does before sprinting, or the arpeggios a vocalist does before singing. He advises repeating the Ten Commandments or words of Christ or Paul to "warm the heart."[43]

Warm-up completed, Luther suggests starting with the Lord's Prayer, repeating and reflecting on each of its seven petitions. He admits the challenge in hearing afresh a prayer so familiar, but this is the only way one truly "tastes" this prayer and "suckles at [it] like a child."[44] Throughout his counsel Luther cautions the Christian to pause when she needs to, lingering over whatever catches her heart. "The Holy Spirit himself preaches here, and one word of his sermon is far better than a thousand of our prayers."[45]

Prayer proceeds then not by talking but by listening and by listening to Scripture. This distinguishes individual worship and prayer from corporate worship and prayer. Throughout *The Book of Concord*, the authors consistently speak of preaching and hearing in regard to corporate worship.[46] In contrast Luther's counsel on individual prayer highlights preaching and listening, listening for the preaching of the Holy Spirit. Receptive listening keeps familiar words from going stale.[47]

From the Lord's Prayer Luther moves on to the Ten Commandments, to which he devotes the bulk of his instruction.[48]* Here he alters the approach of repetition and reflection; he fashions of the Ten Commandments "a garland of four strands," an intricate braid. He presents it first as a school text that instructs the Christian, then as a song book that sings praises of thanksgiving, then as a penitential book that confesses sin, and finally as a prayerbook, offering petitions to the Lord for one's self, for the neighbor, for the world.[49]

The effect of this practice of praying is to give familiar words a new hearing. Luther provides examples from his own world for how a citizen of Wittenberg might braid this four-stranded garland. Lutheran pastors and teachers today are challenged to do the same.

Instruction, thanksgiving, confession, and petition, or, as Luther puts it more lyrically: school book, songbook, penitential book, and prayerbook. After weaving the Ten Commandments into this four-stranded garland, Luther recommends approaching the Apostle's Creed in the same fourfold fashion. He divides the Creed into three petitions for each of the "three great lights," Father, Son, and Holy Spirit, encountered plainly in the world and in prayer.[50] In this final piece of prayer, God is named. To the degree that people become what they worship, Christians naming God also name themselves as creatures of this God and participants in this divine life. Concluding this sequence of prayer, the Creed tells Christians who God is and what they can expect God to continue doing for and with them.

This is a lot to take on. One begins to understand why Luther spent three hours each day in prayer! But Luther constantly cautions against rigidity. He observes that the time one encounters in prayer knows no relation to the time measured by Greenwich mean time. In prayer things happen simultaneously: "For the mind, once it is seriously occupied with a matter, be it good or evil, can ponder more in one moment than the tongue can recite in ten hours or the pen write in ten days."[51] Weaving a four-stranded garland out of the Ten Commandments and the Creed could go very quickly—or it could go nowhere. Cautious about attempts to systematize his counsel, Luther votes for staying with certain phrases or words that animate the soul. In short he recommends "getting stuck" in prayer. Most importantly prayer is the pulpit of the Holy Spirit.

Contours of the Christian Life:
Composing a Way of Life

What would happen if a Christian immersed herself in these practices of prayer on a daily basis? What would she become? Who would he be? Daily exercise in this practice of prayer would compose a way of life shaped by several distinctive dispositions: responsiveness, gratitude, modesty, and joy.

Responsiveness. For Luther prayer is dialogue and direct address. God speaks; Christians respond. In his personal prayerbook and in his counsel on individual prayer, Luther deliberately chooses material that directly addresses either God or the one praying: biblical material like the Ten Commandments, where God speaks to the community, and the Lord's Prayer, where the one praying speaks to God. The Psalms also contain direct address and, as noted, Luther appended several to his personal prayerbook. While not biblical, the creed directly addresses God and names God as Father, Son, and Spirit. Direct address demands response.[52]

Gratitude. Gratitude marks the life of prayer. Significantly in his four-stranded garland, Luther places thanksgiving before confession and petition. Thanksgiving and praise dominate the Christian life. As Luther notes in his Genesis commentary, the God who regarded Joseph in prison was a God who "surely has a record of every drop that falls from our eyes. If you weep, He has a golden basin . . . and catches the tears! But whose tears does He gather? The tears of sinners. Who gathers them? God the creator of all things."[53] Experience of the boundless goodness of God evokes gratitude.

Modesty. Repetition and the penitential character of prayer breed modesty. Christians return to the same rudiments of prayer every day because they need to. The same texts recount the same transgressions: idolatry, gossiping, mean-spiritedness, distraction, disloyalty. Only the disguises change. One never gets "well" or "whole" or "fully realized" in the life of Christian discipleship, except by grasping Christ. Anyone interested in developing the role of the moral virtuoso ought to seek counsel elsewhere.

Indeed Luther determines that perhaps the biggest transgression is the temptation to be a virtuoso of any sort. The Pharisee, he observes, does not really want the publican to be anything but a sinner so that he can compare favorably.[54] The temptation to be better even than God has good precedent. As Luther reads him, Adam goes so far as to blame God for the apple incident: it was God after all who put such a tempting tree in the Garden of Eden. Adam, feigning superior wisdom, would have done things differently.[55] Adam is not an antique exception on these matters.

Joy. Joy marks the Christian life, and to know why, one need only revisit that overly and sadly only partially quoted statement of Luther's: *Pecca fortiter*, "Sin boldly!" Often read as command, it is in reality a sad statement of fact. But Luther went on: *sed fortius fide et gaude in Christo!*, "but even more boldly believe and rejoice in Christ!" Joy replaces the terminal anxiety that is the final fall-out of moral zealotry. The thought world of the overly zealous disciple is all too easy to re-create. The rat wheels of anxiety spin endlessly.

To understand the logic of joy in Christian life, one need only listen to Luther give his rationale for placing the Creed after the Ten Commandments in his catechisms and in his order for prayer. While the Ten Commandments reveal "all that God wishes us to do or not to do, the Creed properly follows, setting forth all that we must expect and receive from God."[56] God gives what God commands, naming God in the Creed identifies God's gifts to God's creatures. How could one be anything but joyful? Don Saliers explains that the peculiar character of Christian joy is neither passing mood nor fleeting emotion but rather "a persistent way of assessing one's life in the light of what God is doing."[57]

Clarifying the Contours. Responsiveness, gratitude, modesty, and joy— sounds oddly like a Lutheran book of virtues. But it would be erroneous to interpret these as habits for which the Christian should strive. That would truly make of these virtues "works," skills appropriate for a technique rather than virtues developed by a practice. Practices, like the practice of prayer described above, compose a way of life. Virtues, like those described above, are the result of daily exercise in the practice of prayer. People who engage daily in this practice move through the world with responsiveness, gratitude, modesty, and joy. This is what happens to people to whom the Holy Spirit preaches. These virtues mark a distinctive way of being in a discipleship shaped by the sort of prayer Luther prescribes.

While much of the academic study of ethics has tended to ignore virtues, moving on to big dilemmas, tough situations, great quandaries, Luther seems more concerned with ordinary life. He pitches his basic instruction in Christian ethics not to battlefields or intensive care units or war rooms but to places where ordinary people show up with regularity and without fanfare: home, school, church, work, and neighborhood.

Prayer and Action

I have used this focus on practices and formation as another point of entry into a discussion that has traditionally taken one of any number of doctrinal starting points. In identifying distinctive features of Lutheran ethics, it has seemed helpful to turn to concrete, congregational practices and to ask, how do these compose a way of life?

Hopefully this analysis will not only help practicing Christians understand the life their practices compose, but it might also reframe critical debates about Lutheran ethics. Citing Luther's concerns about legalism, works-righteousness, and the priority of divine initiative, Ernst Troeltsch characterized Lutheran ethics as an ethic of disposition (*Gesinnungsethik*). He contrasted this with an objective ethic (*Objectivethik*) that would feature rules and principles directing actions.[58] In such cataloguing, however, Troeltsch lost sight of the significance of the practices Luther prescribed and the formation he encouraged. He ignored Luther's intense preoccupation with catechesis or initiation into that way of life. Finally he missed Luther's attention to the role of rules, particularly the Decalogue, in the congregations under his care.

Unfortunately Troeltsch's judgments have set the tone for other evaluations of Luther's ethics. Appropriating Troeltsch's distinctions, James M. Gustafson argues that in his campaign against works righteousness Luther courts the equal and opposite danger of "moral intuitionism," providing little objective direction for the moral life:

> God's love in and through man in faith, gives the end and the shape of Christian moral behavior. Luther did not use the Aristotelian pattern of virtues to program the ways in which love is formed in the self or is the means of its embodiment. The good man does good deeds; the 'substance' of the person must be renewed. But the delineation of that substance is neither as refined nor as clear in Luther. There is less definition of the sieve through which love is to be directed, and this certainly makes for a greater sense of spontaneity and freedom. Whether this is finally due to a lack of interest on Luther's part, to the perception of a theological fault in portraying the self in such intricate terms, or to the overwhelming sense of new life Luther had, is not for us to decide.[59]

In Gustafson's view Luther presents an ethic of character without the requisite attention to formation, namely, to how character is shaped, formed, or molded.

This chapter revisits these judgments by displaying Luther's obvious efforts in the work of formation. Rather than recruiting Aristotle in this enterprise, Luther turns to the practices of Christian discipleship or, in his own words, to the "marks of the church." These practices shape person and community for worship and witness. Virtues like responsiveness, gratitude, modesty, and joy come to characterize people and communities who engage in the practices. The Decalogue is the template for discerning concrete acts on behalf of the neighbor in the world.

As noted earlier in this chapter, Luther names a number of practices that function as "marks of the church": proclamation of the Word and its reception in faith, confession, and deed; baptism; Eucharist; the office of the keys; ordination/offices; prayer/doxology/catechesis; and the way of the cross/discipleship. In their chapter Cynthia Moe-Lobeda and Larry Rasmussen implicitly question whether another practice ought to be added to this list: care for the whole of creation. There may be considerable debate about what practices mark and ought to mark the contemporary church, about the ordering and prioritization of practices, and about the relationship of practices to action. I have not chosen to engage those debates here.

Rather than general talk about Christian practices, I have preferred to tackle a single, concrete practice in detail. While suggesting that worship, catechesis, and personal prayer constitute a trinity at the heart of Luther's work of formation, I focus here on the practice of prayer. Besides addressing a concern central of contemporary Christians, Luther's counsel on prayer represents well his concern for formation in general, his attention to the Decalogue in particular, and his desire to shape Christian action. My conclusion is simultaneously a program for further investigation: a closer examination of the connection between prayer and action.

How does prayer shape action? If it is the case that we can only act in the world that we see, then vision is crucial to action. Prayer forms and informs moral vision in several ways. Most importantly prayer enlarges the scope of moral vision; with prayer the view alters. We live differently depending on whether we think the context of our actions is a neighborhood, a nation, a hemisphere, or a global village. Daily prayer rearranges horizons. If the Decalogue contains "all that God wishes us to do or not to do," the Creed sets forth "all that we must expect and receive from God."[60] If God is acting in and with us, even the global village is too small a context for action. The horizon for action is nothing less than the life of the triune God. Praying daily the Decalogue and the Creed reinforces that scope.

In inscribing a horizon for action, prayer tells Christians what they are looking at. Prayer also tells Christians what they are looking for. Because Luther encouraged the Christian to pray "for yourself and the neighbor" rather than delegating prayer to priests or pastors, he invited Christians to see God in all things and see the stranger as neighbor. If I am lost in thought, I do not see an old and overburdened woman on a crowded bus. The question of coming to her aid is moot since she is invisible to me. Prayer reminds me what to look for and makes the surroundings more visible.

In addition prayer exercises the faculty of attention, the ability to see something as it really is without fantasy or delusion, without calibrating everything in terms of its relationship to the self. The poet Rainer Maria Rilke praised the artist Paul Cézanne for this kind of candor, contrasting his work with a self-indulgent painting of sentiments, "They'd paint: I love this here; instead of painting: here it is."[61] Prayer encourages us to see things—ourselves, God, and our surroundings—as they really are. Prayer both requires and creates attention as one waits on the "preaching of the Holy Spirit."

From attention follows perception, noticing morally distinctive or salient aspects of both situation and person. Only when someone is truthfully seen can certain aspects of her person be assessed as morally significant. The older woman with two heavy grocery bags on a crowded bus is suddenly seen as someone who is suffering. Imagination connects attention and perception by linking something visible—an older woman with two large parcels—with a pattern we have seen before and recognize in a burst of empathy as suffering. The woman is suddenly seen as someone who is uncomfortable. Imagination allows us to see someone as something or someone else: to see this woman as a neighbor whose evident discomfort has a claim on my own comfort.[62]

Often a failure to act or an inappropriate act stems from failing to see something or someone as having a claim on us. Throughout his counsel and catechesis on the Decalogue, Luther talks constantly about "the neighbor," even when the text of the commandment does not mention this. Such repetition cannot fail to aid in perception, that is, in the ability to see another as neighbor not stranger. These exercises in perception not only affect how we see others but also how we see ourselves and God. Praying constantly to "forgive us our trespasses" requires that we name the places of brokenness in our lives, an act that reinforces a spirit of modesty in the face of grandiosity and a spirit a joy in God's unfailing love in the face of creaturely unloveliness.

Perception informs moral judgment, which is the ability to apply general rules to specific situations. Using the Decalogue as a template for action, we discern what to do and how to do it.[63] Once a stranger is seen as the neighbor, perception aids in judging how one might concretely apply the Fifth Commandment on a crowded bus. The commandment gives parameters for action, proscribing actions that fall outside those parameters (killing, back-biting, gossip, unjust economic transactions, uncharitable readings of another's behavior) and prescribing how to "help and befriend [the neighbor] in every necessity of life."[64] Praying the Decalogue on a daily basis primes one for action, imprinting on the heart general rules for responding to the neighbor. Responsiveness, gratitude, modesty, and joy—virtues shaped by prayer—yield instruction in how to act.

Finally prayer locates the moral agent, the one who is acting. Daily prayer with fixed texts invites us to attend to familiar words in changing situations. The elements of daily prayer—the Decalogue, the Creed, the Lord's Prayer— become a sort of moral compass, positioning and repositioning us as we move through the ordinary and extraordinary events of our lives. Through them we see sharply our finite points of view. Through them we are continually reoriented to the One who functions as the polestar of our lives.

"Are you a practicing Christian?" A practicing Christian, particularly a Christian trained in the practice of prayer as Luther counseled it, not only practices but acts in the world and on behalf of the neighbor. Along with the other practices of Christian discipleship, prayer informs moral vision, inviting one to attend, to imagine, to perceive, to judge, and finally to be oriented to the God in whom we place our final faith and trust.[65]

❧ 5 ❧
African American Lutheran Ethical Action
The Will to Build

Richard J. Perry Jr.

> When a man starts out to build a world,
> He starts first with himself
> And the faith that is in his heart—
> The strength there,
> The will there to build.[1]

In the poem "Freedom's Plow," Langston Hughes demonstrates three dimensions of African American ethical action: faith, the will to build, and freedom. Faith pushes freedom's plow. The will to build is a metaphor for African American ethical action. The goal of building is freedom connected with the religious and social advancement of African American people. The will to build reflects a spirituality that stresses survival in any context. It is a call to transcend any context through ethical action by building a community of freedom.

In my focus on this will to build,[2] I will contend that African American Lutheran ethical action is rooted in the African American ethical tradition and similar to the pietistic tradition of Lutheranism articulated in the United States during the mid-nineteenth century. First I identify the sources, norm, content, and goal of ethical action from an African American perspective. Second I explore the ministries of three African Americans: the Rev. Jehu Jones Jr., Sister Emma Francis, and Bishop Daniel Alexander Payne. Third I investigate several official documents of the Franckean Synod, a nineteenth-century synod with pietistic origins. Finally I identify some implications for a "Lutheran" ethic in the twenty-first century.

History and Social Location

My point of view is historical. The story of African American Lutheranism has essentially been a hidden one, especially when told from an African American perspective. The stories of this "great cloud of witnesses" serve as a beacon for contemporary and future ethical action by African American Lutherans. The question about history is more than "What did African American Lutherans do once upon a time?" It also embraces the question "What in the legacy of African American Lutherans can guide ethical action today?" The being and behavior of African American Lutherans cannot have meaning apart from what God in Jesus Christ has done and is doing within the African American community.

Christian ethicists disagree on how much attention they ought to give to social location. For some doing theology or ethics from the perspective of the poor and marginalized contributes to the "secularization" of the church with the danger that the church's core will be lost.[3*] Contemporary liberation theologies, on the other hand, contend that theology and ethics are a reflection on how God acts in particular communities. One cannot make adequate ethical responses without recognizing the social, cultural, economic, and political factors that shape those responses. Ethical action looks different if you are poor, uneducated, a woman, or politically disenfranchised.

Construing the ethical task in this manner enables us as Lutherans to face one of the continuing pressing problems in our context today: racism. Although strides have been made to reduce outward expressions of racist behavior, problems continue to fester in the moral and spiritual soul of America and the church.

One way to discover what constitutes a "Lutheran" ethic is to retrieve how and on what basis Lutherans have responded to institutionalized racism. If it is the case that the core of Lutheran ethics is the "two kingdoms" concept, did African American and Franckean Lutherans employ it as a basis for ethical action? In the midst of the pressing problem of race, did they draw from such doctrines as justification and sanctification? Or did they call upon theological and ethical resources outside of Lutheranism? These and other questions may lead us to some clarity about the foundation of Lutheran ethics, especially African American Lutheran ethical action. This is especially important for Lutherans as we seek to work with others in constructing a just, free, equitable, and equal legacy within Lutheranism and the wider society.

This chapter provides a glimpse into the life, thought, and liberating service of African American Lutherans. It does not claim to be a definitive study of the theological and ethical thought of African American Lutherans. Yet this study confirms that African people within the global Lutheran communion have established a plurality of ways of living out the Christian ethic.

Elements of Ethical Action

Christian theology and ethical action contain various elements that contribute to how we think about God and act in our contexts. These interrelated elements do not constitute the whole of ethical action. We may not be aware that we are employing them in our public practice. Yet they provide a framework for unveiling African American and European American Lutheran ethical action in the nineteenth and early twentieth centuries.

Sources of Ethical Action. *Scripture.* Scripture is essential because it is the primary document of the Christian faith, the record of God's revelation to God's people. For African Americans Scripture provides a view of God, Jesus, human nature, the mission of the church, and how to treat other human beings that sustains the community's struggle for freedom. The scriptural images of God's liberating acts of freedom—especially the Exodus event; Jesus' life, death, and resurrection; and Paul's proclamation in Galations 3:28—provide theological and ethical bases for ethical action. These readings emerged in the nineteenth-century formation of the independent African American church.[4] The scriptural story closely paralleled the African American situation and authenticated the pursuit of freedom with justice.[5]*

Experience. Experience figures prominently in ethical action by African Americans. More than an inward look at the awesome nature of God and Jesus Christ in an individual's life, experience has also to do with the concrete nature of life, with the joys and pains of a community. Since in the United States a disproportionate number of African Americans are poor, the experience of poverty becomes decisive. Race along with economic depravity and limited political power figure prominently in the African American life situation. The relationship between Scripture and the African American experience is a dialectical one. Scripture questions and tests our experience, and our experience questions and tests Scripture.

History. The story of African Americans, on the one hand, tells how the dominant culture systematically controlled and destroyed the life of African people. On the other hand, the story celebrates the ability of a downtrodden people to overcome insurmountable obstacles. The ability to celebrate in spite of being sinned against is grounded in faith—the will to build a world of freedom for all people. History is a source that recalls the story of God's activity in the life of the community.

Tradition. As a fourth source of African American ethical action, tradition has both a universal and particular dimension. The universal aspect begins with the early Christian community. The boundaries for our thinking about God, Jesus Christ, and ethical action are set through the witness of the early Christians. The particularity of tradition is the African American community's appropriation of the person and work of Jesus Christ. African Americans focus on the witness of such people as Sojourner Truth, Frederick Douglass, Shirley Chisholm, and Martin Luther King Jr. and their commitment to build a community of freedom for all people. For African American Lutherans Lutheranism is also a particular tradition. As the 1986 Harare statement declared, "The Lutheran heritage and its doctrinal formulations continue to be a resource for us in our present situation."[6] The Protestant Reformation and Luther's witness are a story that African American Lutherans critically embrace. What makes African American Lutherans distinctive is an ability to combine both traditions through a diversity of ethical responses.

Culture. Culture is a source tied up with a community's experience and history; through it a community expresses its soul, its spirit to the world. Culture is the silky poetry of Maya Angelou, the rhythmic music of the Winans, and the groit-like skills of the comedian Sinbad and the novelist Toni Morrison. It is the arts, literature, songs, hymns, sermons, and worship—the style through which God's incarnated word is expressed by African American people. Culture creatively engages the past with the present.

The Norm of Ethical Action. An interpretative principle, a norm determines how the sources are used and authorizes and guides ethical action taken by an individual Christian or a specific Christian community. Because as Christians we confess with the early Christian community that Jesus Christ is Lord, our norm is universal. It is also particular since each community gives testimony to its encounter with God's action in and through the person and work of Jesus Christ. Throughout the African American experience, the norm has been Jesus Christ the Liberator (Luke 4) who frees us from all oppression.[7]*

The Content of Ethical Action. The content of ethical action is the holistic process through which God justifies and sanctifies. Through God's unmerited grace, we become "new creatures." Sanctification, being empowered by the Holy Spirit, means doing works of justice. While justification focuses on the relationship between God and the individual, sanctification focuses on human relationships, on what we do with each other. The 1986 Harare statement of African and African American Lutherans underscores the unity of justification and sanctification: "We also assert unequivocally that there is an inextricable link and relationship between who one is, namely a baptized and adopted child of God, and what one does, namely living and acting in conformity to the will of God."[8] Justification and working for justice are a total process initiated by God for the people of God.[9]

The Goal of Ethical Action. The goal is to build a community of freedom. Freedom is more than a spiritual freedom involving an ahistorical understanding of God's act of forgiveness and the work of the Holy Spirit. Freedom from an African American perspective is historically situated and includes action to enhance the life of the community. The goal is to assure that God's excluded people are full participants at the Table of Grace and have the opportunity to pursue their dreams. Thus Hughes exhorts: Keep one's hand to the plow. While freedom is manifest in the concreteness of life, it has a "not yet" dimension. The believer strives to make freedom real, knowing that full freedom "comes in the morning."

These five elements of ethical action provide a framework for elaborating ethical action by African American and Franckean Lutherans. Before elaborating their ethical action, we need to probe the African American ethical tradition.

The African American Ethical Tradition

African American ethical action begins in Africa, a huge and diverse continent with many languages, peoples, cultures, and religious beliefs. Although there is diversity, African people constructed a particular view of the world, religion, and ethical action. John Mbiti makes this clear in his description of African religious structure to life. This structure includes an integrated understanding of the sacred and secular, an emphasis on community, and a sense of the ethical as directly connected with religion. Failure to be connected with the religion of one's community "amounts to a self-excommunication from the entire life of the society, and African peoples do not know how to exist without religion."[10]

This pervasive nature of religion is grounded in a concept of God. God the supreme being is the creator and source of everything in the world. God's reality is so pervasive that one does not have to be told the supreme being exists; even children know God exists.[11] A host of lesser divinities, ancestors, and priests mediate the power of God in the community.

African Morality. African conceptions of morality presuppose that God is a moral being. God, the creator of everything, is good and wills good things to happen in the life of the community. Since God called the universe into an orderly and harmonious unity, all creation must be sacred to God. Accordingly African peoples understand God as love since God "would not have created them" if God did not love them.[12]

Implicit in this belief is an emphasis on kinship or community. Kinship or community involves everything that brings human beings together: the extended family, the "living dead," those yet unborn, and nature. Through rituals, ceremonies, stories, and proverbs, the community teaches and trains its members in what constitutes "good" and "bad" behavior. Individuals in the community learn what behavior enhances the life of the community and are encouraged to practice these behaviors.[13]* Thus Mbiti contends that African morality is dynamic rather than static because "it defines what a person does rather than what he is."[14] Ethical or moral action is functional because its goal is to enhance the life of the community, and that is good.

African American Continuity with African Morality. In his important book *The Spirituality of African Peoples,* Peter J. Paris demonstrates the continuity between African and African American ethical action.[15] This continuity is based on a common spirituality, an "animating and integrative power" connected with life.[16] Concepts of God, community, family, and the individual constitute four pillars of this common spirituality. Paris identifies six virtues (beneficence, forbearance, practical wisdom, improvisation, forgiveness, and justice) that appear in the public practice of African and African Americans. These virtues manifest themselves in the lives of people like President Nelson Mandela and Dr. Martin Luther King Jr.[17] Mandela and King share a common spirituality because their public practice exhibits faithfulness to their community's concept of appropriate responses to the world. They remained faithful by working to build a world community of freedom.

The African American Church. Scholars differ on the relationship between the religious and ethical traditions of African people and those of African American people. E. Franklin Frazier believed that the Middle Passage and slavery stripped African people of their African origins. For him Christianity provided "a new basis for social cohesion."[18] On the other hand, Lawrence Levine argues that African people came to the United States with a myriad of beliefs, languages, and religious practices. He further contends that African Americans created a cosmology that reflects a creative response to the reality of being a slave.[19] A third position, put forward by scholars like Paris, contends that African American religious and ethical thought is an amalgam of the encounter between African and European American worldviews.

This amalgam emerges in the African American church. This church became a community where one could freely worship God, exercise leadership, and realize freedom.[20]* It was and still is the primary institution that embodies "the goals and purposes that pertain primarily to the welfare of black people." This unique institution promotes an alternate view of what constitutes humanity and responsible ethical action.[21]

A strength of the African American church is its ability to be flexible in its response to the world. C. Eric Lincoln and Lawrence H. Mamiya attribute this ability to it being a "dialectical church."[22] It is a dynamic institution that constantly struggles with tensions and polarities in changing situations. A dialectical church supports a diversity of viewpoints and responses to the world that enables members to move beyond one interpretation of the church and one response to its context.[23]

Even with its flexibility, the church has maintained its mission to transmit to its members "creative forms of coping."[24] The church embraced the task of teaching members a tradition of ethical action that protested the immoral and amoral nature of European American Christianity. This tradition not only protested against racism in church and in society but also offered a way of plowing a new furrow for freedom's seed to grow. Its emphasis was and is on building a world of freedom, justice, and equality in church and society.

A Tradition of Ethical Responses In outlining the ethical responses of this dialectical institution, I follow the types Peter Paris identifies: priestly, prophetic, political, and nationalist.[25] These ideal types are useful as a framework for identifying and clarifying ethical action by Lutherans.

Priest. The priestly response, whose roots are lodged in Africa, is perhaps the oldest of all responses. The priest represents God to the people, interprets the symbols of the faith, performs the community's rituals, and motivates the people to deeper spiritual convictions. Society is good, despite the racism some practice. The programmatic thrust of the priestly response is guided by the value of racial self-development; programs are created that can build self-esteem within and among the people. The ethic that emerges is realistic accommodationism. In its public practice, the pastoral function is to care for souls and the political function is to work behind the scenes to accomplish the community's goals.[26]

Prophetic. This response with its roots in the Antebellum period emphasizes confrontation with society and church. The prophetic response also views society as good yet recognizes the need to confront evil practices. Since God is a God of justice, the prophetic response seeks a moral end in all of its activity. Reform must be constructive and nonviolent. Its central value is racial self-fulfillment, namely, fulfilling our God-given talents as African Americans. An ethic of idealism emerges. The prophet has a vision of what church and society should be and uses moral persuasion to bring about their transformation. Prophetic ethical action is directed toward building social and racial justice in the world.[27]

Political. The roots of this response are in Reconstruction. It emerges from the experience of powerlessness and tends toward problem-solving and compromise. While the political system may be sinful, the community needs to organize to implement its goals. The political response is guided by the value of racial self-initiation. The African American community like every other community has the right to organize itself politically to achieve its goals. Its ethic is one of realism similar to the priestly response: Know the system and use the system to further the community's goals. African American ministers, especially those elected to public office, view political participation as an extension of their pastoral ministry.[28]

Nationalist. The roots of this response are located primarily in the colonization movement. The nationalist response views all social institutions and society itself as evil and calls for their reordering or complete change. To accomplish this the nationalist supports separation from the past and present experience of evil. Racial self-determination is the guiding value. Once African Americans have discarded how they are defined by the dominant culture, they must move toward defining themselves. When this occurs, a "race first" ideology and group solidarity are embraced. The ethic that emerges is liberation from all human controls external to the African American community.[29]

A Lutheran Connection? When African Americans join European American denominations, questions emerge about their theological perspective. Are African Americans Lutheran or Methodist or Baptist? Questions of this nature become personal affronts when they assume that the theological perspectives African Americans bring with them are second class. How does European American Lutheran tradition converge with the African American tradition?

At the 1986 Harare Conference, James Kenneth Echols suggested one convergence.[30] European American Lutherans speak of "two kingdoms" (or two realms) and African Americans speak of "two worlds."[31]* The former understands that God employs a twofold rule in the world, the law and the gospel. God rules the kingdom on the left through law or the state to restrain sin and to ensure justice for all people. This corresponds with the African American understanding of "this world," where freedom is worked out. The kingdom on the right refers to God's justification of the sinner while the gospel rules. This corresponds to the "other world" in African American thought. Since African American existence is permeated by oppression, the other world is considered a time when slavery will not rule. There is convergence in how the two realms are conceptualized.

While there is convergence, continues Echols, the issue is the public practice that emanates from the two kingdoms concept. Lutherans have placed an emphasis on Romans 13 (submission to human authorities), which led to a public practice of quietism and social conservatism.[32] African Americans, on the other hand, have taken a stance that emphasizes prophetic activism, with a focus on building a world of freedom and transforming the structures of evil. Thus Acts 5 (obedience to God) was invoked rather than Romans 13.

Simon Maimela, a South African Lutheran theologian, also affirms invoking the two kingdoms concept. The church has a responsibility to speak God's word to the state. That word is both law and gospel. It reminds the state that it is "to account for and to justify its actions before God" and in so doing its role is "to establish law and justice, and maintain peace and security for all persons given to its care."[33] As the church confesses and preaches the word of God to the state, it joins in solidarity with the poor and excluded members of society. The church reminds the state that its task is more than its power to harass and punish its citizens. The state is to care for the poor.

Through the church's confession and proclamation of law and gospel, the relative nature of the state is revealed for what it is, a human construct. Law and gospel revealed how the state in apartheid South Africa became an absolute that was deified and oppressed people. The preaching office of the church "relativize[d] and de-divinize[d] the apartheid system" and reminded people that it was a human invention.[34]

African and African American ethical responses to racism then can be compatible with a Lutheran construal of the two kingdoms. From the African American perspective, the priestly and the political responses both seek realistic goals for the community. They cooperate with systems of oppression in order to access resources and benefits for the good of the community. Further, both believe that government has a responsibility to maintain order and execute justice. Their understanding of racism, however, lacks a systemic analysis, and they rarely call for fundamental transformation. In the final analysis, their task is to keep the government focused on its proper role while building harmony among all people.

Prophetic and nationalist responses can also be compatible with a Lutheran construal of the two kingdoms concept. While the priestly and the political responses support the status quo, the prophetic and the nationalist responses challenge the validity of those structures and practices that exclude people. These responses focus on fundamental transformation of society. They speak the law and so reveal the absolute nature of evil structures and practices of society. Racism is systematic and must be eradicated. The prophetic and nationalist responses relativize evil structures and practices that prohibit the free movement and communication among people. The biblical injunction to obey God rather than humans and the doctrine of sanctification play a greater role in authorizing and justifying the activism of these responses.

African American Lutheran Ethical Action

The history of African American Lutheranism reveals at least three ethical responses: priestly, political, and prophetic. These three responses can be illustrated through the ministry of three individuals. The Rev. Jehu Jones Jr., the first African American to be ordained by a Lutheran church body in the United States and the Caribbean, represents the priestly and the political response. Sister Emma Francis, the first African American Lutheran deaconess, represents the priestly response. Bishop Daniel Alexander Payne, the second

African American to be ordained a Lutheran pastor, embodies the prophetic response, particularly in a major speech against slavery in 1839.[35]

The Reverend Jehu Jones, Junior. Jones's ministry began in Charleston, South Carolina.[36] As early as 1816, African Americans approached the Rev. John Bachman about joining St. John's Lutheran Church. By 1860 African Americans constituted more than 30 percent of the membership of St. John's, and by 1859 they had more than 900 members within the South Carolina Synod.[37]

Between 1830 and 1865, the United States was struggling with race issues and slavery. Emigration, the abolitionist and colonization movements, and the Civil War were vehicles meant to remedy the race problem in America. The emigrationists, contending that African people would not obtain full citizenship rights in the United States, advocated return to Africa. The colonizationists argued that since slavery was not about to end, free African people should be relocated to Africa. The abolitionists argued that African people were due immediate emancipation, and they organized and employed moral persuasion to achieve their goal. Clearly moral persuasion failed since only war brought an end to slavery.

Lutherans in Charleston appear to have supported the emigration and colonization movement. Their vision of building a community of freedom included sending a missionary to Liberia. Jones was a promising candidate so Bachman recommended that he be ordained with that in mind. Armed with a letter of recommendation from Bachman, Jones went to New York to be ordained by the New York Synod. Jones returned to Charleston to join an expedition leaving for Liberia, but he was arrested under a law that granted authorities the power to arrest free African people who had left the city and returned.

Although one door closed, another subsequently opened for Jones. He built an "African congregation in Philadelphia."[38] Jones was quite aggressive in his pastoral calling, making over 2,000 visits to African people in Philadelphia, Gettysburg, and Chambersburg. The seeds of the gospel took root in Philadelphia when a congregation known as St. Paul's Evangelical Lutheran Church organized in 1834 and dedicated its building in 1836.[39]

Several elements of ethical action are present throughout Jones's ministry of building an African congregation in Philadelphia. His letters and reports do not contain explicit reference to Scripture, though it was reported that Jones "preached in the Friend's meeting house, on Acts 1, 10, 11."[40] Yet there are implicit references to "burden bearing" and helping "the least of these." Since St. Paul's congregation was always in need of financial support, especially when they were constructing the church, Jones called upon the larger church to support its ministry.

Tradition also figures in Jones's ministry. Although he was a member of St. John's, there is no evidence that he received training in Lutheran theology and ethics. In one of his letters, however, he stated that he wanted to build an African Lutheran congregation. While seeking financial assistance, he wrote "that through great exertions, he has under the blessings of Divine Providence got up a building . . . where The Coloured People can worship God, according to Lutheran Doctrine."[41] Jones was willing to build a congregation in the Lutheran tradition although financial support was not forthcoming from the denomination. Throughout his endeavors he demonstrated his trust in God.

Jones's ministry also embodies two dimensions of a political response. The first was letter writing, a popular tool for exposing life under the conditions of slavery. In a letter reprinted by *The African Repository*, a journal of the American Colonization Movement, Jones called for the repeal of a law that jailed free African South Carolinians who returned to Charleston. He argued that the law ought to be repealed because it would be in "the interest, as well as the dictates of humanity" to do so. Jones reasoned that repeal of the law would "disarm the north of a very important and powerful weapon, now wielded against you." His point was that European Americans in the North, where "freedom" reigned, treated free African people far worse than in Charleston, where slavery existed.[42]

A second dimension of Jones's political activity was organizing African American people. By 1830 independent African American church denominations as well as congregations in European American denominations had been formed. Between 1830 and 1850 Philadelphia became a prominent location for a number of independent African American organizations. A prominent protest movement, the National Negro Convention Movement, was organized. This movement was the African American community's voice against slavery, for the colonization of free African people, and for the uplift of the African race.[43] In 1836 the American Moral Reform Society was formed, and it followed the abolitionism advocated by European Americans.

In 1845 Jones along with several others formed the Colored American National Society as a bridge organization between the Convention Movement and the American Moral Reform Society. This organization sought "to unite the whole family of free colored people in interest and feelings, for the lawful rights to petition to the constituted authorities of our country, for the repeal of every law injurious to native born Americans."[44] In keeping with the practice of the American Moral Reform Society, this organization permitted European Americans to participate in its life.

Jones's public practice exemplifies how the African American ethical tradition and the Lutheran tradition converge. He wanted to bring the word of God to African people because they were "destitute of the word of truth."[45] On the one hand, he had pastoral concern for the souls of African people, exhibited especially in his desire to build an African Lutheran congregation. On the other hand, Jones's political activity in his organizing efforts to obtain the rights of African people reflects the African American ethical tradition. He was willing to confront and work with the political system although it denied African people their basic rights. The goal and content of his ethical activity was freedom for African Americans and European Americans.

Sister Emma Francis. The priestly ministry of Sister Emma Francis is one of the inspirational examples of African American Lutheran ethical action.[46] The passion and energy she gave to the service of young people is striking. Faith in the power of God and Jesus Christ motivated her to make Christ known through service. Her life exhibited her confirmation pledge that she would "give my whole life to God."[47]

Several elements of ethical action are present throughout Sister Emma's ministry. Among the most prominent is Scripture. In preparation for her commissioning as a deaconess, for example, she was asked what led her to become a deaconess. She replied with 2 Cor. 5:14: "For the love of Christ controls us, because we are convinced that one has died for all; therefore all have died."[48] Scripture was so important to Sister Emma that she felt if the Bible were used more around the home, things would be different in the congregation she was serving in Harlem.

The Lutheran tradition is another source that appears to inform Sister Emma's service. This influence is especially evident in her view of society, the mission of the Lutheran church, and her articulation of the doctrine of justification by grace alone. On many occasions she expressed concern about the world. The power of evil was great, prompting her to lament that "something must be done to save the youths."[49] Her ministry in Germany, the West Indies, and Harlem, New York, testifies to her concern for young people.

Sister Emma believed the Lutheran church had a mission to exercise its influence in the lives of people. When the Virgin Islands were going through changes during the 1930s, she assessed the problem as spiritual. She believed, "Our Lutheran Church has now an opportunity to bring a special evangelical message again to the community that has become great in Sabbath breaking and movies, dance & music not suited for the Lord's Day."[50] Sister Emma understood the work of the church as emphasizing personal piety and devotion to the saving message of Jesus Christ.

These were important to Sister Emma during her ministry at the Ebenezer Orphanage, where the young people developed a routine that included prayer and Bible study. During heavy flooding in the United States, she wrote, "May God assist us by His grace to hold fast to the true faith as we have received it in Christ Jesus, our Lord and Saviour."[51] She also wrote "God is God. He alone is All-wise. On Him we must trust for the future although it appears dark to us." Sister Emma knew that she was justified by God's grace and that she could trust God to give her strength as she faced the world. She encouraged others to do the same.

The goal of Sister Emma's public practice was to build up God's people, especially young people. Her priestly concern also extended to people from other racial and ethnic backgrounds. During her ministry in Harlem, she assisted a Cuban family who was homeless and without work. To minister with people from three different racial backgrounds—German, African, and Cuban—she learned their languages.

Like Jones's, Sister Emma's ministry embodies the priestly tradition and its convergence with the Lutheran tradition in two areas. First she understood her calling as service: She was called by God to represent God among the people. Accordingly in her visits to people in the Harlem congregation and through programs developed to build self-esteem and personal responsibility, she showed God's love and care of the people. Second, Sister Emma emphasized spiritual practices. Her public practice of prayer, morning and evening devotions, and regular participation in church became a model for young people. Eventually a young person, Edith Prince, followed in Sister Emma's steps, became a deaconess, and faithfully served with her in Harlem and the Virgin Islands.

The convergence of Sister Emma's ministry with traditional Lutheran ethical thought is both explicit and implicit. She wrote, "One should never seek a work for . . . ease and comfort—or the praise & honor of world, but rather for the glory of God."[52] Besides an explicit understanding of God's act of justification, there is an implicit expression of an African American understanding of the "two worlds" in her analysis of society that recognized evil and sin in the world. Christians must guard against becoming too closely identified with the world or allowing the world to determine what the church ought to believe or teach its members. Sister Emma certainly understood what it meant to be "in the world but not of the world." Faith in God meant acting out that faith with the knowledge that God would supply one's needs. Her ministry reminds us of Article 27 of the Augsburg Confession:

> For this is Christian perfection: honestly to fear God and at the same time to have great faith and to trust that for Christ's sake we have a gracious God; to ask of God, and assuredly to expect from him, help in all things which are to be borne in connection with our callings; meanwhile to be diligent in the performance of good works for others and to attend to our calling.[53]

Sister Emma's will to build was grounded in God's justifying love that empowers active service of the neighbor. God supplies the resources to face the world.

Bishop Daniel Alexander Payne. Although Bishop Daniel Alexander Payne never actually became a Lutheran,[54] his significance for Lutheranism is that he was the second African American to be ordained a Lutheran pastor in the United States and the Caribbean.[55] Moreover Lutherans influenced Payne, especially through his theological education. During Payne's four-year involvement with Lutheranism (1835-1839), his ministry embodied a prophetic response to institutional racism.

Payne's prophetic ethical response began in his youth. He remembered that his parents were quite religious and worshiped at the Cumberland Street Church of the Methodist Episcopal Church. Payne recalled that his father dedicated him when he was born "to the service of the Lord." His spiritual depth continued to develop when at the age of eighteen he joined Cumberland Church. He told of his conversion experience: "I have set thee apart to educate thyself that thou mayest be an educator to thy people."[56] Payne redirected his life vocation to become an educator.

In 1829 Payne's will to build emerged when he started a school for African American children in Charleston. Reactions to events such as the Denmark Vesey and Nat Turner Rebellions, however, caused the South Carolina legislature to enact a law that prohibited teaching African people to read and write. Payne's dream of being an educator was dashed. He lamented that his school had to be closed because of slavery. This experience with racism caused such agony that he questioned God's existence and God's just nature. Although Payne was not a slave, he could identify with the slave, and slavery raised doubts about God's existence. Yet Payne felt the assurance of God who was actively working in history to eradicate slavery. Since God was active in history, Payne could trust God would end slavery.[57] This Job-like struggle over God's existence and just nature reflects not only the biblical tradition but also the African American interpretation of that tradition. This struggle fueled Payne's desire to challenge slavery and build a community of freedom.

The prophetic dimension of Payne's ministry is clearly expressed in a prominent speech he made at the 1839 meeting of the Franckean Synod. After a committee's report, Payne launched into a moving theological and ethical speech against slavery.[58]

Two principles ground Payne's speech: divine moral government and human moral agency. God is the creator of all people, and the human being is "this being God created but a little lower than the angels, and crowned him with glory and honor." Payne argued for a theological anthropology that begins with the goodness of God. God's moral government reflects "the goodness and justice of God" and is expressed through human relationships.

The moral agency of humankind, the ability "to move and act as the breath of Heaven," is grounded in freedom. Human beings are made for freedom, and slavery destroys the ability to choose freely to obey God's law. Slavery is sinful because it puts the person who enslaves and the person enslaved into a relationship that subverts the moral government of God. Without freedom, argued Payne, African Americans cannot be human.

Payne's protest against slavery is linked with his striving to lead the holy life of sanctification. For example, after confessing his own shortcomings, Payne prayed, "I present my soul, body, and spirit [as a] living sacrifice to thee. *O make it holy and acceptable by the unction of the Spirit and the sanctify (sic) energy of thy Grace.* And from hence forth let me be thine to think, to speak, and to act."[59]

This prayer reveals several dimensions of the African American and Lutheran ethical tradition. First, holy living was essential to being a moral person. This was a popular view in the African American community since many felt that through holy living they could prove to European Americans their ability to participate fully in society. Second, being and doing were intimately connected in public practice. Rather than separating being and doing, as some Christians do, Payne brought the two together.

Third, Payne's understanding of sanctification was similar to that of Samuel Schmucker, his teacher and mentor at Gettysburg Seminary. Both understood that faith led to good works and was the work of the Holy Spirit. They differed, however, on when one attained holy living. Payne understood holy living as attainable in the present life; Schmucker, as progressive change. The believer could grieve the work of the Holy Spirit by being unfaithful to God, yet there was possibility of growth toward a holy life.[60]

Payne's experience with Lutherans and his prophetic speech against slavery contain several elements of ethical action. Scripture was a chief source for condemning slavery. Payne's method was to state what Scripture says and show how slavery contradicted Scripture. For example, one of the Ten Commandments says, "Thou shalt not commit adultery" (Ex. 20:14), yet slave masters owned the bodies of African women. Payne's norm for judging everything about slavery is Ps. 8:5, where the Psalmist says that the human being is created a little lower than the angels. Another element was Payne's own experience of slavery. After saying what slavery did, Payne related what he experienced through the closing of his school and what slaves told him about their existence in this condition. The content or aim of his ethical action was complete freedom of the slave.

Payne's protest against slavery was militant. He urged the Franckean Synod to "hurl the hottest thunders of divine truth at the head of this cruel monster."[61] After leaving the Franckean Synod, Payne worked diligently to build a community of freedom for all people. Eliminating race hatred in the United States would contribute to that goal.

A Lutheran Response to Racism

Among European American Lutherans, the Franckean Evangelical Lutheran Synod's response to slavery was similar to the African American prophetic response. This synod sought to reform the practice of church and society regarding institutionalized racism. How did this group of Lutherans ground ethical action?

Slavery was a church-dividing issue in many denominations. Among Lutherans it was the occasion for the formation of a new synod in the mid-1830s. At the 1836 meeting of the Hartwick Synod, one resolution was presented calling for the abolition of slavery and another stating that the church body should not be involved in the matter. After considerable discussion a third resolution passed that "indefinitely postponed" the issue.[62] The action prompted four pastors and their congregations to "come out" of the synod.[63] The Franckean Synod formed as an antislavery synod in 1837.

The Franckean Synod's Stance against Slavery. The Franckean Synod's public stance against slavery was articulated in its constitution and in a pamphlet called "The Fraternal Appeal." Both documents reflect the elements of ethical action discussed earlier as well as the thinking of the abolitionist movement of the 1830s.

Significantly the synodical constitution contains prohibitions against slavery. Delegates and clergy were prohibited a seat in meetings if they were slaveholders or found advocating support of slavery. Four standing resolutions clearly reflect the "comeouter" position on slavery. The final resolution states: "That it is the duty of christians throughout the land, to come out from the BABEL of ruins, according to the Divine command, lest its rotten and crumbling mass should fall on them."[64] Thus the Franckean Synod organized itself as an institution that believed slavery and its supporters contaminated the Christian community.

"The Fraternal Appeal," which outlines clear biblical and theological reasons for the synod's position on slavery, was an even more explosive document.[65] It began by recognizing the autonomy of all Lutheran synods to decide how they would approach the subject of slavery. Nevertheless the Franckean Synod felt it their duty to speak "on the same ground that we preach the Gospel and labor to elevate morally any portion of the inhabitants of this fallen world." The document proceeded to illustrate why slavery should be immediately abolished.

"The Fraternal Appeal" grounded its argument against slavery in two sources, the Bible and the United States Constitution. The appeal opposed slavery on the basis of the concept of the "image of God." "Slavery is the *reduction* of *immortal and godlike* M A N, the crowning glory of this created world, *into a thing,* or a *chattel person."* Slavery denied personhood because "all were created on an equality in the image of God." Genesis 1:26 and the First Article of the Apostles' Creed laid the foundation of their position. The Franckeans drew on the Exodus story and from the Old Testament and engaged constitutional language to help legitimate their position.

The Lutheran tradition, especially implicit understandings of the two kingdoms and law and gospel, are evident in "The Fraternal Appeal." Christians were encouraged to use their "influence and powers to achieve this praiseworthy end" of an equal and free community. This corresponds to how orthodox Lutheranism understood the role of the Christian. Another veiled reference to the Lutheran tradition was lodged in the second reason why Christians ought to support the abolition of slavery. The desire of a "common brotherhood" led the Franckeans to assert that "this is the grand aim of the law and gospel."

Although they did not elaborate the two kingdoms concept, they did use two kingdoms thinking. For example, in 1850 when the government passed the Fugitive Slave Act, the Franckeans vehemently opposed the law. They denounced the law because it was an "ill-shapened and hydra-headed offspring of bold usurpation and unmitigated cruelty."[66] Since it was an unjust law, the Franckeans invoked Acts 5 (obedience to God) in the same manner as did African Americans.

The content of the Franckean Synod's ethical response was liberation. "Has God said, 'Let my people go,' while enduring a comparatively mild system of oppression in the land of Egypt? . . . And shall not the people of this country obey the command of God, 'to let the oppressed go free'?"[67] Jesus' ministry (Luke 4) and the Samaritan story were examples for all Christians to follow in publicly denouncing slavery.

The goal of the Franckean Synod's stance was "universal brotherhood." Again they supported their call by appealing to the Bible and the United States Constitution. "All humanity constitutes one common brotherhood, rich or poor, high or low, honored or dishonored." Slavery violated this right to participate in one community where all people were treated equally. The slave could not say, "MY soul, MY will, MY head, MY body, MY affections, MY hands, and MY feet" because as chattel they belonged to the master. The Franckeans recognized a constitutional protection for the inalienable rights of the slave. In Lutheran terms they contended that the government's job was to provide these rights and thus preserve order in society. Being a master over African people meant that the master "abolished all the personal and inalienable rights of the slave."[68]

Before ending their appeal, the Franckeans made statements that parallel those of two great Christian reformers, Martin Luther and Martin Luther King

Jr. They implored their Lutheran colleagues to speak out and to act "because you have assumed the attitude as reformers of the world, and as lovers of holiness and of God." The Franckeans called upon their colleagues to fulfill their duty in the spirit of Martin Luther. Reformation of the world would come from inheritors of this tradition who acted on their love of Jesus Christ. "The Fraternal Appeal" ended with an eloquence similar to King's "I Have a Dream" speech:

> For the practical establishment of this equalizing principle we should toil and pray until we shall see its matchless efficacy fully demonstrated. Sound abroad this sentiment of inspiration with the pealing notes of Sinai from every hill top and through every valley; let it mingle with every breeze and sweep over every plantation down to the gulf stream, and along the wending Sabine, re-echoed from the Rocky mountains and the growling surges of the Atlantic, till the whole land becomes tremulous with the blessed truth, that in the scale of humanity, all ye are brethren.

Connecting faith and action in a way reminiscent of James 2:14-17, the Franckean Synod admonished other Lutherans to act. They interpreted Lutheranism as leading to the duty to speak out and act against slavery. Because of their fervor in challenging and confronting the Lutheran communion, they were viewed as radicals. One of their founders, the Rev. Nicholas van Alstine, responded: "I glory in assuming the epithets, Radical, Radicalism, instead of hiding my face in shame."[69] The synod gave a positive twist to the change: "Reform would get no where without radicals. In this sense, Jesus Christ was a radical, the apostles and early fathers, Luther and his coadjutors, were radicals; so are abolitionists and we glory in it."[70] At the same time the public practice of the Franckean Synod was limited by its inability to place Bishop Daniel Alexander Payne in a congregation.

Implications for a Contemporary Lutheran Ethic

What are the implications of this study for contemporary Lutheran ethics? I will pursue this question by suggesting three broad categories as they emerged from this inquiry: social analysis (Luke 24:13-35), diversity (Acts 10), and a new ethical direction (Luke 4:18-19).

An Emmaus Road Style of Social Analysis. I begin with the Emmaus road experience. In Luke 24 Jesus joined two disciples and walked and talked with them all the way to Emmaus, but they did not recognize him. When they reached Emmaus, the two disciples invited Jesus to stay with them for the evening. In the act of breaking bread, they recognized their visitor as the risen Christ.

The first implication that emerges from our study is the importance of social analysis. Social analysis is an ability to read the context, both its past and present.[71] It means becoming familiar with the condition, history, traditions, and relationships of people and institutions in a particular context. A truthful social analysis is willing to join people in their walk, to listen to their description of what is happening in the world, and to break bread with them.[72]*

The ethical witness of African Americans shows with whom they identified in the world. The public practice of Jones, Payne, and Francis not only included speaking out against the oppressive conditions of African people and young people; it also included engaging in the African American community's struggle against exploitation and humiliation, and participating in their struggle for freedom. What African American Lutherans did was predicated on telling "the truth about the situation of black people vis-à-vis the structures of oppression and exploitation."[73]

The ethical witness of African American Lutherans contextualizes the question "What ought I to do?" Answers are shaped through a dialectical encounter between Scripture and context. Thus what it means to be ethically responsible is often different for African American Lutherans than it is for European American Lutherans. The oppression and marginalization of African Americans leads inevitably to different questions and answers. As Major Jones suggests, the ethical question "What ought I to do?" must be divided for there to be an authentic African American answer.[74] Consciously importing the questions and answers that emerged from Wittenberg leads to misdiagnosing the context in which African and African Americans exist on a global level.

A Diversity of Ethical Responses. A second implication is that there are diverse ethical responses. Ethics often asks what response is most faithful to the history and the theological and ethical traditions of the dominant culture's religious experience. If one is going to be a Lutheran in the United States and the Caribbean, one is expected to respond to the world according to a European American interpretation of the two kingdoms concept. Many consider uniformity far more important than engaging and affirming a diversity of ethical responses.

The critical question of how Christianity engages a variety of cultures appears when Cornelius sought to become a Christian (Acts 10). At issue was whether he, an uncircumcised Gentile, would have to follow the Judaic way of life. Peter settled the issue by sharing a revelation from God: "Truly I perceive that God shows no partiality, but in every nation any one who fears him and does what is right is acceptable to him" (Acts 10:34-35). Cornelius could remain Roman; he did not have to be circumcised or live according to Judaic culture. Cornelius could respond to God's grace according to how God became incarnated in his community.

The ethical responses of African American Lutherans and the Franckean Synod challenge the Lutheran church to be flexible in its response to the world.[75]* Although there was similarity in their experiences, Jones, Payne, Francis, and the Franckean Synod responded differently. Yet there is common cause with the Lutheran tradition. Jones's ethical response reflects the two kingdoms. Sister Emma Francis's ethical response is consistent with justification by grace alone through faith alone. Payne's prophetic ethical response converges with the pietistic emphasis on sanctification. Conversely the Franckean Synod's ethical response emphasizes sanctification and in a limited way converges with the African American prophetic ethical tradition. Rather than viewing these diverse ethical responses as evidence of ethical relativism or conflict, we should see them as complementary. They are partial responses that together become powerful weapons against social sins in any age. The Lutheran confessional heritage and ethical tradition are broad enough to support a diversity of ethical responses to the world.

The Ethical Paradox of African American Lutherans. A third implication of this study involves questions such as these: Does embracing the cultural heritage and struggle of African American people mean saying no to one's denominational heritage? Does embracing one's denominational heritage mean saying no to one's cultural heritage? Can African American Lutherans be authentically African American and Lutheran?

At the 1986 Harare Conference Albert Pero addressed these questions. African American Lutheran theological and ethical thought is necessarily different because the African American context is "dominated by white racism."[76] Thus theological and ethical action by African American Lutherans must be related to the struggle of African Americans for freedom and justice.

Pero provides a framework for properly analyzing African American Lutheran experience. The framework is built upon W. E. B. Du Bois's "double consciousness" concept. African American Lutherans live a paradoxical existence, one African American (cultural identity) and one Lutheran (denominational identification). Accordingly the African soul leads "beyond the white contradictions of the gospel and discover[s] God's liberation/salvation." The Lutheran soul "helps us engage our African roots" in such a way that African Americans become more than "a mere imitation of Lutheran theology from Europe."[77] In encountering a context dominated by racism, these two souls compete with each other.

The ethical implications of Pero's analysis are formidable. Will African American Lutherans respond to a context dominated by racism based on their African soul or their Lutheran soul? What standard should be used to determine how to respond to the context? The ethical witness of African Americans in this study indicates that they responded to the context based on their

African soul. The context of racism led them to respond in a manner consistent with the African American ethical tradition. The question of whether their response was Lutheran never surfaced in their attempt to build a world of freedom and justice for African American people.

The ethical witness by Jones, Payne, and Francis recalls a piece of ethical wisdom passed on by African American people: "Two wrongs do not make a right." In other words African American people understand that to act like European Americans is alien and inconsistent with the resistance tradition of African Americans. It is alien and inconsistent because European Americans have often employed their culture and religion to oppress people while African Americans have employed culture and religion in the struggle for justice and freedom. To do to European Americans what they have done to African American people is outside the experience, history, and tradition of the African American community. Whenever ethical action is rooted in a religious and cultural tradition other than African American religion and culture, it is useless in the African American journey toward freedom and justice. Ethical action by African Americans is rooted in biblical faith and its organizing principle of the parenthood of God and the kinship of all people, commonly called the "black Christian tradition."[78] To move away from the African American religious and ethical tradition leads to a devaluing of that tradition.

A New Ethical Basis? A fourth implication is the focus on the poor and oppressed with whom African American Lutherans have walked. Although Jones, Payne, and Francis were relatively free African Americans, the condition of African American people loomed large on their ethical horizons. This suggests that a Lutheran ethic for the twenty-first century must be an ethic that emerges from its walking and breaking bread with the poor and marginalized people of the world.

From a global perspective, the chasm between "haves" and "have nots" is widening. In addition the churches that are growing are those that identify with the poor. Some of this growth can be attributed to the compassion of churches to meet the needs of the poor, some to the public practice of churches fulfilling Jesus' first sermon. In his first sermon Jesus clearly outlines his mission: to go to the poor, release the captives, restore sight to the blind, and free those who are oppressed (Luke 4:18-19). Whatever else one may make of Jesus' first sermon, it was about the actual conditions of being poor, captive, blind, and oppressed.

Whatever the cause of the church's growth, the church of the twenty-first century will likely be a church of the poor. This type of understanding demands a new ethical basis. The ethical witness of African American Lutherans tells us that the starting point and goal of ethical action must be thought anew, with the poor and the oppressed at the center of our ethical thinking and behavior. Recognizing that the poor are the church means developing an ethic that confronts the "principalities and powers" that stifle the freedom of God's people.

Conclusion

In focusing on African American Lutheran ethical action, I have shown that the history of African American Lutheranism points to a diversity of ethical responses, rooted in the African American ethical tradition. There is some similarity with the Lutheran tradition, especially with the Franckean Synod. Retrieving the legacy of those who reflect their community of origin while members of the Lutheran church is critical for moving the church from a preoccupation with "right doctrine" to "right practice." African American Lutheran ethical action challenges European American Lutheranism to see that who we are before God is intimately joined with what we do among God's people. Bishop Payne challenges all of us: "Oh, that the Lord Jesus would move the heart of the Lutheran Church to work among the colored people, according to her ability. Luther ought to be as widely and intimately known down South among the colored Christians as Calvin, Knox or Wesley."[79] Not only must Luther be made known. The African American religious and ethical tradition must be made known, lest we forget what brought African Americans to this day. What a challenge Lutherans doing ethics face in the next century as we together join with others in building a community of freedom for all people!

❧ 6 ❧
Ethics and the Promise of God
Moral Authority and the Church's Witness
James M. Childs Jr.

We have lost our moral compass

The ethical consensus of our society has been steadily eroding

The church urgently needs to speak clearly and forthrightly to this situation of growing moral anarchy.

Such concerns and convictions are commonly voiced today. Moreover they have been a perennial complaint in virtually all societies. Within the church, however, there is more to this moral malaise than the widespread perception that our society is in an ethical tailspin. Some persons of faith also fear that the church might too closely resemble society. They are convinced that the church has lost its grip on its own moral authority and with that its moral courage. They fear the church is a trumpet that blows an uncertain sound.

Yet even if the church summoned the moral courage for a powerful witness in our ethically foundering world, it would first face a number of stubborn uncertainties. In matters of both personal choice and public policy, we are constantly mired in the ambiguity of life in a fallen world. How do the theological resources of the Lutheran tradition help us to cope with that reality? Second, Christians often struggle with one another in profound disagreement over the complex issues of contemporary life. Does a Lutheran approach to ethics and authority in ethics speak helpfully to this state of affairs? Third, there are continuing debate and attendant uncertainty over how far and in what ways it is appropriate for the church to engage in social concerns and public policy. Can Lutherans resolve their historical and theological tensions in this regard? Finally, having dealt with our own internal diversity, how do we witness effectively in a world of increasing diversity? Does the Lutheran heritage have something to contribute in this twenty-first-century situation?

Let me combine these concerns into one question to focus the discussion: *How do we as Christian people and as a Lutheran church speak with courage and confidence to ethical issues even in the most complex and disputed of circumstances?* In addressing this question, I will consider some key themes of Lutheran ethics in order to gain a better understanding of moral authority and ethical deliberation in the Lutheran tradition and to encourage our witness as a church.

Ethical Witness and the Vocation of the Church

Lutherans have not always been clear or consistent about their mandate for ethical witness, though we have usually been somewhat more comfortable and confident in the personal sphere than in the realm of public policy. The seeds of this ambivalence are in the thinking of Martin Luther himself and most especially in subsequent interpretations of Luther.

Ethical Witness in the Two Realms Tradition. Although the term "doctrine of the two kingdoms" was not coined until the 1930s, Luther's teaching of God's two modes of governance has certainly been a prominent feature of the Lutheran heritage since the publication of his "Temporal Authority: To What Extent It Should Be Obeyed" in 1522. In this and subsequent writings, such as the "Commentary on the Sermon on the Mount," Luther set forth his well-known distinction between God's two governments, the spiritual and the temporal, and with that the twofold ethical response demanded of Christians. A great deal of scholarship and debate has gone into what Luther really intended and taught.[1] I will first track how his twofold formula became dualistic.

In an influential nineteenth-century essay on Luther's ethics, Christian Ernst Luthardt wrote in connection with Luther's doctrine of two kingdoms that:

> To begin with, the Gospel has absolutely nothing to do with outward existence but only with eternal life, not with external orders and institutions which could come into conflict with the secular orders but only with the heart and its relationship to God, with the grace of God, the forgiveness of sins, etc. . . . Thus Christ's servants, the preachers, likewise have no reason to espouse these secular matters but are only to preach grace and forgiveness of sins in the name of Christ. As for secular concerns, "the jurists may advise and help here on how this should function."[2]

Ulrich Duchrow has written that Luthardt's essay typifies the very dualistic conception of the nineteenth century that still continues to obscure our view of Luther's doctrine. In this understanding of "two spheres of life," "Christianity is restricted to the personal, inner sphere; the preacher is forbidden to comment on political matters."[3]

The extreme consequences of this nineteenth century mindset were observable in the United States. In a statement that seems unimaginable today, the Lutheran Church-Missouri Synod theologian Wilhelm Sihler wrote that the gospel had nothing to say to the issue of slavery. The gospel's message is one of spiritual liberation from the slavery of sin, not external liberation from the bonds of servitude. Thus he concluded, "Nor can the gospel stipulate it to be a matter of faith and of love, that is, a matter of conscience, that the slave-holder grant his slaves their physical freedom on the grounds that they too are his brothers in Christ."[4]

James Echols, while attempting to show points of conceptual convergence between Lutheran two kingdoms thinking and African American Christianity, nonetheless sees the behavior of the two traditions standing in stark contrast. African American Christians have been activists for liberation from oppression since slavery to the present. Lutherans have tended toward quietism and the status quo under the influence of dualistic interpretations of God's twofold governance.[5]*

Helmut Thielicke has spoken of three potential dangers in Luther's doctrine of the two realms: bifurcation, secularization, and harmonization. These seem to be three variations of dualism. Bifurcation is the separation of the two realms into the personal versus the official, leading to a "double morality." Secularization dualistically separates the gospel from the world; the world is divided into autonomous spheres of activity under the sway of totally secular authorities. The final danger of harmonization refers to the impression Luther sometimes gives that the two kingdoms stand side by side in mutual harmony, each having different laws from the other.[6] In all three variations there is a dual morality—personal versus social—and quietism in the church's relation to the world.

Most of us who are the "senior citizens" of Lutheranism in America, or nearly so, can testify to some form of this dualistic thinking as a staple of our theological formation. Citing a 1970 study in the United States, Karl Hertz noted:

> Among the laity and many of the clergy we find an approach that strongly emphasizes the distinction between the secular and spiritual spheres of life. Christians must indeed live in the world, but the church nevertheless—apart from the demand for individual piety—has no ethical advice to direct the conduct of believers in society. . . . The sharp distinction between the two realms (which are often falsely identified as church and state) serves to justify this ethical position.[7]

Certainly the impulses toward dualistic and quietistic interpretations of the two realms are there in Luther himself. In "Temporal Authority" Luther made the provocative comment, "You have the kingdom of heaven; therefore, you should leave the kingdom of earth to anyone who wants to take it."[8] Then again in commenting on Matt. 5:38-42, Luther explained the distinction between seeking justice and turning the other cheek:

> Each should move in its own sphere, and yet both should be effective. A Christian may carry on all sorts of secular business with impunity—not as a Christian but as a secular person—while his heart remains pure in his Christianity, as Christ demands. . . . Thus when a Christian goes to war or when he sits on a judge's bench, punishing his neighbor, or when he registers an official complaint, he is not doing this as a Christian, but as a soldier or a judge or a lawyer.[9]

While it is not difficult to see how these and similar statements by Luther could lead to a double morality of personal versus social and a retreat from the social witness of the church, the larger context of Luther's writings suggests a more balanced perspective. Consequently Thielicke can speak of an objective and subjective link holding the two realms together. The objective link is forged by God ruling in both spheres: God's love is operative in both modes of divine governance. The subjective link is the love with which the people of God respond in both their immediate relationships with their neighbors and in service to their neighbors in fulfilling their vocation in the orders of earthly authority. Love does not belong solely to the personal sphere nor law to the social and political sphere. Love is the determinative principle in all spheres.[10]

Earlier in this century, the great Luther scholar Karl Holl made a similar point regarding love: "By interpreting the orders of secular life as means for the exercise of love, and by charging Christians to keep improving them in this sense, [Luther] demonstrated the possibility of retaining love as the ruling motive in every situation and every moment."[11] Holl's insight is echoed in the splendid essay on the two kingdoms doctrine by Heinrich Bornkamm. Bornkamm rejects the notion offered by some interpreters that the love involved in seeking justice is different from the love of sacrifice for the neighbor. Love is indivisible even though it takes on different forms for different tasks.[12] Finally Gustaf Wingren says: "It is the neighbor who stands at the center of Luther's ethics. . . . Vocation and the law benefit the neighbor, as does love born of faith. . . . Love born of faith and the Spirit effects a complete breakthrough of the boundary between the two kingdoms, the wall of partition between heaven and earth, as did God's incarnation in Christ."[13]

More recent interpretations of Luther echo Wingren's judgment. José Míguez Bonino, while critical of the more quietistic versions of Luther's thought, follows Wingren on vocation. "At the ethical level gospel and law, power and love, come together in the life of individual Christians, in whatever *Stand* (social or vocational location) they may find themselves in society."[14] In a similar vein David Steinmetz wrote, "For Luther, the vertical relationship to God and the horizontal relationship to the neighbor are so inseparably joined in the act of faith that one is unthinkable without the other. . . . Freedom in faith and freedom to love can only be isolated from each other with disastrous results for both."[15]

The common emphasis of these Luther scholars on the indivisibility of love and the linkage of the two realms in God's comprehensive love and our response in all venues of life mitigates the influence of dualistic thinking. It opens the door to a renewal of the church's social conscience and involvement. It helps us to avoid the danger of double morality by showing the intimate connection between personal and social ethics in the concept and dynamic of Christian neighbor love. "Faith active in love" is simultaneously "faith active in love seeking justice."

The quest for justice driven by love is also shaped by the realism that is so much a part of Luther's two realms thought. There would not be a "left hand" rule of law if true Christian love really prevailed. Yet it does not, and therefore in providential love God has provided for government and other forms of authority. As Miguez has pointed out, Luther had a positive view of the purpose of government and could therefore call it to be true to its God-given mission of keeping justice.[16] Indeed Dietrich Bonhoeffer in his resistance to the Nazi regime took this very tack. While recognizing the proper and distinct roles of church and government, he nonetheless claims it is the duty of the church to confront the state and even become involved in direct political action when it is apparent that the state has failed in its function.[17] While the distinction between Luther's two kingdoms remains among the thinkers we have sampled, their separation in the ethical witness of the Christian community is precluded.

Reappraising Luther's thought and the force of courageous witnesses like Bonhoeffer have helped Lutherans find their way into the church's social witness in our time. The social statements that multiplied in the churches of American Lutheranism since the socially turbulent sixties display a new sense that both Luther and the Augsburg Confession provide encouragement for taking up the cause of justice and peace. The distinction between the two realms remains, and with it a distinction between the church's ethical witness and its gospel witness. Nonetheless there is a clear statement that the church and the secular order operate in "functional interaction" and that the church has the authority and vocation to speak to ethical issues in the secular sphere even while respecting its integrity.[18] William Lazareth's essay, "Luther's 'Two Kingdoms' Ethic Reconsidered," written for the World Council of Churches, is reflective of the new consciousness of the sixties. Lazareth concludes his reconsideration this way:

In short, what Lutherans need desperately today is a prophetic counterpart to the priesthood of all believers. Evangelical Christians will be reverent to God's Word as well as relevant to God's world by expressing both their priestly Yes, through faith active in love, and their prophetic No, through love seeking justice.[19]

Significantly Lazareth unites the concerns of the two realms in the vocation of the church and defines the activities of the church in both realms as activities of love. At the same time he distinguishes between the church's priestly vocation as belonging to one realm and its prophetic vocation as appropriate to the other. For many this is probably a satisfactory solution. It overcomes the social quietism of the past and avoids what many fear could be a confusion of law and gospel if the cause of justice were linked too closely with the message of justification. For others the ethical witness of the church—including the cause of justice—and the gospel witness of the church are more closely linked. They see faith active in love seeking justice as a single, unified vocation of the church. Within this vocation distinctions of law and gospel and of the ultimate and penultimate can be maintained.

The Eschatological Perspective. Hertz recognized an attitude of negativity toward the world that is hard to escape in much of the two kingdoms tradition. He picked up the insight of Paul Tillich that a truly transforming or revolutionary social ethic was not possible as long as the realm of creation and that of redemption did not share the same eschatological future. Identifying salvation with the individual apart from any expressed hope for the human community and the universe frustrates efforts to mount an ethical witness that takes the future of worldly matters with utmost seriousness. Hertz believed that necessary distinctions between the ultimate and penultimate in the two realms tradition can be sustained within the framework of an eschatological ethic that unites the ethical vocation of the church with its evangelical calling.[20]

Lutheran theologians during the past several decades have been prominent among those systematically appropriating the importance of biblical eschatology. The recovery of the Bible's historical-eschatological character placed new emphasis on the promise of God's coming future reign as the fulfillment rather than the antithesis of history. As the whole of God's historical creation comes under the promise of God's future, ethical striving within the world becomes more than a holding operation; it is suffused with hope. In short these theological developments move us toward Hertz's hope for a closer relationship of the church's ethical vocation to its evangelical calling.

Wolfhart Pannenberg has developed this eschatological perspective most powerfully in Lutheran theology. Reflecting on the two kingdoms doctrine, Pannenberg has observed: "Like Augustine before him, Luther did not do justice to the positive relationship between the hope for the Kingdom of God and the themes of political life, but instead regarded the latter as only an emergency measure against sin."[21] Pannenberg recognizes the validity of Luther's distinctions in defining and respecting the different roles of church and government. Luther's realism is important because secular force is needed as a hedge against fanaticism and unrealistic enthusiasm for social transformation. Yet Pannenberg laments that "nowhere in Luther can we find any inspiration to transform political conditions by the powerful vision of the eschatological vision of the Lordship of Christ which already illumines the present world."[22]

In an earlier essay on Augustine's influence, Pannenberg observes that Augustinian ethics are marked by a dualism and pessimism regarding the world. This seems to correlate with Augustine's eschatology that Pannenberg describes as suffering from an "otherworldly distortion." Eschatological hope is understood to be with God in God's transcendent otherness and separateness from the world. Yet if consistent with biblical eschatology we understand God to be the future of the world, then the promise and hope of eschatology is for the transformation and fulfillment of the world in the kingdom of God. Pious striving for God is no longer a matter of leaving the world behind for God's sake. Rather our striving in love is converted into concern for the world: "The most constructive consequence of this conversion to the world is the Christian idea of love that affirms the present world in transforming it."[23]

Carl Braaten has also recognized a critical point made by Pannenberg. The idea of the transforming activity of love in Christian "conversion to the world" is not to be construed as a retread of liberal Christianity's overly optimistic hope that the kingdom of God can be the product of our ethical striving.[24] Rather:

> The clue to the relationship of eschatology to ethics may be discovered by establishing the nature of the presence of the eschatological future in the person and activity of the historical Jesus. The key term is *proleptic;* there is a proleptic presence of the eschatological kingdom in the activity of the historical Jesus. The kingdom of God which is really future retains its futurity in the very historical events which anticipate it in the present. Christian ethics is not to be understood as the means of producing the future kingdom of God, but only as annunciation, anticipation, and approximation, let us say as "signs of the coming kingdom.[25]

I have picked up these themes in my writings by speaking of the church as the community of promise called to live out an ethic of anticipation. When our hope for God's final reign is recast in biblical terms as a hope for the fulfillment of God's intention for the whole creation, then the gospel promise by which the church is established becomes a promise for the whole person and the whole world. The worldly ethical concerns for both the spiritual and physical well-being of individuals, the common good of society, and the care of the earth point to or anticipate dimensions of the gospel promise for God's reign. The kingdom of God provides a vision, a horizon within which we can see the purpose and trajectory of our ethical endeavors. At the same time this promise gives birth to the faith, hope, and love that strain toward that future. Thus the church's ethical vocation is one of anticipation. As such its ethical vocation works in tandem with its evangelical vocation.[26]

The various trends sampled here lead from dualistic thinking to a more unitive vision of the relationship of love and justice, personal and social ethics, and ethical and evangelical witness. This vision seems evident at various key points in the Evangelical Lutheran Church in America's social statement, "The Church in Society: A Lutheran Perspective." The statement sees the witness of the church in society as flowing from the community's life in the gospel.

> "Faith is active in love; love calls for justice in the relationships and structures of society. . . . The Gospel does not take the Church out of the world but instead calls it to affirm and enter more deeply into the world. Although in bondage to sin and death, the world is God's good creation, where, because of love, God in Jesus Christ became flesh. The Church and the world have a common destiny in the reign of God."[27]

By What Authority and by What Criteria?

The ethical witness of the church in society regarding issues of both personal choice and corporate life is an integral part of the church's vocation to witness to the gospel of God's coming reign. Understanding the vocation of the church as the community of anticipation is fundamental to what we can and cannot say about the church's moral authority and ethical voice.

Authority and Certitude. In an eschatological perspective, the realism of Luther's two realms doctrine is preserved in the tension between the future revealed and present in Christ's victory and the present of brokenness and sin. The existential tension of the individual as *simul iustus et peccator* projected on the large screen of human history shows the very pattern of our world's eschatological existence.[28] Again the ELCA social statement on "Church in Society":

> "Through faith in the Gospel the Church already takes part in the reign of God announced by and embodied in Jesus. Yet, it still awaits the resurrection of the dead and the fulfillment of the whole creation in God's promised future. In this time of 'now . . . not yet,' the Church lives in two ages—the present age and the age to come."[29]

Within this perspective Luther's ethic is reframed in temporal rather than spatial terms. The horizon is a holistic vision of God's promise for the future of history, revealed definitively in the person and work of Jesus the Christ.

This reframing serves to mitigate the dualistic tendencies traced above. Yet two key theological insights at the heart of Luther's formula remain intact: its realism (already noted) and the distinction but constant interaction between the two realms. The distinction and interaction are sustained in the dynamic of the "now . . . not yet" structure of reality. The "not yet" character of our sinful world requires the structures of God's "left hand" rule and marks them off from any confusion with the ultimate reign of God announced in the gospel. At the same time the "now" reality of that promise creates and sustains Christian love in its zeal for transforming the conditions of our world as a witness to its hope and in obedience to God's Word. Embedded in this tension and distinction is a realism concerning the fragmentary and anticipatory character of our fallen, not-yet world. The interplay of law and gospel, the pulsebeat of both corporate and individual life, remains in the interplay of the "now . . . not yet."[30]

The coincidence of the *simul* of our personal existence and the *simul* of the world's eschatological existence corresponds to the unity of personal and social ethics in a Lutheran understanding of the ethics of the kingdom of God. Both personal and social ethics are an integral part of the church's witness to both God's judgment and promise. Both personal and social ethics participate in the ambiguous character of our "not yet" reality and must deal with the uncertainty that often comes with it.

Also central to a Lutheran understanding is that Christians have the freedom in the gospel to face this reality in the confidence of God's favor. We thus take the responsibility to make our ethical witness to the world even when that means "bold sinning." According to Luther's "Treatise on Christian Liberty," we are perfectly free in the gospel from the judgment of the law and therefore free to bind ourselves in love to the needs of our neighbor.[31]* The gospel promise, the faith it engenders, and the love that springs from faith are the beginning and sustaining ground of the Christian ethic. We are free in the gospel to embrace the commands of God with appreciation and expectation, not fear and trepidation, even though they continue to accuse us and the world in which we live continues to drive us into circumstances fraught with terrible and uncertain choices.

Dietrich Bonhoeffer was particularly insightful in discussing Luther's famous statement, "Sin boldly, yet more boldly still believe." If we take the statement as a premise, he wrote, it becomes a license for "cheap grace." If, however, we see the statement as Luther did, as a sum, it looks very different. As a sum it indicates that, being sinners, even our best efforts in life's tangled circumstances will add up to sin, but at the same time God's gracious promise attends us and calls us to live boldly and with courage and trust in that assurance.[32] Paul Althaus's comment punctuates this line of thought:

Just as God—paradoxically—accepts me as righteous and looks upon me with favor even though I am and remain a sinner, so God also accepts and approves my works. Empirically, what the Christian does is never so good as to be right and acceptable in the sight of God, for man's sinful nature continues to contaminate everything he does. Nevertheless, the deeds are right in the sight of God because in his grace he approves them—even as he approves the man who in faith lays hold of his wondrous grace and favor.[33]

The point is not that there are no reliable ethical standards. God's Word is a rich resource for that. Nor is it that Christians are inherently incapable of moral discernment. We are called and empowered to speak to the issues of our world, as I have already made clear. The point is rather that our confidence in the moral life is rooted not in the certainty of our judgments but in the assurance of God's promise. Authority is not established by certitude, especially in a world where our theological realism suggests that certitude is a scarce commodity.[34]*

Authority and Authorization, and the Good. By what authority do we speak, then? The authority by which we speak resides in the vocation we are graciously given as a people of God to witness to God's eschatological promise. This is our authorization to speak. The message with which we are entrusted gives foundation and substance to our ethical voice.

The revelation of the reign of God, centered in the person and work of the Christ, is a word that confronts us and our world as both law and gospel. It evokes prophetic judgment and guides and inspires the positive efforts of love. It judges our present existence and conduct in its resistance to God's coming future, God's righteous rule in our world and lives. At the same time the revelation of God's dominion is the promise of its fulfillment. This promise is sealed in the blood of the cross and assured in the triumph of the resurrection. Our brokenness is disclosed both in the suffering of our Savior and in the contrast of our world to the wholeness of God's future dominion. At the same time, however, the assurance of the future in the victory of Easter is a promise generative of faith, hope, and love.

Furthermore the promise and vision of God's future set the course for faith active in love striving in hope and seeking justice. As the Bible develops its portrait of God's promised future, we discover a variety of values that are integral to that ultimate good. These values become the focus of Christian love as it battles all that negates them and strives for those things that contribute to their realization. Any ethic must identify what is right, good, and virtuous. The good is that toward which we strive in our efforts to do the right. The virtues are those traits of character that incline us toward the right and the good. The Bible provides content and guidance in all three components of an ethic. I look first at how it speaks to the good.

For the prophet Isaiah the reign of God will be one of unbroken peace (2:2-4) and justice (11:3-5). When Christians become active agents of reconciliation at every level of life, from the nuclear to the international family, they anticipate the promise of peace in the dominion of God. When in love they concern themselves with such issues as economic justice and equal treatment under the law, they anticipate the perfect justice of God's kingdom that will be beyond the need for coercive law. In Christ God has made peace with the world and promised a world of peace in which hostility and estrangement are supplanted by community and unity. God has called the eschatological community, the church, to work at this now (2 Cor. 5:19). We do so in the expectation of its coming, even as we eat the meal of the future in the Eucharist of the present.

In the reign of God there is equality beyond any distinctions (Gal. 3:28). When Christians work to break down barriers of race, gender, and ethnicity, attacking all the "isms" that exclude and denigrate people because of who they are, they anticipate this promised equality in the hope of its final realization.

At key points in his ministry, Jesus identified his person and work with prophetic expectations for the reign of God. These expectations include the triumph of life over death, healing of infirmities, good news for the poor, and the end of oppression (Matt. 11:4-5, Luke 4:17-21). When Christians stand for the value of life by opposing the wanton use of abortion or by supporting the acceptance, rights, and opportunities of the disabled, they anticipate the triumph of life in the reign of God. When Christians visit the sick, comfort the suffering, and actively pursue health care for all, they bear witness to the health and wholeness of the kingdom foreshadowed in Jesus' healing works. When in the face of exploitation and predation Christians promote a sexual ethic that celebrates the unity and integrity of our spiritual-physical creation in God's image, they anticipate in yet another way that wholeness that is the promise of our eschatological perfection in the *imago Dei*.[35] Finally when Christians, like their Lord, identify with the poor and their needs and oppose all forms of oppression, they anticipate the *shalom* of God's kingdom, where our final freedom from sin dissolves all oppression in perfect freedom with God. These and other diverse activities are evidences of the Christian ethic of love reaching out for the values that express God's will and promise.

Beyond the hope of life and wholeness in the human community is the promise that all creation will find healing and new life (Rom. 8:21), as the prophet Isaiah foresaw in his proleptic vision of the peaceable kingdom. The fulfillment of all creation as eschatologically promised is the final grounding for the intrinsic value of all historical, created reality. Thus when Christians speak out on behalf of the whole creation and extend Christian love to include love for nature, they anticipate the truth that God's future is the future of the whole world.[36]*

The values I discern then are life, the wholeness of all creation, peace, equality, community, unity in reconciliation, and freedom. The Bible itself and the issues of our day associated with these values give them concreteness.

The promise of God for the future energizes our present ethical resolve even in the face of disappointment and adversity. The ELCA study on economic life picks this up nicely:

> The purposes of God will not be thwarted. The disappointed promises of economic life can be faced and addressed. Hope emerges out of despair, life out of death. The coming of God's reign is not dependent on our achievements, but on the faithful promises of God. The heart of this vision provides substance and direction for actions and policies that can bear witness to God's righteousness and justice in economic life today. [37]

The criteria by which the church must select those ethical issues that it will address are the values revealed for God's promised future in the person and work of Jesus Christ. From matters of personal conduct to those of public policy, the church is in constant dialogue with the world around it and within its own community, discerning prophetically where these values are being compromised and discerning constructively how they may be better anticipated. The ethical authority of the church is further consolidated when, faithful to its vocation, it is faithful to the values of God's reign.

Discerning when these values are at stake and what responses are right and possible is not always easy for "not yet" people in a "not yet" world. The opening reflections of this chapter gave us a glimpse of this challenge. We have a vision, but in the midst of complexity and conflict how do we move from vision to decision?

Facing Our Conflicts:
Courage and Confidence in Decision and Action

Scripture, as it permeates the whole life of the Christian community in Word and Sacrament, is the generative ground and wellspring of our faith. This faith is the beginning of our ethical vocation. Scripture is the resource through which we experience God's self-disclosure and come to know Jesus. God's Word is alive among us in the community of faith; it nurtures us in this faith, and it shapes us in the love that Christ displays as the Son of God and the prototype of true humanity.[38] Joseph Sittler's words are fitting: "Love and Faith are not, in the New Testament, alternative or opposing terms. Faith is the name for the new God-relationship whereby the will of God, who himself establishes the relationship, is made actual. And that will is love. Faith active in love is alone faith; and love is the function of faith horizontally just as prayer is the function of faith vertically."[39]

The faith-creating, faith-nurturing, love-shaping power of Scripture points us toward the vital role of the Bible in shaping Christian character individually and as a community. In many respects this is the Bible's most important contribution in shaping the Christian ethic. Since what we do is an expression of who we are, we must take note of character and the virtues that describe it before discussing ethical decisions.[40*]

The character in which we are shaped as individuals and as a Christian community is the character of neighbor love embodied in our Lord (for example, Phil. 2:5-7). Luther makes this point quite eloquently:

> Behold, from faith thus flow forth love and joy in the Lord, and from love a joyful, willing, and free mind that serves one's neighbor willingly and takes no account of gratitude or ingratitude, praise or blame, of gain or loss. . . . Hence as our heavenly Father has in Christ freely come to our aid, we also ought to help freely our neighbor through our body and its works, and each one should become a Christ to the other that we may be Christ to one another and Christ may be the same in all, that is, that we may be truly Christians.[41]

The Beatitudes help to spell out the sorts of virtues that describe the disposition of love. These blessings or endowments of grace point to virtues like openness to the neighbor's need and worth, mercy, peacemaking, solidarity with the suffering, and honesty. Consistent with the idea that Christian character is formation in the love of Christ, Gustavo Gutiérrez has remarked that the Beatitudes display the attitude of Christ to whom they all fundamentally refer.[42] These beatitudinal virtues are corollaries of the values we have identified and the norms of love to which we now turn.

The Bible not only provides us with the wellspring for our formation in faith and love and with a vision of the good as the goal of love in its portrayal of God's future; it also gives content to love and definition and direction to the way love behaves in response to the ethical issues of life.

To be sure, the New Testament idea of Christian neighbor love has considerable content in itself. No one is excluded from our caring, not even our enemies (Matt. 5:43-44). Having ourselves been affirmed by God, we are free to embrace the way of love as self-giving in the manner of the Christ (Phil. 2:4ff.). In Christ we have a self to give! We know that love drives toward unity and community through reconciliation even as we have been reconciled to God in Christ (2 Cor. 5:19).[43] There is much here on which to build an ethic. We can extrapolate from this core disposition of the Christian moral life norms that speak to life choices. Yet the Bible gives even further guidance for love.

For much of the life of the church this guidance has been defined by the Decalogue and the church's catechetical development of the Decalogue as it correlates with other scriptural resources. The Decalogue speaks to love's concerns for the neighbor. I have attempted to translate the content of the commandments into five general rules that embody love's concern for the neighbor and the world: respect for autonomy, commitment to justice, respect for the sanctity of life, truth-telling, and promise-keeping (including fidelity in marriage). They require further clarification in the process of applying them to situations of moral choice. The church has been doing this for centuries in the development of its catechesis and in its response to new moral challenges.[44]* For the Christian who lives the life of agape love in the freedom of the gospel, the commandments of God provide direction and possibility. They also continue to accuse us in the reality of our lingering sinfulness and serve as the foundation of law for a society that does not live by love.[45]

The Word of God provides rich, clear indications of the will of God for the life of love. Moreover we have confidence in the guidance of the Holy Spirit as we reflect on that Word and seek its direction. In the assurance of the promises of God and the presence of the Spirit, the church struggles to understand and apply rightly the ethical mandates of its faith under the ambiguous conditions of historical existence. We take part in a continual process of dialogue between the commandments of love and the situations individuals engage as they face personal choices. Simultaneously we take part in a continual process of dialogue for the church as it seeks to refine its ethical understandings in the crucible of worldly engagement. Both processes require our reason along with our obedience. Indeed Luther saw reason as essential to the well-being of society and at its best discerning what is consistent with love and natural law.[46] In both processes we are aware of how culture and experience influence and can shed light on the obligations of Christian love, even when love runs counter to culture and experience. Both processes are in the service of our vocation individually and corporately, and both point to decision and action.

Dialogue and Decision in the Community of Promise. The dialogical interchange between text and context takes on a variety of aspects as the church and the dictates of the Christian ethic face different challenges. Often the application of norms embodying love is clear and straightforward. The obligations to be honest, keep promises, or maintain marital fidelity, for example, are seldom difficult to discern. Any struggles we have with these obligations are more likely due to our own self-serving rationalizations than to any ambiguity about the normative requirements of our ethic.

Yet sometimes the dialogue is one of resolving conflicting claims or obligations, resulting in painful and sometimes tragic choices. What do we do toward the end of life when relief of suffering and preservation of life seem incompatible? How do we balance the obligations of work and family life?

Resolving some of these dilemmas does not occur without lingering doubt and anxiety. In the end we have only the assurance of God's love and presence to sustain us.

The community of the church is a place where such dilemmas can be shared. Through this sharing, ministry to one another can occur and the ethical vocation and resolve of the people of God be strengthened. The section on the church as a community of moral deliberation in the social statement "The Church in Society" spells out the kind of dialogue to which I am pointing. It recognizes the diversity of gifts and experiences among believers that can lead to difference of opinion on moral matters. It points to the resources of Scripture and tradition, as I have. It lifts up the necessity of seeing the Word in the context of the world and vice versa. It stresses the need for full participation by those affected, those in positions of leadership, and those with expertise. From these ingredients come the kind of dialogue or deliberation the church requires for the guidance of its members and for its witness in the world. The statement sees clearly that the dialogue engaged in is not for the negotiation of opinions but for discerning the will of God (Rom. 12:2).[47]* Ethical dialogue in the church serves as both a form of ministry among members and a resource for mission in the world.

It is not uncommon that individuals face questions of public policy and professional practice, leading the church to develop a social statement. Such a statement relates text and context in critical interaction and usually produces a number of "middle axioms." These are somewhat more specific ethical directions than the most general principles of love on which they are based. Middle axioms develop those general principles to interpret concretely their meaning for the dilemmas and decisions at stake. Because social statements and middle axioms do not prescribe or anticipate all decisions that may be entailed by a given issue or set of issues, dialogue among the people of God and with the world will continue in an effort to clarify our prophetic and constructive witness.

The problem of abortion illustrates these various forms of dialogue. Women and couples can face terrible conflictual choices when considering abortion. The dialogue about personal choice in these conflicts is likely to be an agonizing one. Christians in the health care professions must also search their hearts to find the parameters of their participation in this procedure. Reflecting the larger social debate, Christians within the church community differ over the meaning of the scientific data regarding the development of prenatal life and therefore the moral status of that life. Christians also remain divided over the clarity with which Scripture speaks to abortion with respect to the relative status of prenatal life in the biblical prohibition of killing. Out of this critical and multifaceted dialogue, the ELCA has produced a social statement on abortion asserting the strong Christian bias for life, setting some parameters for when abortion might be a morally defensible albeit sorrowful choice, and committing the church to seek legislation more reflective of these values than the current state of affairs under the U.S. Supreme Court's 1973 decision in *Roe v. Wade.*

Dialogue and Witness in the World. Through the dialogue that led to the social statement, we are better equipped ethically to continue that conversation within the church, in our individual struggles, and better equipped to engage the world with a prophetic critique of its wanton use of abortion and with a constructive effort to seek better laws.

Christian advocacy for better laws and public policies—pursuing the values love seeks in its God-given vision of the good—has an ironic dimension. The laws we advocate are a testimony to the goodness and dignity of humankind and of the whole creation. Yet the necessity of the coercive use of civil law reminds us that humanity is also a fallen race that, if unrestrained, will rob creation and one another of their dignity. In its quest for more just public policy, the church lives with that irony and does not confuse any proximate gains with the full realization of divine will. Yet this realism, though sobering, does not dampen our resolve to do still better. Nor should it obscure the recognition that these efforts, however, proximate and fragmentary, are a genuine expression of love and the hope that is within us.

Christians in dialogue with the world may also discover in new ways the proximate character of their own existence and insight as the world fills the forms of love with its demands for justice. New ethical insights regarding racism and sexism, stemming from the voices of those who suffer and further informed by the social and political sciences, have reversed the prejudicial attitudes and practices of the church's past and its less than benign neglect of urgent matters of injustice in our society.[48]*

Such occasions are times for repentance, but they are also times to appreciate once more that we live our ethic and embrace our vocation in the confidence of the assurance of God's promise and not in the certainty of our judgments. In the assurance of the promise, we are open to the Spirit and to the learnings of our various dialogical encounters. We are open because in the freedom of the gospel and in obedience to the law of love we can seek the good of our neighbor rather than feel compelled at every turn to show how right we are.

This freedom and openness, simultaneously to God's call and the world's voice, are what equip us well for witness in a pluralistic world such as ours. In our global society the manifold diversity of religions and cultures, competing and intersecting, creates a situation that makes a greater moral consensus seem both necessary and unlikely. Increasingly theologians and ethicists are advocating the need for the church to bring its views into a process of public dialogue both as a witness to its faith and as a means of facilitating a public moral conversation.

While Luther may not have expected much in the way of social and political transformation, he did see that the structures of governance and the economy by God's loving initiative have a vocation to serve the common good. As B.A. Gerrish pointed out in his landmark study on grace and reason in Luther, Luther had a positive evaluation of reason in public affairs and in moral deliberation, notwithstanding the corruption of sin and the limits of human finitude. Reason was primarily problematic when allowed to intrude into matters of salvation in theologically inappropriate ways.[49] From this vantage point, those who are involved in the institutions of society and culture are potentially good dialogue partners. It is well within our Lutheran tradition to engage in dialogue with them for the common good. We, of course, enter into this process always attempting to discern the will of God. We are open to our partners in dialogue while always cognizant that dialogue may need to be coupled with prophetic confrontation.[50]*

The pluralism of our world and the attendant threat of ethical relativism make the church's ethical witness an urgent requirement. The dialogue that pluralism generates provides the opportunity for that witness. Hans Küng has argued that the staggering pluralism of our global society requires a dialogue among the world's religions if there is to be peace and global moral responsibility. He counsels religious leaders to dialogue with "steadfastness," sticking to the integrity of their convictions. Dialogue is not compromise but a quest for mutually acceptable truths.[51] Ronald Thiemann has demonstrated that religious participation in public policy in America is desirable, can be done with integrity, and is consistent with the liberal tradition of our constitutional life.[52]

An ethic of openness to new discovery in the assurance of God's promise and the Spirit's presence in the life of the church is good equipment for dialogue. Being a "community of moral deliberation" is good practice. If we are clear about our vocation and our existential situation in the church and the world, as this chapter has sought to help us be, then we should be ready to embrace the responsibility of public dialogue in a diverse world. We have peculiar theological gifts for this task.

A final word on authority seems in order. While the authorization in our vocation as a church is the keystone of our authority, and the Word of God gives us guidance and voice, the final piece in the authority puzzle is the integrity of our witness. Integrity requires faithfulness to the truth of our faith, that is, an unremitting devotion to an ethic grounded in the promise and the love that follows. Integrity means that we eschew a false certitude that would belie the theological truth of our radical dependence on grace in a fallen world. At the same time it means refusing to yield to the world's comfort with relativism, moral drift, and systemic injustice, not to mention cruelty and perversity, wherever they are found.

In Conclusion

I have looked at the way in which the ambiguity of human existence, the complexities of moral choice in this ambiguous life, and the developments of our own ethical tradition create the demand for a renewed understanding of our ethical vocation and nurture our moral courage and authority. The vision and the promise of the reign of God revealed in the Christ are the focal point. Standing over against our historical existence, God's future gives birth to faith, hope, and love, the energy of the Christian ethic. The form and texture of this future vision portray an array of values that set the agenda for love. Our pursuit of these values as a community of faith is an integral part of our vocation to witness to the hope within us. In the contrast between that future and our present, we recognize that the dominion of God also stands in judgment on even our best efforts. The realism that follows from that realization delivers us from false assumptions about our own moral certainty and naive notions about making social progress. Yet in the encouragement and freedom of the gospel, we are open to the neighbor and the world for dialogue and discovery. It is an ethic whose courage and confidence reside in the assurance of divine promise and whose authority resides in the call to serve that promise and in the faithfulness of our response.

Pauline Ethics
Congregations as Communities of Moral Deliberation
David Fredrickson

Introduction

A founder and nurturer of congregations, St. Paul thought and wrote about moral matters for these same congregations. Recent interpreters have shown that the apostle's ethical statements were shaped to fit the needs and circumstances of the particular group of believers to whom he was writing. This chapter does not seek coherence in various moral topics in Paul's letters and then apply his views as guidelines for individuals.[1] Nor does it focus on the specific cultural and historical identities of the congregations he was addressing. Instead I will draw out ethical significance from the fact that Paul placed congregations at the very center of his thought. In this approach congregations are neither obstacles to the reconstruction of coherent moral opinions nor the passive recipients of already worked out answers. Rather they are places where moral reflection, formulation, and action occur. Pauline ethics grow out of the apostle's vision of the church as persons gathered and empowered for moral deliberation by the Spirit in the name of Jesus.

Why is Paul's ethical thought a pertinent topic in a book on Lutheran ethics? One reason is that many Lutheran ethicists have appealed to Paul's writings as an authoritative source for such key teachings as Christian freedom, justification by grace through faith, and vocation. Ethics is Lutheran, it is claimed, if the individual believer is motivated for good works through the forgiveness of sin. Ethics speaks first about the individual before God and the conscience that has been freed from guilt. It has also been a Lutheran belief that God has structured the world and called individuals into roles, relationships, or as Robert Benne has aptly put it, "places of responsibility." Paul's writings have served as a biblical basis for this dual focus on individual motivation and the role of the individual in the orders of creation.[2] Most Lutheran interpreters of Paul have appropriated him to legitimate this scheme of ethics.

Another reason to turn to Paul, and the one behind this essay, is the belief that Paul provides an alternative to that kind of Lutheran ethics. While not ignoring the issue of individual motivation for good works, my approach makes thematic the power of persons in community to influence their corporate lives and the world for good or for ill. Instead of assuming stable and meaningful structures into which individuals are called, this ethic explores the way humans use power to create structures that are sometimes beneficial and sometimes oppressive and destructive. The moral task that lies before the church is the testing of all things by those who must bear the consequences of the decisions reached. Taking up this task in the power of the Spirit, the church aligns itself with the reforming work of Martin Luther.[3*]

My approach requires me to give more attention than is usual in the Lutheran appropriation of Paul to the political dimension of his thought. By "political" I mean to evoke the Greek city-state and its democratic procedures for decisionmaking.[4] I will pursue the thesis that an adequate account of Pauline ethics must begin with the instructive parallel that exists between Paul's conceptualization of the local church and the assembly (*ekklēsia*) of the Greek city. This parallel does not explain all of Paul's thinking about the church, but it does underscore that for Paul the chief ethical problem has to do with the kind of politics the church practices internally.

The three passages I examine (2 Cor. 3; Phil. 1:27—2:18; and Rom. 12–15) are rich in political imagery for the internal actions of the congregation. 2 Cor. 3 and Rom. 12–15 also have theoretical treatments of the use of Scripture in the church, while Phil. 1:27—2:18 helps us understand Paul's appropriation of the theory of example in Greco-Roman moral philosophy. His commitment to the theory of example influences the way he uses Scripture. Furthermore his use of Scripture coordinates well with his understanding of the congregation as a democratic community.

Free Speech and the Letter/Spirit Distinction in 2 Corinthians 3

The political metaphor of the congregation as assembly shapes Paul's ecclesiology.[5] This is most easily demonstrated in 2 Cor. 3, where we also encounter Paul's theory about the proper use of Scripture.

It is somewhat artificial to think of 2 Corinthians as Paul's discussion of Christian community. Paul is engaged in self-defense in which he gives an account of his ministry. Yet there is a connection between Paul's ministry and the community. Some within the Corinthian church have charged him with flattery and a lack of free speech (*parrēsia*). To answer this charge, Paul views his possessing free speech as dependent not upon his own moral virtue, as the philosophers did, nor upon his social standing, as did political theorists. Rather he uses much free speech (*pollę, parrēsia, chrōmetha* 3:12) because of the Spirit. In 3:18 it is clear that the Spirit is the possession of all in the community. The source of Paul's free speech and the free speech of his audience is the Spirit. Thus Paul's apology helps us understand the political dimension of his ecclesiology.

The Christian Congregation as Open and Inclusive Political Community. Because of its associations with ancient democracy, the term "free speech" (*parrēsia*) in 3:12 implies that Paul understands the congregation as analogous to the Greek assembly.[6*] The community of believers is a speaking place, where the future of the community is determined through unhindered conversation that seeks to arrive at consensus through persuasion. As we will see when examining another political term (*politeuesthai*) in Phil. 1:27, modern translators are usually deaf to the political overtones in Paul's language. They turn *parrēsia* into a subjective state, and the analogy between Pauline congregation and democratic assembly disappears. The Revised Standard Version, New Revised Standard Version, and a host of commentators have encouraged an existentialist reading of Paul by taking this term out of its political setting and making it merely a matter of confidence.[7]

Free speech was in fact the heart of ancient democracy. It was the right of all to whom Greek cities granted citizenship and was the most effective means of preserving the city's freedom and safety. After Alexander's conquest, as the centers of decision making shifted away from cities to regional capitals, philosophers imagined free speech independently of waning city life. The good conscience based upon the wise man's virtue gave him confidence to speak the truth no matter what the personal risk. Free speech also had an important role to play in friendship. Friends spoke the truth to one another to confront shortcomings and bring moral improvement. Frank speech was the language of friendship.[8] At political, philosophical, and interpersonal levels, *parrēsia* was always a matter of speaking and never simply confidence.

To grasp the radical openness of the Christian congregation as a political community, it is important to note who was not granted freedom of speech in ancient democracies: women, slaves, foreigners, and children. Because of its inclusiveness, Paul's vision of the church as a democratic community is an extreme form of democracy by the standards of the ancient world. He tore down the barriers to full participation through his conviction that the Spirit grants free speech to all who belong to Christ. For the church to be the church, the voices of all must be heard.[9*] Even though Paul uses the imagery of the Greek assembly in which those trained in rhetoric had an advantage in promoting their purposes, he does not grant this privilege. Paul takes from the assembly the ideal of free speech and leaves behind the social status and educational distinctions that favored the speech of some to the exclusion of others.

Shame Brings Silence: The Spirit Brings Speech. Paul rejects the way his culture limited the power of free speech to upper class, free males. Although free speech as a rhetorical activity cannot be reduced to subjectivity, it nonetheless did rest upon a state of mind known as *pepoithēsis* (confidence), which Paul mentions in 3:4.[10] A fruitful way of interpreting 2 Corinthians 3 is to trace the way confidence for free speech is created. For Paul this is a theological question. Social standing and moral virtue were the two confidence-creating factors in Greek society. For Paul they play no role in making persons free and thus capable of using free speech. Instead the Spirit of the Lord creates this freedom (3:17) and does so by removing shame.

2 Cor. 3:4-18 traces how the written code, or letter (*gramma*), brings about shame and silence, the very opposite of free speech. The letter is the death of the church as a democratic community resting on free speech. The Spirit, on the other hand, is the source of its life: "The letter kills but the Spirit makes alive." The letter/Spirit distinction is not a hermeneutic distinction as many scholars have argued. Paul's point is not that persons who have the Spirit have access to the meaning of Old Testament texts by transcending the literal sense. Rather the letter/Spirit distinction should be understood in political terms.[11] Paul is asking what makes participation in the community possible for all its members. What is the source of the community's freedom and free speech?

To amplify his claim in 2 Cor. 3:6 that the letter kills while the Spirit gives life, Paul employs a common rhetorical device called comparison (*sugkrisis*). In 3:7-18 he freely adopts the story of Moses' veiled face in Exodus 34. If it is the case that code written on stone and resulting in death occurred in glory, how much more glorious is the ministry of the Spirit (3:7-8). In 3:9 letter is renamed the ministry of condemnation and contrasted with the Spirit's ministry of justification. In 3:10 the old covenant is being nullified. If glory attaches to it in spite of its temporal limitation, then how much more will glory attach to work of the Spirit that remains forever. Based upon the enduring work of the Spirit to create justice, Paul concludes the first comparison in 3:12: "Therefore having such hope, we use much free speech." It is not written code that creates the confidence or hope upon which free speech and democratic community are based. Only the Spirit with its promise of enduring transformation accomplishes this.[12]*

In 3:13-18 the comparison turns from the two ministries to the two ministers, Moses and Paul. In 3:13-15 Moses begins as a negative example but in 3:16 emerges as a positive example.[13] In 3:13 Paul tells his hearers that he is not like Moses insofar as Moses veiled his face so that the sons of Israel might not stare at the result of the old covenant. This self-veiling suggests that Moses hid himself from a sense of shame, since in ancient philosophy and literature there was a frequent connection between shame and concealment of the face.[14] In Paul's retelling of the story, Moses does not want the people of Israel to see the result (*telos*) of the old covenant—shame. Nevertheless the fact that Moses' veil is removed in 3:16 signifies an end to his shame, and he exemplifies its very opposite—freedom. The connection between Moses' unveiled face and freedom reflects a popular notion that freedom was dependent on a good conscience. Free speech in turn finds its legitimate basis in the freedom granted by a good conscience. The person having no cause to be ashamed is empowered to use free speech.[15]

Scripture Samples the Spirit's Work. The unveiled Moses and the unveiled Paul, both made free by the Spirit, are models of the church. Not that they are patterns for imitation. Rather they are samples of the reality that the Spirit is creating in the church. Thus Paul can begin 3:18 with the inclusive and emphatic "we *all* with uncovered face . . ." Freedom and free speech are the possessions of all in the congregation. The remainder of 3:18 depicts what happens when this freedom is allowed to run unhindered. The main event is ongoing transformation. The one image into which all members of the community are being shaped is Christ, who is himself the image of God (4:4). This transformation does not, however, happen behind the backs of the members of the congregation. It happens in, with, and under the exercise of freedom. It is accomplished as they gaze without shame into each other's faces as if into a mirror, simultaneously seeing themselves and the glory of the Lord. They become the face they see.[16*]

2 Cor. 3 teaches us that for Paul each member of the congregation is empowered by the Spirit to use free speech. The shame that in the Greco-Roman world was attached to being poor, female, and slave is removed by the Spirit. The Spirit makes it possible for each in the church to look directly at the other, to speak, and to be transformed into the image of Christ. Furthermore the use of Scripture must harmonize with this experience of liberation. Transformation to an image rather than obedience to an authority is the key to Paul's use of Scripture. To the extent that Scripture is used as written code and precludes the shaping of the community's will through free speech, it functions as the letter that kills. Yet when Scripture is read for examples of shame being removed, it offers samples of the reality of the Spirit's work in the church.

Moral Action Means Extending Freedom:
Philippians 1:27—2:18

So far we have seen that for Paul the congregation is a community of persons empowered by the Spirit to speak freely. The use of Scripture must conform to the community's experience of all being freed for speech by the Spirit. As important as the inclusion of all voices is, there is more that needs to be said about the concrete good of the community. What is worthy action in a community whose future is determined by the inclusion of all voices in conversation? How does Scripture help to bring about this moral action? How is this moral action shaped by God's action in Christ?

The Moral Good of a Testing Community. In Phil. 1:27 Paul encourages the community of believers in Philippi to "engage politically in a manner worthy of the gospel of Christ." The reference to worthy action establishes the moral good in relation to a political process. Unfortunately modern translations of *politeuesthe* as "behave yourselves" or "conduct yourselves" do not help us understand that Paul portrays his audience's action in political terminology. The term carries the notion of initiation of policy in matters of the city's welfare.[17] The King James translation is revealing: "Only let your conversation be as it becometh the gospel of Christ." The background for this term is democracy. It refers to citizen action within the assembly, the deliberating and legislative body of ancient democracies. What goes on in the community of those belonging to Christ is analogous to the popular assemblies of democratic governments.[18] Paul exhorts his readers to engage actively through speech in the affairs of their own assembly, the local church. The nature of moral goodness rests on this political understanding of the community.

Phil. 1:9-11 deserves our attention since it also speaks of communal interaction and the moral good. In 1:10 the community's central activity is called "testing (*dokimazein*) the things that really matter."[19] The things that really matter carry conviction only through a procedure in which all participants are free to raise questions, offer objections, and make alternative recommendations that are themselves subject to the testing of the other members. The significance of Paul's emphasis on testing cannot be overestimated, especially when compared with the other ethical paradigms of the ancient world. Paul is not asserting that the moral life is an imitation of universal order; nor is it conformity to a particular historical tradition. Neither is it obedience to divine command. Instead persons in community pursue consensus through testing.[20]* Paul understands the moral good as what enhances the whole community taking up the task of testing. Accordingly he prays for the community to abound in love, knowledge, and perception in order that testing might go forward. Most importantly testing is a privilege and responsibility of all members of the community rather than the possession of an elite group.

Paul's ethics is concerned with the way communities arrive at moral decisions through the full and free participation of individuals. Placing *dokimazein* and *politeuesthai* in their ancient political context liberates us from the modern preoccupation with the moral formation of the solitary self and its accompanying distortion of Pauline ethical thought. Furthermore exhortation in Phil.1:27 has to do with how individuals engage politically within the community that is constituted by the narrative of Christ. Paul directs his hearers to evaluate their participation from a perspective that is established by the narrative of Christ Jesus in 2:5-11.

Christ Creates Our Freedom. Paul introduces the Christ hymn in Philippians 2 by exhorting the community to adopt the same mind as exists in Christ Jesus. The narrative begins in 2:6 with a political community composed of God and Christ Jesus. We are justified in speaking of the relationship between God and Christ Jesus as a political community if we interpret the concept of equality in the phrase "to be equal with God" in an adverbial sense rather than adjectival. Equality refers to the way God and Christ Jesus exist with one another rather than the identity of some quality, often described by commentators as "divinity." Paul is speaking of equality as equal participation in the governance of the community, or as Aristotle called it, "reciprocal equality."[21]

We need to re-conceptualize the Christ hymn from the perspective of equality employed in the discourse of democracy. Phil. 2:6b-8 narrates Christ Jesus' decision not to keep his equality with God in himself but as something that must be extended to others. Christ Jesus opens the limits on equality with God. Notice what is not said. The pattern of the Father sending the Son, which plays an important a role in Paul's other letters (for example, Rom. 8:3), is not the hymn's underlying narrative. Rather the emphasis falls on Christ's refusal to limit the political community to himself and God. The story is not of Jesus' conformity to God's will but of his own initiative to extend equality with God to others.

To extend equality with God, Christ Jesus takes on the form of a slave. How is his slavery able to communicate equality in participation with God? This is impossible to grasp if it is assumed, as in the case of many interpreters, that Christ's slavery is to God as master.[22] There is, however, another interpretation of 2:7-8 that makes better sense of the narrative. Christ's obedience is given to humans not to God. Similarly his voluntary slavery is directed to humanity.[23] To understand the significance of Christ's voluntary slavery, we need to recall the origin of freedom according to ancient political philosophy.

Freedom has a material foundation. Civic freedom depended on freedom from daily tasks. Aristotle emphasizes the dependence of the master's freedom upon the slave's labor: "Therefore all people rich enough to be able to avoid personal trouble have a steward who takes this office, while they themselves engage in politics (*politeuovrai*) or philosophy."[24] In the narrative Christ Jesus becomes humanity's obedient slave and thus creates freedom for his masters at the expense of his own body. He empties himself to create freedom for others.

The Moral Life as a Shared Paradox of Power. The first half of the Christ hymn helps us understand what it means for the church to "engage politically in a manner worthy of the gospel of Christ" (Phil. 1:27). Christ extends to others democratic participation in the divine community. The means to this end is his voluntary enslavement to those he wishes to free.[25] Thus to engage in the affairs of the community worthily of the gospel of Christ, each member, conscious of freedom, must take up the same goal: to extend participation to the other. Each will employ the same means to this end: voluntary slavery to the other.

What significance might this notion of mutual slavery have had for Paul's hearers? The answer is in the paradoxical character of the communal relations implied by mutual obedience. Each person in the community is simultaneously master and slave, ruler and ruled. This paradox has an antecedent in the understanding of sharing power in ancient democracies. Aristotle pointed out that the distinguishing mark of political rule (as opposed to the rule of master over slave or male over household) was an exchange of ruling and being ruled. Citizens must learn both to exercise authority over others and to obey the authority of those whom they once ruled or would rule.[26] In democratic arrangements of power a citizen could expect over time to be both ruler and ruled. Paul introduces a new factor by removing the temporal succession, but there is enough similarity between his understanding of the Christian community and power sharing in Greek democracies to make a meaningful comparison. By removing temporal succession, Paul makes more complex the relationships between the members of the community. While each is a master—a full participant in the divine community—each is also a slave to the others. Yet since this slavery is mutual within the congregation, the slave is again made a master.[27]

We are now able to state the relation between ethics and politics in Paul based upon the exhortation to "engage politically in a manner worthy of the gospel of Christ." If we focus on the verb, each member of the community is exhorted to play an active role in the formation of the group's plans, policies, and objectives. What is remarkable about this exhortation is the predominance of a process of participation to work out a mutually acceptable form of life over assimilation to an already determined form of life or obedience to divine command. There is an openness that is to be limited by the participants themselves through speech and persuasion.

Nevertheless modifying (but not retracting!) the high degree of individual participation and initiative is the adverbial phrase "worthily of the gospel of Christ." In, with, and under the moral claims and testing initiated by community members, another activity goes on in which each individual extends freedom for equal participation in the community of God and Christ Jesus to the other. It must be acknowledged that this activity, initiated by and modeled on the voluntary slavery of Christ to humanity and his self-lowering in obscurity, is in tension with the verb *politeuesthai*. How can I assert my freedom by proposing and defending controversial moral claims and simultaneously empty myself for the other in slavelike obedience? One might reject this tension as a Pauline blunder or mystification through paradox, but taking it seriously could be the beginning of fruitful reflection on the character of the moral good in Christian congregations. What concretely does it mean to extend freedom to the other? What kind of community is this that presumes both individual initiative and mutual obedience?

The Christ Hymn and Paul's Use of Scripture. Before leaving Philippians we note the absence in 1:27—2:18 of Scripture as a norm for moral action.[28] Paul does not show the slightest interest in applying an already established moral code to the life of the Philippian congregation. This we should expect in light of his critique of written code in 2 Cor. 3. It is also consistent with his vision of all the members of the community engaging in political action through speech and the testing of things that matter. We must not, however, make the mistake of equating Scripture with written code and think that Paul throws the former out with the latter. As we saw in the story of Moses' veil, Scripture is full of both positive and negative examples that embody the attitudes and behavior appropriate to a community whose members are simultaneously free and slave to one another.

Even though there is no explicit use of Scripture for exhortation purposes in Phil. 1:27—2:18, the theory lying behind the way Paul employs Scripture in other letters is present. In other words, the way he uses the narrative of Christ in 2:5-11 is the way he uses Scripture in general. Certain terms in 1:27—2:18 are drawn from the theory of example in Greco-Roman moral exhortation.[29] Rather than code, Scripture provides examples of character. Paul offers the examples to the church for imitation and thus for the formation of the character that is the source of appropriate action in the community established by Christ's extension of freedom through his own slavery. In Philippians Paul surrounds the Christ hymn with two of the main technical terms for moral exhortation employed by the philosophers of his day: *paraklēsis* and *paramythion*.[30] Also borrowing from the ancient conventions of moral exhortation, he offers himself to the congregation as an example in 1:30.

The significance of Paul relying on example rather than code cannot be overestimated. Paul does not demand obedience to an authoritative set of rules, to his own apostolic authority, or even to Christ as the teacher who knows God's will. Instead he exhorts his hearers to be transformed into the pattern of Christ's liberating action narrated in the hymn.[31] This transformation begins by the Spirit's free gift of the mind of Christ to the community.[32*] As we will see in Rom. 15:1-6, Paul regards Scripture as a repository of this transformed mind, a collection of stories displaying Christ's mind. Christ's mind, of course, is not only or even primarily example.[33] It is not simply a goal to be striven toward. Christ's mind already exists in his hearers by virtue of their participation in the Spirit (2:1), or as we read in 2:5: "Have this mind among you which is yours in Christ Jesus."

Bearing Difference to the World: Romans 12–15

Connecting morality so closely with Christian congregations may lead some to suspect that such an ethic is naïve in two ways. First, does the church have the capacity to test all things when there is radical difference among the members? What happens when Paul's exhortation to test all things comes to members who regard some moral matters so firmly established as to be exempt from testing? What if speaking about them is unnecessary, if not itself immoral? Second is the suspicion of a kind of churchly isolationism. Does Paul's political church have the resources to create public significance out of an ethic that concerns itself primarily with the internal interactions of the members of the body of Christ?

Difference Does Not Put an End to Testing. In Romans 12–15 Paul responds to these challenges. He does so first by the test case of an audience composed of two groups: the weak in faith (14:1) and the powerful (15:1). Paul identifies himself with the latter group, for whom the distinction of clean and unclean is meaningless. They are convinced that nothing in itself is unclean (14:14). The weak in faith, however, hold that certain foods are polluting (14:2) and certain times are sacred (14:5). The clash of worldviews could hardly be more striking. The weak judge the strong, and the strong count the weak as nobodies, attitudes that reveal the additional dynamic of social class. It should be underscored that the Pauline exhortation to test all things is inherently biased toward the strong. They possess a knowledge of things in which no division of space and time into sacred and profane stands in the way of questioning and searching out God's will. The weak, on the other hand, cannot place all matters on the table without first giving up the way they believe the world to be in relation to God. The openness toward change that is assumed in the Pauline vision of the church as the location of the Spirit's liberating presence (2 Cor. 3:17-18) is at odds with the perception of the world in categories of clean and unclean.

Yet Paul does not ask the strong to back away from the centrality of testing in the community's life. In fact in 12:1-2 Paul lets it be known that the church's chief activity is to "test (*dokimazein*) what is the will of God, the good and pleasing and perfect."[34] Notice, however, that the capacity for testing is not given with the knowledge or social structures of "this age." Testing the will of God depends upon a prior transformation that in turn depends upon a renewing of the mind. Here we see how Paul addresses the question of what becomes of testing in a community in which some are not committed to the testability of all things while others already engage in critical reflection. One of the tasks Paul takes up in Romans 12–15 is to delineate the character of mind that responds in love to those who must restrict the scope of matters in which God's will is to be tested. Paul thus maintains the pattern he established in Phil. 1:27. Free participation in the community's life is both asserted and modified by practical reasoning not given in the natural course of things but only in the narrative of Christ and through the Spirit.

The other challenge to Paul's political conception of the church is the apparent isolation of the congregation's ethics from the broader society. If what counts in Christian morality is the process through which decisions are reached and the insistence that all voices are to be heard, then it becomes a real problem to conceive how the church as the body of Christ acts in the world at all. Romans 13 provides a link between the inner working of congregational life and society.

Public Sphere and the Metaphor of Debt. Paul's most original contribution to Christian ethics is the way he weaves together testing in a heterogeneous community with the community's relationship with the world. He is forced to deal with the complexity of the church's relation to society because he does not have the simple solution provided by a church speaking with one voice to the world about moral matters, as if all its members (or at least the ones who count) had privileged access to truth. This notion of a single voice on moral matters would violate his notion that the church is a place of ongoing moral conversation in which no voice may be shamed into silence. It also minimizes his belief that the law is written on the hearts of all people (Rom. 2:12-16). Most of all, to conceptualize the church as a monolithic source of moral facts prevents it from making its unique contribution to civil society. Paul argues in Romans 13–15 that the church models for the world a way of carrying forth in unity in the presence of conflicting moral claims.

Romans 13 has been interpreted to speak of two separate matters.[35] Supposedly in verses 1-7 Paul deals with the believer's responsibility to obey civil government and in verses 8-14 with the individual's moral life in general. In this interpretation Paul advocates a quietist ethic with respect to Christian involvement in society. One obeys the civil authorities to avoid drawing attention to the small band of believers. What is missing in this interpretation is careful attention to God's creation and preservation of the public sphere. The issue in Rom. 13:1-7 is not whether one should obey the government but how one conceives of the public sphere in the first place. 13:8-14 goes on to speak of the way the congregation contributes to and transforms the public sphere.

God creates and preserves public life. We should note that Paul does not describe his readers' actual experience of political rule in first-century Rome. Rather he builds upon the ideology of kingship originating in the philosophic response to the rule exercised by Alexander the Great and his successors. After Alexander's conquest, public spheres were created and preserved less frequently through democratic means and more often by monarchical rule. Before Paul can conceptualize how the church's inner life contributes to and transforms society (13:8-15:13), he has to provide his readers with a theory of the public sphere that is intelligible and poses no insurmountable obstacles to the church's influence. The Hellenistic ideology of kingship with its subordination of power to justice provides such a theoretical beginning.

When Paul says in Rom. 13:4 that the ruler is "God's servant for you for the good," he has captured the basic insight of Hellenistic theorists of monarchical rule who sought to place limits on the king's power. Ruling authority exists for the sake of the public good not for the ambitions of those who occupy the office. As God orders and creates harmony in the heavens, so the good king brings about peace and friendship among persons on earth by executing justice, honoring those who contribute to the common good, and conducting his affairs in an exemplary manner. The good king's rule mirrors divine rule.[36] The coercive dimension of rule, to which Paul alludes with such terms as judgment, fear, and sword, exists to suppress evil. Paul also emphasizes in 13:3 that the role of the ruler is to honor those who make a positive contribution to the community's life. Finally in 13:6 Paul mentions that the rule is undertaken at great expense and personal trouble to the ruler.

Paul also makes a connection between the account of the public sphere offered in 13:1-7 to the inner life of the church in 13:8. The glue that binds the ruled to the ruler is the obligation to repay debt. In 13:5 subordination to civil authority is necessary not merely out of fear of punishment but more importantly from a sense of fairness. The reason that taxes are paid and respect given (13:6-7) is that the rulers have put forth great personal effort on behalf of the ruled. Justice therefore demands that something is owed them. From this reasoning comes the Pauline exhortation: "Repay the debts to all (*apodote pasin tas opheilas*)."

Paul's exhortation in Rom. 13:8 must be interpreted in the context of obligation within the public sphere discussed in 13:5-7. Although debts generated by the civil authority's effort to bring about justice must be repaid, one obligation toward the ruling authority can never be fully discharged. Members of the community of believers are in a perpetual state of obligation to the broader human community to love one another: "Owe no one anything, except to love one another." Paul does not exhort his hearers to love persons outside of the community of believers, although the notion of doing good to outsiders is certainly not an idea foreign to his thought (Gal. 6:10). The point is that the congregation is a debtor to civil authority. The way it attempts to repay—but never thinking it has fully discharged its obligation—is through mutual loving relations within the congregation itself (which I will examine shortly). Note the unique way Paul is conceptualizing the relation between church and civil society. The metaphor of debt presents a complex interplay between the church's inner life and its relationship to the public sphere.[37] It is the medium through which the church's ethic, built up around its politics, can have an effect on the greater society.

Christ, Scripture, and the Meaning of Love. In Rom. 15:1 we read, "We who are powerful ought to carry the weaknesses of those who are not powerful and not please ourselves." Standing behind the word "ought" is the Greek word *opheilō*. With a word play, Paul connects the obligation described in 15:1 to his earlier discussion of the public sphere in 13:7-8 where debt (*opheilē*) is repaid and his hearers are to owe (*opheilete*) nothing to anyone except to love one another. The terms "good" and "neighbor" in 15:2 also remind the reader of the transition between the public and the church in 13:7-10. Love within the community, the perpetual debt to the wider society, is made concrete in the phrase "to carry (*bastazein*)" weaknesses.[38] But what does this mean?

In a negative sense it means that the powerful are not to cause the weak to violate their own conscience. Paul alludes to this principle in 14:5: "Let each be fully convinced in their own mind." The worst thing that can happen is for the powerful to cause the weak to be grieved (14:15) or to stumble (14:20). This amounts to the destruction of the ones for whom Christ died (14:15), who are the creation of God (14:19). To love is not to bring the other into self-judgment and self-condemnation in the matter that is being tested (14:22-23). Paul offers a theory about the use of Scripture in 13:8-10 that correlates with his idea about what love does not do. Love fulfills the law because it "does not work evil toward the neighbor" (13:10). Love summarizes the prohibitions of the law (13:9). But the logic of summary and fulfillment leads the congregation away from actually reading Scripture since the prohibitions are already contained in the command to love.

Paul develops the positive sense of "carry" in Rom. 15:3-6. In doing so he comes up with a fuller theory of the use of Scripture.[39] As in 2 Cor. 3 and Phil. 1:27—2:18, the theory prefers example/transformation to command/obedience. Christ's example of not pleasing himself is cited in 15:3, and this is expanded by discovering in Scripture (Ps. 69:9) the mind of Christ. With this turn to Scripture as the repository of Christ's mind, "bearing" another person comes into clearer focus: "The reproaches of those reproaching you fell upon me." This is not sympathy or toleration but the actual feeling, thinking, and living in the world of the other as experienced in shame, which was the result of a rebuke as severe as a reproach (*oneidismos*). Reminiscent of mutual slavery as the mark of the entire community in Philippians 2, the prayer in Rom. 15:5 makes clear that the gift of Christ's mind is finally for all the members. Thus the congregation's unity does not rest in its agreement about moral topics, although each member has the right to initiate testing with the hope of consensus. Rather the church's unity resides in the gift of God, in each member sharing the mind of Christ, in each bearing in himself or herself the reproach that falls upon the other. This unity brings glory to God (15:6). When perceived by the world, the church's obligation to society is perpetually discharged (15:7-13).

Paul and Lutheran Ethics

I have a made a case for understanding Pauline ethics in terms of two distinct but related activities. Both are carried out in the church by means of the Spirit.

The first activity is political. It is the church's testing of values received from tradition or culture. Paul takes from the history of Greek democracy the vision of a community whose members are free to initiate discussion about any matter yet also responsible to give reasons for any claim made. Paul radicalizes this vision in two ways. First he is convinced that the Spirit gives the right of testing to all for whom Christ died regardless of the status markers that they bear in the world. Second, testing goes on in a community that is composed of God, Christ, and the church. Testing then is not just a good idea or an effective means to build community (it may sometimes seem otherwise!); it is a theological activity. God's life can no longer be understood apart from the life of the community that lives in the freedom for testing extended to it by Christ's death.

The second activity is ethical. The moral good is the mutual extension of freedom within the community. Paul uses the images of slavery and burden bearing to depict the freedom creating action of Christ for us. Living out of this narrative, the church is a place where persons are mutually and voluntarily enslaved to one another, dedicated to the other's freedom. It is also the place where real differences are present and the other's shame carried. The world sees this ethos and glorifies God.

Paul's chief contribution to Lutheran ethics is his vision of the church as a community of moral deliberation in which the political and the ethical exist simultaneously and energize each other. It is crucial not to break them apart. Any approach to Lutheran ethics that emphasizes simply the process of coming to moral decisions and ignores the ethos of the community—its living out of the story of Christ—will not reflect the Pauline vision since it will have lost sight of the moral task of extending freedom to the other and bearing the other's difference. Conversely any proposal that thinks only in terms of the community's identity and the ethos it has received from the tradition will abandon the critical principle within Paul's ethics and fail to do justice to the freedom granted by the Spirit through the death of Christ for us. Lutherans must discover from Paul what they already know—to live simultaneously free and bound.

🌿 8 🌿

The Reform Dynamic
Addressing New Issues in Uncertain Times

Larry Rasmussen with Cynthia Moe-Lobeda

Where We Are, Perhaps

Imagine. Imagine that you, like Martin Luther, live in a time when the institutions of one age creak in the beams (feudalism in Luther's case, modernity in ours) but those of the coming era are not yet established (modernity in Luther's case, something postmodern in ours). Imagine you live in a world that is not adding up well on its own. Many people seek frameworks of sure meaning at the same time that traditional moral and doctrinal positions are being questioned anew. Not all the pieces to the puzzle of life can be found; some that are found do not fit.

Or imagine you find yourself suddenly akin to early Christians around the Mediterranean basin. The world is religiously eclectic, multiethnic, multiracial, multilinguistic, and crowded. It breeds a thousand competing spiritualities, philosophies, and ways of life, worries over fraying moral and social fiber, and suffers more than a little world-weariness and violence. Then imagine that, like Augustine of Hippo, your challenge is to forge an ethic of civic responsibility from the heart of a radical and otherworldly faith for a world experiencing both cataclysm and new opportunity.

Now jump the centuries. Imagine that, like the early Christians, Augustine, and Luther, you too live in a time of discontinuity. Unsettling news arrives that they did not face. The unsettling news is that earth can industrialize only once in the manner and on the scale it has, and that both the rate of change and its global reach are unprecedented.[1]* The unsettling news is that for the first time since humans appeared on the scene, soil loss is exceeding soil formation, freshwater use is exceeding aquifer replenishment, forest destruction is exceeding forest regeneration, fish catches are exceeding fish reproduction, carbon emissions are exceeding carbon fixation, and species extinction is exceeding species evolution. Some of the effects, the news continues, are or may be irreversible. Species loss is one example, accelerated global climate change possibly another. In short, cumulative human power to destroy is gradually outstripping earth's power to restore in ways hospitable for life as we know and desire it.

The world's population, the report goes on, has tripled since 1900 and doubled since 1950. If you were born before 1950 you have seen more population growth than occurred during the preceding 4 million years! Production and consumption have also accelerated dramatically since 1950—grain three-fold, seafood fourfold, water threefold, firewood threefold, lumber twice, paper six times, fossil fuels fourfold since 1950, thirtyfold since 1900. The world's economy has quintupled since 1950; it has grown twentyfold since 1900.[2] Moreover the income gap is widening. In 1960 the richest 20 percent of the global population received thirty times more than the poorest; in 1991 the richest received sixty-one times more. The poorest one-fifth of the world's peoples saw their share of global income drop from 2.3 percent to 1.4 in this period, the richest one-fifth saw theirs rise from 70 to 85 percent. In 1996 the assets of the 358 billionaires in the world exceeded the combined annual incomes of countries with the poorest 45 percent of the world's population. "The meek show no signs of inheriting the Earth," quips one commentator.[3]

Imagine in short that the present world is unsustainable, that you are part of it, and that to your surprise the human world's relationship to the rest of earth has changed fundamentally in a mere wink of time, namely, from the onset of this century to its close. Life-as-we-know-it turns up unable to meet the needs of the expanding human world and the rest of nature for present and future generations. And the factors that create unsustainability—social disintegration, economic disparities, and environmental degradation—are systemic rather than episodic.

Then imagine our task is to help create a sustainable world. Clearly a task for generations, it nonetheless begins now, when many are disoriented and focused on the short term, urgent about protecting what they have, and not readily given to consensus about what to do. How will we go about this? How should we broach re-formation in off-balance times?

What the Tradition Offers, Perhaps

Next imagine you belong to a Christian tradition that confesses a reforming dynamic as the way of living faith itself. Imagine first that you cannot escape

the political, economic, social, and religious upheaval of your time. Even if
you wanted to "start from scratch," in a world long underway, there is no
"scratch" to start from. Then imagine you belong to the specific confessional
tradition that takes its name from a sixteenth-century German reformer whose
faith led him to become a "protest-ant" and stand up to and against the dominant institution of his society, all the while proclaiming an inexhaustible grace
sufficient to sustain his life in protracted struggle. Imagine as well what you
might do with his theological linkage of this grace to oppositional and reconstructive Christian practices.[4]* In his case, these practices boldly urged believers to reread the Scriptures and tradition through different lenses,[5]* to recast
liturgy dramatically, to articulate new philosophies and theologies, and to
write new confessions that protesting Christians would stake their lives upon.
They asked the church "to decapitate and democratize itself,"[6] clergy to leave
behind some of the vows of their ordination, scholars to render the Scriptures
such that the simplest reader might discover the power of the Word, and
laypersons to take responsibility for their lives, rituals, neighbors, theology,
and conscience. They established the Protestant principle of prophetic criticism and creative protest in the name of a "gospel for every present,"[7] a gospel
that relativized all claims to the finality of human knowledge and institutions,
including those of the Protestants. These practices revalued the common life
and daily experience of ordinary people in ways that affirmed and unleashed
their energy, all in the realization that while dirty hands are inevitable and the
moral life complex, the amazing grace and forgiveness of God in Jesus Christ
is pardon and power for courage, daring, and indeterminate responsibility.[8]*

Imagine all this as faith's own hard-won effort to discern the systems of
bondage that entrap and hold us, to throw them off in the power of the Spirit,
and to turn our attention to the creative task of reform. For Luther, the loci of
bondage included scholastic theology and its confidence in human reason and
free will, the sale of indulgences and other means of rescue from purgatory,
corruption of the church, oppression of the poor, and the papacy's control of
people's lives through fear of condemnation and the saving power of righteous
works. For us the task is the long, difficult transition from an unsustainable
way of life to an economically, environmentally, politically, socially, morally,
and spiritually sustainable world.

Imagine in brief that the style of a Lutheran ethic facing new issues in a
time of discontinuity is that of a reformed church always reforming, sparked
by returning to its sources boldly, with new eyes and the sturdy confidence of
faith. How will we go about reform? What does the legacy offer to aid and
abet the constructive task?

Some Theological-Ethical Resources, Perhaps

The resources of a reforming Lutheran ethic for a sustainable world have two distinct elements. One is the theological and ethical deposit of Luther and the Reformation. This deposit is clustered around notions of creation, cross, sin, and human response and action. The second element is how the church treats this legacy in order to face new challenges. This is the element of method that we illustrate as we discuss the theological and ethical legacy, rather than treat separately. Nonetheless, some comment on method is in order since a chief purpose of this chapter is to identify a reforming dynamic integral to Lutheran theology and ethics and to claim this as a gift of the tradition itself for Christian ethics in uncertain times.

The Reformation brought altered church practices and fierce theological argument and innovation to a religiously intense culture. Consequences reverberated throughout society, causing change on a grand scale. Without really intending it, Luther and the Reformation found themselves pushing a dialectic of continuity and discontinuity that fashioned an age. While it was not clear to its contemporaries, it is clear in retrospect that the Reformation was both continuous and discontinuous with the medieval world from which it was born and the modern world it helped shape.

Part of this dialectic was the dynamic of reform itself. Highly knowledgeable of the tradition and planted in it as firmly as a healthy tree, Luther drew upon it to reform that very tradition imaginatively and boldly. This we will illustrate is *the proper dynamic of a Lutheran ethic for our time.*

Ours is not an effort to offer a different Luther or Augustine or any other past authority. Their perspectives and judgments stand. Nor are we assessing the validity of their perspectives and judgments for their own time and place. Rather we are asking which aspects of the Lutheran legacy are valid for our lives and how in light of the issues we face today. Sometimes that legacy may provide us new eyes to see what we as Christians also living in an age of continuity/discontinuity have been well trained to overlook. At other times portions of that legacy may need to be abandoned as part of self-inflicted bondage, given what we need to do. Yet for this very process of handling the past in the present for the sake of the future, while living in an unsteady time, the Reformation's own gift of reform dynamics offers itself. Though it has been carefully kept under a bushel by Lutherans who have preferred the Reformation as a settled deposit, the choice between "deposit" and "dynamic" is itself false. The task here is to show how the Reformation offers its own way, or perhaps pushes us to find our own way, of using the tradition to reform the tradition in order to address new issues and provide "a gospel for every present."[9]

We propose a method then that combines three strong voices as a way of "doing ethics": the theological-ethical deposit of the Reformation, its reform dynamic, and the signs of the times as read in and by the believing community. The believing community is itself the scene of deliberation and recommended actions. With this in mind, we turn to the tradition and to our own times in light of this method.

Creation: "They Also Have Nice Ponies." From the point of view of sustainability's requirements, a deep fault line runs through Lutheran ethics.[10*] The soteriologically significant is limited to what happens between God and the human, the morally significant focuses on what happens among human beings. Salvation is a divine-human transaction in the inherited scheme, morality a human-human one.

But ethics is not a matter of societal relationships only, nor redemption a matter of human well-being alone.[11*] The sociocommunal is only one of three crucial arenas that make for life and affect it. The biophysical and the geo-planetary are equally vital to the community of life and equally the subject of theological and moral concern and reflection. The well-being of the life systems of the planet itself, and our bodily existence as part and parcel of the larger body of life, belong with the sociocommunal to the essentials of a sustainable society and world.

This means that any Lutheran ethic that fails in its assumptions or conclusions to recognize the complicated and interdependent relationships of humankind and the rest of nature is faulty from the start. We are not so much at home on earth as we with all else are home as earth. There can be no apartheid segregation of the human from the nonhuman in a creation that is one. Creation is one from both a scientific point of view and a confessional one.

Likewise any Lutheran ethic that fails to respond benevolently and justly to the fact of human kinship "with all creatures" (Luther's recurrent phrase) has not properly answered the lawyer's question to Jesus, "Who is my neighbor?" For a sustainable world, the scope of moral responsibility necessarily encompasses "all that participates in being" (H. Richard Niebuhr) as that is touched by human presence. "All that participates in being" includes elements and processes that began eons before the arrival of humans as a species. If our God-talk and theological framework begin and end with the human species, our God is too small for a fifteen-billion-year universe and our moral universe too quaint for words.

The crimped focus of Lutheran theology and ethics is there from its beginnings. While the Protestant Reformers believed that God is revealed in two "books"—the book of nature and the Holy Scriptures—faith's concentration was on the knowledge of God and the human self in such a way as to push aside consideration of the world as inevitably a configuration of nature, ourselves included. The human subject, even individual consciousness, became the place of encounter with God. The axis of faith was God and humanity, with salvation before a judging God the preoccupying issue. So while the cir-cumference of Martin Luther's and John Calvin's thinking implicitly took in the whole created order—the sociocommunal, the biophysical, and the geo-planetary—the center of their thought restricted itself to God, the human, and justification. Such thinking, quite understandable in the medieval world, now stands in need of serious reformation as we face the task of creating an eco-nomically and ecologically sustainable world.

Were this not faulty enough on its own terms, the Protestant derailment of the doctrine of creation unwittingly played into the secularization of nature in the industrialized West in the nineteenth and twentieth centuries. As mod-erns we live as though we were a species apart, with the rest of nature a col-lection of objects for our use. We have surpassed the Reformation by far in this domineering, manipulating, and alienated posture. We have effectively reduced creation to nature, and then drained nature of intrinsic value and meaning. Re-formation of both our sense of ourselves as creatures in a vast creation and the moral standing of that creation is needed.

Such reformation can drink from its own wells, in this case from Luther's understanding of creation. For Luther life itself is a precious, unmerited, and awesome gift, and all creation is the very abode of God. All nature, not just we, is fearfully and wonderfully made, and all of it masks and wraps God. God is truly and powerfully in, with, and under all that is creaturely. God is "sub-stantially present everywhere,"[12] the reformer says. The creator is "with all creatures, flowing and pouring into them, filling all things."[13] Luther even says the divine majesty is wholly present "in a grain, on a grain, over a grain, through a grain, within and without, and that, although it is a single Majesty, it nevertheless is entirely in each grain separately, no matter how immeasur-ably numerous these grain may be."[14] The awesome secret of creation is the indwelling of God within it.

There is horror here as well as beauty, mercy as well as cruelty, terror as well as mystery and ecstasy. Nature is not sweet nor life a symphony. Nonetheless the proper response to the gift of life is everlasting gratitude, not everlasting fear, much less everlasting possessiveness. Annie Dillard's last page of *Pilgrim at Tinker Creek* says it nicely: "I think the dying pray at the last not 'please,' but 'thank you,' as a guest thanks his host at the door."[15]

In short Luther's is a sacramentalist, panentheistic notion of creation that begs in our time for a more expansive notion of redemption of "all things"[16]— the sociocommunal, the biophysical, and the geoplanetary. Obligation extends "to the poor, to future generations, to sentient life, to organic life, to endangered species, and to ecosystems as a whole," to cite one Lutheran ethi-cist's effort to line out the appropriate moral framework.[17]

The orbit of creation as simultaneously the orbit of redemption is reinforced when we see how Luther recasts the theology and ethic of his own education and religious order, the Augustinians. Augustine's enormous influence
had helped create the medieval church's preoccupation with human salvation
and its search for a gracious God in a demon-infested world. This we noted
was Luther's preoccupation and drive as well. Yet Augustine had fostered
human estrangement from earth and a turn from the biophysical and geoplanetary, even society, as the locus of redemption. Communion with God meant
the ascetic ascent of the soul from earth and body to higher spirit in a creation
ordered hierarchically from lower to higher (rather than ecologically). Christ
descended, claimed Augustine, so that we might ascend. This is Augustine's
picture and his essentially monastic ethic. He hews to it even when it issues in
high praise for the beauties of creation as descending emanations of the
divine. As part of that creation, our bodies are "the earth we carry," he says in
a lovely image meant to affirm earth and body.

Luther also pictures an ordering of creation in the manner of a Great
Chain of Being, but he rejects an ethic of ascetic ascent. Christ descends so
that we do not even try to ascend! God is found "in, with, and under" all things
creaturely. Sin in fact is our refusal to accept our finitude and earthiness. We
are to rejoice in our bodiliness as the very place the utterly incarnate God is
with us, not sever our souls from the biophysical in an attempt to leave earth
behind and incant our way to supposedly "higher" places.

Luther's rejection of Augustine's ascent theology and ethics is nicely pic-
tured in contrasting sketches. Both of these tortured monks are geniuses of
religious faith and compelling portrayers of the Christian life. But their renditions move in opposite directions.

In Augustine's famed *Confessions*, the theologian pours out his love of God.
Then with characteristic introspection, he asks, "But what am I loving when I
love you?" His reply:

> Not beauty of body nor transient grace, not this fair light which is now so
> friendly to my eyes, not melodious song in all its lovely harmonies, not the
> sweet fragrance of flowers or ointments or spices, not manna or honey, not
> limbs that draw me to carnal embrace: none of these do I love when I love
> my God.[18]

Like other Latin Africans of his age, Augustine goes on to say that there
is nonetheless a "kind of light, a kind of voice, a certain fragrance, food and
embrace"[19] to the love of God. But they are not earthly. So he asks yet again
what it is he loves when he loves God. Most of all he knows what it is not, and
where it is not. He poses a series of questions to "earth," to "the sea and the
great deep," to "the teeming live creatures that crawl," and they all reply, "We

are not God, seek higher." The answer is the same for "the gusty winds," "sun, moon, and stars," and "all things which stood around the portals of my flesh."[20]

By contrast Luther's refusal to sever spiritual from material finds God precisely in and through "the sea and the great deep," "the teeming live creatures that crawl," "the gusty winds and every breeze." These are not themselves God; on that Luther and Augustine wholly agree. But because the transcendent God is present as divine power in all places, "nothing can be more truly present and within all creatures than God himself with his power,"[21] says Luther. God is present to us, and we to one another and to all creatures as bodies in creation, God's own abode. Christ "must be, orally and bodily, in places and localities,"[22] Luther insists.

This is God's happy accommodation to our creatureliness, and we ought not try "to improve upon what God has made,"[23] neglect it, or leave it behind. Yes, Luther writes, Christ ascended to heaven. But "he is present in the sacrament and in the hearts of believers not really because he wants to be worshiped there [in the sacrament], but because he wants there to work with us and help us."[24] Christ works with us and helps us as bodily creatures.

Differently said, God is always present to creation in creation as and through creation, hidden in nature as the mask of God. God's ways are always the ways of bodiliness: "Nothing can be more truly present and within all creatures than God himself with his power."[25]

Such is Luther's reformation of Augustine and the theology of leaving body and earth behind. Heiko Oberman argues that this is an ethical alternative that rejects both monasticism and puritanism.[26] As it does so, it is more than a statement about God's nature as incarnate Word. It is also a profound affirmation of our creatureliness and that of other creatures.

Affirmation of body and creation is expressed often in Luther, not least in the catechism's "I believe God has created me, together *with all creatures*." Luther, never timid, vague, or without imagination as he recasts theology and ethics, not only lists the mouse "as a divine creature" "with such pretty feet and such delicate hair" that "it is clear that it was created by the Word of God with a definite plan in view";[27] he even details the items of our own anatomy—"flesh, bone, skin, and hair"— as among "God's good creatures."[28] The body, indeed the biophysical and geoplanetary in every part, is God's good creaturely creation. Pure spirit is nothing we can know, and ought not try to know. We live through our senses, in our bodies, where God is with us. Luther even chides Erasmus, the humanist, for not caring much about the knowledge of the details of natural life. "It interests him little how the fetus is made in the womb," Luther complains, and goes on to say we ponder God's own goodness and power when we ponder flowers or other of God's mighty works.[29] Trying to transcend them is for Luther the work of the devil. The devil tempts us from Eden on to try to

"improve upon what God has made." This is part of the devil's churchly theological work whereby we think we can know God through "de-natured" reason,
speculation, and earth-denying ascetic spirituality.

Even Luther's picture of heaven is saturated with the earthly; heaven is
earth renewed and refashioned. "The flowers, leaves and grass will be as beautiful, pleasant, and delightful as an emerald," Luther writes, "and all creatures
most beautiful."[30] Asked whether there will be animals in heaven, he replies:
"You must not think that heaven and earth will be made of nothing but air and
sand, but there will be whatever belongs to it—sheep, oxen, beasts, fish, without which the earth and sky or air cannot be."[31] For his son Hans, Luther paints
a picture resonant with a child's dreams: heaven is "a pretty, beautiful and
delightful garden where there are many children wearing little golden coats.
They pick up fine apples, pears, cherries, and yellow and blue plums under the
trees. They sing, jump, and are merry. They also have nice ponies."[32]
Augustine's heaven has no ponies, and loving ponies on earth is not the way
to love God.

Luther's reforming dynamic in theology and ethics shows itself in other
places as he recasts his own heritage. Suffice here to add but one more
instance of the dynamics of method we are advocating. It turns on the matter
of our creation in the image of God, *imago dei.*

As always Luther gives due consideration for the needs of the hour as he
does biblical interpretation. In his scriptural, theological, and moral judgments, he is keenly aware that the present age and context shape decisions.
Even similar issues faced across a relatively short time may call for different
responses. In "On War against the Turk," he roundly scolds those who claim
he was morally inconsistent just because he rendered different judgments at
different times: "But it is not fair to forget what the situation was then and what
my grounds and reasons were, and to take my words and apply them to
another situation where those grounds and reasons do not exist. With this
kind of skill who could not make the gospel a pack of lies or pretend that it
contradicted itself?"[33]

If one does not account for the existential dynamic of the living word in
the moral life, the gospel might well appear "a pack of lies" or a bundle of "contradictions." Scripture and tradition are always read interactively with the
signs of the times. And well they should be. Otherwise the power of Scripture
to guide in the face of the challenges and issues before us is lost. Authority
resides not in the texts per se, nor does it rest in the readers. It emerges over
and again in the relationship of these to and in God, as living word come to
expression in the believing, discerning community.

When Luther teaches his students about humans created in the image of
God, he has them read the church fathers. As with all authorities, Luther

relativizes their renditions and issues a caution. In this instance he does not find the fathers persuasive when they propose that the image of God consists in certain distinctive capacities of humans as a species, such as intellect, memory, or will. He does acknowledge that these "opinions of the fathers were discussed in all the churches and schools." They thus carry the weight of theological and catechetical tradition. But he says: "My advice is to read [the fathers] with discretion. They often speak as the result of an emotion and of a particular mood which we do not have and cannot have, since we do not have similar situations."[34]

Luther goes on to render "the image of God" differently, preferring to emphasize not internal human capacities as a species—intellect, memory, will—but the quality of life Adam and Eve lived. They had *securitas* and lived free from anxiety and fear. Luther with his usual penchant for specifics names fear of fire, of other animals, of discomforts, and, above all, fear of God.[35] Eden's life included peace and harmony between humans and other creatures. Kristen Kvam concludes that "right relationship" rather than internal human capacities is what creation in "the image of God" means for Luther.

Kvam goes on to cite a second difference from Augustine and the tradition in which Luther stood. Augustine had lifted up chiefly mental capacities and attributes as God's image in us. Luther by contrast incorporates physical capacities, once again reflecting his down-to-earth doctrine of creation and the presence of the infinite in the finite. He even says that the image of God includes "the most beautiful and superb qualities of body and of all the limbs."[36] Against the tradition of such as Augustine, Tertullian, and Chrysostom, he argues, sexual partnership and activity were not created by God as a post-fall antidote for sin. Rather they belong to the goodness of creation from the beginning.[37]

Through all of his bold, imaginative, and selective reinterpreting of tradition and recasting of church practices and teachings, Luther is no romantic. Nor is our quest for a mutually enhancing relationship with earth in the interests of a sustainable world served by nature romanticism. Yes, Luther's is an extraordinary, sacramentalist celebration of all creatures as God's, ourselves included. But nature is also cursed. In fact Luther fancies himself living in the last days, with the whole cosmos running down. The nature he sees is under God's "left hand," and the God he discerns in that nature is the wrathful, alien, and hidden God of doom and judgment. Dillard's "We wake in terror, eat in hunger, sleep with a mouthful of blood,"[38] would have been understood by Luther and his age as utter realism. The compelling revelation of God is not, then, in cursed nature as creation, despite creation as the genuine abode of God and Luther's conviction that life is pure and precious gift. The telling encounter is elsewhere, in the cross and resurrection of Jesus Christ.

Cross: Tree of Life. Christians in quest of a sustainable world certainly need a theology of creation different from the one that effectively prevails in the globalized economy, where nature is little more than capital, resources, information, sink, and stage for a world in the effective hands of one species only. But a theology of creation with a strong sense of the image of God as reflective of the wisdom of God present throughout the created order and with human goodness as smoothly continuous with divine goodness crashes headlong into the twentieth century. At least by sheer numbers, this century has been easily the deadliest. Perhaps as many as 187,000,000 people have died as a result of warfare alone in this century, the equivalent of one-tenth of the total world population when the century began.[39] "Every flag that flies today is a cry of pain," the poet Adrienne Rich writes. We have lost our moorings. We are unsure of what "behooves us."[40] So it is not the slow, steady triumph of creation's goodness that meets us. It is the brute reality of public suffering at human hands, suffering that encompasses human and nonhuman life together. A theology of creation thus requires somewhere near its own center a theology of cross and resurrection. If there is no hope for a tree of life from the dead wood of Golgotha—life itself on the home turf of death—then there is no hope, period.

Twentieth-century suffering is neither unique nor the first convincing evidence that life resists happy endings and is tragic. Luther's own grim experience of the late Middle Ages is one reason the cross is compelling for him, as it has been for the pious poor in so many places. What Augustine had said of the Roman Empire held for the Reformation as well: "You cannot show that men lived in happiness, as they passed their lives amid the horrors of war, amid the shedding of men's blood—whether the blood of enemies or fellow-citizens—under the shadow of fear and amid the terror of ruthless ambition. The only joy to be attained had the fragile brilliance of glass, a joy outweighed by the fear that it may be shattered in a moment."[41]

In brief a Lutheran ethic will not find it convincing simply to affirm human goodness and emphasize its continuity with creation in God's image, only to jump from there to the modern assertion of the autonomous human subject. The devil "and all his works and all his empty promises" practices an ethics of death that we know too well, personally and systemically, from the inside out and the outside in. The cross—death by torture at the hands of political, religious, and popular authorities—is graphic witness to the destruction of the innocent and the good at human hands.[42] Any ethic facing the daunting tasks of effecting a sustainable world on the home turf of death is impotent if it does not confront the reality of evil and suffering—humankind's and otherkind's—at the center of its morality. The further one is removed, by denial or apartheid, from the suffering present in creation, the further one is from its central moral reality. The closer one is to creation's suffering, the more difficult it is to refuse participation in that afflicted life.[43]*

But the cross is more than a witness to the depth of human sinfulness. It is a witness to the depth of God. God is, deep down, a suffering God. God's heart (*cor*) is full of the suffering (*miserum*) that creation experiences, and mercy (*misericordia*) is the response of the gracious One. God enters into the suffering and injustice in such a way as not to perpetuate the violence that creates them. Compassionate solidarity and unmerited forgiveness sufficient for a new start, even new creation, issues from the heart of being itself. Luther's admonition to "be Christ to the neighbor" does not have less in view than the imitation of God.

That said, we once again face the need for reform of the tradition by the tradition. Suffering and the cross are theologically and morally fraught with danger in the Lutheran legacy, especially when the cross is a sign of victory by those who "make" history rather than simply "take" it. (W. H. Auden comes to mind: "Only the sated and well-fed enjoy Calvary, as a verbal event.") If the cross is a symbol of "home" at the center of a culture rather than a shocking sign from the periphery about injustice and death at the hands of that culture, then the cross—and God—have been domesticated. Then the cross perversely confirms two joined assumptions that have sanctioned conquest and oppression: the assumption of the unity of civilization on the basis of Christianity and the assumption of the cultural superiority of that civilization. Or in another perversion of the tradition, the cross sometimes contributes to submission and self-denigration. A sturdy vein of masochism in Christianity runs deep in pieties of crucifixion and in cross theology as "I-am-a-worm" and "we-all-have-our-crosses-to-bear" theology. In Lutheranism this legitimated suffering has reinforced patriarchal orders-of-creation that survived Luther's antidualist and antihierarchical polemics against the medieval church and its ascent theology. Luther's radical teaching on the justification of the godless and his cross theology did not recast his social theory. He remained medieval, Constantinian, patriarchal, and anti-Semitic. This composite stance legitimized oppression and submission to suffering rather than resisting them, and it often did so in the name of the cross itself. To cite one example, the good wife in Catholic ethics was described in exactly the same way in Protestant ethics: obedient, silent, and pious. Jews were labeled Christ-killers in both traditions as well and considered proper objects of ghettoization and vilification.

Differently said, a Lutheran ethic must say which cross we take up in following Jesus. It is not ancient Rome's cross, the cross of imperial power wielded against those it brands criminals, rebels, and traitors. Nor is it Constantine's cross, that fusion of Christianity and imperial rule which turns the cross into the emblem of victorious conquest and colonization in a mission of self-defined "civilization." This mission was easily given to declaring and killing heretics, pagans, witches, and the infidel. It is not the cross of bearing suffering we can do nothing about—"We all have our crosses to bear." Finally it is not the cross of self-negation, erasing "as thyself" from the command to love the neighbor. Rather the cross of Jesus is the cross of life as resistance to suffering and oppression that need not be. It is the price sometimes paid for facing down the culture and ethics of death in the name of life, even radically new life where it is not expected, among persons (like us) from whom it is not expected.[44] In a word Jesus' cross discloses the power of life-creating solidarity with all who suffer as the gracious God's own power.[45]

Sin: The Strangled Heart. The heart of God is open, embracing, and compassionate. This is manifest in Jesus in his life and ministry, and on the cross, and confirmed in the resurrection as God's own way. The sinful heart is self-strangling as it pridefully excludes (*cor curvatus in se*). The strangled heart essentially affirms oneself and one's group but not the other as a value and acknowledges others only in relation to one's own. *Cor curvatus in se* is thus the fundamental dynamic by which "we" are established over against "they." "They" are judged by norms established by the collective "we." Normative "whiteness" becomes the basis for judging other "races." Euro-American civilization becomes the norm for measuring other cultures. Heterosexism becomes the norm for assessing proper sexual orientation and behavior. And value to humans becomes the means for measuring the worth of the rest of nature. This is the individual and collective pride that objectifies the other as "other," then judges the other on the basis of the heart turned inward rather than outward. A sustainable world cannot be effected if "otherness" means this kind of exclusion and use.

God as the transcendent wholly Other is also God immanent, for us, with us, even in us and the rest of nature. This God establishes community among those who are "other" to one another. This is only maintained as "comm-unity" when the heart-turned-in-on-itself is shattered open. It is shattered open by the foolishness and power of the cross and daily dying and rising with Christ in baptism. The cross shatters reason's grip in its overreaching effort to control the world.[46] It exposes our understandings as provisional, tentative, distorted, and parochially reflective of changing time and place. Faith by contrast begins in the darkness, where it does not see well. It is the kind of knowledge that exposes our unknowing, so as to avoid the pretense that lays our truth on reality and confuses it with reality. Faith is less a claim on knowledge than the simple, profound trust with one's whole being that God is there in the darkness in ways that through Jesus and in the Spirit make for life.

Once again Lutherans facing what sustainability requires need to bring reform dynamics to their own moral legacy. In addition to the "we/they" exclusions intimated above, the reformers failed to recognize as sin's own construction the collective human "we" over against objectified nature as "other." This "other" is then measured by our norms and judged by its utilitarian value to us. In this manifestation of the inward-turned human heart, nature is no "Thou" and masked presence of God but an objectified "it." Less than Calvin, but nonetheless powerfully, Luther articulates a doctrine of callings that over the course of the next few centuries in the West results in an ethic of domination of the earth. This occurs despite Luther's own sacramentalist reserve and his awe, fear, and reverence in the face of life. The Reformation preoccupation with human-centered salvation (another instance of *cor curvatus in se!*) ends up emphasizing human agency, especially male human agency. In the name of election, stewardship, and vocation this emphasis helped bolster the forces of modernity as the human conquest and configuration of the rest of nature. Reformation insights about sin as overweening pride are not extended here, as they now must be, to the relationship of human beings as a species living with other species in a common community of life.

A tradition that understands bondage and perversity will acknowledge how the preoccupation with salvation can easily become the instance of the self-strangling heart. This preoccupation can easily epitomize selfishness in which nothing other than salvation truly matters, and it cannot be shared. It can foster a sense of election of peoples and cultures that holds others in contempt or treats them as the lost and unenlightened. In its transcendent other-worldliness, it can denigrate creation as a realm of secondary value that is finally to be abandoned. Even when Lutherans have proclaimed the gospel as the liberating news that in Jesus Christ we no longer need be preoccupied at all with our salvation, the preoccupation continues institutionalized in ways that subtly devalue earth and say no to its well-being. The relationship of creation to salvation in Lutheran ethics needs thoughtful and far-reaching attention, for the sake of a sustainable world.

Human Response: Glad, Bold, Busy Faith. The Augustinian-Reformation teaching on sin gives a conservative bent to human action in times of uncertainty and transition. "Carefully" is an important qualifier for a Lutheran ethic addressing new issues. Luther stands in a long line from Plato well beyond Augustine that renders a cautious reply to the desire for order in the face of widespread, deep change. No doubt the coming apart of feudalism is the pressure here for Luther, as the cataclysm of Rome facing barbarian invasions was for Augustine. In Luther's case this was complicated by the real threat of anarchy from those who with his fiery teachings sought to upend prince, priest, and landowner in an already plagued order. The devil was already wreaking sufficient havoc with the help of a corrupt papacy, thought Luther, and needed no additional allies from peasants who heard political and economic freedom in Luther's teaching on Christian freedom and in his corollary demolition of hegemonic authorities.

Yet a turbulent age with an already shaky social order does not so much explain Luther's analysis as confirm it. His conservatism—the priority of order over justice as the latter's precondition—has its grounds elsewhere. It surfaces in more settled times as well. We are fundamentally anxious souls, Luther is convinced, in constant search of *securitas*. We are condemned to a certain finite freedom and yearning that is the occasion, though not cause, of sin. Other species are spared this. They "buzz, sing, [and] mate not because they choose to but because they cannot choose not to."[47] With "Adam's hapless seed,"[48] however, it is different. Consigned to freedom, we must choose. We will err and regret, retaliate and forgive and try something else, only to choose and err all over again. We cannot choose not to choose, though invariably it means we run to deities and despots, fad and fashion, to relieve the burden of uncertainty and responsibility. We close an open circle in the effort to ensure a fixed meaning and a stable world.

Yet the uncertainty of life is inescapable; we are "stuck" as moral beings condemned to choice. Given sin's genius for self-inflicted bondage, the best we can do is maintain a modicum of order and learn to live by the dim light of half-knowledge and of truth and happiness as fragile as glass.

Faith is the ultimate trust that answers to our idolatrous propensity to close the circle and fix the universe. Faith lets God be God and us be mortal, finite, and restless. Morality is penultimate action that keeps a vulnerable order intact, an order that by grace, luck, and hard work can be moved incrementally toward justice. Faith is the gracious gift of God to those who would receive it; morality is the shape of our responsibility for the orderly address of the neighbor's welfare. Faith is a freedom from all authorities but God; morality structures and limits our freedom so that we attend to the welfare of others.

On issues of sustainability and threatened life systems, the cautionary stream of a Reformation ethic might say: Do not act in such a way as to make the planet the laboratory in a trial-and-error experiment. Instead employ the "precautionary principle" and protect the integrity of the biosphere. In the face of uncertain fallout from accelerated climate change, for example, reduce carbon emissions and other greenhouse gases rather than wait to see what might happen. If an entity cannot be reclaimed, reused, and recycled, do not make it. If it cannot be reproduced without deleterious, degrading effects, do not grow it. If the probable consequences of its use cannot be reasonably known, tracked, and paid for, do not venture it. Or to shift examples yet again, if the context of cloning is an economic culture that treats virtually everything human and nonhuman as information, capital, and resources to be manipulated in a world that cannot agree on regulations or ensure their enforcement,

do not pursue it. In sum, human sinfulness and the limitations of finite knowledge mean that a reform ethic is "careful" as well as "bold" and "imaginative."

The strong conservative bent in Lutheran ethics has often issued not only
in the precautionary principle but in quietism vis-à-vis those in authority.
While there are good as well as bad reasons for this, it later badly obscured the
Reformation's own enormous release of human energy to create a different
world, precisely in uncertain times when precaution is appropriate. Another
look at Luther on faith and works is helpful. "The Preface to the Epistle of St.
Paul to the Romans" describes the moral agency and courage that issues from
genuine faith:

> Faith is a living, daring confidence in God's grace, so sure and certain that the
> believer would stake his life on it a thousand times. This knowledge of and
> confidence in God's grace makes men glad and bold and happy in dealing
> with God and with all creatures. And this is the work which the Holy Spirit
> performs in faith. Because of it, and without compulsion, a person is ready
> and glad to do good to everyone, to serve everyone, to suffer everything, out
> of love and praise to God who has shown him this grace. Thus it is impossi-
> ble to separate works from faith, quite as impossible as to separate heat and
> light from fire.[49]

"Heat and light" mean energy. "Fire" is faith's issue. Faith in God and love
toward neighbor cannot be separated. By God's grace faith "changes us and
makes us to be born anew of God,"[50] writes Luther. "Oh, it is a living, busy,
active mighty thing, this faith," he goes on. "It is impossible for it not to be
doing good works incessantly. It does not ask whether good works are to be
done, but before the question is asked, it has already done them, and is constantly doing them."[51]

The error, Luther explains, is to confuse faith and works. "When [people]
see that no improvement of life and no good works follow—although they can
hear and say much about faith—they fall into the error of saying, 'Faith is not
enough; one must do works in order to be righteous and be saved.'"[52] Faith is
enough to be judged righteous by God and saved in Christ. The response is
the outpouring of works. In the moral life this renders faith "a living, busy,
active mighty thing" directed to the needs of the neighbor as "all that participates in being."[53] Justification by grace through faith means the increase of
power in the life of the believer, precisely for good works.

The starting point for ethics is what Luther in "The Freedom of a
Christian" calls "the third power of faith," namely, unity with Christ.[54]* A new
life in Christ occurs in which the attributes of Christ and the believer are
exchanged. The Christian moral life issues from this relationship. We are to
"be Christ" to the neighbor. What Christ now does in, with, and through us
are good works. With characteristic bombast and charm, Luther says, "Only

raving fanatics think Christ has no other glory than to sit at the right hand of God on a velvet cushion and let the angels sing and fiddle and ring bells and play before him."[55] Through faith refreshed daily in a life of dying and rising with Christ, we as Christ's are "made strong and equipped to do all good works and to resist sin and all the temptations of the devil. Since faith cannot be idle, it must demonstrate the fruits of love by doing good and avoiding evil."[56]

True, society cannot be governed by the gospel. The free giving of the gospel by God in Christ, however, creates faith, saves, and empowers. It empowers neighbor love in life's varied and overlapping spheres. Here Christians recognize and honor systems of worldly authority and are subject to them. Christians do not make use of worldly authority in their own cases; they renounce their own interests and rights and suffer injustice, according to Luther. But they do use worldly authority to put neighbor love into practice for the well-being of the neighbor, whether Christian or not. The full range of secular duties, from spouse to judge to executioner to pig farmer, is the realm of moral responsibility. Especially in times of widespread change, this entails sinning boldly and creatively. What is key is believing in Christ, and rejoicing more boldly still.

It is important for any reform movement to recognize that this two-sphere ethic has been socially and historically conservative in much of Lutheran ethics.[57]* Its orders of creation reflect Luther's feudalism. Thus it has been patriarchal in spousal and parental relationships. Moreover it has largely identified social ethics with the ethics of governance, and then reduced governance to matters of "the sword." Citizenship is defined with a view to legitimizing coercive power and its limits; the normal posture of citizens is as obedient subjects. Given this reductionism and the settledness of medieval society, "orders of creation" ethics foster little ethical critique along vital lines of race, class, gender, culture, and treatment of nature. Neither does it emphasize "civil society" as citizen-based democratic initiatives, despite Luther's strong doctrine of the laity. In the end its basic moral posture is to accommodate to dominant Western culture as normative, without fundamentally challenging the basic patterns of systemic and culturally structured power. When this happens, baptism and cathechesis are no longer the early church's "great renunciations" of one way of life (as the baptized faced Rome), and the "great affirmations" of a counter-cultural Christian way (as the baptized faced Jerusalem). Instead they are socialized into the patterns of prevailing power, as powers given the benefit of the doubt. Because the Imperial Reformation continued this Constantinian marriage of throne and altar (in contrast to the Radical Reformation), Lutheran ethics ironically has often turned anti-reform. This occurred despite Luther's feisty equal freedom of each and every Christian and an empowering faith focused upon neighborly needs.[58]*

Conclusion, Perhaps

How does a Lutheran ethic address new issues? Imaginatively, boldly, carefully, in a dialogue of three strong voices: reform dynamics, the Lutheran theological-ethical deposit, and the signs of the times as read by the believing community addressing the issues at hand.[59]* Yes, the community proceeds carefully, attentive to the needs of justice for order in an uncertain age. At the same time the strokes can be bold and imaginative and often will need to be— politically, economically, and socially as well as culturally, liturgically, theologically, and ethically. A sustainable world requires that large-scale systems and we ourselves be changed. Although we cannot yet foresee the details of this change, it involves:

- a demographic transition from an unprecedented population explosion to a roughly stable world population;
- an economic transition that lives off nature's "income" rather than its "capital" and builds into all economic activity, including the cost of goods, what is required indefinitely for nature's regeneration and renewal;
- a social transition to a broader sharing of nature's income and human wealth, along with increased opportunities for sustaining livelihoods for all;
- an institutional transition that combines greater cross-national cooperation in order to address global problems with greater attention to what makes for sustainable local communities and regions;
- an informational transition in which research, education, and global monitoring allow large numbers of people to understand the problems they face and offer them the means to address these problems;
- a technological transition that effectively means minimal environmental impact per person;
- a moral transition to a framework that includes the sociocommunal, the biophysical, and the geoplanetary—the whole community of life—as the arena of daily human responsibility and accountability; and
- a religious transition to earthkeeping as a religious calling and vocation common to all the world's religions.[60]

For all this, faith means energy and hope. Christ really does have other glory than to sit "at the right hand of God on a velvet cushion and let the angels sing and fiddle and ring bells and play before him."

Any and every ethic must attend to moral formation, the formation of human character and conscience and the structures and institutions that so profoundly shape these, whether social, political, or economic. A way of life is not accidental or random. So if Lutheran ethics are to contribute to creation of a sustainable world, the substance of sustainability and its necessary transitions must itself find its way into moral formation as a matter of gospel and law. Law, including its third use, is far more than ardent commendations to the single believer about the love of God and neighbor. It includes creating and shaping corporate identity and consciousness; forming social, political, and economic organization; and the channeling of responsibility. The function of law is not only deep critique but positive construction as well.

What we have tried to do here is include some of the material resources of the Lutheran legacy on creation, cross, and moral agency. Re-formed, they might aid and abet a sustainable world. We have also argued that a reforming dynamic itself belongs at the heart of that legacy. It offers a way to address new challenges in uncertain times. It does so in ways that revivify that legacy by drawing deeply from it. None of this is a simple yes or no to Lutheran traditions. We reject the reformer's denigration of women's bodies and of sexuality in the post-fall state, just as we reject his admonitions about physically subjugating the body in order to repress its passions. We certainly do not share racial, ethnic, and religious assumptions that mirror convictions of superiority sanctioned with biblical and theological backing. Indeed much of the point of this chapter is to bring the reform dynamic to Lutheran ethics itself and let it work in a church that claims and welcomes it.

The following stanzas and prayer seem a fitting match and closing. They lift up faith's call to trust in God no matter what and morality's call to answer with oppositional and reconstructive Christian practices. They exemplify the meaning of faith for ethics in a Lutheran way: By grace Christians are secure enough to risk justice in an uncertain time—carefully, imaginatively, boldly. The stanzas are the third and fourth of Luther's battle hymn of the Reformation; the prayer is W. E. B. Du Bois' from 1909 or 1910.

> Though hordes of devils fill the land, All threat'ning to devour us,
> We tremble not, unmoved we stand; They cannot overpow'r us.
> Let this world's tyrant rage; In battle we'll engage!
> His might is doomed to fail; God's judgment will prevail!
> One little word subdues him.
>
> God's Word forever shall abide, No thanks to foes, who fear it;
> For God himself fights by our side, With weapons of the Spirit.
> Were they to take our house, Goods, honor, child, or spouse.
> Though life be wrenched away, They cannot win the day.
> The Kingdom's ours forever.[61]
>
> Give us grace, O God, to dare to do the deed which we well know
> cries to be done. Let us not hesitate because of ease, or the words
> of men's mouths, or our own lives. Mighty causes are calling us -
> the freeing of women, the training of children, the putting down of
> hate and murder and poverty—all these and more. But they call

with voices that mean work and sacrifice and death. Mercifully grant us, O God, the spirit of Esther, that we say: I will go unto the King and if I perish, I perish—Amen.[62]

9
A Table Talk on Lutheran Ethics

At their final meeting together the writers of this volume participated in a daylong discussion with one another that built upon what they had written in their chapters. The following is an abbreviated (one-fourth the original length) and somewhat reconstructed version of their recorded oral conversation, such that some complexities and nuances may be lost. An attempt has been made, however, to preserve important threads of what was said as the writers interacted with one another and in ways that communicate their common, complementary, and differing emphases. This Table Talk is offered as an example of what needs to be an ongoing, deepening moral conversation in the life of the church. Edited by Karen Bloomquist (KB).

Our Social Location Makes a Difference

David Fredrickson (DF): I have been teaching at Luther Seminary for about ten years. One of the challenges church leaders are facing, and I in my teaching, is that of leading congregations in moral conversation. In the Southwestern Minnesota Synod a number of congregations have given attention to how they face ethical issues, ranging from large hog confinement facilities to sexuality questions. These congregations want to be places where moral discussion occurs. I have been part of a group that has tried to help congregations think about what goes into this. I have thought about how the Bible makes this moral deliberation a Christian theological activity, and have found the Pauline epistles very helpful. Paul is writing to congregations and, between the lines, trying to establish them as places of moral conversation.

Reinhard Hütter (RH): My primary thought is shaped by my being a teacher of the church, training future clergy in the late twentieth century. We face deep moral insecurity both inside the church and in the broader society. Sometimes this is expressed as an affirmation of license, of "anything goes," in order to cover up an uneasiness about complex contexts. On the other side, it is covered over by a somewhat fundamentalistic return to securities. What provides a rich matrix for thinking about morality today is the recent Roman Catholic encyclical, *Veritatis Splendor*. This has led me to reconsider what has been somewhat forgotten in the Lutheran tradition: the theme of God's law.

Martha Stortz (MS): I teach at a Lutheran seminary in a context that is both ecumenical and interfaith, and in many ways very secular. Being Christian in a highly secular, almost post-Christian culture places me a lot to the right of center, whereas some of the positions I articulate in my own communion place me somewhat to the left of center. This is a very ambiguous and sometimes frustrating position to be, but also very rich. My chapter is addressed to those who are seeking spiritual formation, many by going to other traditions. I attempt to point them to their own tradition as Lutherans for spiritual formation.

Richard Perry (RP): The seminary at which I teach is located in an urban context that is ecumenical and influenced by a major university but also in a community that is economically and racially diverse, with a history of political activism. Students ask: How do we handle all of this? What does it mean to live in an urban, multicultural, politically diverse context? I teach public ministry, the church in society, and urban ministry, where we encounter concrete issues. What I try to do in my chapter is to lift up the particular ethical background of African American Lutherans. This is an area that has not been investigated in our church and would benefit not only African American Lutherans but also the wider church. It was important for me to re-cover this so as to provide a foundation for leading and teaching in congregations.

Robert Benne (RB): I am the only one here who teaches in a college context. That is a very important starting point for me. I taught in a seminary for seventeen years, and my perceptions toward the end of those years were that the mainstream traditions of Christianity were losing their capacity to transmit their traditions. My experience with college students of the mainstream, whether Catholic or Protestant, is that they know very little about their position, have very few serious patterns of piety, and are on their way out of the tradition, or only mildly connected to it. They may return someday, but probably not, given the tremendous competition in the culture. This contrasts with evangelical and fundamentalist Christians who know the Bible, pray, and seriously maintain a piety. So I get this sinking feeling that we're not carrying our tradition to the next generation. My job is to try to re-enter that element into the college enterprise. My recent writings have been an attempt to make a straightforward, uncomplicated, unrevised portrayal of the Lutheran moral teachings. That's also why I wrote what I did for this book.

James Childs (JC): Back in the sixties, when I was a young inner-city pastor in an African American congregation in the South, at a time of great turbulence, it became very evident to me how quietistic the attitudes of my church at that time (Lutheran Church—Missouri Synod) were when it came to social change, and how isolated I felt as a pastor who was concerned about such matters. This created in me a deep concern for a more aggressive, fully integrated approach to social concerns in the church. Subsequently as a young professor of theology, I became embroiled in issues of authority in that church body. Many people were trying to overlay the power of Scripture to speak for itself with dogmatic requirements designed to guarantee the certitude of that witness on other grounds than the innate power of that witness to convert and shape people's lives. Now much later, I find these issues resurfacing as I teach students who will be pastors a genuinely Lutheran approach to Christian ethics that is also sensitive to the concerns that people have for authority.

Cynthia Moe-Lobeda (CML): Two dimensions of my personal vocation have shaped me theologically and my work in this project. One is my vocation as a Lutheran. A theologically formative event occurred at a point in my early adulthood when justification by grace through faith became so real to me that I felt as though it saved my life. God's unconditional love became the home out of which I work. A second formative event was my experience as a missionary in Central America, and subsequent Central American work in this country. I have been seared by that experience, by encountering tortured people and realizing that my government supported the torturers, and by encountering deadly poverty and realizing that it was linked to the global economic order by which middle- and upper-strata North Americans benefit. I cannot escape knowing these things. I can only go deeper into them and understand them as parts of my call, though they torment me. Now in reading Luther, I ask what neighbor-love means in a world in which our affluence spells death for many global neighbors.

Larry Rasmussen (LR): I've spent nearly my whole teaching career in non-Lutheran settings. Teaching social ethics now at an urban ecumenical seminary means that I as a genuinely marinated Lutheran must come to terms with urban reality and with pluralism. This has led me to a social analysis that sees the dynamics of the modern world, especially the economic, as dynamics that undermine rooted, stable relations. So I want to know as a Lutheran how one can address this. Participation in the ecumenical movement (through the World Council of Churches) has reinforced the need I feel to be a Christian pluralist, honoring diverse understandings of the Christian story, without becoming a moral relativist. My ecumenical involvements have also held before me the massive public suffering that has to be addressed. So I want to work at how the richness of the Lutheran tradition can address a range of issues in an unstable world. How can that be done with a sense of commitment and confidence, even when the one thing you can be sure about is that there aren't unambiguous answers? How can we do ethics in the "time between times" and not lose the traditions that can provide guidance?

The Distinctiveness of Lutheran Ethics

(RB:) I was moved by Cynthia's impression of how important is justification by grace. For Lutherans that belief is pivotal both theologically and ethically. From there flow a number of other important categories, like law and gospel as two ways God rules the world and operates dynamically in it. The commonality that is probably most decisive for us is that we've all been formed and shaped in Lutheran communities. The same liturgy and sacraments have shaped us, and we have an ethos in which these notions have been important.

(JC:) The interplay of law and gospel, the pulse beat of life in Christ, means that ethics is never divorced from that core reality of our existence. That vital center of our existence dictates that some methods are appropriate and others are not. We act faithfully out of the assurance of God's promise that is at the core of our ethics, rather than acting skillfully out of a method. We also frequently refer to Luther's notion of Christian liberty—that the Gospel frees us to act out of love toward the neighbor and at the same time binds us in love to the needs and concerns of the neighbor.

(RP:) There has been a disjunction between what we claim to be our core and what we actually do. If God has forgiven and accepts us, then why do we who have this belief still mistreat a whole lot of people in the world? What drives me is to try to bring together what we believe and what we do so that the world can see that God is the one who is in control of everything and not human beings.

(RH:) I agree with what has been said but, to put the accent a bit differently, there are moral realities in the world that have an effect on us and to which we are to respond. We fail or succeed morally insofar as we recognize what is due to others. In order to balance the sometimes rigidly subjectivist bent of Lutheran ethics I see the need to retrieve the objective side—the law. I call this the bone structure of Lutheran ethics. We don't even know what justification by grace means if we haven't encountered God's law. God's law is nothing else than God's wonderful, beautiful creation as ordered in the Torah and providentially laid out in creation. That is as essential as God's encounter with humanity in Christ. The basic moral demand on us is not relativized by wherever we find ourselves. There is an element in the United States but also in Germany of broad relaxedness about the moral demand: "If I have not been truthful, so what? No one has been!" The key element of the remembrance of God's law is to keep alive in the human community the sense of what it means to be human before God.

(DF:) Paul's notion of testing is what the law is about. You don't have to talk about law from the pulpit as individual commands, although you can do

that, but law also is the reality of the neighbor and his or her moral claim on me. That can be the most terrifying experience of the law.

(RP:) A contemporary example would be a Jesse Jackson who gets up and preaches in a way that "thus saith the Lord" comes out of his mouth. It's an attempt on his part and others like him to get corporations to do what's right: "Your practices are hurting people; treat your workers with respect and dignity." The bottom line is to be able to hear God's law speaking here, and then for the parties to sit down and begin to work through their differences.

(RB:) Realism within the Lutheran framework has led Lutheranism, more than some other traditions, to be less sentimental about certain things. An example was the debate on deterrence that took place in the LCA [Lutheran Church in America] over its social statement on peace, giving deterrence a kind of tentative legitimacy. Reinhold Niebuhr best articulates this realism.

(JC:) But this realism should not be equated with a cautionary, conservative approach to social change. Realism can deter Lutherans from the imperative to participate in the causes of peace and justice, although it did not deter Niebuhr. Realism reminds us of what's possible. What we seek may be out of reach, but that kind of realism should not be set over against the hope or dynamic of anticipation that I think fills the Christian ethic. The two are not incompatible because the hope rests in the confidence we have in God's ultimate reign, brought in through God's power. We don't realize these possibilities through our own actions. Nonetheless this hope impels us to reach out for these possibilities, even in the face of realistic assessments and setbacks.

(RH:) Here I disagree because this only gets us back to some of the conventional wisdom of interpreting Luther in the line of a reforming dynamic. An important implicit element of Lutheran ethics is to explode some of the conventional categories with which we operate. One of them is the progressive/conservative distinction in this country, which I find very unhelpful.

(LR:) I come at this in part out of the teaching on sin, because I think the Lutheran teaching on sin makes for a disposition that on the one hand emphasizes humility in what we can really know. The future is hidden from us. I too am deeply suspicious of grand narratives, big plans. At the same time this goes hand in hand with radical questioning. Because of the doctrine of sin, you have to ask absolutely the most probing basic questions. There also are resources for affirming moral agency and for a kind of daring bold action even in the face of an uncertain future, not knowing the grand plan. This kind of collective disposition is important. As we argue in our chapter, this seems particularly apropos when all sorts of things are up for grabs.

(RB:) Glenn Tinder articulates the Reformation tradition by arguing that in our creation we are given eternal and temporal destiny and by our redemption we are given worth before God who immeasurably cares for us such that each one counts. He argues that's the spiritual center of Western democratic political life. I believe the Lutheran tradition carries the deontological consideration that each one counts, which is helpful in countering the tendency in modern society to adopt an utilitarian ethic.

(*JC:*) For Lutherans, there is also the central idea of vocation. Occupation, seen through the lens of vocation, should lead persons toward seeing the dimension of service to neighbor in what we do rather than just getting ahead or accumulating wealth. It's not that we don't want to attain excellence in our jobs or be successful in our businesses but that we see this as subsidiary or instrumental to the possibility of service to the neighbor. In that sense ethics is a way of living. On the macro level, there is a desire to see whatever system works for the common good, or at least for a better distribution of opportunities and goods. The dimension of neighbor love embedded in vocation is a Reformation contribution that bears directly on some aspects of economic life, both personally and corporately.

(*LR:*) One of the strengths of Lutheran ethics has been the theme of freedom—the insistence that our performance in the moral life does not establish the nature of our relationship to God. Salvation is God's initiative. God's action frees us from always asking, "How am I doing in relation to God in my life?" I hold that as one of the treasures of Lutheran ethics. Freedom is formed for the upbuilding of community life together.

(*DF:*) Do we understand the important category of freedom as the individual's freedom from pangs of conscience or as grounded in the community process that precedes the existence of the individual? My sense is that Lutheran ethics has historically gone after the first option. That doesn't work so well when you read Paul's epistles. He assumes that freedom is somehow located and granted by the Spirit in the context of the community rather than in an individual's relationship before God.

(*JC:*) It seems that freedom as we understand it, for example, Luther's twofold formula that we are perfectly free and yet bound to the neighbor, is freedom *for* empowerment to be God's people rather than freedom *from* whatever. For so much of contemporary culture freedom has meant individuality over against community. If we understand Luther in this respect, we can forestall some of the individualistic tendencies that very easily creep into our own tradition by understanding the communitarian slant to Luther's formula as part of the overall understanding of empowerment to be the people of God in the world.

(*CML:*) How does empowerment to be the people of God occur? I am drawn to Luther's conviction expressed in "The Freedom of a Christian" that one of the powers of faith is union with Christ in which Jesus Christ becomes the active subject within the believer in community. That presence is morally empowering.

(*MS:*) One could say that at the heart of Lutheran ethics is the relationship to God that has been rectified in Christ. Every relationship is both a gift and a challenge. It makes a demand on us—to live up to this relationship in the world. Too often justification is understood as unconditional acceptance and love in such a way that the example of Christ gets lost.

(*RB:*) The life of gratitude in response to God's grace must involve works of love. Faith without works is dead. On this we all agree.

(*LR:*) Yet there's still a notion lurking that works to address the neighbor's need to re-establish the moral life as a qualifier of a person's standing before God. Faith and works aren't properly related. Another tendency is to insist that if God is doing it human beings can't be doing it, and if we're doing it God isn't. I run across this either/or thinking a lot.

(*CML:*) I have difficulty with the sharp distinction between God's saving action in Christ and all human efforts to improve the world. The call to be a part of God's redeeming work in creation is ignored by much traditional Lutheranism. I know I am made right with God through God's saving action, but I transgress this by conforming to a world which demands that I continue to desecrate God's people and the earth. As one who is saved, I am somehow called, invited, embraced by the grace of God into radical resistance. Christian communities throughout history have embraced a vaster, deeper sense of moral agency than has North American Lutheranism. We have not offered a distinctive ethos in American society.

(*RB:*) I don't think that's true. Lutherans have created an ethos in which one responds to justifying the grace of God by exercising one's calling toward the neighbor. Something very powerful has been at work driving so many Lutherans into teaching, social work, education, as well as being parents, for example.

(*CML:*) Yes, there has been formation into deep caring, into an ethos of service, but it has been crippled by our inability to see the ramifications that our lives of privilege have on the lives of our neighbors.

(*JC:*) Maybe it is the forensic stress we place on justification that fails to move us in the direction of action. This feeds a kind of individual salvation tradition that doesn't strengthen our sense that the message of the gospel is for the whole world, and into which we are drawn. The horizon of the reign of God in its comprehensiveness is a corrective to that individualism. It is the horizon on which to locate that larger sense of connectedness. Also a lot of people are just simply overwhelmed by the world. They can't take too much more and process it. They are just trying to get through the day and hope there's not another fight at home, or that one of the spouses doesn't drink too much again that night, or hope that somehow they can hang onto their job. Because we do become overwhelmed, it really is good news that we're not saved by ourselves.

On Retrieving, Teaching, and Critiquing a Tradition

(RB:) If there is one thing we have in common, it's a fascination with Luther. Traditions have exemplars, and he certainly stands as a giant among exemplars. Everybody here finds some way to relate to Luther, hopefully not in a slavish way, nor by doing an end run around Lutheran theology to get to Luther.

(CML:) The core of a Lutheran ethic is a faithfully critical relationship to the tradition that juxtaposes reform of the tradition with reclaiming it for each new time. Faithful disbelief is held in tension with belief. The Lutheran tradition entails a dialectic between remaining rooted in those aspects of the tradition that convey the gospel, even at the cost of life itself, and ferreting out those aspects of the tradition that betray the gospel, in the context of a central reforming dynamic as method. Luther himself is a model of remaining faithful to the tradition but challenging the principle assumed categories of the tradition. Central is his notion of the living Word, which is dynamic. The testing of the faith and the relationship to the living Word through Scripture is only a reality in community, a community that includes the testimony and the witness of those who are oppressed.

(LR:) On the question of tradition, I like the point David raised in his chapter. If we don't test, we become naive and gullible. When we test, there is an opportunity to check perception, to check understanding within community. That is vital in today's world. We do not live when Luther lived. And so what Luther encountered we could appropriate, but we do that through testing with other people, through dialogue and conversation. Furthermore, since the gospel is at the heart of the Lutheran ethic, a transformed and transforming life is possible. The other categories are different ways of trying to articulate what the gospel means. Do all the critiquing you need to because these other categories and concepts and ethics are in the service of the gospel. There is the freedom to critique them in such a way as to draw out their richness.

(KB:) It is in the midst of ethical dilemmas that not only the theological questions arise, but also the impetus to really challenge and expand how we understand some of the theological categories.

(LR:) A critical theory of religion and society requires that we not only ask about the teachings as if they stood on their own, but also ask what they mean in a particular time and place as they're interacting with other factors.

(DF:) People are critiquing because there's something fundamentally wrong with the way the tradition has been passed on, some fundamentally deep things that don't match up with the Bible. An example is the focus on the relationship between God and the individual, and moving on to the social only after this is taken care of. Paul doesn't work that way. It's God and humans, God and earth, God and cosmos. The sequencing of God and individual and then moving to the social is wrong. So my problem in teaching the tradition is do I teach something that I believe is a misperception of what's going on in the New Testament?

(RH:) But modern Lutherans don't have much of a tradition to critique! In Lutheran seminaries, at least the one I teach in, there is one required course in Christian ethics. At the Roman Catholic seminary near us there are four required courses in moral theology. It's been very hard for Lutheran or even Protestant ethicists to build up and maintain a tradition of discourse, which is one reason why I am so excited about this ELCA project. What we often think is a tradition is nothing else than the reproduction of Luther. We have virtually nothing accessible by Phillip Melanchthon, who was the professional ethicist of the Reformation movement in ways Luther was not. The tradition from then on through Lutheran orthodoxy is pretty obscure, with very little translated from Latin. We know very little about it. Compare that with the self-awareness of Roman Catholic moral theology as an ongoing tradition of discourse. Before we can even think of critiquing, we must retrieve the tradition. A wonderful example is the recovery of Luther's notion of God's two ways of governing the world. It was a critique of key elements of the tradition, but also a compelling retrieval of something that was very close to the heart of Luther's own practice of engaging political and practical matters.

(RB:) I see a deficiency in the teaching of congregations. I ask every class I have, "What are the commandments?" and they do not know. We used to be able to count on a generalized Protestant culture to inculcate people with these notions, but that's gone in most places. Congregations are in a new teaching position and it isn't happening. In seminaries the focus is on critique and revision. I fully agree that in the Lutheran tradition there is the notion of critique, but there's little catholic substance left to critique. One of the problems I have with mainstream Christianity and all you fine critics is that if all the energy and talent goes to that, we're not transmitting real substance.

(JC:) I don't think the critique is what's getting in the way. Whatever critique of the tradition I've been engaged in is not uppermost in my teaching of ethics at the seminary. I'm trying to get across what is a fundamentally faithful rendition of doing ethics out of a Lutheran context. My main point is there's a vicious circle going on here, and I don't know how we break it. Because it's not happening in the congregations, it's frustrating its development in seminaries. After seminary, it is difficult to get people out for continuing education on theology and ethics, unless of course it's a hot button issue.

(RP:) We have students who come to the seminary who are not even aware of the two kingdoms. I perceive that my role as a teacher is to have students encounter this and then draw them to encounter how Luther talks about the two realms. But I also want them to develop the capacity to critique that.

I present them not just one view of the tradition, but various interpretations, to get them to encounter it in a way that helps them understand themselves and to understand how people may be functioning in the world.

Sometimes we as African American Lutherans encounter Lutheranism presented to us as a litmus test as to whether we are really Lutherans, and that becomes problematic for us. It raises the question, can anything good come out of Savannah, Georgia [where one of the first African American churches organized]? We have to balance and integrate what comes out of Germany with what's developed from Savannah. Yes, there is a Lutheran tradition, but we have to critique and test that tradition because it's been oppressive and kept us out of the church.

(CML:) Given our increased knowledge of the Jesus movement and the pre-Augustinian and pre-Constantinian churches, we now know and are shaped by thinking to which Luther did not have access. Understandings related to original sin, human destiny, and moral agency that preceded Augustine were significantly different from those Luther developed. How would he have shaped his theology differently in light of these understandings?

(RH:) I have no idea what Luther would think apart from what we have received in his writings. A reading of Luther's "mind" always remains our reading. Therefore I distinguish theologically between, on the one side, Luther's authority as the authority of a particular theologian and, on the other side, the authority of doctrine. A doctrine would be a binding theological teaching under Scripture, as in the *Book of Concord*. Some of Luther's writings are included there, others not.

(JC:) The tradition is living and continually revitalizing. Faithfulness to the Lutheran Confessions is certainly not a process of repristinization. It is to deal with the realities as we confront them in a way as faithful as the reformers did with what they confronted. So would Luther have revised some of his own thinking? Probably so, if he were true to himself. But now we are Luther's heirs so we try to be faithful in the same way as he was. Confessions endure as the deposit of the Reformation coming together at a critical point in history. Luther is part of and yet an individual alongside of them. What endures about him is the evocative character of what he says.

How does what is authoritative or normative sustain itself? What is revelatory just stands forth as truth. There is a core there which comes out and grabs you. Jesus "spoke with authority," which is christological. What he brought was something revelatory that made him authoritative. What is revelatory becomes authoritative in the life of the church.

The Role of Scripture in Lutheran Ethics

(RH:) When we talk about how Scripture shapes ethics, the first thing that comes to mind is whether you can find the passages that will tell you what's right or wrong. In some cases, yes, but that isn't the only or even perhaps the most prominent way in which Scripture shapes the Christian ethic and becomes its source and norm. First of all, Scripture is the medium in and through which we come to know God, Jesus Christ, the promises of God, and justification. We come to know the interplay of law and gospel, the commandments of God as the way of love in the life of freedom. It's the way in which we get some sense of God's intention for the world and that toward which we should be striving in our own life as disciples.

(JC:) We may disagree on how to interpret texts and what hermeneutical moves are or are not acceptable, but we are very concerned to ground our ethical insights in Scripture. In recent times we have learned more about the variety of roles that Scripture plays in the shaping of the Christian ethic, how Scripture informs our ethics without simply being a manual for developing a code. One of the obvious ways the character of love is formed by Scripture is through the Beatitudes—a poverty of spirit, a kind of openness and absence of pretense that underlies our capacity in the freedom of the gospel to seek truthfulness. Therefore we are open to the reform of our own tradition and our own thoughts under the impetus of gospel freedom and formation in love that is not presumptuous or pretentious. Scripture forms the attitude that Marty [Martha Stortz] expressed in her chapter.

(LR:) So much more has to be done in the way of basic biblical literacy because Scripture is so important to moral formation—shaping the way people see the world, their moral agency, motivating, directing, guiding ethical reflection and action across the whole spectrum from teaching virtues to giving us perspective on particular issues. Scripture is formative of the church's identity.

(CML:) You don't turn to Scripture as shaping moral agency or norms without knowing it deeply and well. An evangelical ethicist once said to me, "Never say 'thus saith the Lord' until you've read the entire canon a number of times." The way Scripture shapes us is by drawing us deeply into a longstanding, intimate relationship with the living God.

(RB:) I find enormously helpful Luther's notion that the center of Scripture is what refers us to Christ. In a lot of the conversations I have had with very conservative fundamentalists, one of the first things I try to establish as a common ground is whether we share the notion of Christ as Savior. There is an interpretation of Scripture in Lutheranism that gets at essentials and provides a commonality that even fundamentalists can agree with.

(JC:) The hermeneutical key of what confesses Christ helps us interpret what is not so clear. We rightly construe the authority of Scripture in our own tradition by letting Scripture speak on its own terms through the power of its own message, rather that trying to impose upon it rationalistic structures of authority which have to do with empirical truthfulness or rational consistency. Scripture as source and norm is always understood within the community of the faithful as a tradition-forming process within which there is a role for critical scholarship. There is a certain freedom to pursue that critical test because we're not banking on some other notion of certitude than what Scripture itself offers us.

(RH:) The fundamental way I see Scripture is that it constitutes the horizon in which we operate. I compare this use of Scripture with the use of the icon in the Eastern Orthodox tradition. The icon inverts our perspective and draws us into God's own reality from God's perspective, into God's economy of salvation. Our primary relationship to Scripture is an extension of our worshiping relationship to God. We are not reading Scripture primarily as we would read the telephone book or a novel or a philosophical treatise, but we are drawn into submitting to what God is doing.

(DF:) When you talk about submitting to Scripture, I worry where the critical voices or critical analysis comes in. Scripture is an ancient text in ancient languages. Even more, it has ways of conceiving the world that we don't accept any more. If we don't enter into it critically from the beginning, I wonder if what comes as the Word of God to us, or God's drawing us in, means accepting frames of reference that we cannot accept today. An example is Paul's sexual ethic, where his main metaphor for sex is use. In Romans 1 he talks about the use of females. Now as I read this material I don't want to enter into that world as I would enter into an icon. I've got to have my thinking cap on from the very beginning. But with all the critical tools I bring to the text, I have this utter confidence that it's going to be really interesting and better news than I could possibly imagine. That may be what you're talking about, Reinhard, with icons.

(RH:) What it means to be drawn into Scripture through theological critique and self-critique is that in the end we are the ones who remain critiqued.

(CML:) As we see Scripture revealing the will and ways of God, at the same time we must seek where Scripture obscures God and reveals human brokenness and finitude.

(KB:) What are the implications for ethics of some of the very diverse readings of Scripture in current scholarly circles?

(JC:) Two things strike me. One is that we've had a proliferation of methodological developments beyond historical-critical developments. Each has brought its own particular set of insights. We have a kind of norming of critical scholarship going on within the life of the church. There is a greater affinity to holistic readings in which the reaction of the community and the reader become part of the interpretation of the text. My second point is I believe that this norming will go on because the church here on earth has been given the gifts of the Spirit. Sorting that out through the guidance of the Spirit will happen, although not without a lot of pain and argument. Under the conditions of finitude and fallenness, it's going to be messy. Nonetheless we need to bank on the gifts of the Spirit and then go about the process as a community working to norm that which is inside the theological circle.

(CML:) Many of the methodological developments mirror the postmodern turn and are the work of scholars who do not know the Bible as Scripture. I am troubled by the extent to which biblical interpretation within Christian circles may be shaped by the scholarship of those who do not hold the Bible to be Scripture.

(MS:) We all stand in this wonderful schizophrenia where on one hand as scholars we see this diversity of readings and proliferation of methodologies, and on the other hand as church people we're constantly asked what does the Bible say about something. We have this conviction that Scripture somehow does speak to our contemporary world. What scares me so much about that question is the assumption that there is a simple solution.

(KB:) But members of our church still ask for clear Scripture-based answers to the ethical dilemmas they face. What guidance can we provide for pastors and others who are hit with these kind of questions?

(JC:) The first thing I'd say is that Scripture says a lot that is as plain as the nose on your face, such as how high on God's agenda are concerns for the poor. Scripture talks about sexuality in terms consistent with the meaning of agape love. But it doesn't tell you how to relate to your spouse in order to keep your marriage alive and forestall its erosion into what is tantamount to an adulterous circumstance. Those are the things that we hammer out in dialogue with Scripture. A lot of moral concerns involve connecting up life issues with hints and directions in Scripture. That's another level where Scripture engages us in everyday moral discourse but doesn't necessarily settle our issues for us. Finally there is a narrow band of issues where we simply disagree over what Scripture actually says about them.

(RB:) Those things that are plain as the nose on your face are also quite plainly consistent with how we understand God's actions in our lives through Christ. Where we sharply disagree is over what is ambiguous and what is unambiguous. On some things, we would probably have a big disagreement over what betrays the gospel. I tend to see the things that are less ambiguous in the realm of personal ethics and the more ambiguous things in social ethics, particularly when getting into public policy with all the unintended effects.

For example, I think it is obvious that there is a heterosexual structure to God's will. But I don't think it is obvious how we then should deal with or what kinds of relationship we have with gays and lesbians. The pastoral problem is very complex. For a lot of you, it probably is not so clear that heterosexual relations are the will of God, and therefore we have differences over what is ambiguous and what is unambiguous.

(RP:) What I disagree with is how we treat people who may be gay or lesbian. If these are persons created by God, then we are to treat them with respect. I have to raise the question, what are the public policies and church practices that are hurting them? I don't want to separate personal ethics from social ethics. If Scriptures give us some indication of how we are to relate, then the only question I would bring is why aren't we doing what Scripture is talking about? People have major problems with the church saying that Scripture is normative but behaving in ways inconsistent with Scripture. The African American religious tradition rose up in direct opposition to a church that said that we were creatures of God but then turned that around and said no, not really.

(JC:) I quite agree with Bob that public policy decisions with all their unintended results represent an area of great ambiguity. But I would emphasize that while the church has no particular competence to judge a specific public policy, it does have the competence to say two things. One, when people are hurting, something has to be changed. Two, we call upon society to make the moral commitment through public policy action, rather than simply through political or economic exigencies. There are many ways, for example, to imagine universal health coverage in our society. We're not particularly competent as a church to say which one is going to work best. But we are competent to say there is something wrong in this society like ours where 37 million people don't have it, and there needs to be a societal commitment to make sure it happens.

In Addition to Scripture

(LR:) One of the complicating factors involved in the use of Scripture is that on virtually all of the issues Scripture is not the only source. So then the question becomes, how does Scripture interact with other sources? Scripture is always a part of a matrix of sources. This becomes especially difficult when some of the other sources give us information that runs against what we get from Scripture. Homosexuality is an example. If biblical communities assume a certain understanding of the will of God as heterosexual, and understand heterosexuality in a particular way, and then other information tells us something else about homosexuality, we've got a conflict of sources. That makes it difficult to make decisions together. Whatever the example, there are always more sources operating, which can be in conflict with each other.

(RP:) One of the critical sources that came through in what I looked at here was the role of experience. There's a critical relationship between Scripture and experience for African American Lutherans. We also bring an identification of the dilemma we encounter as human beings: loving self versus loving others. If I love others more than I love myself, does that mean that I am denying my tradition or culture? Does loving self mean I am denying the tradition or culture of others? African American Lutherans bring to the table an ability to help us face these dilemmas individually and corporately. Bob's earlier point about realism is translated into our community as we name what we see for what it is.

(MS:) There are intersecting circles of Scripture, church tradition, experience, culture, and so forth. The community needs to take seriously the witness of each of these and somehow come to a point where it can say, "It seems right to the Holy Spirit and to us." All these pieces are present and shape one another. I find that people appeal to experience as if it were raw. But experience is always already shaped, for example, by Lutheran and biblical understandings. There's enormous reflexivity between the way I read Scripture and the way Scripture then "reads" me. This happens in the context of a community.

(CML:) An epistemology of the cross, as Mary Solberg has written, reminds us that knowing is morally freighted, and that we know God most fully in the most broken places of life. That locus of knowing is an important Lutheran contribution to moral discernment.

(MS:) Moral formation allows and demands that we see things differently. When something presents itself to us as an issue, we need to see who's configuring the issue. My best work has come from standing back to see if this issue is really what it is cracked up to be, or what else is going on here. In moral discernment you can only choose and act within the world you can see, so the way we as Lutherans see the world may shape a rather different approach. Perception is really important in helping us to discern and decide.

(JC:) Social analysis, which is an aspect of rational reflection upon the world in which we live, is not itself normative but is highly revelatory of where we plug into what is normative out of our biblical and traditional foundation.

(LR:) I want to push for a larger amount of attention to systemic analysis. I think Bob and I have a basic disagreement here. I don't accept the separateness of an economic sphere, a political sphere, and a cultural sphere. For me these have very little autonomy of themselves, they're so interacting. The economic order is so productive of the kind of market culture that so affects the moral formation we associate with culture.

(RB:) That would be one place we don't disagree. I agree with what you said.

(LR:) Well, okay. In any case we have to be even more self-conscious about lifting that element into our ethics when we talk about moral formation, or when we talk about whatever action is appropriate. There is a deficit in most Lutheran ethics at the point of doing systemic analysis as a part of ethical method so that we don't quite get the degree to which systems and practices form us. Dynamics in society erode the traditions we used to count on. The kind of formation that Bob and others have talked about, and that was a part of my growing up, is no longer present even in those communities. But that's not because all sorts of dissenting groups within the Lutheran church are pulling apart the traditions. It's because a whole lot of factors in the large systems, especially the impact of the economy on family life, pull them apart. Instead you have moral formation going on by way of mass culture.

(RH:) This whole area of systemic analysis would fall into what I would understand as an extended first use of the law, the political use of the law. The political connection can only rightly be applied along with systemic analysis, which is a form of discernment. A problem in relation to social and political analysis is which analyses are the accurate ones, for example, regarding the economy.

(CML:) But the ambiguity about social analysis doesn't render it unnecessary. Theological discernment and biblical reflection also entail ambiguity. Moral issues about which there is ambiguity in the Bible are often enormous, crucial, life-and-death matters.

(RB:) When we talk about social or systemic analysis, I want to emphasize that the door should be open to different kinds of analysis. When I hear the word systemic analysis associated with causes, I immediately think of left-wing social analysis. I think one of the reasons the church doesn't speak with much authority for laypeople is because laypeople sniff out where these systemic analyses come from, and so I want to keep a more open discussion of social analysis and systemic reflection.

(LR:) The common form of what I call systemic analysis in the process of moral discernment as it takes place in congregations and other church settings is not, at least to my mind, something carried out by a small group of people who are highly sophisticated in social theory. I think more about getting out the varieties of experience of people in the society, which is why having folks representing a wide spectrum of interests around the same table is crucial, because with facilitation people can be involved in deliberation. People can tell you what they see where they are, how they understand things to be working. That's the kind of systemic analysis that I want to be encouraging. If among those folks are people who have given it a whole lot of time and attention because of their own particular professional training, all the better, but the key is the range of experience at the table of what's happening in the society. That's why setting the table of community is for me the key to discernment itself.

(*CML:*) I take seriously the challenge that truth is fatally embroiled in power. Discernment about the moral guidance in Scripture must include the voices of the disenfranchised. The table at which we sit includes invisible people; we need to seek out and hear their voices. I think of the experience my husband and I had at Luther Place Memorial Church in Washington, D.C., with homeless women, many of whom had been sexually abused as children or had been trapped in prostitution. They contributed rich biblical interpretation and moral discernment. Part of our interpretation and discernment involves welcoming to the table voices that we simply have not yet learned to hear.

(*RP:*) I agree, and sometimes that will push the church to act when the church is not ready to speak or act as an institution. People who are in situations of being poor or homeless may not have the time that we think we have to wait. It can be read as not caring to say the church can't speak or act because we haven't had time to study the issue or to call upon "our experts" to help us understand the dynamics and complexities of the issues.

(*DF:*) Cynthia is saying what I proposed Paul was up to. Getting all the voices at the table was a critical issue for him. It's creating a situation in which anything can be challenged. Nobody can control what can't be said.

(*JC:*) There's an inherently ethical character at stake here: justice as participation. Those closest to issues we're discussing need to have their voices heard. Our own social location and experience influence what we have written here. Where we're coming from is a lens through which we look at these things. This relates of course to power, to how different stories form communities and shape their moral vision. What counts as experience is deserving of a decisive role in the discussion.

(*RP:*) What I am concerned about is the support and complicity with structures that hurt people, and our own responsibility to challenge them and create structures that promote and enhance life and the common good.

(*RB:*) But the more you get into social transformation, the more you realize there are a lot of different viewpoints on what it is. Christians disagree sharply about what constitutes the common good and what public policies move in that direction. Yet our disagreements don't absolve us from doing deeds of charity for the neighbor. Charity is great, and for a lot of Christians that's as far as they're going to go.

(*RH:*) I don't know what it means when we say we want to radically transform something. We are constantly transformed anyway, whether we like it or not. Luther wonders sometimes about whether some changes will be improvements. In terms of government, people seek radical change, get their own people in, then what's happening afterwards is that just another group exploits. That doesn't lead to cynicism; I think it leads to a deep soberness. Or we seek to control by just holding the pieces together and putting one little piece on the other one until we finally have reached this wonderful society. We need to ask basic questions afresh: What after all is the state for? In the present situation where the global economy and big corporations are in place, why would we reinvent the state? Let's get the progressive/conservative spectrum out of the way and get to the core ethical questions.

(CML:) I'm challenged by the witness of communities who have been morally formed to resist evil, for example, the Huguenot village in southern France that decided to save about 4,000 Jews. Fifty years later a woman was asked why she risked her life to save others. She said, "Why wouldn't I have done it?" What was different about the moral formation of this community from that of other communities who didn't decide to save Jews? That Huguenot community was shaped by stories of persecution and resistance. In our Lutheran communities here in North America, to what extent are we shaped by stories that equip us for stances of resistance?

(RB:) Garrison Keillor may not be too far off in suggesting there is a kind of modesty in Lutherans that accepts an incremental vision of life, doing good in a very nonostentatious, nonheroic way. This doesn't encourage people to get out there on the edge, either imaginatively, constructively, or in terms of resistance. There is much more of a sense of enduring rather than resisting.

(LR:) We need to push harder on what are the dynamics that in fact are forming the next generation. There's been a remarkable consensus in our discussions that ethics is a way of life, and an increased concern on our part to nurture a particular way of life that was largely taken for granted. We have to do moral formation now in a very self-conscious way because other forces of formation are more compelling. That's why there's also remarkable agreement about the need for a counter-cultural way of life. We disagree about some of the particulars, but we need to be fostering a community whose own formation is often at odds with what's happening.

Continuing Deliberations Regarding Homosexuality

(KB:) Building upon what you have written in your chapters and what you have been discussing here, let's make this more concrete by engaging in some deliberations regarding the difficult topic of homosexuality.

(RH:) Students in my basic Christian ethics course, who care relatively little about rethinking other matters, are so focused on what I am going to say about human sexuality. I am puzzled by the assumption that we can talk about human sexuality in a "naked," unmediated way. Human sexuality is never just "out there." It is always configured and mediated through distinct institutions and practices that make up the matrix of the Christian vocation.

Marriage is a distinct vocation in the Christian community, and celibacy is another vocation. There also are a whole range of friendships that are different from marriage. I have reservations about rushing into a broad range of acceptance of homosexual activity, especially when it is included in the divinely mandated institution of marriage. Yet the concept of "friendship" might be a constructive perspective that could offer a possible mediation in this regard, instead of just focusing on sexual acts or orientation per se.

(RB:) At a recent event where both sides of the theological argument were presented, someone suggested that we extend the blessing of households to people who live together. That could be sisters and brothers, parents and children, all the way through gays and lesbians. I was amazed at the amount of interesting consensus that had.

(DF:) Looking at the New Testament material, I've come to realize that those writers did not have a concept of sexuality with which to work. It's just not there, although it is translated that way in English. It may be a very modern move to even conceptualize sexuality, and to read that back into the text and have that come back to us as "the Word of God."

It's also problematic when the whole issue is construed from the male perspective of passion and the control of passion. When I think about sex I think about mutuality and communication and deep love and commitment. That's coming from the friendship tradition that you're talking about, Reinhard. The friendship tradition infiltrated marriage. But I also have to realize that Paul didn't think that way.

(RH:) I think the psychological and social studies regarding sexuality in all its aspects are far from being unambiguous or clear. We need to take time to discern, to grant ourselves time as a church to work out areas of disagreement or uncertainty on some matters. I have learned from Roman Catholics that certain processes takes a century. It's the church's time, and it is especially hard in our present culture to take that into account. We want to have answers right now, solutions right now.

(MS:) But particularly on this whole issue of sexuality, there have been memorials to the church for the past few decades that have not been acted on. For some people it's almost midnight and for other people it's almost dawn, or the dawn is just breaking. Our sense of timing is very different.

(JC:) What is at stake in gay and lesbian relationships? Is it some innate violation of sexuality, or is it a matter of understanding sexual relationships of mutuality and love? I take the latter approach. As I look at what the New Testament says about sexuality, what is affirmed is what is loving and mutual;

condemned is what occurs outside of that kind of a relationship, or what is exploitative. What is affirmed is consistent with neighbor love or agape, namely, regard for the other and refusal to violate the integrity of the person. When we come to gay and lesbian relationships, if we posit a relationship of mutuality, commitment, and love analogous to that in heterosexual marriage, albeit in the absence of procreative possibilities, in what respect does that line up with other prohibitions that fit the category of agape? And if it doesn't seem to be a natural or logical entailment of agape, then where does it come from and do we have more than one ethical tradition in the New Testament to which we are beholden?

(RH:) I would like to go along in many ways with what you say, but it makes it difficult for me to understand Genesis 1, namely the heterosexual nature of the marital bond between female and male for the sake of union and procreation. There also is a certain natural teleology to the sexual organs; they are made for a certain purpose or end, precisely for procreation.

(CML:) The fact that an organ isn't used for its most "natural" purpose doesn't make the use immoral. I don't think we can locate immorality in whether an organ is used for its "primary natural" purpose. Many bodily organs—include sexual organs—don't have a singular use. As to whether homosexual marriage would detract from the heterosexual institution of marriage, that notion is challenged by the existence of faithful, lifelong homosexual "marriages" that are mutual and loving. The definition of "m-a-r-r-i-a-g-e" as exclusively heterosexual is itself a human construct.

(RH:) You're running into a postmodern construction of reality through language: whatever "we" decide something to be and mean "is" that thing. What disappears is a moral reality that is not just the arbitrary construct of our language.

(CML:) But having always defined marriage as heterosexual isn't what makes either marriage or heterosexual orientation moral.

(RH:) How modern marriage has disconnected sexual activity from procreation is already for me a deep problem, a subversion of the very moral purpose of marriage. Marriage includes an openness to new life.

(CML:) In a context of overpopulation is it immoral to decide not to be open to new life? Are marriages that can't generate "new life" immoral?

(RH:) No, I would differentiate there.

(CML:) To me there is a way of reshaping the question that I find useful, namely, to talk about the morality of heterosexism. Is it moral or not? Regarding the seven passages in the Bible [which are usually used to oppose homosexuality], why so much furor about those seven passages—none of which is out of the mouth of Jesus—when we don't take seriously so many of Jesus' moral teachings regarding wealth and poverty?

(*RP:*) The African American community over the years has come to accept people who happen to be homosexual. This is based on two things. One is on anthropology—this person is a human being and needs to be treated on that basis. The other is theological—it was God who created this individual and Jesus who died for them. Yet my perception is that within the African American community there has not been adequate theological or ethical reflection on the behavior. Personally I think homosexual behavior is wrong. This is a sensitive issue because of the high profile of some leaders in our community, and it doesn't get talked about sufficiently. Homosexual behavior has not been sufficiently discussed in public.

(*MS:*) I don't know what it means to legitimize homosexuality or homosexual acts, as I don't know what it means to legitimize heterosexuality or heterosexual acts. That doesn't quite make sense to me. The question for me is whether it is possible for a committed and faithful relationship between two gay men or two lesbian women to be acknowledged as a relationship that mirrors the love of God. It's the relationship question. Marriage does not necessarily mean that a relationship will be committed and faithful. What are the resources in the tradition, in the community, and in Scripture that can help our marriages to be committed and faithful?

(*JC:*) It is very important to stress those things that we can say with some certainty. Everybody, heterosexual and homosexual alike, has need of counsel and mutual reflection in light of our best understanding of Christian love and mutuality. We do not reject persons who are gay or lesbian from the community. The unfinished business is the question of the moral status of homosexual activity itself. The historical record of attitudes toward same-sex relationships is very mixed and in some cases very hostile. I recognize that one of the key arguments against the affirmation of gay and lesbian sexuality is the silence of the tradition in affirming it, whereas we don't have such silence in terms of heterosexual relationships. That's not insignificant. At the same time, a point at which to start as a Christian ethicist is the role of Scripture and the centrality of agape love, and to ask in what respect is the prohibition supposedly issued by Paul based on a violation of the canons of agape love. A lot of people condemn homosexual relationships simply because the Bible says it. They don't ask the question about the vital center of biblical ethics in the New Testament, and that's the question I want answered.

(*RB:*) I have great fear and trepidation that indeed this could split the church. To me it is an open and shut case that God meant for man and woman to be together in marriage and that in some sense something has gone awry in persons who are homosexual. It's also clear that love in its various forms is appropriate to form. If there is a form and a given structure about createdness, that has to be respected. It is interesting that people who are ready to be ecologically sensitive on other matters all of a sudden lose their sense of ecology here. This is an age-old wisdom from thousands of years. Now during the last part of the twentieth century there are attempts to overturn the moral presumption. There's a great deal of discernment in the whole body of Christian tradition and the biblical witness on this that you'd better be awfully careful about overturning. I can work through a lot of accommodations, but if the normative teaching of the church finds itself saying it really doesn't matter whether it's male with male and female with female, then I take seriously the option of whether I can be in this church. I feel that strongly about it.

(CML:) One concern I have about censuring homosexual behavior is the body of research indicating that some people are born homosexual. If that's the way some people are created as God's good creatures, then to say they can't behave as they've been created is to censor God's good creation. Also, Bob, you say there is a heterosexual structure to Scripture. There's also a patriarchal structure to Scripture. The overriding patriarchal structure doesn't make patriarchy morally right.

(KB:) I want to ask about the either/or logic behind some of what has been said here. What is it about possibly giving a positive moral evaluation to committed homosexual relationships that jeopardizes or threatens the normativity of heterosexual marriage? There are gay or lesbian persons who've been in heterosexual marriages and then "came out" and left their marriages. In these cases, there was a far more negative effect on the vocation of marriage, and especially on the spouse they left, than if there had been greater acceptance for them to live in a faithful gay or lesbian relationship in the first place. Why would the possibility of evaluating homosexual relationships more positively be so threatening to the basic moral core?

(RB:) I do not deny that there are goods in homosexual relationships. But even if it were proven that genetic makeup leads to this condition, that doesn't cut any moral ice with me because creation is flawed; it's disordered from the beginning.

(RH:) I'm generally in agreement regarding the basic heterosexual structure to the created order. At the same time Cynthia's questions haunt me, and I would like to find constructive answers to them. I'm also haunted by questions of bisexuality, or of man/boy [pederastic or pedophilic] relationships, which conceivably can be voluntary and mutual in character.

(CML:) I suggest that man/boy homosexual relationships no more implicate homosexuality than the longstanding proliferation of man/girl heterosexual relationships implicates heterosexual relationships. To legitimize and bless love within homosexuality does not suggest that we then legitimize and bless abusive forms of sexuality. It doesn't lead on a slippery slope to bestiality or incest or anything else. To find unabusive homosexuality to be moral does not suggest that abusive behavior between any combination of sexes becomes moral. There are different categories for immorality in sex than gender, categories having to do with power relationships and violence and lack of consent.

(LR:) This kind of issue raises a whole other kind of question for Lutheran ethics, namely, how we deliberate as the church on such an issue. There are both pressures for urgent responses or action, and we need to think through the long-term implications. It's an issue where we still are sort of at "flat earth" knowledge: what we know about sexuality with some kind of consensus and certitude is precious little. Yet we must decide; we can't just say we don't know enough here. There are enough differences, sides, and feelings showing up, and enough thinking has been going on that there is a serious questioning of a position that has been by and large regarded as a part of the moral core. Disagreements here raise the question of how we should proceed ethically. Is there a way of being a body together and staying with one another on this issue, and doing all sorts of things at once? What are the resources in the tradition that say we shall remain together on this? Certain dispositions will be helpful or conducive to this. One example where we as a church did this quite positively was on the abortion issue [at the 1991 Churchwide Assembly].

The Church as a Community of Moral Deliberation

(LR:) There are many circumstances in families and communities where people find themselves at odds with one another, in conflict and argument with one another, but because there are bonds of love it goes on and is handled in a particular way that is not the case where they're absent. The church is the kind of community that is to nurture those bonds. Given the character of the church, how does that set the terms for a kind of public ethic, where the church is the "public"? Are there stipulations of respect and hearing one another that are laid down by virtue of this being an ecclesial conversation?

(CML:) I am reminded that the bonds of love are not just human love, but the love of God present in the Spirit with us. The presence of prayer and communion as reminders of the bonds of love can make the difference between being a constructive community of moral deliberation and a destructive one.

(DF:) That's what Paul is getting at when he uses the imagery of "carrying" in Romans 15. Recent translations are "to put up with the neighbor." Christian love is far more than toleration.

(RH:) In my experience the bonds of faith are stronger than the bonds of love, because love can fail and there might be conflicts in which it's hard to maintain the bonds of love. But what constitutes them and the framework in which bonds of love can be renewed are the bonds of faith. Being in Christ is what holds us together.

(JC:) It strikes me that the bonds of faith and love establish some things that are essential for dialogue, namely, mutual respect and acceptance as persons of value whose voices need to be heard and understood. The bonds of faith and love were operative as this group progressed through its work. It is threatening to bring together a number of scholars who have various degrees of activity and achievement. This could have turned into a game of one-upmanship, of who can be more Lutheran or more clever or more learned, but that did not happen. There was a desire to respect the work of each other. As a consequence, when it came to identifying commonalities we were able to celebrate them. When it came to identifying differences we were able to deal with them at a level of interchange that was never antagonistic but always in a quest for the truth. As a consequence of that attitude of respect and mutual acceptance as sisters and brothers in Christ, in many instances we found that we may have misunderstood or not fully appreciated one another's views. As a result there was a kind of corrective that may not have eradicated the differences but eliminated those that are false and distorting among us.

(RB:) I agree and want to reflect for a moment on the prism of the calling. There is a kind of technical excellence demanded in our calling. I've really been impressed and comforted by the technical competence of people in this group. I've been reconvinced or reconfirmed that people here are faithful to their calling to be Lutheran teachers, and that's comforting and exhilarating.

(MS:) What I'm reminded of again in being a part of this group is how difficult and awesome it is to arrive at being able to say, "It seems right to the Holy Spirit and to us." How hard that is to say and how much time and conversation and prayer and worship must occur before we can finally reach that conclusion!

(RP:) I always go back to Acts 15 as a model of how the Christian community handled issues of great importance. When people feel they can share their point of view within the Christian community and talk and work through their differences, recognizing that they've been saved by Jesus Christ and that it's our faith that keeps us together, eventually the mission and ministry get accomplished. The Holy Spirit works, and God is working. This whole process has helped me understand even more that it is possible for there to be a diversity of opinion, and that what binds us and what holds us together is our faith, and that we can talk about it.

(JC:) For the life of the church in congregations and in other settings, it's important to remember the strength of these bonds in providing an atmosphere in which people can work through the issues openly and honestly, sharing their misgivings and their disagreements and their questions. The fear is that if we do this people will fight and leave, and I suppose that risk is always there. But if we don't do it, then people in their callings in the world, where they face so many of these issues of the moral life, are left unprepared. They are left without the benefit of reflection on this within the gathered community.

(DF.) The question is whether we really believe that our future is open, that it is shaped by our speech with one another, which at the same time is speech with God.

(MS.) My plea would be that as congregations and church leaders take the work we have done back into congregations they would, in their discussions, make room for the presence of the Spirit to move and work through their conversation. I feel the Spirit was speaking through all of you around this table.

Abbreviations

BC
The Book of Concord: The Confessions of the Evangelical Lutheran Church, trans. and ed. Theodore G. Tappert, et al. Philadelphia: Fortress Press, 1959.

LW, 1-30
Luther's Works, ed. Jaroslav Pelikan. St. Louis: Concordia Publishing, 1955–1967.

LW, 31-55
Luther's Works, ed. Helmut T. Lehmann. Philadelphia: Fortress Press, 1957–1986.

WA
D. Martin Luthers Werke: Kritische Gesamtausgabe. 60 vols. to date. Weimar: Hermann Bâhlaus Nachfolger, 1883ff.

Notes

Endnotes in which the authors dialogue with one another are introduced by an asterisk (*).

Chapter 1: Introduction

1. "The Augsburg Confession," IV, *BC*, 30.

2. "The Augsburg Confession," VI, 31.

3. Ed. Harold C. Letts (Philadelphia: Muhlenberg Press, 1957). See Bibliography.

4. Gene Outka, "The Particularist Turn inTheological and Philosophical Ethics" in *Christian Ethics*, ed. Lisa Sowle Cahill and James F. Childress (Cleveland, Ohio: Pilgrim, 1996), 95.

5. Valerie Saiving Goldstein, "The Human Condition: A Feminine View" in *The Journal of Religion* 40 (April 1960), 100–112.

6. Elizabeth Bettenhausen, "The Concept of Justice and a Feminist Lutheran Social Ethics" in *The Annual of the Society of Christian Ethics. 1986* (Washington, D.C.: Georgetown University Press, 1987), 178–80.

7. Lisa Sowle Cahill, "Particular Experiences, Shared Goods" in *Sex, Gender, and Christian Ethics* (Cambridge: Cambridge University Press, 1996), 54, 55.

Chapter 2: Lutheran Ethics

1. *After Virtue* (Notre Dame: University of Notre Dame Press, 1981), 207

2.* This definition of ethics identifies ethics as a second-order intellectual practice. It implies that ethics (the theoretical activity) has a moral ethos (the practical, lived dimension of moral existence) upon which to reflect. Its major emphasis is reflection on a way of life, though it also takes up specific issues in the light of this way of life. This manner of defining ethics is distinguished from more rationalist and deductive ways of construing ethics. I suspect that all the writers in this volume operate from such an ethical approach. They are located in a living tradition. Further it is important to note that the perennial themes that I will be delineating emerge from an American Lutheran ethos, though there would be much overlap with the themes from other Lutheran communities around the world. But there are Lutheran communities both in America and in other places that approach moral existence from a different angle than will be represented in this essay.

3. I have used "Lutheran tradition" in a way that needs clarification. The themes I will elaborate are drawn from what I consider to be the "dominant" or "normative" ethics of the major Lutheran churches of the United States. These ethics drew upon the classic traditions of European Lutheranism but refracted them through an American context much affected by other Christian traditions and by our peculiar American experience. These North American traditions contained many "minority voices" within them. One could catalogue the particular perspectives of smaller American Lutheran churches—such as the American Evangelical Lutheran Church or the Suomi Synod—as well as strong voices of individual theologians who did not easily fit the classical mode—those of Joseph Sittler and A. D. Mattson come to mind. In recent times "minority voices" also include African American and feminist perspectives. Some of these latter voices are represented in this book. But I have chosen not to delve into these minority perspectives in this essay, partly because of space and partly because of my understanding of my task, which is to elucidate the dominant themes carried officially by the major Lutheran church bodies of North America. These bodies include the predecessor bodies of the Evangelical Lutheran Church in America as well as the ELCA itself. Indeed the crucial ELCA document, "The Church in Society: A Lutheran Perspective" (1989), clearly manifests many of the themes that I will identify in this essay.

4. George Forell, *Faith Active in Love* (Minneapolis: Augsburg Publishing House, 1954), 84.

5. Einar Billing, *Our Calling*, trans. Conrad Bergendoff (Rock Island, Ill.: Augustana Book Concern, 1951), 7.

6. Dietrich Bonhoeffer, *Ethics*, trans. N. H. Smith and ed. Eberhard Bethge (New York: Macmillan, 1955), 73ff.

7. Forell, *Faith*, 112ff.

8. Robert Benne, *Ordinary Saints: An Introduction to the Christian Life* (Minneapolis: Fortress Press, 1988), 69ff.

9. Gustaf Wingren, *Creation and Law* (London: Oliver and Boyd, 1961).

10. Joseph Sittler, *The Structure of Christian Ethics* (Baton Rouge: Louisiana State University Press, 1958), 76.

11. Anders Nygren, *Agape and Eros* (London: SPCK, 1932).

12. Reinhold Niebuhr, *The Nature and Destiny of Man* (New York: Charles Scribner's Sons, 1941), 1:220. Niebuhr was reflecting on what he termed "Lutheran quietism." He notes that Lutheranism has a profound estimation of both human sinfulness and divine grace. The two fit together; the miserable condition of humans must be addressed by a radical divine grace. This grace he compares to a peak that is so high and glorious that it makes foothills (the relative distinctions so important to political judgments and responsibilities) seem flat and undifferentiated. Thus, he claims, Lutherans tend to bask in the wonder of grace and ignore political responsibilities. Niebuhr contrasts this with what he calls the "more superficial" doctrines of sin and grace of British and American Protestant Christianity, which ironically lead to more activism in the political sphere.

13. Martin Luther, *Martin Luther*, ed. John Dillenberger (New York: Anchor Books, 1961), 53.

14. Forell, *Faith*, 86.

15. Ibid., 122ff.

16. Bonhoeffer, *Ethics*, 73; and Benne, *Ordinary Saints*, 69.

17. I realize this construal of the work of love seems to give it a "liberal" or "progressive" bias. That is not necessarily the case. When the structures of "covenantal existence" are being damaged by permissiveness or lack of realism about human motives and behavior, love may in fact adapt more "conservative" strategies to help the neighbor. The main point is that love is always asking the question: Which of my actions will bring good to the neighbor? The answer to that question does not always lead toward more "liberal" or "open" attitudes and actions.

18. Luther exposited the Decalogue in both the Small and Large Catechisms as a guide to the Christian life. George Forell in his durable *Ethics of Decision* (Philadelphia: Fortress, 1955) follows a similar path.

19. Bonhoeffer is particularly instructive in elaborating this notion of "conformation" with Christ. The Christian is conformed to Christ incarnate, crucified, and resurrected. See his *Ethics*, 17ff.

20. Billing is particularly interesting on this point. He argues that the Lutheran idea of the calling is concretely focused on daily duties. We live out our callings with the hope that they will contribute to God's reign. "We can never foresee the results of our acts, least of all when the goal is the Kingdom of God. To maintain that our feeble deeds do serve this infinite goal is and remains a matter of faith. Our day's work lies ahead of us. It seems small and inconsequential. But God who gave it to us must also know its value, so go to it!" *Our Calling*, 26.

21. Luther, "Defense and Explanation of All the Articles," 1521, *LW* 32, 24.

22. Ernst Troeltsch, *The Social Teaching of the Christian Churches* (New York: Harper Torchbooks, 1960), 2:569–76.

23. R. Niebuhr, *Nature*, 1:184–98.

24. Foremost among them is Mark Noll in his "The Lutheran Difference," in *First Things* 20 (February 1992): 31–40.

25. The social ethics of the Lutheran Church in America, as articulated in its social statements, tended in a mildly left-of-center political direction, though it is interesting that its "Peace and Politics" statement was the only mainstream church statement that morally legitimated a deterrence-based nuclear ethic. William Lazareth, George Forell, and Richard Niebanck, whose theological counsel was formative in those documents, were political liberals. Right-of-center social ethics are more difficult to find in official Lutheran statements but are well represented in the writings of individual Lutherans such as Gilbert Meilaender, Richard John Neuhaus (before his conversion to Catholicism), James Nuechterlein, and Benne.

26. These four themes are drawn from my reading of Lutheran social statements, from suggestions made by a large number of Lutheran ethicists who were asked to enumerate key

Lutheran themes by the ELCA Division for Church in Society, and from the American Lutheran ethical writings of Forell and Lazareth in particular. All these it seems have been shaped by the dynamic portrayal of Lutheran social ethics manifested in Scandinavian writers such as Gustaf Aulen, Billing, and Wingren, and German writers such as Dietrich Bonhoeffer and Helmut Thielicke.

27. Stanley Hauerwas, *The Peaceable Kingdom* (Notre Dame: Notre Dame University Press, 1983), 99ff.

28. As claimed by Carl Braaten in his *Principles of Lutheran Theology* (Philadelphia: Fortress, 1983), 124.

29. Ibid.

30. Ibid., 135.

31. H. Richard Niebuhr, *Christ and Culture* (New York: Harper and Brothers, 1956).

32.* I offer these preceding paragraphs as counter-evidence to the criticism made by Larry Rasmussen and Cynthia Moe-Lobeda in n.58 in chap. 8 that my presentation of Lutheran theology leads to undue social conservatism. I believe I have argued in this entire essay that worldly institutions and practices are under constant judgment by both the law and the gospel. Both law and gospel prod Christians not to conform to the world as it is but to work incessantly for a better one. I therefore cannot see how the theology I elaborated has intrinsically conservative implications. It is more likely that we disagree on how we employ these basic theological themes than on the themes themselves. Our argument may be one less in principle than in application. The employment of theological principles will be affected by one's political and philosophical orientation, as well as one's situation in life, and I certainly admit to differences with Rasmussen and Moe-Lobeda on that front.

33. The concepts of "exalted individual" and "destiny" are developed by Glenn Tinder in his *The Political Meaning of Christianity* (Baton Rouge: Louisiana State University Press, 1989), 19ff. Tinder's key categories are modern articulations of Reformation ideas.

34. R. Niebuhr, *Nature*, 2:318.

35.* This weakness is being addressed in this volume by Reinhard Hütter, whose essay on the commandments in the Christian life is a salutary step forward.

36.* Rasmussen deals constructively with this issue in chap. 8 and in his *Earth Community, Earth Ethics* (Maryknoll: Orbis Books, 1996). Meilaender, another leading Lutheran ethicist, employs a rich understanding of a theology of creation in his *Bio-Ethics: A Primer for Christians* (Grand Rapids, Mich.: Eerdmans, 1996).

37. For example see Tuomo Mannermaa's "Theosis as a Subject of Finnish Luther Research," *Pro Ecclesia* 4, 1 (Winter 1995); 37–48.

38.* Martha Stortz in chap. 4 develops a strong link between religious practice and moral formation. In doing so, she goes around Lutheranism to Luther himself, who evidently saw certain Christian practices as contributing to moral virtue. See also the important article by David Yeago, "The Promise of God and the Desires of Our Hearts" *Lutheran Forum* 30, 2 (Pentecost 1996): 21–30.

39. It is pleasing to note that Lutherans have grappled with the challenge of ethical decision-making. James Childs, a writer in this book, and Paul Jersild have dealt with decisionmaking issues. Childs has written *Faith, Formation, and Decision* (Minneapolis: Fortress, 1991); and Jersild, *Making Moral Decisions* (Minneapolis: Fortress, 1990).

40.* Childs engages the problem of moral authority in chap. 6.

41. A number of Lutherans are writing on the relation of ecclesiology to ethics. Among the most important are Hütter, a contributor to this book, in his "Ecclesial Ethics: The Church's Vocation and Paraclesis," *Pro Ecclesia* 2, 4 (Fall 1993): 433–52; and in his "The Church as Public: Dogma, Practice, and the Holy Spirit," *Pro Ecclesia* 3, 3 (Summer 1994): 334–61, and David Yeago, "Messiah's People: The Culture of the Church in the Midst of Nations," *Pro Ecclesia* 6, 2 (Spring 1997): 146–71.

Chapter 3: The Twofold Center of Lutheran Ethics

1. For the range of Lutheran accounts of Christian ethics and their history in Germany from the middle of the last century, see the works of Chr. Ernst Luthardt, Ernst Sartorius, Albrecht

Ritschl, G.Chr.A. von Harleß, A.F.C. Vilmar, J. Chr. von Hofmann, Fr. H. R. Frank, Isaak August Dorner, Wilhelm Herrmann, Ernst Troeltsch, Dietrich Bonhoeffer, Werner Elert, Paul Althaus, Helmut Thielicke, Emanuel Hirsch, Wolfgang Trillhaas, Ernst Wolf, Trutz Rendtorff, Wolfhart Pannenberg, Dietz Lange, Oswald Bayer, and Hans G. Ulrich. For detailed bibliographical information on these authors, see, in addition to the Bibliography in this book, Rendtorf, "Ethik: VII. Neuzeit," in *Theologische Realenzyklopädie* 10, 481–517; *Evangelische Ethik: Diskussionsbeiträge zu ihrer Grundlegung und ihren Aufgaben*, ed. Hans G. Ulrich (Munich: Kaiser, 1990), 412–53; *Freiheit im Leben mit Gott: Texte zur Tradition evangelischer Ethik* (Gütersloh: Gütersloher, 1993), ed. Ulrich, 431–78. For the United States, see especially Johann Michael Reu and Paul Buehring, George Forell, Joseph Sittler, William Lazareth, Carl Braaten, Robert Benne, Gilbert Meilaender, Albert Pero, Paul Jersild, and James Childs. The Bibliography in this book contains information about the publications of these authors. Looking at this array of approaches, accounts, and readings, one is hard pressed to see any coherent tradition of discourse among these authors. There are, of course, clear overlaps and strong areas of agreement but also significant and remarkable disagreements in fundamental questions. An interesting volume that documents the emergence of a distinguishable tradition of discourse around the theme of "freedom" is Ulrich's *Freiheit im Leben mit Gott*. For a comprehensive account of the history of Protestant ethics since the Reformation, which is in its very consistency and penetration a lively witness to the fact that there is no narrative of the history of ethics without putting forward a substantive and systematic claim about the very content and nature of the subject matter, cf. Rendtorff's article cited above.

2.* Cf. Edmund Pincoffs, "Quandary Ethics," in *Revisions: Changing Perspectives in Moral Philosophy*, eds. Stanley Hauerwas and Alasdair MacIntyre (Notre Dame: University of Notre Dame Press, 1983), 92–112; Hauerwas, "On Keeping Theological Ethics Theological," in ibid. 16–42; Alasdair MacIntyre, *After Virtue* (Notre Dame: University of Notre Dame Press, 1984), 63–78. Cf. also Martha Stortz's concern as raised in her contribution under "Formation Tackles the Ordinary."

3. Cf. Ulrich Beck, *Risk-Society: Towards a New Modernity*, trans. Mark Ritter (London/Newbury Park: Sage Publications, 1992).

4. Christopher Lasch's *The Culture of Narcissism: American Life in an Age of Diminishing Expectations* (New York: W. W. Norton, 1978); and idem, *The Minimal Self: Psychic Survival in Troubled Times* (New York: W. W. Norton, 1984); and Robert Bellah et al., *Habits of the Heart: Individualism and Commitment in American Life* (Berkeley: University of California Press, 1985) are still accurate and relevant commentaries on and analyses of our society and its hegemonic middle-class ideals.

5. For a constructive and critical engagement of *Veritatis Splendor* from the perspective of Protestant—mainly Lutheran—ethics, cf. *Ecumenical Ventures in Ethics: Protestants Engage Pope John Paul II's Moral Encyclicals*, eds. Reinhard Hütter and Theodor Dieter (Grand Rapids, Mich.: Eerdmans, 1998).

6. "Modern Protestantism" refers to that significant strand of mainline Protestantism in which the contours of modernity define its self-understanding. Other strands of Protestantism also live "in" modernity, for example, evangelical Protestantism and Anabaptist Protestantism, but do not necessarily fall under this category.

7. Nevertheless *Veritatis Splendor*'s conceptualization is not without its own serious problems. For a discussion of the encyclical's more problematic aspects regarding the relationship between justification by faith alone, God's law, and human freedom, cf. Lois Malcolm, Gilbert Meilaender, or my own contribution in *Ecumenical Ventures in Ethics*.

8.* For my ecclesiological presuppositions concerning "Lutheranism" as a confessing movement in the church catholic, cf. "The Church's Public Ministry in Her Babylonian Captivity," in *Pro Ecclesia* 2, 1 (Winter 1993), 18–20. The following engagement with both "classical" Protestant ethics since the Enlightenment and the Roman Catholic tradition comes from this understanding of Lutheranism's vocation in the church universal. In other words, instead of "reifying" something into a "Lutheran ethos" or ideologizing Lutheranism, this engagement with contemporary Protestantism, Roman Catholicism, and moral philosophy is what identifies "Lutheran ethics." I have deep reservations concerning the "reform dynamic" that Larry Rasmussen and Cynthia Moe-Lobeda in their chapter consider to be at the center of the " 'way of living' in a Lutheran tradition." To understand the Lutheran tradition in this way means to read it through the categories of that modernity which is the very problem they rightly identify and challenge.

According to my understanding, the whole logic of a "reform dynamic at the very center of the tradition" precisely puts humans into the seat of judgment and criticism. What we receive becomes endlessly "formable" and "re-formable." Luther's Diet of Worms statement, "Here I stand," is profoundly misunderstood in modernity. Luther continued by saying that his conscience was bound by the Word of God, that is, he was unfree to change according to the emperor's will. The "reformatio" was for Luther anything but a "reform"—although it included some "reforms." In the *Book of Concord*, one does not find any awareness or claim of a "reform dynamic." One simply confesses the faith of the Catholic church according to the Augsburg Confession. The very notion of "an ongoing dynamic of reform" as an abstract principle strikes me to be the very invention of modernity itself, the "new age" ("*Neuzeit*"), in which everything will be "(re)formed" according to the critical principle of human reason alone. Seventeenth- and eighteenth-century Protestantism, especially Calvinism, participated in this "enlightening" movement of modernity, and later in an apologetic move claimed it as its own invention. This Protestantism thereby placed itself as both the initiator and *avant garde* of modernity by integrating modernity's principle of "reform" into its own Protestant "genetic code." "Modern Protestantism" precisely with its "reforming dynamic"—so accurately analyzed by Max Weber—is at the root of the problems that Rasmussen and Moe-Lobeda tackle in their chapter. All of this is not to say, of course, that reforms cannot or should not happen in the church. A human institution is reformable. Our awareness that the church is a church of sinners should keep the question of potential reforms always before us. But reforms are always matters of particular and concrete questions, decided case by case. If a question of reform is emerging or put before the church, it can as well be an act of faithfulness not to reform as it can be to reform. Claiming that a principled "reform dynamic" belongs to the core of the tradition itself can make the concrete discernment—whether a reform really is appropriate or just a way to give in to the *Zeitgeist*—very difficult if not impossible. Instead of assuming an inherent "reform dynamic," the Christian's eyes are opened to those reforms that are needed due to the nature of the subject matter at hand and its inherent problematic, regardless of any "dynamic" that might obligate or impel us to reform whether the reform is appropriate or not.

9. Cf. Walter von Loewenich's poignant formulation: "*Das sola fide ist für Luther der articulus stantis et cadentis ecclesiae, das bedeutet aber für ihn nicht die Versklavung der Wirklichkeit des christlichen Lebens unter ein systematisches Prinzip.*" In *Duplex Iustitia: Luthers Stellung zu einer Unionsformel des 16. Jahrhunderts* (Wiesbaden: Steiner, 1972), 72. "For Luther, the *sola fide* is the article by which the church stands and falls. Yet this does not mean for him the enslavement of the reality of the Christian life under a systematic principle."

10. Gerhard Forde's chapter "Christian Life" in *Christian Dogmatics*, 2, eds. Carl Braaten and Robert Jenson (Philadelphia: Fortress, 1984), 395–469, is one case where this problematic concentration on and thereby overstretching of the doctrine of justification become quite evident. While I profoundly agree with most of what Forde lays out under the doctrine of justification, it nevertheless swallows up everything else pertinent to the Christian life. This rendition neither captures the richness and complexity of the way Luther addressed the Christian life in its manifold layers, nor can it give an account of the way the whole Melanchthonian trajectory developed. Rather it is reflective of a particular way of retrieving Luther in the tradition of Rudolf Hermann and his student Hans Joachim Iwand, a tradition tacitly but deeply indebted to Kant's philosophy. Cf. nn.11, 12 for some bibliographic references. While Forde clearly sees the trap of antinomianism and affirms the law's truth, he nevertheless does not spell out the latter in a way that successfully diverts the danger of the first. It seems to be impossible for him to do so because of his exclusive focus on the doctrine of justification by faith as the sole "descriptor" of the Christian life.

11. The point that through faith we are not only declared righteous on the grounds of Christ's righteousness but that by receiving Christ himself in faith we are actually beginning to become righteous was expressed by Luther early on in his "Sermo de duplex iustitia" (1519). While he later modified his thinking, he maintained a clear emphasis on Christ as the very "form" of faith, as himself present in faith, in his *Lectures on Galatians* and in the notion of a "*iustitia incepta*" in his late disputations. Cf. Walter von Loewenich, *Duplex;* Paul Althaus, *The Theology of Martin Luther,* trans. Robert C. Schultz (Philadelphia: Fortress Press, 1966), 234–41; and esp. Tuomo Mannermaa, *Der im Glauben gegenwärtige Christus: Rechtfertigung und Vergottung—Zum ökumenischen Dialog* (Hannover: Lutherisches Verlagshaus, 1989). Cf. also David Yeago, "The Bread of Life: Patristic

Christology and Evangelical Soteriology in Martin Luther's Sermons on John 6," in *St. Vladimir's Theological Quarterly* 39, 3 (1995): 257–79, esp. 271ff.

12. What I am attempting to address here is a complex phenomenon that is observable across the board of Protestant theological "camps." It can be observed, for example, in Werner Elert and Rudolf Bultmann, in Gerhard Forde and Paul Tillich. It has to do with the particular core-assumptions of Kantian philosophy as they found their way via Kant-Lotze-Ritschl-Herrmann into the central construals of the Luther renaissance in the 1920s. For an analysis of this phenomenon, cf. Risto Saarinen, *Gottes Wirken auf uns: die transzendentale Deutung des Gegenwart- Christi-Motivs in der Lutherforschung* (Stuttgart: Steiner, 1990); and in a more accessible way, David Yeago, "Gnosticism, Antinomianism, and Reformation Theology: Reflections on the Costs of a Construal," in *Pro Ecclesia* 2, 1 (Winter 1993): 37–49. For seeing the problem more clearly, I am indebted to Yeago's analysis and also to his forthcoming book on the theology of Martin Luther.

13. Cf. David Yeago, "Gnosticism", 40–41: "Since the law/gospel distinction is placed in no wider context, but is itself the context into which everything else in theology must be integrated, the grounds for the oppressiveness of the law must be sought in the law itself. . . . If it is true that the law oppresses simply because of its formal character as ordered demand, then the converse would seem also to hold: anything with the formal character of ordered demand oppresses. That is to say, anything which proposes some particular ordering of our existence or calls for a determinate response from us will be perceived as being, simply put, the oppressive law from which the gospel delivers us. And since the gospel's liberating character is defined in terms of its antithesis to the law, it will not be our sinful abuse of the law and hostility to the commandment, and God's wrath against us on that account, from which the gospel liberates us. Rather, the gospel will liberate us from the situation of having to hear commandment at all, from having to reckon with any word whatsoever which has the formal character of ordered demand." For Luther—in contrast to neo-Protestantism—this meant two things: first the insistence of the ongoing presence of the "law" in the church for Christ's sake (its "second use") and second the insistence that the Decalogue as remembrance of what is written in our hearts is the way of life for humanity intended by God. As such it is to be taught to all humans, whether believers or unbelievers. Regarding the first point, cf. Luther's *Fifth Disputation against the Antinomians* (1538), WA 39/I, 357, thesis 61 and 62, where he states that God's law, which we do not fulfill, reflects God's own goodness, and precisely because God's law is good and perfect, it condemns us. Without God's law being continuously proclaimed and taught, we do not understand what it means that Christ fulfilled God's law *pro nobis* and that we are always in need of Christ's fulfillment of God's law. Regarding the second point, cf. George Lindbeck, "Martin Luther and the Rabbinic Mind," in *Understanding the Rabbinic Mind: Essays on the Hermeneutics of Max Kadushin*, ed. Peter Ochs (Atlanta: Scholars Press, 1990), 141–64, esp. 149–55; cf. also Luther's "Second Disputation against the Antinomians" (1538), WA 39/I, 454, 4–16, where he claims that the Decalogue has to serve as a visible remembrance of what humans were before Adam's fall and what they will be in Christ!

14.* Robert Benne raises a similar concern in his contribution—under "Contemporary Challenges."

15. For the crucial distinction between *libertas* and *libentia* in Luther's understanding of "freedom," cf. Robert W. Jenson, "An Ontology of Freedom in the *De Servo Arbitrio* of Luther," in *Modern Theology* 10 (1994): 247–52.

16. A short note on the "third" or "pedagogical" use of the law is in order. While I agree with the insight that the "third use of the law" intends to maintain, it is crucial to distinguish between "law" on the one hand and "commandment," "mandate," "torah" on the other hand. Due to the condition of sin, "law" in both its first and second use has an enforcing, restraining, and convicting character. This is not inherent in God's law but is the result of the radical human estrangement from God. As the *gestalt* of the way of life with God—the embodiment of genuine human freedom—the enforcing, restraining, and convicting elements are lost. The "commandment" in distinction from "law," as suggested by Paul Althaus, embodies the goods constitutive of the way of life in communion with God. It is the *usus practicus evangelii* (in Wilfried Joest's terminology) or the "second use of the gospel" (in William Lazareth's words). Let me be clear: In this life the struggle between "spirit" and "flesh" is not yet over. The estrangement from God is broken "in faith" but not yet fully overcome. Therefore the substantive dialectic between "law" and "gospel" still applies

to Christians. In our still ongoing estrangement from God, God's law encounters us as restraining and convicting. Yet by grasping Christ in faith, Christian freedom receives its distinct *gestalt* through a way of life according to the commandments: the Decalogue, the Sermon on the Mount, and the double-love-commandment. Here I am basically drawing upon Article VI of the *Solid Declaration, Formula of Concord*. For the "substantive dialectic" between "law" and "gospel" due to the not yet complete renewal of the Christian, cf. 964,11–965,29; for the struggle between "flesh" and "spirit," cf. 967,25–37; and for God's commandments as the embodiment of Christian freedom, cf. 965,36–966,42. In *Die Bekenntnisschriften der Evangelisch- Lutherischen Kirche* (Göttingen: Vandenhoeck & Ruprecht, 8th ed., 1979). Cf, *BC*, 564, 6–565, 9; 567, 18; 565, 11–566, 15.

17. Still the clearest and most "successful" account is Joseph Fletcher's, *Situation Ethics: The New Morality* (Philadelphia: Westminster, 1974).

18. Cf. the chs. "Emotivism: Social Content and Social Context," " 'Fact', Explanation and Expertise," and "The Character of Generalizations in Social Science and their Lack of Predictive Power" in MacIntyre, *After Virtue*, 23–35, 79–87, and 88–108, for a fascinating analysis of these complex problems.

19. For three fine accounts of various aspects of its history, cf. John Mahoney, *The Making of Moral Theology: A Study of the Roman Catholic Tradition* (Oxford: Clarendon Press, 1987); Servais Pinckaers, O.P., *The Sources of Christian Ethics* (Washington, D.C.: Catholic University of America Press, 1995), 191–323; and Donal Dorr, *Option for the Poor: A Hundred Years of Catholic Social Teaching* (Maryknoll: Orbis, 1983, exp. 1992).

20. Immanuel Kant stated: "Autonomy of the will is that property of it by which it is a law to itself independently of any property of objects of volition. Hence the principle of autonomy is: Never choose except in such a way that the maxims of the choice are comprehended in the same volition as a universal law." In *Foundations of the Metaphysics of Morals*, trans. and introduced by L. W. Beck (New York: Liberal Arts Press, 1959), 59. Martin Heidegger put it in a shorter form: "To give the law to oneself is supreme freedom." In "Die Selbstbehauptung der deutschen Universität. Rede, gehalten bei der feierlichen Übernahme des Rektorats der Universität: Freiburg i.Br. am 27.5.1933," in *Das Rektorat 1933/34: Tatsachen und Gedanken*, ed. H. Heidegger (Frankfurt/M. 1983), 14f.

21. For a fascinating attempt to recover this insight "after modernity," cf. Karl Barth, *The Holy Spirit and the Christian Life: The Theological Basis of Ethics* (Louisville: Westminster John Knox, 1993; orig. German 1929; orig. English 1938).

22.* Cf. Benne's poignant formulation in his contribution in the section "Salvation versus Human Effort": "When the God-man Jesus Christ is refused as Savior, the man-god in many different guises rushes in." In their contribution Rasmussen and Moe-Lobeda rightly decry the derailment of the doctrine of creation. It is the eclipse of the creator—the mode of operation *etsi Deus non daretur*—that in consequence eclipses "creation" and that is then replaced by "nature" as the object of human conquest and exploitation. They poignantly express this undergirding revolutionary dynamic of modernity when they say: "We have effectively reduced creation to nature and then drained nature of intrinsic value and meaning." Nevertheless I deeply disagree with their attempt of getting God, so to speak, "back into nature" by extending the notion of "sacrament" to creation, so that Luther's account of creation can be described by them as a "sacramentalist, panentheistic notion." This move, I fear, ultimately obfuscates the difference between God's presence as creator in creation and God's salvific presence in baptism and the Lord's Supper, a decisive distinction that Luther always maintained. "Sacrament" stands for God's salvific activity through the tangible elements of baptism and the Lord's Supper, both rooted in the triune God's self-giving in Christ. In other words, the sacrament is God's salvific gift "for us." God, however, is not present for us in precisely this way in creation in general. Rasmussen and Moe-Lobeda point to an issue of crucial importance in their worthy attempt to retrieve an awareness of God's presence in creation. But while this presence surely is a mirror of God's glory, holiness, and hiddenness, it is not therefore "sacramental," that is, both unambiguously communicating who God is in relationship to us humans and at the same time drawing us into God's own triune life. They rightly point to Jesus' cross and resurrection as God's saving activity, that is, the ground and content of the sacraments.

23. Gerhard Forde captures this modern self's self-assertion as "will to power" very well when he writes: "But what is false is that it is always the law that is negated, not the old Adam. The old

Adam escapes unscathed and appears on the stage of history as the one who embodies, understands, and eventually carries out the negation. Unnegated themselves, old beings appear now in the role of arch-negators, revolutionaries, the arbiters over the lives and deaths of other beings. The truth, the law, is relative to their vision. Human beings are expendable." "Christian Life," 468.

24. Cf. Immanuel Kant, *Critique of Practical Reason and Other Writings in Moral Philosophy*, trans. and ed. L. W. Beck (Chicago: University of Chicago Press, 1949), 227–34. It is necessary to emphasize Friedrich Nietzsche's work as a radical critique of the "Kantian Christianity" of the nineteenth century and its way of "saving" God as a transcendental idea of practical reason. For Nietzsche the rationally justified moral agent of the eighteenth century is a fiction. Cf. *The Joyful Wisdom* (1882) section 335, where toward the end Nietzsche writes: "Let us *confine* ourselves, therefore, to the purification of our opinions and appreciations, and to the *construction of new tables of value of our own:*—we will, however, brood no longer over the 'moral worth of our actions'! Yes, my friends! As regards the whole moral twaddle of people about one another, it is time to be disgusted with it! To sit in judgment morally ought to be opposed to our taste! Let us leave this nonsense and this bad taste to those who have nothing else to do, save to drag the past a little distance further through time, and who are never themselves the present—consequently to the many, to the majority! We, however, *would seek to become what we are,*—the new, the unique, the incomparable, making laws for ourselves and creating ourselves! And for this purpose we must become the best students and discoverers of all the laws and necessities of the world. We must be *physicists* in order to be *creators* in that sense." In *Joyful Wisdom*, trans. Thomas Common (New York: Frederick Ungar, 1960), 262f.

25. Cf. among his numerous works especially *The Philosophical Discourse of Modernity: Twelve Lectures* (Cambridge: MIT Press, 1987); and *Moral Consciousness and Communicative Action* (Cambridge: MIT Press, 1990). The relationship between Jürgen Habermas' and K. O. Apel's "discourse ethics" and theology is quite complex. For fine engagements, criticisms, and constructive ways to draw upon Habermas' and Apel's work, cf. *Habermas, Modernity, and Public Theology*, eds. Don S. Browning and Francis Schüssler Fiorenza (New York: Crossroad, 1992), esp. the essays by Helmut Peukert, Matthew Lamb, and Gary M. Simpson.

26. But cf. Franklin I. Gamwell, *The Divine Good: Modern Moral Theory and the Necessity of God* (New York: HarperCollins, 1990); Glenn Tinder, *The Political Meaning of Christianity: The Prophetic Stance* (New York: HarperCollins, 1991); David Walsh, *After Ideology: Recovering the Spiritual Foundations of Freedom* (New York: HarperCollins, 1990); and Václav Havel, *Living in Truth*, ed. by Jan Vladislav (London: Faber & Faber, 1987).

27. *Church Dogmatics* II/2 (Edinburgh: T. & T. Clark, 1957), 518. Cf. also *Epistle to the Romans*, (London/New York: Oxford University Press, 1933), 425–526; and "The Problem of Ethics Today" in Barth, *The Word of God and the Word of Man* (Grand Rapids, Mich.: Zondervan, 1935): 136–82.

28. For Barth's late ethics and its impact on the reading of the whole *Church Dogmatics*, cf. the excellent study by John Webster, *Barth's Ethics of Reconciliation* (Cambridge: Cambridge University Press, 1995); for Bonhoeffer, cf. his *Ethics* (New York: Simon & Schuster, 1995); and for a fine exposition of the implications of Bonhoeffer's theology and personal witness for today, cf. Larry L. Rasmussen (with Renate Bethge), *Dietrich Bonhoeffer—His Significance for North Americans* (Minneapolis: Fortress, 1990), esp. 144–73.

29. Cf. George F. Thomas, *Christian Ethics and Moral Philosophy* (New York: Charles Scribner's Sons, 1955), 485–522; Paul Ramsey, *Basic Christian Ethics* (reprinted in the series: Library in Theological Ethics: Knoxville: Westminster John Knox, 1993), 191–23 and most notably Stanley Hauerwas. Among his numerous books on these topics, cf. especially *Character and the Christian Life: A Study in Theological Ethics* (San Antonio: Trinity University Press, third printing with new introduction, 1985) and (with Charles Pinches) *Christians among the Virtues: Theological Conversations with Ancient and Modern Ethics* (Notre Dame: University of Notre Dame Press, 1997). From a Lutheran perspective, see Gilbert Meilaender, *The Theory and Practice of Virtue* (Notre Dame: University of Notre Dame Press, 1984). For a good summary and analysis of the "comeback" of the virtues in philosophical ethics, cf. Wybo J. Dondorp, *The Rehabilitation of Virtue* (Amsterdam: VU University Press, 1994).

30. I borrow this expression from Charles Taylor, *The Sources of the Self* (Cambridge: Harvard University Press, 1989), 159. He uses this expression as a heading for his discussion of John

Locke, who is arguably more important for the success of individualism and its related concept of freedom in the Anglo-Saxon world than Immanuel Kant.

31. Cf. among many, Enrique Dussel, *Ethics and the Theology of Liberation* (Maryknoll: Orbis, 1978); and idem, *Ethics and Community* (Maryknoll: Orbis, 1988), and from a Lutheran perspective, Walter Altmann, *Luther and Liberation: A Latin American Perspective* (Minneapolis: Fortress, 1992).

32. Among many, cf. Mary McClintock Fulkerson, *Changing the Subject: Women's Discourses and Feminist Theology* (Minneapolis: Fortress, 1994); and from the angle of political theory and practice, Jean Bethke Elshtain, *Public Man—Private Woman: Women in Social and Political Thought* (Princeton: Princeton University Press, 1981); and idem, *Women and War* (with a new epilogue; Chicago: University of Chicago Press, 1995).

33.* Cf. Rasmussen's and Moe-Lobeda's chapter as one example. For other explicitly Lutheran approaches to this new "recontextualization of the human in creation," see *Concern for Creation: Voices on the Theology of Creation*, ed. Viggo Mortensen (Uppsala: Tro & Tanke/Svenska kyrkan, 1995). Among many others, cf. Larry L. Rasmussen, *Earth Community, Earth Ethics* (Maryknoll: Orbis, 1996); and *Good News for Animals? Christian Approaches to Animal Well-Being*, eds. Charles Pinches and Jay B. McDaniel (Maryknoll: Orbis, 1993). For this new recontextualization in creation in an explicitly trinitarian framework, cf. Jürgen Moltmann, *God in Creation: A New Theology of Creation and the Spirit of God* (Minneapolis: Fortress, 1993).

34. One can find early indications of this move in the ecclesiology and ethics of Karl Barth, *Church Dogmatics* III/4 par. 53 and par. 55.3 and the fragment *The Christian Life. Church Dogmatics IV/4: Lecture Fragments* (Grand Rapids, Mich.: Eerdmans, 1981); Bonhoeffer, *Ethics*, 199ff. and 294ff.; and Paul Lehmann, *Ethics in a Christian Context* (New York: Harper & Row, 1967), 45–73. On Paul Lehmann's work, cf. the recent study by Nancy Duff, *Humanization and the Politics of God: The Koinonia Ethics of Paul Lehmann* (Grand Rapids, Mich.: Eerdmans, 1992). This approach was developed more strongly in John H. Yoder, *The Politics of Jesus: Vicit Agnus Noster* (Grand Rapids, Mich.: Eerdmans, 1972); idem, *The Priestly Kingdom: Social Ethics as Gospel* (Notre Dame: University of Notre Dame Press, 1984); idem, *The Royal Priesthood: Essays Ecclesiological and Ecumenical*, ed. Michael G. Cartwright (Grand Rapids, Mich.: Eerdmans, 1994); and in Stanley Hauerwas, *A Community of Character: Toward a Constructive Social Ethic* (Notre Dame: University of Notre Dame Press 1981); idem, *The Peaceable Kingdom: A Primer in Christian Ethics* (Notre Dame: University of Notre Dame Press, 1983); idem, *Christian Existence Today: Essays on Church, World and Living in Between* (Durham: The Labyrinth Press, 1988); and idem, *In Good Company: The Church as Polis* (Notre Dame: University of Notre Dame Press, 1995). For detailed discussions of this new approach to Protestant ethics, cf. Reinhard Hütter, *Evangelische Ethik als kirchliches Zeugnis* (Neukirchen-Vluyn: Neukirchener Verlag, 1993); Arne Rasmusson, *The Church as Polis* (Notre Dame: University of Notre Dame Press, 1995); and Martin Walton, *Marginal Communities: The Ethical Enterprise of the Followers of Jesus* (Kampen: Kok Pharos, 1994). But cf. also Timothy F. Sedgwick, *Sacramental Ethics: Paschal Identity and the Christian Life* (Philadelphia: Fortress, 1987); Vigen Guroian, *Ethics after Christendom: Toward an Ecclesial Christian Ethic* (Grand Rapids, Mich.: Eerdmans, 1994); Sally Purvis, *The Power of the Cross: Foundations for Christian Feminist Ethic of Community* (Nashville: Abingdon, 1993); and Larry L. Rasmussen, *Moral Fragments and Moral Community: A Proposal for Church in Society* (Minneapolis: Fortress, 1993).

35. Cf. Oswald Bayer, *Freiheit als Antwort: Zur theologischen Ethik* (Tübingen: J.C.B. Mohr, 1995); and idem, *Freiheit im Leben mit Gott: Texte zur Tradition evangelischer Ethik*, ed. Hans G. Ulrich (Gütersloh: Gütersloher Verlagshaus, 1993).

36. *LW*, 31, 344; *WA* 7:21 and 7:49.

37.* For a sustained critique of this pervasive but deeply distorted reading of Luther's so-called "two kingdoms doctrine," cf. Ulrich Duchrow, *Christenheit und Weltverantwortung: Traditionsgeschichte und systematische Struktur der Zweireichelehre* (Stuttgart: Klett Cotta, 1983). For more accessible studies and source collections, cf. *Lutheran Churches — Salt or Mirror of Society? Case Studies on the Theory and Practice of the Two Kingdoms Doctrine*, ed. Ulrich Duchrow (Geneva: LWF Department of Studies, 1977) and *Two Kingdoms and One World*, ed. Karl H. Hertz (Minneapolis: Augsburg, 1976). Cf. also the dissertations on this topic by Thomas W. Strieter and Molefe S. Tsele, both listed in the Bibliography. For an accurate representation of Luther's so-called two kingdoms doctrine and for an interpretation of it that is congenial to Luther, cf. Benne's contribution, and for the importance of its eschatological dynamic, cf. Childs's contribution. Richard Perry's historical narrative of the

African American Lutheran tradition provides both a telling critique of a distorted "two-realms" thinking and a compelling African American application of a correct understanding of Luther's distinction between and inherent relatedness of God's two governances.

38. For Luther this "happy exchange" (Christ receiving our sin, and we receiving Christ's holiness, righteousness, truthfulness, peacefulness, and freedom) has its root in baptism, the preached word of the gospel received in faith, and the reception of the Lord's Supper. This "happy exchange" constitutes the very root of Christian freedom. For Luther, then, Christian freedom is rooted in the practices of Christian worship; it is a freedom received in and through Word and Sacrament. This insight has been convincingly developed by Bernd Wannenwetsch, *Gottesdienst als Lebensform: Ethik für Christenbürger* (Stuttgart: Kohlhammer, 1997), 189f. Cf. also his more accessible essay "The Political Worship of the Church: A Critical and Empowering Practice," in *Modern Theology* 12 (1996): 269–99.

39. *LW*, 31, 365–67; *WA* 7, 64f.

40.* As David Yeago has rightly pointed out to me, the christological pole of Luther's account of Christian freedom is obviously much more protected from the thinness of "Protestantism lite" than I seem to allow here in my brief discussion, which focuses only on the treatise "The Freedom of a Christian." For other important places where this substantive christological pole comes to the fore, one might see the distinction and relation between Christ as gift and Christ as example in Luther's "Brief Instruction on What to Look for and Expect in the Gospels" (1522). First the gospel-proclamation brings the Christ of the Gospels to us as gift: His life is not his own but "for us." This evangelical "pro me" grounds the return to the Christ of the Gospels as example: The very life that has become my own is depicted as an example and paradigm for me. Christian freedom is not tied simply to a general notion of "self-giving love" but to a concrete and detailed narrative paradigm. There is a move within the christological pole between gift and example that parallels the movement that I describe between Christian freedom and the remembrance of the commandments. Inherently connected with this is, of course, the meditation of the life of Christ. For a detailed account of that, cf. Martin Nicol, *Meditation bei Luther* (Göttingen: Vandenhoeck & Ruprecht, 1984), and Stortz's contribution in this book.

41. *LW*, 31, 360. The section continues: "Since, however, we are not wholly recreated, and our faith and love are not yet perfect, these are to be increased, not by external works, however, but of themselves." Cf. *WA* 7, 61.

42. *LW*, 1, 9; *WA* 42:71.

43. David Yeago, "Martin Luther on Grace, Law, and Moral Life: Prolegomena to an Ecumenical Discussion of *Veritatis Splendor*," in *The Thomist*, 62 (1998), 176–78. That the commandment is the form of Adam's and Eve's *cultus dei* is reflected in the importance that the Third Commandment has for Luther in the Decalogue, so that the exposition of the First Commandment takes place in light of the Third Commandment. Cf. Wannenwetsch, *Gottesdienst*, 85–87.

44. I tend to use the term "commandment" for pointing to the *gestalt* of freedom both in the state of original grace and "in faith." This *gestalt* extends from the Decalogue to the Sermon on the Mount. I reserve the term "law" in its first and second use (see n.16) for the human encounter with God's will under the condition of sin. "Law" has an inherently heteronomous character because humans in their estrangement from God resent it. Since Christians are still involved in the eschatological struggle between "spirit" and "flesh" (Gal. 5:17), the notions of "law" and "commandment" both apply to their existence, although in different ways. In other words, there is no substantive difference between God's "law" and God's "commandments." The difference is one of reception: either under the condition of sin as encounter with God's will or as the *gestalt* of freedom in communion with God (see n.13). For Luther a decisive outcome of the eschatological fulfillment of faith in Christ is the *dilectio legis*, the delight in the law, "where the law is not anymore law" (*WA* 50, 565,18f). For this reason Ps. 119 with its rich and mixed use of "law," "commandment," "mandate," and "torah" remained for Luther the center of the Psalter. For a fine study on the complexity of the usage of "law" in Luther's theology, cf. Andreas H. Wöhle, "Dilectio legis: Zur Oszillation des Gesetzesbegriffes Martin Luthers im Licht seiner alttestamentlichen Predigten. Eine Quellenstudie" (Amsterdam: Unpublished PhD. diss., University of Amsterdam, 1995).

45. Yeago, "Martin Luther," 180.

46. *WA* 8: 458. *De abroganda missa privata Martini Lutheri sententia* (1521); Yeago's translation. For a discussion of the so-called "third use of the law," see n.16. Luther's way of relating Christ and the law is paralleled in the way the Spirit and the law are related in Article VI of the *Solid Declaration, Formula of Concord.* Cf. 965,36–966,8, in *Die Bekenntnisschriften der Evangelisch-Lutherischen Kirche* (Göttingen: Vandenhoeck & Ruprecht, 8th ed., 1979). Cf. *BC* 565, 11–566,12.

47. See n.16 on the question of a "third use of the law."

48. Regarding the interpretation of the Decalogue in Luther as a form of *halakah*, I am indebted to George Lindbeck's essay, "Martin Luther and the Rabbinic Mind," in *Understanding the Rabbinic Mind: Essays on the Hermeneutic of Max Kadushin,* ed. Peter Ochs (Atlanta: Scholars Press, 1990): 141–64. In addition Yeago has helped me to see that the "ethics" of the catechisms is found in the interconnections among (1) the exposition of the commandments (which form a unit with the First Article of the Creed); (2) the notion of Christ's lordship developed in the exposition of the Second Article of the Creed; and (3) the exposition of the Lord's Prayer, which describes the conflictual nature of the "holiness on earth" initiated by the Spirit (in the exposition of the Third Article). I attempt to exemplify all five of my points in this "ethics": the role of the commandments as the concrete form of a life with God, the ecclesial context, the connection between ethos and truth (*halakah* and *haggadah*, commandments and creed), the focus on desire (not only in Luther's reading of the final commandment(s) as prohibitions of the cupidity that breeds violence but especially in the realization of the Decalogue in the Our Father), and the equation of life according to the commandments and the freedom Christ has given us.

49. *BC,* 366.

50. Stanley Hauerwas, *The Peaceable Kingdom: A Primer in Christian Ethics* (Notre Dame: University of Notre Dame Press, 1983), 30–34.

51. This passage is found in Luther's exposition of the Second Article of the Creed in his Large Catechism, *BC,* 414.

52.* Cf. David Fredrickson's masterful reconstrual of a Pauline ecclesiology from the perspective of an "economy of power" for central elements that an ecclesial hermeneutics has to take into account. Nevertheless I remain unconvinced by the congregational exclusiveness with which he presents his central thesis. Despite a whole range of crucial insights, his account of the Pauline congregation seems to me to be ultimately too influenced by Habermasian assumptions and a theologically unexamined modernist agenda that guides the reconstructive exegesis. Why, for example, can a historicist argument be made, on the one hand, regarding Paul's asceticism—in order to question the use of his authority for a contemporary Christian defense of the institution of marriage—yet, on the other hand, the suggestion be made that Paul was concerned about something so utterly modern as "the self's becoming"? This influence becomes quite clear in his n.20, where he acknowledges his indebtedness to Habermas in his account of dokimazein. Yet Heinrich Schlier, for example, interprets Paul's use of *dokimazein* in relationship to the *nous,* which, according to Schlier, is for Paul the "sense of perception" of God's will, both for Jews and Gentiles. In "Vom Wesen der apostolischen Ermahnung nach Römerbrief 12,1–2," *Die Zeit der Kirche: Exegetische Aufsätze und Vorträge* (Freiburg: Herder, 2nd ed., 1958), 88ff. In contrast to Habermas' formal and procedural account of reason, the assumption here is a *nous* that is related to a reality that the individual and/or communal *dokimazein* can meet or miss. In addition I wonder whether a Pauline vision can be convincingly presented as a guide to moral deliberation in Lutheran ethics that brackets (1) the apostle's own authority in relationship to his congregations, (2) the canon's authority in relationship to the deliberating congregation, and (3) those "structures of responsibility" in which humans find themselves and to which both the Decalogue and the natural law tradition clearly point.

53.* I do assume that analyses of political, social, and economic life are always to a lesser or greater extent included in any form of ethical reflection and moral deliberation. Yet I do not want to make them an abstractly required element of an ecclesial hermeneutics because these analyses are far from unambiguous. Some are very obvious, some less so, and others are quite debatable or downright questionable. In difference with Rasmussen and Moe-Lobeda, I am also hesitant to include the "signs of the times" as an explicit principle in ecclesial hermeneutics. The reason is that everyone perceives something as "signs of the times" and regards those or a selection of them as decisive, but what they are is most often far from clear. The classical case that has cured me from using this concept is how both Paul Tillich and Emanuel Hirsch applied the concept of "kairos" in the early 1930s in opposite ways in relationship to the early National-Socialist movement. At that point it was far from obvious that Tillich's reading would turn out to be the right one and that the "liberation" and "people's movement" for freeing Germany from economic and political oppression would turn out to be a disastrous and demonic enterprise. For an introduction, cf. John Stroup, "Political Theology and Secularization Theory in Germany, 1918–1939: Emanuel Hirsch as a Phenomenon of His Time," in *Harvard Theological Review* 80, 3 (1987): 321–68; Robert P. Ericksen, *Theologians under Hitler* (New Haven: Yale University Press, 1985), 120–97; Jack Forstman, *Christian Faith in Dark Times: Theological Conflicts in the Shadow of Hitler* (Louisville: Westminster John Knox Press, 1992), 210–21. In other words, either certain problematics are so obvious that they demand serious attention by themselves (as the ecological crisis does), which makes the concept of "signs of the times" unnecessary, or certain problematics are complex and not quite so obvious, so that the concept "sign of the times" is not able to make them less ambiguous by classifying them under this category. Of course I am in favor of "calling things as they are," but placing a particular discernment backed by particular social and political analyses under the category "signs of the times" simply does not save it from contestation and potential error. It only implies some kind of "prophetic lead" that in some cases might be right, in others wrong. For example, when we read the encyclical *Evangelium Vitae*, does Pope John Paul II read the "signs of the times" correctly in seeing our Western world increasingly involved in a "culture of death"? I tend to agree with this perception and also with much of what he has to say as a consequence about abortion and euthanasia. But his reading is something that is contested by many Christians who tend to read "the signs of the times" quite differently.

54. I have in mind Bonhoeffer's stressing the importance of learning how to read Scripture over against ourselves instead of for ourselves. "The Presentation of New Testament Texts," in *No Rusty Swords* (London: Collins, 1970), 302–20. An ongoing ecclesial hermeneutics of the Decalogue and of the Sermon on the Mount especially will require this self-decentering exercise of reading Scripture over against ourselves. For a broader discussion of these issues, cf. the suggestive approach in Stephen E. Fowl and L. Gregory Jones, *Reading in Communion: Scripture and Ethics in Christian Life* (Grand Rapids, Mich.: Eerdmans, 1991).

55. *BC*, 368.

56.* Cf. Stortz's contribution for the importance of spiritual discipline embodied in particular practices as a central element of a Lutheran ethos.

57.* This is an important area of conversation and reflection in light of the challenge that Rasmussen and Moe-Lobeda's essay presents to the approach offered here. One can rightly argue that the Decalogue does not explicitly articulate the moral obligation to love and serve nonhuman creation. Nevertheless I think that an ongoing exegesis and scrutiny of God's commandments certainly implies unambiguous directives toward the right stewardship of creation. I am, however, quite hesitant to think of a "moral obligation" toward the nonhuman creation. "Morality" is a constitutive element of the inherently inter-human reality. It is constitutive neither of our primary relationship to God nor of our relationship to nonhuman creatures—except insofar as nonhuman creation is again related to other humans, for example, to future human generations. (Concerning our relationship to God, I distinguish between a constitutive primary relationship—God's relationship to us as creator—which is one of pure passivity from the human side—and a secondary relationship, comprising our human vocation as stewards, which is one of responsibility and accountability.) Now to assume that where no strictly moral obligation is found, license sets in, means one is seeing the world not as "creation" but as a bunch of "things" for free perusal and disposal, which is the very mode of existence *etsi Deus non daretur*. The Decalogue prohibits this mode of existence: In the First Commandment all of us are identified as creatures (cf. Luther's wonderful exposition of the First Commandment in his Small Catechism); the Third Commandment commands the honoring of the Sabbath, which should include all creatures in the resting of creation (cf. Moltmann, *God in Creation*, 276–96, and esp. the interesting reflections of Wannenwetsch, *Gottesdienst*, 328–38, on the relationship between the scope and limit of human responsibility and the Third Commandment); the commandment not to steal relates to all future generations; and the last commandments are directed to our coveting, our unchecked desires. The First Commandment also implies a fundamental and radical relationship of accountability to God for all that depends on our care and attention. That is what it means to be both a steward and a co-creature. The more that depends upon us, the more are we account-able and responsible. Therefore in relation to God, humans as co-creatures and as stewards are increasingly accountable and responsible to care for creation; in relation to our forebears, we have the obligation not to squander what we have received; and in relation to future generations, we have the obligation to pass on what we received. While humans as stewards undoubtedly are responsible to God also for nonhuman creation, we do not, however, have a direct moral oblig-ation to the forests and rivers, the atmosphere and wildlife. Nevertheless our scope of responsi-bility for them widens with their ever-increasing dependency on the right or wrong of our activ-ity. For the ethical implications of this widening of human responsibility, cf. especially Hans Jonas, *The Imperative of Responsibility: In Search of an Ethics for the Technological Age* (Chicago: University of Chicago Press, 1984); and William Schweiker, *Responsibility and Christian Ethics* (Cambridge: Cambridge University Press, 1995).

58.* Stanley Hauerwas has most successfully introduced the importance of "vision" for Christian ethics. Cf. esp. his "The Significance of Vision: Toward an Aesthetic Ethic," in *Vision and Virtue: Essays in Christian Ethical Reflection* (Notre Dame: University of Notre Dame Press, 1981), 30–47. But cf. also Stortz, who rightly emphasizes the importance of "seeing" (and thus forma-tion) in the section "Formation Tackles the Ordinary."

59. *BC*, 377.

60.* Stortz points out the importance of formation and the practice of individual prayer in for mation. The practice is understood as probably the most central practice through which our desires are continually redirected toward God as their source and goal. Only in and through this redirection do they receive their right measure in relationship to all the goods of creation.

61.* St. Augustine, *The Confessions*. Introduction, trans. and notes by Maria Boulding O.S.B. (Hyde Park, N.Y.: New City Press, 1997), 39. I have deep reservations about the presently fash-ionable but I think essentially misconceived reading of Augustine as denigrating the "body" and regarding "sex" as a post-fall phenomenon. Concerning the first issue, cf. the differentiated and nuanced account given by Margaret Miles in her books *Augustine on the Body* (Missoula: Scholars Press, 1979) and *Fulness of Life: Historical Foundations for a New Asceticism* (Philadelphia: Westminster Press, 1981), 62–78; and by Jean Bethke Elshtain, *Augustine and the Limits of Politics* (Notre Dame: University of Notre Dame Press, 1995). Augustine actually unmasked the hypocrisy behind the claim commonly found in late antiquity that the body was to be despised: "Neither does anyone hate his own body. For the apostle truly said, 'No one ever hated his own flesh.' And when some say that they would rather be without a body altogether, they entirely deceive themselves. For it is not their body but its heaviness and corruption which they hate. And so it is not no body, but an uncorrupted and very light body that they want" (*De Doctrina Christiana* I.24.24). Regarding sexuality, Augustine assumed that sexual intercourse inherently belonged to human life in par-adise (*City of God* XIV.26); after the fall sexuality had become disjunctive and incongruent with reason. Cf. Miles, *Augustine on the Body*, 70–77 for a differentiated discussion of Augustine's increasingly harsher views regarding "fallen sexuality" close to the end of his life. This complex-ity in Augustine's thought regarding "body" and "sexuality" leaves me unconvinced by the way Augustine's thought is characterized and criticized in Rasmussen's and Moe-Lobeda's chapter.

62. Cf. the interesting gestures toward a "new asceticism" in Miles, *Fulness of Life*.

63. For how seriously Luther took "covetousness" and for how much it mattered in his anthro-pology and economic ethics, cf. the study of Ricardo Rieth, *"Habsucht" bei Martin Luther: Ökonomi-sches und theologisches Denken, Tradition und soziale Wirklichkeit im Zeitalter der Reformation* (Weimar: Verlag Hermann Böhlaus Nachfolger, 1996), esp. the discussion of covetousness in the catechisms, 98–101.

64. The First Commandment's fulfillment in faith has its own distinct practice, which is the-matized in the Third Commandment—the sabbath-sanctification! Cf. Wannenwetsch, *Gottesdienst*, 328ff.

65. Bonhoeffer starts the first fragment of his *Ethics*, 21ff., with this startling, unforgettable insight into the radical nature of Christian ethics by presupposing Luther's "back in paradise" of Christian freedom: "The knowledge of good and evil seems to be the aim of all ethical reflec-tion. The first task of Christian ethics is to invalidate this knowledge. . . . Already in the possi-bility of the knowledge of good and evil Christian ethics discerns a falling away from the ori-gin. Man at his origin knows only one thing: God. It is only in the unity of this knowledge of

God that he knows of other men, of things, and of himself. He knows all things only in God, and God in all things. The knowledge of good and evil shows that he is no longer at one with this origin. In the knowledge of good and evil man does not understand himself in the reality of the destiny appointed in his origin, but rather in his own possibilities, his possibility of being good or evil. . . . The knowledge of good and evil is therefore separation from God. Only against God can man know good and evil."

66. The idea that the "natural law" is something "at hand" to be read from the structure of our rationality or the structure of our human nature is a modern phenomenon. For that reason natural law has been taken in modern times as an account of "how" to reach moral agreement that is neutral over against different worldviews and basic beliefs; it is seen as an ethical methodology transcending particularities. Yet for theologians such as Augustine, Aquinas, and Luther, albeit to different degrees, it is precisely *sub conditione peccati* that the "natural law" is decisively weakened. Russell Hittinger in *A Preserving Grace: Protestants, Catholics, and Natural Law*, ed. Michael Cromartie, 7, points to Aquinas' affirmation: "Now although God in creating man gave him this law of nature, the devil oversowed another law in man, namely, the law of concupiscence. . . . Since the law of nature was destroyed by concupiscence, man needed to be brought back to works of virtue, and to be drawn away from vice: for which purpose he needed the written law." (Grand Rapids, Mich.: Eerdmans, 1997). Thus for Aquinas the "old law" was a training in the natural law, which is not simply available to human reason. Pamela Hall puts Aquinas's view succinctly: "We must learn (or relearn) the natural law because sin obscures our understanding of it and of our end; at the same time, we discover that we cannot do what we know to be good. The work of the Old Law is to teach us the natural law." In *Narrative and the Natural Law: An Interpretation of Thomistic Ethics* (Notre Dame: University of Notre Dame Press, 1994), 48. These key elements of a theology of natural law were the ones eclipsed in the modern era. Natural law was no longer something essentially lost, something to be "remembered" under the guidance and tutorship of God's commandments. Rather it was simply "at hand," the self-evident principles of practical reason inherently accessible to every human agent per se. This explains why the "project of modernity" sought to reach a societal consensus on moral matters irrespective of particular religious convictions. Yet neither Aquinas's nor Luther's theological doctrine of natural law as such was intended to tell us much about "how" to reach moral agreement with non-Christians. For both such agreement is not reached *a priori*, at the universal level, but right in and through all kinds of ad hoc discussions of particular issues in positive law.

67.* Cf. the converging analysis of this matter under the heading "Epistemological" in the last section "Contemporary Challenges" of Benne's contribution.

68. For a good introduction, cf. *Catechism of the Catholic Church*, §§1776–1802 (New York: Doubleday, 1995), 490–95.

69. To be sure, the traditional Roman Catholic concept of conscience is also fundamentally an address by God. Yet when one listens to *Gaudium et Spes* (# 16), one gets the impression that God's voice just seems to be somewhat unclear and distant yet nevertheless genuinely "at hand": "His conscience is man's most secret core and his sanctuary. There he is alone with God whose voice echoes in his depths." Not so for Luther. Our estrangement from God has turned our conscience into a deeply ambiguous reality. It tends to frighten us, make the world close in on us, because, as Forde aptly put it, "It does not represent God's presence within us, it represents his absence, that we are left to ourselves." "Christian Life," 417.

70. Forde, "Christian Life," 417.

71. Exactly because of our essentially frightened conscience, the world tends to close in on us and becomes "too small." Luther described it with the image of "rustling leaf" of Lev. 26:36: "There is nothing smaller and more ignored than a dry leaf lying on the ground crawled on by worms and unable to protect itself from the dust. . . . But when the moment comes, horse, rider, lance, armor, king, princes, all the strength of the army and all power is frightened by its rustling. Are we not fine people? We have no fear of God's wrath and stand proudly, but yet are terrified and flee before the wrath of an impotent dry leaf. And such rustling of the leaf makes the world too small and becomes our wrathful God, whom we otherwise poopoo and defy in heaven and on earth," *WA* 19, 126,16ff; Forde's translation from "Christian Life," 418.

72.* Cf. Benne's discussion under "Ecclesiological" in "Contemporary Challenges" on why this points to a problem in Lutheranism.

73. An assumption strongly visible in Philip Melanchthon's work, for example.

74. Cf., for example, the material content of Kant's *Metaphysics of Ethics*, trans. J.W. Semple (Edinburgh: T&T Clark, 3rd ed., 1871).

75. I am aware that I am gesturing toward a wide field with these all too short intimations. For an accessible introduction into the concept of "moral notions," cf. Stanley Hauerwas, *Vision and Virtue* (Notre Dame: University of Notre Dame Press, 1981), 14–22; for a fine application of what I have in mind, cf. Bernd Wannenwetsch's essay, "'Intrinsically Evil Acts' or: Why Abortion and Euthanasia Cannot Be Justified," in *Ecumenical Ventures in Ethics*, eds. Reinhard Hütter and Theodor Dieter (Grand Rapids, Mich.: Eerdmans, 1998). For an excellent introduction to the concept of "intrinsically evil acts," cf. Martin Rhonheimer, "Intrinsically Evil Acts and the Moral Viewpoint: Clarifying a Central Teaching of *Veritatis Splendor*," in *The Thomist* 58 (1994), 1–39.

76.* It is true that Luther could say extremely positive things about the power of human reason, used in its proper limits, as Childs points out in the section "Dialogue and Witness in the World." If one thinks of the basic workings of theoretical reason (logic, mathematics), of the "poetic" reason of creating artifacts (buildings, machines), and of "practical" reason (conducting a meeting, governing, acting according to law and custom), Childs and his reference, Gerrish, are correct. One thinks especially of the positve role of reason in Luther's *Disputatio de homine* (1536), theses 4–6. Yet none of this means that Luther assumed humans would be able to act freely and well simply on grounds of the insights of reason (1. Disp. de hom. 18; 25–27. For a more detailed discussion of this topic, cf. Gerhard Ebeling, *Lutherstudien*. Vol. 2: *Disputatio De Homine*. 2nd Part (Tübingen: J.C.B.Mohr, 1982): 263–77. The most telling evidence concerning Luther's basic assumption about reason wounded by our sinful desires, habits, and practices can be found in a manual for the Christian prince, his *Commentary on Psalm 101* (1534). "This is not to condemn or reject law, sound reason, or Holy Scripture but rather the miserable admixture of the filth of our arrogance—the fact that we do not begin such a plan and proceeding with the fear of God and with a humble, earnest prayer, just as if it were enough to have a right and proper proposal and the intention to convert this plan into action speedily according to one's own ability. To do this is to despise God and to seek glory for yourself as the man who can do it. It is contrary to the First Commandment. Therefore such an admixture changes the best law into the greatest injustice, the finest reason into the greatest folly, and the Holy Scripture into the greatest error. For if the First Commandment is missing and does not give light, then none of the others will give proper light, and the understanding will be entirely faulty," *LW*, 13, 152f.

77.* Cf. Benne's nuanced and balanced interpretation of the concept of "vocation" in relationship to the places of responsibility in his section, "The Christian's Calling in the World."

78. In his *Commentary on Psalm 101* (n.76), Luther also addresses the question of natural law. It is not for him an abstract *a priori* "inherent in all heads that resemble human heads," *LW* 13:161. Instead the knowledge of natural law comes through contingent insights gained by particular people in particular historical circumstances. Natural gifts are granted contingently by God's providence, and virtues and skills are acquired through particular education and practices. Persons in whom these gifts, virtues, and skills coincide in an extraordinary way so as to achieve significant historical deeds are "heroes." Now and then God sends a "hero" who "knows how" to get society to work as it should in some respect or other. Yet "heroes" are primarily a way for Luther to account for exceptional moral character and/or political genius. Most of the time our access to natural law comes by way of the messiness of life in human community. "The world is indeed a sick thing; it is the kind of fur on which neither hide nor hair is any good. The healthy heroes are rare, and God provides them at a dear price. Still the world must be ruled, if men are not to become wild beasts. So things in the world in general remain mere patchwork and beggary" (164). Now while Luther's main concern obviously is with the practical matter of governing lawfully under predemocratic conditions, his basic insight into the moral phenomenon of the "hero" still makes sense, as long as it is not misunderstood in the sense of an *Übermensch* who stands above God's law.

79.* Perry provides excellent case studies of this kind of particular witness on the local level in the lives of Rev. Jehu Jones Jr., Sister Emma Francis, and in the Franckean Synod's stance against slavery.

80. Stanley Hauerwas, "The Truth about God: The Decalogue as Condition for Truthful Speech," in *Neue Zeitschrift für Systematishe Theologie und Religious philosophic* 40 (1998), 25.

81. *WA* 50, 659f; cf. Oswald Bayer, *Theologie* (Gütersloh: Gütersloher Verlagshaus, 1994), 61ff.

82. I am indebted to the suggestions and criticisms from the co-authors and the editors of this volume. In addition, I would like to thank Michael Cartwright, Stanley Hauerwas, Lois Malcolm, Bernd Wannenwetsch, and David Yeago for their comments and suggestions on an earlier draft.

Chapter 4: Practicing Christians

1.* All the authors in this book show concern for the transmission and reception of the Lutheran ethos. Robert Benne argues that the Holy Spirit enlivens a tradition that is marked by a dynamic ethos or way of life. Ethics is the systematic reflection on that way of life. I argue that practices are the instruments a tradition uses to articulate that distinctive ethos.

2. James M. Childs Jr. emphasizes the role of formation in Lutheran ethics in his *Faith, Formation, and Decision* (Minneapolis: Fortress Press, 1991).

3.* Cf. Alasdair MacIntyre, *After Virtue* (Notre Dame: University of Notre Dame Press, 1981), 175ff. A technique requires certain skills and is judged by the quality of the good produced, while a practice is a good in itself and is judged by standards internal to it. If prayer is assessed in terms of what it produces, it is no longer a practice, but a technique. If prayer is expected to achieve some goal, no matter how important the goal, it is probably being judged by standards external to it. To require that prayer be "liberatory," "oppositional," or "reconstructive" is to render prayer a technique. See n.4 in the chapter by Larry Rasmussen and Cynthia Moe-Lobeda. Matthew Lamb comments: "Unfortunately, much of the modern instrumentalist orientation has deformed Christian asceticism, prayer, and piety . . . into techniques rather than the genuine practices they are meant to be," in *The New Dictionary of Theology*, "Praxis," eds. Joseph A. Komonchak, Mary Collins, Dermot A. Lane (Collegeville: The Liturgical Press, 1987), 787.

4. Craig Dykstra and Dorothy C. Bass, "Times of Yearning, Practices of Faith," in *Practicing Our Faith*, ed. Bass (San Francisco: Jossey-Bass, 1997), 6–8.

5. See the suggestions of Timothy F. Lull, "The (Normative) Sexual Hole," *Dialog* 32, 1 (Winter 1993), 65–68.

6. Larry Rasmussen framed this question for me most powerfully. See our article "A Coast-to-Coast Conversation on Sexuality," in *A Reforming Church . . . Gift and Task: Essays from a Free Conference*, ed. Charles P. Lutz (Minneapolis: Kirk House Publishers, 1995), 151–72.

7. Cf. Reinhard Hütter, "The Church as Public: Dogma, Practice, and the Holy Spirit," *Pro Ecclesia* 3, 3 (Summer 1994), esp. 352–57.

8. Martin Luther, "On the Councils and the Church," LW 41, 150ff.

9.* Hütter, "Church," 354. In developing the notion of practices, I am exploring enactment of some of the key themes treated in other essays in this book: the doctrine of vocation (Benne, Childs); the doctrine of creation (Rasmussen and Moe-Lobeda); and the doctrine of the two kingdoms (Childs).

10. Hütter, "Church," 354–56.

11. Martin Luther, "Lectures on Galatians 1535, Chapters 1–4," LW 26, 256.

12. Leif Grane, "Luther, Baptism and Christian Formation," *Encounters with Luther* 2 (Gettysburg: Institute for Luther Studies, 1982), 217.

13. Robert W. Jenson, "The Return to Baptism," *Encounters with Luther* 2 (Gettysburg: Institute for Luther Studies, 1982), 225.

14. Gilbert C. Meilander, *The Theory and Practice of Virtue* (Notre Dame: University of Notre Dame Press, 1984), 100–126.

15. "Preface to the Small Catechism," BC, 340.

16.* For similar emphases in this book, see the chapter by David Fredrickson, who explores the Pauline emphasis on character rather than code, and Richard Perry, who traces the close link between who one is and what one does in African-American Lutheran ethics.

17. Martin Luther, "The Sermon on the Mount (Sermons) and The Magnificat," LW 21, 245.

18. "Large Catechism," BC, 411.

19. Robert Bellah, Richard Madsen, William M. Sullivan, Ann Swidler, and Steven M. Tipton, *Habits of the Heart* (Berkeley: University of California Press, 1985), 142ff.

20. H. Richard Niebuhr, *The Responsible Self* (San Francisco: Harper & Row, 1963).

21. "Large Catechism," BC, 379–98.

22. Cf. Stanley Hauerwas and David Burrell, "From System to Story," in *Truthfulness and Tragedy*, ed. Hauerwas (Notre Dame: University of Notre Dame Press, 1977), 15–39.

23. Iris Murdoch, *The Sovereignty of Good* (New York: Routledge & Kegan Paul, 1970), 37.

24. Luther, "Sermon," *LW* 21, 216.

25. Joseph Kotva, *The Christian Case for Virtue Ethics* (Washington, D.C.: Georgetown University Press, 1996), 87.

26. Cf. Karl Holl, *The Reconstruction of Morality*, trans. Fred W. Meuser and Walter R. Wietzke (Minneapolis: Augsburg Publishing House, 1979), 26, 36ff.

27.* Dietrich Bonhoeffer, *Ethics*, trans. Neville Horton Smith (New York: Macmillan, 1955), 84. In his chapter Fredrickson elaborates Pauline dimensions of christological formation in his exegesis of Phil. 2:5.

28.* Cf. Steven Ozment, *The Reformation in the Cities* (New Haven: Yale University Press, 1975), 152. In his chapter Benne underscores a similar problem of transmission for the contemporary church.

29. *Dr. Martin Luther's Large Catechism*, trans. J.L. Lenker (Minneapolis: Augsburg Publishing House, 1935), 35, 39, 59, 56.

30. Quoted in M. Reu, *Catechetics* (Chicago: Wartburg Publishing House, 1927), 86.

31. Martin Luther, "A Simple Way to Pray," *LW* 43, 193.

32. Ibid., 209.

33. Several resources translate Luther's practices of personal prayer into contemporary congregational use: Robin Maas, "A Simple Way to Pray: Luther's Instructions on the Devotional Use of the Catechism," in *Spiritual Traditions for the Contemporary Church*, eds. Maas and Gabriel O'Donnell, O.P. (Nashville: Abingdon, 1990), 162–70; Donald W. Johnson, *Praying the Catechism* (Winnipeg, Manitoba: Wallingford, 1995), and *Daily Texts: 1997* (Bethlehem, Pa.: The Interprovincial Board of Publications and Communications, Moravian Church in America, 1996).

34. George Lindbeck, "Martin Luther and the Rabbinic Mind," *Understanding the Rabbinic Mind*, ed. Peter Ochs (Atlanta: Scholars Press, 1990), 141.

35. Marc Lienhard, "Luther and Beginnings of Reformation," in *Christian Spirituality, vol 2: High Middle Ages and Reformation*, ed. Jill Raitt (New York: Crossroad, 1988), 288.

36. Luther, "Sermon on the Mount," *LW* 21, 357.

37. Luther, "Personal Prayer Book," *LW* 43, 13.

38. Jean Leclerq, "Monasticism and Asceticism: Western Christianity," in *Christian Spirituality*, vol. 1: *Origins to the Twelfth Century*, eds. Bernard McGinn, John Meyendorff, and Leclerq (New York: Crossroad, 1992), 113.

39. Martin Luther, "Preface to the Wittenberg Edition of Luther's German Writings (1539)," in *Martin Luther's Basic Theological Writings*, ed. Timothy F. Lull (Minneapolis: Fortress, 1989), 67.

40. Quoted in Richard Foster, *Celebration of Discipline* (San Francisco: HarperCollins, 1988), 34.

41. Luther, "A Simple Way to Pray," *LW* 43, 193.

42. Murdoch, *Sovereignty*, 37.

43. Luther, "A Simple Way to Pray," *LW* 43, 193–94.

44. Ibid., 200.

45. Ibid., 200.

46. "Augsburg Confession," V, VII, *BC*, 31–32.

47. Luther, "A Simple Way to Pray," *LW* 43, 200. A Jesuit who has prayed for years in the tradition of Ignatian spirituality talks about the journey of prayer being a journey from talking to listening. "I started out talking *at* God; then, it became talking *to* God; then, it was talking *with* God. As time wore on, prayer became a matter of listening *to* God, and now I find myself listening *for* God."

48.* In his counsel on prayer as in his catechisms, the Decalogue commands Luther's attention. Hütter develops this attention to the Decalogue in terms of law and commandments in his chapter.

49. Luther, "A Simple Way to Pray," *LW* 43, 200.

50. Ibid., 209–10.

51. Ibid., 207.

52. Robert Alter observes that particularly in the Hebrew Scriptures speech is "finally a technique for getting at the essence of things." Alter, *The Art of Biblical Narrative* (New York: Basic Books, 1981), 70.

53. Martin Luther, "Lectures on Genesis, Chapters 38–44," *LW* 7, 138.

54. Martin Luther, "Lectures on Galatians, 1519: Chapters 1–6," *LW* 27, 394.

55. Martin Luther, "Lectures on Genesis: Chapters 1–5," *LW* 1, 175.

56. "Large Catechism," *BC*, 411.

57. Don Saliers, *The Soul in Paraphrase: Prayer and the Religious Affections* (Cleveland: OSL Publications, 1991), 76.

58. Ernst Troeltsch, "Grundprobleme der Ethik," in *Gesammelte Schriften*, vol. 2 (Aalen, The Netherlands: Scientia, 1962), 621ff.

59. Cf. James M. Gustafson, *Christ and the Moral Life* (Chicago: University of Chicago Press, 1968), 130.

60. Luther, "The Large Catechism," *BC*, 411.

61. Rainer Maria Rilke, *Letters on Cézanne* (New York: Fromm International, 1985), 51. Cf. Simone Weil, *Waiting for God* (New York: Harper & Row, 1951), 105–16.

62. "I take 'as' to be the 'copula of imagination.'" Garrett Green, *Imagining God* (New York: Harper & Row, 1989), 73.

63. Lawrence A. Blum, *Moral Perception and Particularity* (New York: Cambridge University Press, 1994), 38–41, 57–61.

64. Luther, "The Small Catechism," *BC*, 343.

65. I am grateful for critical and constructive comment from the other authors of this book; from its editors, John Stumme and Karen Bloomquist; from my colleagues in the Lutheran diaspora: Aana Vigen, Christian Scharen, and Michael B. Aune; and from my on-site editor, William C. Spohn.

Chapter 5: African American Lutheran Ethical Action

1. Langston Hughes, *Selected Poems* (New York: Vintage, 1974), 291.

2. Drafts of this chapter were discussed with the Conference of International Black Lutherans whose members made helpful suggestions and corrections. I also want to express my appreciation to the staff of the Archives of the Evangelical Lutheran Church in America and the JKM Library of the Lutheran School of Theology at Chicago who assisted in locating material contained in this chapter. Finally I wish to acknowledge the Deaconess Community of the ELCA who in 1992 permitted me to study archival material on Sister Emma Francis.

3.* Robert Benne makes a persuasive case for why Lutheranism may be in danger of losing its core. Since, however, the Lutheran communion is growing worldwide, especially in Asia, Latin America, and Africa, the core of Lutheranism will be enhanced by the voices of feminists, womanists, and the multicultural movement. See sections three and four of his chapter.

4. See Vincent L. Wimbush, "The Bible and African Americans: An Outline of an Interpretive History," in *Stony the Road We Trod: African American Biblical Interpretation*, ed. Cain Hope Felder (Minneapolis: Fortress Press, 1991), 81–97, here 89–93.

5.* David Fredrickson's chapter points to the value of "testing." It is an important dimension for African American people. Political activity (which I understand as ethical action) must be tested by Scripture and the African American interpretation of Scripture if it is to be persuasive among African American people.

6. "A Harare Message of Black Lutherans," in *Theology and the Black Experience: The Lutheran Heritage Interpreted by African and African-American Theologians*, eds. Albert Pero and Ambrose Moyo (Minneapolis: Augsburg Publishing House, 1988), 265.

7.* James Childs's chapter raises an important question concerning our authority to speak on issues that matter to the Christian community. See his discussion in the section "By What Authority and by What Criteria?"

8. "Harare Message," 266.

9. Similar findings were made at the consultation "Justification and Justice: A Meeting of Lutheran Theologians of the Americas," held in Mexico City, Mexico (December 7–14, 1985).

10. John S. Mbiti, *African Religions and Philosophy* (Garden City, N.Y.: Doubleday Anchor Books, 1970), 3.

11. Ibid., 38.

12. Ibid., 49.

13.* Martha Stortz's chapter brings to the forefront a central dimension of African American ethics: training in appropriate practices. The Civil Rights Movement is a prime example of how important prayer was in the formation of people in their struggle for justice.

14. Mbitu, 279. Manas Buthelezi makes a similar point in "Theological Grounds for an Ethic of Hope," in *The Challenge of Black Theology in South Africa*, ed. Basil Moore (Atlanta: John Knox Press, 1973), 147–56.

15. Peter J. Paris, *The Spirituality of African Peoples: The Search for a Common Moral Discourse* (Minneapolis: Fortress Press, 1995).

16. Ibid., 22.

17. Ibid, chap. 6.

18. E. Franklin Frazier, *The Negro Church in America* (New York: Schocken Books, 1974), chap. 1.

19. Lawrence W. Levine, *Black Culture and Black Consciousness: Afro-American Folk Thought from Slavery to Freedom* (Oxford: Oxford University Press, 1977), 4–5.

20.* Fredrickson's chapter makes an important observation concerning the congregation as a place of moral deliberation. For African Americans the congregation (church) was often the only place where one could reflect upon, critically examine, and determine appropriate actions in a context determined by racism.

21. Peter J. Paris, *The Social Teaching of the Black Churches* (Philadelphia: Fortress Press, 1986), 9–10.

22. C. Eric Lincoln and Lawrence H. Mamiya, *The Black Church in the African American Experience* (Durham and London: Duke University Press, 1990), 10–16.

23. Ibid., 15–16.

24. Paris, *The Social Teaching*, 6.

25. I am indebted to Peter J. Paris and his work in this area. What follows reflects a heavy reliance on his thinking. Paris developed "ideal typical" responses of priest, prophet, political, and nationalist in "The Bible and the Black Churches," in *The Bible and Social Reform*, ed. Ernest R. Sandeen (Philadelphia: Fortress Press, 1982), 133–54; in *Black Religious Leaders: Conflict in Unity* (Knoxville: Westminster/John Knox, 1991), 15–28; and in "The Public Role of the Black Churches," in *The Church's Public Role: Retrospect and Prospect* (Grand Rapids, Mich.: Eerdmans, 1993), 43–62.

26. Paris, "The Bible," 136–40; *Black Religious Leaders*, 17–19; and "The Public Role," 47–49.

27. Idem, "The Bible," 140–44; *Black Religious Leaders*, 20–21; and "The Public Role," 49–51.

28. Idem, "The Bible," 144–48; *Black Religious Leaders*, 21–22; and "The Public Role," 51–54.

29. Idem, "The Bible," 148–51; *Black Religious Leaders*, 22–24; and "The Public Role," 54–56.

30. James Kenneth Echols, "The Two Kingdoms: A Black American Lutheran Perspective," in *Theology and the Black Experience*, 110–32.

31.* In this book Childs provides a helpful summary of "two kingdoms" thinking in the section "Ethical Witness in the Two Realms Tradition."

32. Echols, "The Two Kingdoms," 119–23.

33. Simon S. Maimela, "The Twofold Kingdom: An African Perspective," in *Theology and the Black Experience*, 105–6.

34. Ibid., 107–8.

35. Bishop Payne's ministry also has political dimensions to it. I have limited myself to his "Lutheran" years.

36. Jones was one of several children born to Jehu and Abigail Jones Sr., free African Americans. Jones's family was part of the African American elite of Charleston, South Carolina, because of their wealth. See Larry Koger, *Black Slaveowners: Free Black Slave Masters of South Carolina, 1790–1860* (Jefferson, N.C.: McFarland & Co., 1985), 153.

37. Jeff G. Johnson, *Black Christians: The Untold Lutheran Story* (St. Louis: Concordia Publishing House, 1991), 105–29. Johnson argues that Bachman succeeded in developing an "urban strategy" for reaching African Americans in Charleston. I disagree. African American churches were closed in Charleston because of the Denmark Vesey and Nat Turner Rebellions. I contend that the rise of African American membership at St. John's was due to that fact rather than to other factors.

38. "The Colored Ev. Luth. Church in Philadelphia, Pennsylvania," *The Lutheran Observer* 1, No. 27 (March 1, 1834), 212.

39. *The Lutheran Observer* 3, 37 (May 6, 1836), 174.

40. *The Lutheran Observer* 2 (1833), 181.

41. Jones, "Letter 'To the Rev'd Ministers & Vestrymen of the German Lutheran Churches St. Michael & Zion,'" Lutheran Archives Center at the Lutheran Theological Seminary at Philadelphia (October 9, 1834).

42. Jehu Jones Jr., "Slaves without Masters," in *The African Repository and Colonial Journal* 15, 11 (June 1839), 178–80.

43. See Gayraud Wilmore, *Black Religion and Black Radicalism: An Interpretation of the Religious History of Afro-American People* 2d ed. (Maryknoll, N.Y.: Orbis Books, 1983), 92–95; and Julie Winch, *Philadelphia's Black Elite: Activism, Accommodation, and the Struggle for Autonomy, 1787–1848* (Philadelphia: Temple University Press, 1988).

44. Winch, *Philadelphia's Black Elite,* 202 n.65.

45. "A New Ev. Luth. Church for Colored people in Philadelphia," 212.

46. Sister Emma Francis (1875–1945) was born on St. Kitts Island to the Rev. Joseph and Mary H. Francis. See "A Short Sketch of My Life," written about 1922 (Archives, Lutheran Deaconess House, Philadelphia).

47. Ibid., 1.

48. Ibid., 5.

49. Sister Emma Francis letter to Director Sister Anna Ebert (D.), 2.

50. Letter to Rev. E. F. Bachmann, D.D., (N.D.), 4.

51. Letter to Sister Anna (January 29, 1937), 2, 4.

52. Letter to Sister Anna (July 16, 1931), 2.

53. *BC,* 78–79.

54. One journal entry indicates that Payne was expecting to join by confirmation, but there is no record this occurred. See Daniel Alexander Payne, "Journal, 1835–1837," in Josephus Coan, *Daniel Alexander Payne: Christian Educator* (Philadelphia: A. M. E. Book Concern, 1935), 20–47, here 27.

55. Daniel Alexander Payne, *Recollections of Seventy Years* (New York: Arno Press and The New York Times, 1968), chap. 6. Payne was licensed by the Franckean Synod in 1837 and ordained in 1839.

56. Ibid., 17.

57. Ibid., 28.

58. Daniel Alexander Payne, "A Speech Favoring the Adoption of the Report on Slavery," *Lutheran Herald and Journal of the Franckean Synod* 1, 15 (August 1, 1839), 113–14. The quotes that follow in the text also come from this speech.

59. Payne, "Journal," 31. Emphasis added.

60. Samuel S. Schmucker, *Elements of Popular Theology.* 5th ed. (Philadelphia: J. S. Miles, 1845), 199.

61. Payne, "A Speech Favoring the Adoption," 114.

62. Proceedings of the Hartwick Synod (1836), 21.

63. The phrase "Comeouter" has its origins in Revelation 18:4, "Come out from her, my people, that you receive not of her plagues." Congregations "came out" of their denominations because the denominations failed to take a strong public stance against slavery. See John R. McKivigan's *The War against Proslavery Religion: Abolitionism and the Northern Churches, 1830–1865* (Ithaca: Cornell University Press, 1984); and idem, "The Antislavery 'Comeouter' Sects: A Neglected Dimension of the Abolitionist Movement," *Civil War History* 26, 2 (1980), 142–60.

64. Constitution (1839), Art. VII, Sec. 3, 9, 53.

65. Douglas C. Stange, "The One Hundred and Twenty-fifth Anniversary of a Fraternal Appeal," *Concordia Historical Institute Quarterly* 40 (1967), 43–47. The quotes that follow in the text also come from this document.

66. Douglas C. Stange, *Radicalism for Humanity: A Study of Lutheran Abolitionism* (St. Louis: Oliver Slave, 1970), 34, as quoted from the *Journal of the Franckean Synod of the Evangelic Lutheran Church* (1851), 16.

67. Stange, "Anniversary," 46.

68. Ibid., 45. The quotes that follow in the text also come from this document.

69. Stange, *Radicalism for Humanity,* 27, as quoted from *The Lutheran Herald,* 4 (1842), 42.

70. Ibid., 27–28, as quoted from *The Lutheran Herald N.S.* I, 2 (1844), (n. p.).

71. See Joe Holland and Peter Henriot, S.J.'s *Social Analysis: Linking Faith with Justice,* rev. and

enlarged ed. (Maryknoll, N.Y. and Washington, D. C.: Orbis Books and Dove Communications, 1983).

72.* Reinhard Hütter's discussion of God's commandments as a way to see rightly a situation correlates well with my discussion of social analysis.

73. Herbert O. Edwards, "Toward a Black Christian Social Ethic," *Journal of the Interdenominational Theological Center* 40, 2 (Spring 1975), 97–108, here 107.

74. Major Jones, *Christian Ethics for Black Theology* (Nashville: Abingdon Press, 1974), chap. 1.

75.* Larry Rasmussen and Cynthia Moe-Lobeda emphasize precisely what African American Lutherans present to the Lutheran Church. The challenge is always discerning what aspects of the Lutheran legacy are appropriate for our context. As a matter of fact, African Americans have always understood themselves as a "re-forming" body within Christianity.

76. Albert Pero, "Black, Lutheran, and American," in *Theology and the Black Experience*, 150–69.

77. Ibid., 152–53.

78. Peter J. Paris, *The Social Teaching*, 10–13.

79. Daniel Alexander Payne, "Letter to Rev. Dr. W. A. Passavant" (Nov. 7, 1888), in G. H. Gerberding, *Life and Letters of W.A. Passavant, D.D.* (Greenville: Young Lutheran Co., 1906), 531.

Chapter 6. Ethics and the Promise of God

1. In an article by Brent Sockness entitled, "Luther's Two Kingdoms Revisited: A Response to Reinhold Niebuhr's Criticism of Luther," *The Journal of Religious Ethics* 20, 1 (Spring 1992): 93–110, the author tracks the fluidity of Luther's thought from the first part of "Temporal Authority" to the later work on the Sermon on the Mount as a way of demonstrating how difficult it is to interpret Luther's doctrine. Although his concern is to engage Niebuhr's criticism, his discussion helps to explain the extensive debates about what Luther really thought.

2. Quoted in *Two Kingdoms and One World*, ed. Karl H. Hertz (Minneapolis: Augsburg, 1976), 83–84.

3. *Lutheran Churches: Salt or Mirror of Society?* ed. Ulrich Duchrow (Geneva: Lutheran World Federation,1977), 12.

4. Quoted in Hertz, ed., *Two Kingdoms*, 128.

5.* James Kenneth Echols, "The Two Kingdoms: A Black American Perspective," in *Theology and the Black Experience*, ed. Albert Pero and Ambrose Moyo (Minneapolis: Augsburg, 1988): 110–32. See in Richard Perry's chapter his helpful and more extensive discussion of James Echols's work on the two realms doctrine and the African American tradition.

6. Helmut Thielicke, *Theological Ethics*, 1, ed. William H. Lazareth (Philadelphia: Fortress Press, 1966), 364–73.

7. See Duchrow, ed., *Lutheran Churches*, 244. For Paul Tillich the two realms vision of orthodox Lutheranism represents an inadequate view of history in which history has become no more than the scene of the saving of God in Christ. That having been done, nothing new can be expected from it; individual salvation is all that is really significant in God's activity. *Systematic Theology*, 3 (Chicago: University of Chicago Press, 1963), 355.

8. Martin Luther, "Temporal Authority: To What Extent It Should Be Obeyed," in *LW*, 45, 102.

9. Martin Luther, "The Sermon on the Mount," in *LW*, 21, 113.

10. Thielicke, *Theological Ethics*, 1, 373–78.

11. Karl Holl, *The Reconstruction of Morality*, eds. James Luther Adams and Walter F. Bense, trans. Fred W. Meuser and Walter R. Wietzke (Minneapolis: Augsburg, 1979), 133.

12. Heinrich Bornkamm, *Luther's Doctrine of the Two Kingdoms in the Context of His Faith*, trans. Karl H. Hertz (Philadelphia: Fortress Press, 1964), 34.

13. Gustaf Wingren, *Lutheran Vocation*, trans. Carl C. Rasmussen (Philadelphia: Muhlenberg Press, 1957), 46.

14. José Míguez Bonino, *Toward a Christian Political Ethics* (Philadelphia: Fortress Press, 1983), 25.

15. David C. Steinmetz, *Luther in Context* (Bloomington: Indiana University Press, 1986),124. Quoted in Sockness, "Luther's Two Kingdoms Revisited," 107.

16. Míguez, *Toward a Christian*, 23.

17. See the discussion of Bonhoeffer in Charles E. Ford, "Dietrich Bonhoeffer, the Resistance, and the Two Kingdoms," *Lutheran Forum* 27, 3 (August 1993), 28–34.

18. See James M. Childs Jr., "The Confession's Impact on Recent Social Ethics," *Lutheran Forum* 14, 2 (Pentecost 1980),16–22. This article was a review of the social statements of American Lutheran churches in light of the two kingdoms dimensions of the Augsburg Confession.

19. William H. Lazareth, "Luther's 'Two Kingdoms' Ethic Reconsidered," in *Christian Social Ethics in a Changing World*, ed. John C. Bennett (New York: Association Press, 1966), 131.

20. Hertz, *Two Kingdoms*, 342–46; Paul Tillich, *Systematic Theology*, 3, 354–61.

21. Wolfhart Pannenberg, *Ethics*, trans. Keith Crim (Philadelphia: Westminster, 1981), 129.

22. Ibid., 130.

23. Wolfhart Pannenberg, "The Kingdom of God and the Foundation of Ethics," in *Theology and the Kingdom of God* (Philadelphia: Westminster, 1969), 110–12.

24. James M. Childs, Jr., *Faith, Formation, and Decision* (Minneapolis: Fortress Press, 1992), 22–23. This is a crucial point on which I have tried to be very clear in my own writing.

25. Carl E. Braaten, *Eschatology and Ethics* (Minneapolis: Augsburg, 1974), 110.

26. Childs, *Faith, Formation*, especially chs. 2 and 3.

27. "The Church in Society: A Lutheran Perspective," a Social Statement of the Evangelical Lutheran Church in America, adopted at the Churchwide Assembly, August 28–September 4, 1991, 2.

28. Braaten, *Eschatology and Ethics*, 117.

29. "Church in Society," 2.

30. Thielicke is a forerunner of this understanding in his description of our time as living between the ages or within the overlapping of the ages: the old age of our perduring fallen world and the new age of God's rule that Christ has brought into our history. Thielicke wants to recast Luther's two realms in terms of these two ages. *Theological Ethics*, 1, 379–82.

31.* Martin Luther, *A Treatise on Christian Liberty*, trans. W. A. Lambert; Rev. Harold J. Grimm (Philadelphia: Fortress Press, 1957), 7. I find myself very much in accord with Reinhard Hütter's critique of much of modern, mainstream Protestant ethics and with his account of freedom and the law. I would simply add, as I have tried to do in this chapter, that the freedom of the Christian is a basis not for setting aside the law but for dealing with the terrors of interpreting and acting in love in accordance with the law in an ambiguous and conflicted world. Robert Benne's discussion of the "theological challenge" in his chapter corresponds to Hütter's critique of Protestantism and would also seem to lead us into affirming the law in the life of Christian freedom.

32. Dietrich Bonhoeffer, *The Cost of Discipleship*, rev. ed., trans. R. H. Fuller (New York: Macmillan Co., 1967), 55ff.

33. Paul Althaus, *The Ethics of Martin Luther*, trans. Robert C. Schultz (Philadelphia: Fortress Press, 1972), 5–6.

34.* Benne, whose account of Lutheran ethics in the two kingdoms tradition in this book exemplifies the best of contemporary Lutheran faithfulness to that tradition, is certainly correct in emphasizing Luther's realism as well as the fact that Lutheran ethics does not lead to specific public policy resolution. These are correlated with his further observation that public policy pronouncements are on the outermost concentric circle of the church's purposes and have less authority, since they are further away from the religious and moral core. I do not contest this analysis; it is consistent with my own comments on decision in an ambiguous world. Nonetheless I have tried to suggest an alternative model of authority to that of certitude that I believe draws the church's moral struggles with ambiguous but important ethical issues more directly into its authoritative witness in the world. Indeed Benne himself suggests that there are Christian perspectives that bear upon public policy debates even if there are no Christian public policies per se. Presumably these perspectives are drawn from the "core" and are witnessed to as the church engages the issues.

35. For a discussion of our fulfillment in the image of God as a hope for the resurrection in the kingdom of God, see my book, *Christian Anthropology and Ethics* (Philadelphia: Fortress Press, 1978), 98–100; 116–17.

36.* In *Ethics in Business: Faith at Work* (Minneapolis: Fortress Press, 1995), ch. 8, I have a lengthier discussion of the theological foundations of environmental ethics in the context of the responsibilities of business. In this book the chapter by Larry Rasmussen and Cynthia Moe-Lobeda eloquently takes up the challenge of an earthly ethic, adding the critical dimension of the theology of the cross. In n.51 of Hütter's chapter, in response to Rasmussen and Moe-Lobeda, he expresses reluctance to entertain the notion of a "moral obligation" toward nonhuman creation, since morality "is an inherently interhuman reality." The analysis that follows upon that contention is certainly cogent. I would ask, however, whether my claim that the values of God's promised future are normative for our pursuit of the good in the present does not create a moral obligation to seek the good of the whole creation as an ecological unity, given the added point that God's future salvation is for the whole person and the whole world.

37. "Give Us this Day Our Daily Bread: Sufficient, Sustainable Livelihood for All" (Division for Church in Society, Evangelical Lutheran Church in America, October 1996), 19.

38. Childs, Christian Anthropology, 117–21.

39. Joseph A. Sittler, The Structure of Christian Ethics (Baton Rouge: Louisiana State University, 1958), 64.

40.* Martha Stortz's chapter serves us well in this regard and helps us to see the resources within the Lutheran tradition for character formation.

41. Luther, A Treatise on Christian Liberty, 30–31.

42. Childs, Faith, Formation, chaps. 4–7 deal with character formation and the Beatitudes. Gutiérrez is cited on 41.

43. I am much indebted in my understanding of the meaning of agape to Gene Outka, Agape (New Haven: Yale University Press, 1972); and to Victor Paul Furnish, The Love Command in the New Testament (Nashville: Abingdon Press, 1972). Outka provides a threefold analysis of love that involves equal regard, self-sacrifice, and mutuality.

44.* Outka, Agape, Part 3. David Fredrickson's chapter provides a vivid portrait of this sort of development and deliberation in the Pauline church. His account also dovetails nicely with the remarks I will presently share on the dialogical nature of the Christian ethic.

45. See Jan Milic Lochman, Signposts to Freedom, trans. David Lewis (Minneapolis: Augsburg Publishing House, 1982), passim; Paul Althaus, The Divine Command (Philadelphia: Fortress Press, 1966); and Walter R. Bouman, "The Concept of the 'Law' in the Lutheran Tradition," Word and World, 3, 4 (Fall 1983): 413–22 for helpful discussions of the role of law in the moral life of the redeemed.

46. Elizabeth Bettenhausen, "The Concept of Justice and a Feminist Lutheran Social Ethic," in The Annual of the Society of Christian Ethics, 1986, 173.

47.* "Church in Society," 5–6. Fredrickson's chapter also makes the point that moral deliberation or dialogue in the Pauline congregations was for the purpose of discerning the will of God Overall Fredrickson's research appears to provide New Testament underpinnings in the Pauline tradition for the kind of "dialogue in community" or "community of moral deliberation" that I have been trying to lay out. It seems also that the approach to ethics by Paul and his congregations reflects an understanding of authority commensurate with the idea of authority that I have been exploring in this chapter. Moreover it may not only be the Pauline tradition that displays this pattern. Research by my colleague Mark Allan Powell on the "binding and loosing" passages in Matthew also supports a program for community-based ethical discernment in the Matthean church (as yet unpublished).

48.* In his chapter Perry has called our attention to the importance of social location. This and his discussion of the "elements of ethical action" serve to underscore the particularities in and through which ethical perspectives are shaped. The dialogue I am urging inside the community of faith and in public witness is needed both to appreciate the texture that such influences provide for the ethical fabric of the Christian community and to discern common and new directions that all can embrace.

49. B. A. Gerrish, Grace and Reason: A Study in the Theology of Luther (Oxford: Clarendon Press, 1962), 25–26.

50.* Childs, Ethics in Business, 143, discusses the limits of dialogue. Though this book develops the concept of dialogue in the pluralistic world of business as an avenue of Christian witness, I have tried throughout to maintain a sense of realism and the necessity of faithfulness to the integrity of the faith. I find the discussion in Hütter's chapter on recovering the natural law under the conditions of pluralism to be a helpful adjunct to my discussion of dialogue in public Christian witness in a world of diversity.

51. Hans Küng, Global Responsibility: In Search of a New World Ethic (New York: Crossroad, 1991).

52. Ronald F. Thiemann, *Religion in Public Life* (Washington, D.C.: Georgetown University Press, 1996).

Chapter 7: Pauline Ethics

1. If one undertakes this task expecting to find specific teachings normative for individuals, then one must be prepared for surprises. Conservatives and liberals alike will be dismayed to find Paul advocating ethical positions that are unsuited to their own causes. A good example of this is Paul's view of the human body, which informs the statements he makes about sexual practice. Dale Martin in *The Corinthian Body* (New Haven: Yale University Press, 1995) demonstrates that only with the blinders of anachronism can Paul's asceticism be ignored and the apostle be regarded as the champion of heterosexuality. Yet who in current sexuality debates advocates Paul's position: ascetic control of the body and marriage as preventative measure against desire?

2.* For the challenges to this approach in Lutheran ethics and an outline for moving forward, see Robert Benne's concluding remarks in his chapter.

3.* This approach to Lutheran ethics is illustrated by Larry Rasmussen and Cynthia Moe-Lobeda's chapter.

4. Today the term "political" is often used derisively as a synonym for deceitful and secretive power plays. I emphasize just the opposite. To be political means to conduct oneself publicly and to put power in the context of persuasion with a strict avoidance of force. "Democracy" has suffered almost as much as "political" in the common notion that it simply means voting on already established options. I use the term "democratic" in line with the classical sense of power in the hands of the people. This means that "democratic" includes raising issues and public argument aiming toward consensus.

5. For a previous attempt to interpret Paul's thought in political categories, see D. Fredrickson, "Free Speech in Pauline Political Theology," *Word & World* 12 (1992): 345–51.

6.* Free speech in the modern period tends to loose its political mooring and drift into the right of individual "self-expression." Reinhard Hütter in this book sees something like this turn as the core fallacy of Protestant ethics. His masterful detection of self-legislation under the cover of traditional Lutheran themes is an appropriate warning against individualism in my attempt to think about Lutheran ethics in terms of Pauline free speech. Yet his constructive proposal for a decentered self does not fit with Paul, who was concerned that persons not considered selves in the ancient world be empowered to speak, in fact to become selves. Today this is as pressing an issue as dethroning the autonomous self. Since for Paul the self's becoming always takes place in the context of other voices, he is not defending autonomy by promoting free speech. Furthermore as we will see below, he emphasizes the right of all believers to initiate moral discussion in all matters. Decentering the self goes too far if it discourages such initiation.

7. See R. Bultmann, *The Second Letter to the Corinthians* (Minneapolis: Augsburg, 1985), 85. Luther favored free speech, but beginning in the last part of the nineteenth century, interest in subjectivity took over, and the ancient definition as "boldness in words" was dropped. See D. Fredrickson, "*Parrēsia* in the Pauline Epistles," in *Friendship, Flattery, and Frankness of Speech: Studies on Friendship in the New Testament World*, ed. J. Fitzgerald (Leiden: E. J. Brill, 1996), 163–65.

8. Plutarch, *How to Tell a Flatterer from a Friend* 51 C; Philo, *Who Is the Heir?* 21. Unless otherwise indicated, references to ancient literature are to the Loeb Classical Library.

9.* Richard Perry's chapter traces the abolitionist argument in Lutheran synods prior to the Civil War. He tells of the power of African American Lutherans to change minds through argument; he also narrates the exclusion of their voices and resistance even to their claims being made public. Both stories are necessary memories for Lutherans. His essay raises the critical question of how Paul's vision of the church can be realized when groups of persons are excluded from speech or intimidated into silence. Can others speak for them until they are permitted to speak openly? Can their suffering itself be presented to the church as an argument? In Pauline terms, can their groaning become the church's prayer in the presence of God (Rom. 8:18-27)?

10. For *pepoithēsis* as the psychological basis for free speech, see Josephus, *Jewish Antiquities* 19.317–18; 1 Clement 35.2; Phil. 1:14; Eph. 3:12.

11. Against E. Käsemann, *Perspectives on Paul* (Philadelphia: Fortress, 1971): 138–66. For a critique of Käsemann and an alternative proposal stressing moral formation as the key to the letter/Spirit distinction, see S. Westerholm, "Letter and Spirit: The Foundation of Pauline Ethics,"

New Testament Studies 30 (1984): 229–48. Something like Paul's letter/Spirit distinction existed in the philosophic critique of the written code's coercion and inability to bring about justice in the city. For remarkable parallels to 2 Cor. 3 on this point, see Dio Chrysostom, *Oration* 76.1–4.

12.* James M. Childs in this book documents the rediscovery of God's future (what Paul points to by "Spirit") as a critical component in Christian ethics, especially as it overcomes the dichotomy of personal faith and social action often associated with the Lutheran doctrine of two kingdoms. Childs's emphasis on God's promise energizing persons for witness captures the Pauline move to ground confidence in the work of the Spirit and to place it in the context of the church as assembly rather than in the individual's consciousness of God.

13. "Example" here is not for imitation but for proof. For this use of example in rhetoric, see B. Fiore, *The Function of Personal Example in the Socratic and Pastoral Epistles* (Rome: Biblical Institute, 1986), 26–33.

14. See Fredrickson, "*Parrēsia* in the Pauline Epistles," 177–78. See Plato, *Phaedrus* 243B; Epictetus, *Discourse* 3.22.15–16. By the face the person can be known. According to ancient physiognomists, there was no better part of the human body for detecting character traits and temperament.

15. Epictetus, *Discourse* 3.22.18–19, 93–95; Dio Chrysostom, *Oration* 32.11.

16.* The mirror played an important role in the theory of example in Greco-Roman moral exhortation. The person progressing in virtue was to look at a worthy person from the past as if looking in a mirror. The image was simultaneously the goal to be striven toward and the face of the one looking. Such gazing worked transformation. Paul's reference to the mirror reinforces his rejection of Scripture as written code and underscores his reliance both upon face to face relations in the church and upon a theory of example in his appropriation of Scripture as witness of the Spirit's work. For Luther's similar emphasis on transformation within a communal setting as progress into the image of Christ, see Martha Stortz's chapter.

17. Aside from some Cynics and Clement of Alexandria, ancient authors used this term for linguistic interaction between persons rather than the conformity of the individual to an ethical ideal. For the term in democratic Athens, see N. Loraux, "Reflections of the Greek City on Unity and Division," in *City States in Classical Antiquity and Medieval Italy*, eds. A. Molho, K. Raaflaub, and J. Emlen (Ann Arbor: University of Michigan, 1991), 35. For later developments, see E. Gruen, "The Polis in the Hellenistic World," in *Nomodeiktes: Greek Studies in Honor of Martin Ostwald*, eds. R. Rosen and J. Farrell (Ann Arbor: University of Michigan, 1993): 339–54. The sense of initiation and even innovation is underscored by the fact that by the fourth century B.C.E. the term was defined in opposition to *idiōtēs*: a citizen present at the assembly who participated by voting only, not by speeches and other forms of influence. See J. Ober, *Mass and Elite in Democratic Athens: Rhetoric, Ideology, and the Power of the People* (Princeton: Princeton University, 1989), 106–9.

18. Wayne Meeks appropriately draws attention to the boldness of early Christians naming themselves *ekklēsia* in light of this term's association with democracy. See *The First Urban Christians: The Social World of the Apostle Paul* (New Haven: Yale University Press, 1983), 108. He does not, however, develop this insight into a principle of Paul's ecclesiology as I am proposing here. At times Luther's ecclesiology is expressed with the help of political imagery; see "On the Papacy in Rome" (1520), *LW* 39, 65; "On the Councils and the Church" (1539), *LW* 41, 143–45. This is especially the case when the Lord's Supper as the foundation of Christian community is stressed; see "The Blessed Sacrament of the Holy and True Body of Christ, and the Brotherhoods" (1519), *LW* 35,51: "Hence it is that Christ and all saints are one spiritual body, just as the inhabitants of a city are one community and body, each citizen being a member of the other and of the entire city. All the saints, therefore, are members of Christ and of the church, which is a spiritual and eternal city of God. . . . To receive this sacrament in bread and wine, then, is nothing else than to receive a sure sign of this fellowship and incorporation with Christ and all the saints. It is as if a citizen were given a sign, a document, or some other token to assure him that he is a citizen of the city, a member of that particular community." For the church as a freedom bestowing community in analogy to the city, see *LW* 35, 57, 60.

19. The occurrence of *dokimazein* in 1 Thess. 5:21 deserves a brief comment. Although there is some support for thinking of "testing all things" as a precaution against an overzealous attitude toward the work of the Spirit, it makes better sense here to interpret testing itself as spiritual on the same order as not despising prophecy and not quenching the Spirit. As such it is the neces-

sary precondition to the moral life defined by Paul in terms found also in Greco-Roman moral philosophy: "Hold fast to the good and abstain from every form of evil."

20.* My debt to the moral theory of Jürgen Habermas for interpreting *dokimazein* needs to be recognized. For testing in Habermas, see W. Rehg, *Insight and Solidarity: A Study in the Discourse Ethics of Jürgen Habermas* (Berkeley: University of California Press, 1994), 56–83. It is an intriguing question whether communicative ethics has Luther as one of its ancestors. The connection is the reformer's insistence that the local congregation has the right and responsibility to test all things. Luther regarded the congregation's office of judging doctrine as the foundation of the other offices of ministry that the baptized share; see "Concerning the Ministry" (1523), *LW* 40, 31–34; and "Temporal Authority: To What Extent It Should Be Obeyed" (1523), *LW* 45, 117. The reform of the church depends upon this freedom to test; see "Against the Roman Papacy, An Institution of the Devil" (1545), *LW* 41, 269. For testing in congregations, see Gert Haendler, *Luther on Ministerial Office and Congregational Function* (Philadelphia: Fortress, 1981), 55–66. I thank my colleague Gary Simpson for pointing out the similarity between this aspect of Luther's ecclesiology and communicative ethics. Childs's call in this book for "dialogue among the people of God and with the world" implements the Pauline notion of testing.

21. Aristotle, *Politics* 2.1.5.

22. See, for example, S. Fowl, *The Story of Christ in the Ethics of Paul: An Analysis of the Function of the Hymnic Material in the Pauline Corpus* (Sheffield: JSOT Press, 1990), 58–59. The danger of this reading is that it can and indeed has been taken to grant theological legitimacy to domination among humans: Persons of little social power must be submissive to those of higher status just as Christ was obedient to the Father. This danger is usually ignored by white, male commentators who do not seem to be aware of the way their praise of Christ's obedience to the higher power is heard by groups traditionally excluded from power. Sheila Briggs in "Can an Enslaved God Liberate?" *Semeia* 47 (1989): 142–51, unmasks this idealization of slavery and hierarchical roles in the prevailing interpretation of the Christ hymn. I hope to preserve Paul from her valid critique of his interpreters by stressing that Christ's slavery is voluntary, given to humans, and is the model for mutual slavery within the church. The latter notion, seldom stressed, most powerfully removes the Christ hymn from the arsenal of oppression.

23. Luther's interpretation of the Christ hymn generally favors the notion that Christ became our slave and not that he gave obedience to the Father. His opinion on this is not uniform, however; see "Sermon on the Man Born Blind, John 9:1-38" (1518), *LW* 51, 38. Moreover, he does not develop this idea in conversation with the political theory with which Paul seems to have been familiar. Rather the *communicatio idiomatum* is at stake. Nevertheless there is compatibility between Luther and Paul on this point. Through his voluntary slavery to us, Christ wanted to be seen "living as if all the evils which were ours were actually his own." "Two Kinds of Righteousness" (1519), *LW* 31, 301–2. Luther comes closest to Paul's notion of Christ's slavery creating our freedom when he emphasizes the "from Christ to us" direction in the exchange of properties; see *Lectures on Galatians* (1535) *LW* 26, 288; "The Freedom of a Christian" (1520), *LW* 31, 349, 351–55, 366. Luther holds to the idea of Christ's slavery to us outside of commenting on the Christ hymn; see *First Lectures on the Psalms* (1513–15), *LW* 10, 324. The resurrected and ascended Jesus still serves us; see *Sermons on the Gospel of St. John* (1537), *LW* 24, 190.

24. Aristotle, *Politics* 1.2.23. Cf. ibid., 2.6.2; 2.8.5–6; 4.5.2–6; 6.2.1; 7.8.2–3; Plutarch, *Lycurgus* 24.2; idem, *Comparison of Aristide and Cato* 3–4; Philo, *Special Laws* 2.123.

25. Readers may have difficulty accepting the notion that Christ's slavery grants us freedom in the divine community. Indeed the equality with God that Christ communicates to us is ludicrous if one adheres to the substance theory of equality. If, however, equality is viewed in terms of access to conversation as I have argued above, then there is no necessity for us to become omniscient, omnipresent, and so on. We remain creatures even as we are taken into God's life and join with God in the creation of the future through speech. Luther does not hesitate to follow Paul in this regard. The Christian through faith has obtained the form of God; see "The Freedom of the Christian" (1520), *LW* 31, 366. See further *Sermons on the First Epistle of St. Peter* (1522), *LW* 30, 67; *Sermons on the Second Epistle of St. Peter* (1523), *LW* 30, 155. Most striking is "The Magnificat" (1521), *LW* 21, 351: "Through Christ she [Christendom] is joined to God as a bride to her bridegroom, so that the bride has a right to, and power over, her Bridegroom's body and all His possessions; all of this happens through faith. By faith man does what God wills; God in turn does what man wills."

26. Aristotle, *Politics* 1.5.1–2; 2.1.5; 3.2.7; 3.2.11. Cf. Plutarch, *Agesilaus* 1.1–3;2.1; idem, *To an Uneducated Ruler* 780B; idem, *Old Men in Public Affairs* 783D.

27. The Christian as simultaneously free and slave is at the heart of Luther's ethical thought, and for this paradox he looks frequently to the Christ hymn, often in conjunction with 1 Cor. 9:19. The critical question is whether Luther understood slavery in the same way Paul did, as the basis of the other's freedom. For Luther the slavery motif sometimes pertains to the consciousness in which a good work is done, pointing to the removal of arrogance when the powerful help the weak and in its place the joy of giving and the absence of obligation generated by the gift; see "Two Kinds of Righteousness" (1519), *LW* 31, 302–3; "The Freedom of a Christian" (1520), *LW* 31, 356–57. In these instances Luther does not reflect Paul's notion of the mutual slavery of all in the congregation. Yet in other passages when Luther discusses the relationship between sacraments and the life of the church, he sounds more Pauline by moving beyond attitude, employing the notion of the communication of properties and assuming that the context is the congregation in which all are free and slave; see "The Blessed Sacrament of the Holy and True Body of Christ, and the Brotherhoods" (1519), *LW* 35, 58–59, 67; "The Adoration of the Sacrament" (1523), *LW* 36, 286–87.

28. In 2:7 "slave" is not a reference to Isa. 53. While Phil. 2:10-11 is clearly an allusion to Isa. 45:23, it does not function to shape the moral life of the community.

29. See A. Malherbe, "Exhortation in First Thessalonians," *Novum Testamentum* 25 (1983), 238–56.

30. To understand these terms in their proper context of the ancient care of souls, see I. Hadot, *Seneca und die griechisch-römische Tradition der Seelenleitung* (Berlin: Walter de Gruter, 1969). For the many terms Paul borrows from the Greco-Roman hortatory tradition, see Fiore, *The Function*, 165–90.

31. For a critique of the view that example implies obedience to an authority, see Fiore, *The Function*, 45–100, 164–90.

32.* Stortz in her chapter helpfully draws attention to the foundation of ethics in perception: Action proceeds from the way one imagines the world to be. This insight helps interpret Paul's use of the Christ hymn. Paul exhorts his hearers to imagine the world to be as Christ has imagined it—as a place where it is fitting to extend freedom in the divine life to others.

33. Luther's distinction, borrowed from Augustine, between Christ as sacrament and example is pertinent here; see *Lectures on Hebrews* (1518), *LW* 29, 123–24; *Lectures on Romans* (1516–1517), *LW* 25, 309–11; "A Brief Instruction on What to Look for and Expect in the Gospels" (1521), *LW* 35, 119–220. His insistence that the order be first sacrament and only then example captures the Pauline grounding of exhortation in narrative.

34. The terms "good," "pleasing," and "perfect" have a long history in Greek philosophy as the context of what human rationality seeks to discover and live by. We will see that these terms, the first two of which are mentioned again in the following chapters, point to the public significance of the church's process of coming to moral decisions.

35. See, for example, J. Fitzmyer, *Romans* (Anchor Bible 33; New York: Doubleday, 1992), 662–64, 677–78.

36. For Stoic interest in kingship after Alexander, see B. D. Shaw, "The Divine Economy: Stoicism as Ideology," *Latomus* 44 (1985): 16–54. Dio Chrysostom's four orations on kingship (*Orations* 1–4) are evidence of ideas about rule worked out in the Hellenistic period lasting at least through the beginning of the second century of the common era.

37. Paul does not specify how the inner life of the church becomes visible to those on the outside. He simply assumes that it does. In 14:16 he imagines the criticism by an outsider rightly aimed at some member's failure to love. In 14:18 Paul is confident the one who serves Christ by loving the other is acceptable to the testing of human beings in general. Finally in 15:7-13 there is at least the implication that the gentiles' glorification of God flows out of members of the believing community welcoming one another.

38. The New Revised Standard Version is very misleading when it translates *bastazein* with "tolerate." Such a condescending attitude is not present in this verb, which has the sense of "bear" or "carry."

39. Rom. 15:4 is yet another instance of Paul conceptualizing the use of Scripture in terms of Greco-Roman moral exhortation. Note especially the phrase "through the exhortation of the

Scriptures." The term teaching *(didaskalía)* should be understood in terms of the power of examples to shape character. This is similar to Paul's other explicit grounding of the congregations' use of Scripture in the theoretical structure of moral exhortation in 1 Cor. 10:6,11 where the usual connection between type *(typos)* and "instilling mind" *(nouthesia)* is made. Most interesting in the Romans passage is the result Paul envisions when Scripture is used by the congregation: hope. Here he departs radically from the philosophers who saw the goal of moral exhortation to be the rational, stable mind. For him the goal is opening the congregation to the future in which the mind of Christ unites the church.

Chapter 8: The Reform Dynamic

1.* We share with Reinhard Hütter the problematizing of modernity. We do so on the basis of the unsustainability of the modern world; he questions modernity's notion of "individual freedom . . . understood as the fulfillment of whatever personal desires we might have" and modernity's placement of the autonomous human agent—rather than God with and for us—at the center of the moral universe. We agree with Hütter and understand the two critiques of modernity as complementary.

2. Lester Brown, "The Acceleration of History," *State of the World 1996* (New York & London: W. W. Norton), 3–20.

3. Robin Wright, cited by Hal Kane in "Gap in Income Distribution Widening," *Vital Signs 1997: The Environmental Trends That Are Shaping Our Future* (New York and London: W. W. Norton, 1997), 116. The statistical data are from this page as well.

4.* The implication that the subject of Lutheran ethics is a set of "Christian practices" and a "way of living faith" is paralleled in Hütter's contention that the Christian moral life is essentially "the concrete social practices which allow us as believers to embody . . . our communion with God" in a "way of life." We differ with Hütter, or complement him, in perceiving a reform dynamic at the center of a way of living the Lutheran tradition. Martha Stortz also addresses the link between faith and practice(s). She too sees Christian faith as a "way of life" shaped by and shaping "practices embedded in a particular community of faith" as well as doctrine (Lutheran doctrine and community, in this case). Yet the "contours of the Christian life . . . (and) the characteristics of Lutheran ethics" that she suggests emerge from the "practice" of prayer do not seem to be "oppositional and reconstructive," as we suggest.

5.* The chapter by James Childs demonstrates an instance of rereading the tradition. While emphasizing continuity, he tracks how Luther's formula regarding two realms has developed in modern times from dualistic thinking to a more united vision of the relationship of love and justice. He has also reoriented the spatial image to accommodate an emphasis on eschatology and its time-orientation. A more dramatic instance of returning to the sources with new eyes is David Frederickson's treatment of Paul, who has been the biblical theologian for the Lutheran Confessions, theology, and preaching. In his chapter Frederickson presents Paul as the facilitator of congregations as proto-democratic moral communities that, in effect, constitute counter-cultural societies in miniature. Though Frederickson does not raise it, a question emerges here. Since Pauline scholarship now presents a very different Paul from the source used in the Lutheran Confessions and basic categories of Lutheran thought, how do we now treat those presentations, the Confessions, and that thought? If the Confessions themselves declare, as they do, that their own norms are normed by the Scriptures, what do we do when either (a) biblical scholarship presents very different norms from the ones the tradition used, or (b) biblical scholarship itself offers no consensus about those norms?

6. Cornel West, "Martin Luther as Prophet," *Prophetic Fragments* (Grand Rapids, Mich.: Eerdmans; Trenton: Africa World Press, 1988), 257. Much of this sketch of Luther's stance is paraphrased from West, 257–59.

7. John Dillenberger and Claude Welch, *Protestant Christianity* (New York: Charles Scribner's Sons, 1954), 323.

8.* Childs explicitly poses the dilemma of exercising moral agency with courage and confidence in the face of the ambiguity of human existence and the complexities of moral choice. His assertion that the source of moral courage and agency is the assurance of God's promise in Jesus Christ rather than the certainty of our judgments coheres with our sense of Luther's theological linkage of grace and Christian practice. In many ways our chapter offers another complementary reply to his organizing question: "How do we, as Christian people, and as a church, speak with courage and confidence to ethical issues, even in the most complex and disputed of circumstances?"

9. The phrase cited earlier from Dillenberger and Welch.

10.* There is a significant conversation to consider between this chapter and Hütter's. Both address the problem of moral quietism and the range of moral concern. Both link this to a "deep fault line"

(Rasmussen and Moe-Lobeda) or "fallacy" (Hütter) running through Lutheran (Rasmussen and Moe-Lobeda) or Protestant (Hütter) ethics. Yet where we locate the origin of the problem in the Reformers themselves, Luther included, Hütter locates it in later interpreters' failure to maintain the steep dialectic in Luther's twofold statement regarding Christian freedom. In both essays the fallacy/fault line is closely linked to anthropocentricity, and this is where further conversation could prove fruitful. As it stands, we fault notions of salvation and morality that limit their universe to humanity only, rather than creation as a whole. We see this limitation occurring well before modernity, while Hütter concentrates on how modernity replaced theocentrism with anthropocentrism.

11.* Drawing upon Karl Hertz, Wolfhart Pannenberg, and Carl Braaten, Childs makes this point in sketching modern interpretations of the two realms tradition that recover an eschatological vision of the reign of God. He reiterates Hertz's assertion that a "transforming or revolutionary social ethic was not possible as long as the realm of creation and that of redemption did not share the same eschatological future. The identification of salvation with the individual apart from any expressed hope for the human community and the universe" frustrates ethical witness that takes the world and its future seriously. Childs claims, as do we, that God's promise as promise for all of creation "converts us to the world" (Pannenberg) and that the biblical vision of faith active in love seeks the well-being of the whole creation. Hütter also says, in his discussion about "recontextualizing the moral agent," that one dimension of recontextualizing is the emerging focus on creation and the "embeddedness of the human agent into an intricate network of natural habitats on earth, of which the human is only one." Robert Benne's very helpful section on "Contemporary Challenges" to Lutheran ethics includes a call for a "more fulsome theological explication of the First Article." This "will aid in giving more content to an ecological ethic." A "richer doctrine of creation" in Lutheran ethics is needed. This is our plea as well.

12. Martin Luther, *WA*, 23.134.24–23.236.36, as cited by Paul Santmire, *The Travail of Nature: The Ambiguous Ecological Promise of Christian Theology* (Philadelphia: Fortress Press, 1985), 129.

13. Martin Luther, *Sermons on the Gospel of John* (chapters 1–4), *LW*, 22, 26.

14. Martin Luther, *WA*, 32.234.34–236.36, as cited by Santmire, *The Travail of Nature*, 189.

15. Annie Dillard, *Pilgrim at Tinker Creek: A Mystical Excursion into the Natural World* (New York: Bantam Books, 1975), 273, as cited by Sallie McFague, *Super, Natural Christians* (Minneapolis: Fortress Press, 1997), 147.

16. The reference is to the refrain of *ta panta* ("all things") in the Pauline corpus, most prominently in the cosmic Christology of the Letter to the Colossians.

17. James Martin-Schramm, "Population-Consumption Issues: The State of the Debate in Christian Ethics," in *Theology for Earth Community: A Field Guide*, ed. Dieter Hessel (Maryknoll: Orbis Books, 1996), 140.

18. St. Augustine, *The Confessions*, trans. Maria Boulding (Hyde Park, N.Y.: New City Press, 1997), 242.

19. Ibid.

20. Ibid.

21. Martin Luther, "That These Words of Christ, 'This is My Body,' etc., Still Stand Firm against the Fanatics," *LW*, 37, 55.

22. Martin Luther, "Against the Heavenly Prophets," 221 (*WA* 18:211), as cited by Kyle A. Pasewark, *A Theology of Power: Being beyond Domination* (Minneapolis: Fortress Press, 1993), 90.

23. Martin Luther, a writing of 27 March 1525, as translated from *WA* 18:275: 26–36 by Heiko Oberman in his *Luther: Man between God and the Devil* (New York: Doubleday Image Books, 1992), 272.

24. Martin Luther, "Adoration of the Sacrament," 294 (*WA* 11:446), as cited by Pasewark, *A Theology of Power*, 80.

25. Cited above.

26. See Oberman, *Luther*, esp. ch. X, 272ff.

27. Martin Luther, *Lectures on Genesis*, chapters 1–5, *LW*, 1, 52.

28. Martin Luther, "Confession Concerning Christ's Supper," 287 (*WA* 26: 351), as cited by Pasewark, *A Theology of Power*, 93.

29. Cited from Santmire, *The Travail of Nature*, 131.

30. Martin Luther as cited by Colleen McDannell and Bernhard Lang, *Heaven: A History* (New Haven and London: Yale University Press, 1988), 153.

31. Ibid.

32. Ibid.

33. Martin Luther, "On War against the Turk," in *Selected Writings of Martin Luther, 1529–1546*, ed. Theodore G. Tappert (Philadelphia: Fortress Press, 1967), 10.

34. Martin Luther, *LW*, 1, 61, as cited by Kristen E. Kvam, "'Honoring God's Handiwork': Challenges of Luther's Doctrine of Creation," in *A Reforming Church: Gift and Task*, ed. Charles P. Lutz (Minneapolis: Kirk House Publishers, 1995), 178.

35. As cited and summarized by Kvam in *A Reforming Church*, 179.

36. Martin Luther, *LW* 1, 62, as cited by Kvam in *A Reforming Church*, 179.

37. Kvam, "Honoring God's Handiwork," in *A Reforming Church*, 180–81.

38. Dillard, *Pilgrim at Tinker Creek*, 178, as cited by McFague, *Super, Natural Christians*, 143.

39. Eric Hobsbawm, *The Age of Extremes: A History of the World, 1914–1991* (New York: Random House, 1994), 12.

40. Adrienne Rich, "One Night on Monterey Bay the Death-Freeze of the Century," in *An Atlas of the Difficult World: Poems 1988–1991* (New York: Norton, 1992), 23.

41. Augustine, *The City of God*, trans. Henry Bettenson (London and New York: Penguin, 1984), IV, 3, 138.

42. See David Hollenbach's excellent discussion, "Social Ethics under the Sign of the Cross," *The Annual: Society of Christian Ethics* (Washington, D.C.: Georgetown University Press, 1996), 11–13.

43.* Childs, while not explicitly placing creation's suffering at the center of morality, does point to the ethical insight and agency engendered in the church when it hears "the voices of those who suffer."

44. These comments on suffering and the cross are a shortened version of portions of the discussion in Larry Rasmussen, *Earth Community, Earth Ethics* (Maryknoll: Orbis Books, 1996), in the chapter titled "The Cross of Reality," 282ff.

45. For an extended treatment of what this means for social ethics, see the discussion of Hollenbach, *The Annual*, 15–18.

46. The best treatment of this by a Lutheran theologian is Mary Solberg's *Compelling Knowledge: A Feminist Proposal for an Epistemology of the Cross* (Albany: State University of New York Press, 1997).

47. Jacob Epstein, "White Mischief," *The New York Review of Books* (October 17, 1996), 30.

48. Ibid.

49. Martin Luther, "Preface to the Epistle of St. Paul to the Romans," *LW* 35, 370–71.

50. Ibid., 370.

51. Ibid.

52. Ibid.

53. The phrase of H. Richard Niebuhr used above.

54.* Hütter also appeals to "The Freedom of the Christian" as one of the foundational texts for Christian ethics and affirms this treatise's assertion that the moral life issues from union with Christ in loving service to neighbor as our participation in God's own freedom, that is, in God's love that "aims at drawing all of creation into communion with the triune God." He goes on to underline that loving service is given concrete historical shape by the commandments of God, that "allow us as believers to embody . . . our communion with God, which always includes God's other creatures." Hütter's focus on the relationship of freedom to commandment and his placing both at the "center of Christian ethics in the Augsburg Confession's Catholic tradition" are an important complement to our treatment and one with which we heartily agree.

55. Martin Luther, *This Is My Body*, 70 (*WA* 23:155), as cited by Pasewark, *A Theology of Power*, 106.

56. Martin Luther, *Admonition Concerning the Sacrament*, 126 (*WA* 30 [II]: 617), as cited by Pasewark, *A Theology of Power*, 106.

57.* See Childs' very helpful sketch of the development of dualistic and conservative modern interpretations of two-realms thinking.

58.* In our judgment the logic of this long and deep tradition in Lutheran ethics is reflected in Robert Benne's chapter, giving it a very different tone and logic from ours. The moral bent and logic of Benne's portrayal of a Lutheran ethic seem to be as follows. (1) The individual Christian's calling and the personal ethics of the individual believer are the center of moral attention, even when both the personal and the social are morally important. (2) The given structures of society are largely assumed as the sites of this calling and personal responsibility. (3) "Firm steps for the better" as incremental steps are commended as the normal and proper expression of moral agency. And (4) the moral substance for all this rests in a "moral core" that is "constant throughout time." To us the lean of this complex is toward a burden of proof that favors "Christian socialization into the patterns of prevailing power" when those patterns are not in direct and obvious opposition to elements of the unchanging moral core.

59.* An apparent difference with Hütter arises here. We argue for the inclusion of voices that yield "the signs of the times" as necessary to ecclesial hermeneutics and method in ethics, while he evidently does not. On this same matter of "voices," we also differ from Benne. We agree with Benne that "the

Lutheran tradition may be at risk" in a homogenized and vapid Protestantism. We concur as well in his call for "a counterculture that implants in its members a comprehensive vision of life out of which they live their whole lives." Much of his agenda of theological, ecclesiological, and epistemological challenges would also be ours. Benne, however, views as threats to a presumably uncontested moral core and the Lutheran tradition "feminists, liberationists, and multiculturalists." We want these among the voices at the table and view them as among the persons who bring new life and vitality to the tradition and its reformation.

60. These transitions and what they mean for life together are the subject of Rasmussen's *Earth Community, Earth Ethics*. The use of Lutheran resources for this is the focus of three chapters, esp.: "Returning to Our Senses," "The Cross of Reality," and "Song of Songs." The particular listing of transitions above is, however, an adaptation of those listed in M. Mitchell Waldrop, *Complexity: The Emerging Science at the Edge of Order and Chaos* (New York: Simon & Schuster, 1992), 350–51.

61. *Lutheran Book of Worship*, # 229.

62. William Edward Burghardt Du Bois, "Give Us Grace," in *Conversations with God: Two Centuries of Prayers of African Americans*, ed. James Melvin Washington (New York: Harper Collins, 1994), 105. Du Bois's reference is to Est. 4:15-16: "Whereupon Esther sent this reply to Mordecai, 'Go and assemble all the Jews now in Susa and fast for me. Do not eat or drink day or night for three days. For my part, I and my maids will keep the same fast, after which I shall go to the king in spite of the law; and if I perish, I perish.'"

Bibliography of Lutheran Ethics

John R. Stumme

This listing provides guidance for people interested in further study in English of the Lutheran ethical tradition.* Its focus is on writings that define or examine the basic character, stance, approach, and concepts of Lutheran ethics. Beginning with a limited selection of writings from the Lutheran Reformation, the bibliography notes some significant works from subsequent centuries and concentrates on writings from the second half of the twentieth century. The largest number of books and articles appear in the subsection from 1975 to the present.

Most selections are written by individuals who consider themselves Lutherans, while some offer the perspectives of non-Lutherans. In addition, the bibliography highlights "ethical material" in the Lutheran Confessions and includes a section on official social-ethical documents of Lutheran churches and studies about them. A final section is devoted to historical studies of Lutheran ethics. The few selections included on specific ethical issues develop or illustrate fundamental Lutheran themes. The bibliography contains scholarly studies as well as some writings aimed at a general audience. It offers a broad-ranging view of writings in the Lutheran ethical tradition without being exhaustive, under the following headings:

Lutheran Reformation
   Martin Luther
   Philip Melanchthon
   Lutheran Confessions
   Sourcebooks with Selections from Luther and the Lutheran
   Tradition

Early Lutheranism through the Nineteenth Century

Twentieth Century
   1900–1949
   1950–1974
   1975–1997

Church Documents and Studies about Them

Studies of the Lutheran Ethical Tradition
   On the Reformation and the Tradition as a Whole
   On Later Persons and Developments

---

  *I am grateful to the co-editor, the authors in this book, and others who reviewed drafts of this bibliography and offered their ideas and suggestions. I also thank Claire Buettner, director of the ELCA Library at the Lutheran Center, for her help in locating books, dissertations, and articles.

This bibliography, along with occasional updates, can be found on the web page of the Division for Church in Society of the Evangelical Lutheran Church in America—www.elca.org/dcs/studies/.

Lutheran Reformation

Martin Luther

Luther, Martin. "*The Christian in Society.*" *Luther's Works*, 44–47. Philadelphia: Fortress Press, 1962–1971. 44: Five treatises of 1519–21; 45: 12 treatises of 1522–44; 46: Eight treatises of 1525–30; 47: Four treatises of 1521–43.

———. "*Devotional Writings.*" *Luther's Works*, 43, ed. Gustav K. Wiencke. Philadelphia: Fortress Press, 1968. Includes "A Simple Way to Pray," 1535, 187–212.

———. "The Freedom of a Christian," 1520. In *Luther's Works*, 31, ed. Harold J. Grimm, 327–77. Trans. from the Latin by W. A. Lambert and rev. by Grimm. Philadelphia: Muhlenberg Press, 1957.

———. *Lectures on Galatians*, 1535. In *Luther's Works*, 26, 27. Ed. and trans. from the Latin by Jaroslav Pelikan. St. Louis: Concordia Publishing House, 1963, 1964.

———. *Letters of Spiritual Counsel.* Ed. and trans. from the German by Theodore G. Tappert. Philadelphia: Westminster Press, 1955.

———. "The Sermon on the Mount (Sermons)," 1532, and "The Magnificat," 1521. In *Luther's Works*, 21, ed. Jaroslav Pelikan. Trans. from the German by Pelikan and A. T. W. Steinhaeuser. Philadelphia: Fortress Press, 1956.

———. "Temporal Authority: To What Extent It Should be Obeyed," 1523. In *Luther's Works* 45, ed. Walther I. Brandt, 75–129. Trans. from the German by J.J. Schindel and rev. by Brandt. Philadelphia: Muhlenberg Press, 1962. [For another translation with an Introduction and glossary see, *Luther and Calvin on Secular Authority*, ed. and trans. Harro Hopfel, 1–46. New York: Cambridge University Press, 1991.]

———. "To the Christian Nobility of the German Nation Concerning the Reform of the Christian Estate," 1520. In *Luther's Works*, 44, ed. James Atkinson, 115–217. Trans. from the German by W. A. Lambert and rev. by Atkinson. Philadelphia: Fortress Press, 1966.

———. "Treatise on Good Works," 1520. In *Luther's Works*, 44, ed. James Atkinson, 15–114. Trans. from the German by W. A. Lambert and rev. by Atkinson. Philadelphia: Fortress Press, 1966.

———. "*Word and Sacrament*" III, *Luther's Works*, 37. Ed. and trans. from the German by Robert H. Fischer. Philadelphia: Muhlenberg Press, 1961.

Philip Melanchthon

Melanchthon, Philip. "*Loci Communes Theologici,*" 1521. In *Melanchthon and Bucer*, ed. with an Introduction by Wilhelm Pauck, 3–152. Trans. from the Latin by Lowell J. Satre, 3–152. Philadelphia: Westminster Press, 1969. Topics in this first Lutheran dogmatic include law, divine laws, counsels, human laws, love, and hope.

———. *Melanchthon on Christian Doctrine: Loci Communes 1555*, 83–129, 130–40, 175–86, 323–43. Ed. and trans. by Clyde L. Manschreck. Introduction by Hans Engelland. New York: Oxford University Press, 1965. Topics include divine law, the distinction of commandment and counsel, good works, and worldly authority.

———. *A Melanchthon Reader*, 179–238. Ed. and trans. from the German and Latin with an Introduction by Ralph Keen. New York: Peter Lang, 1988. "Commentary on Aristotle's Ethics, Bk. 1," and "Summary of Ethics." Bibliography.

Lutheran Confessions

The Book of Concord: The Confessions of the Evangelical Lutheran Church. Trans. from the German and Latin and ed. by Theodore G. Tappert in collaboration with Jaroslav Pelikan, Robert H. Fischer, and Arthur C. Piepkorn. Philadelphia: Fortress Press, 1959. Note especially: "The Augsburg Confession," Articles IV, VI, XVI, XVIII, XX, XXVII, XXVIII. "Apology of the Augsburg Confession," Articles IV, XVI, XVIII, XX, XXVII, XXVIII. "The Small Catechism." "The Large Catechism," especially "The First Part: The Ten Commandments." "Formula of Concord," "Part 1: Epitome," relevant parts of Articles II, III, IV, V, VI; "Part II: Solid Declaration," relevant parts of Articles II, III, IV, V, VI.

Sourcebooks with Selections from Luther and the Lutheran Tradition

Beach, Waldo, and H. Richard Niebuhr, eds. *Christian Ethics: Sources of the Living Tradition*. 2nd ed. New York: Ronald Press, 1973. Selections from Luther and Søren Kierkegaard.

Forell, George W., ed. *Christian Social Teachings: A Reader in Christian Social Ethics from the Bible to the Present*. Garden City, N. Y.: Doubleday, 1966. Includes selections from Luther, German Pietism, Paul Tillich, and Dietrich Bonhoeffer.

Gill, Robin. *A Textbook of Christian Ethics*. Edinburgh: T. & T. Clark, 1985. Includes four selections from Luther and one from Bonhoeffer. Bibliography.

Hertz, Karl, ed. *Two Kingdoms and One World: A Sourcebook in Christian Social Ethics*. Minneapolis: Augsburg Publishing House, 1976. Brief selections from the Bible to the twentieth century and from around the world. Numerous nineteenth and twentieth century American Lutheran sources. Bibliography.

Lull, Timothy F., ed. *Martin Luther's Basic Theological Writings*. Foreword by Jaroslav Pelikan. Minneapolis: Fortress Press, 1989. The final section is "Living and Dying as a Christian" (577–755). The selections also include "Heidelberg Disputation" (30–49), "How Christians Should Regard Moses" (135–48), and the sermon "Two Kinds of Righteousness" (155–64).

Schrey, H.-H., ed. *Faith & Action: Basic Problems in Christian Ethics: A Selection of Contemporary Discussions*. Introduction by H. H. Thielicke. Trans. from the German by Carl Schuenemann. Edinburgh: Oliver & Boyd, 1961. Selections from twenty theologians and ethicists on foundational themes.

Wogaman, Philip, and Douglas Strong, eds. *Readings in Christian Ethics: A Historical Sourcebook*. Louisville: Westminster John Knox Press, 1996. Includes selections from Luther, Bonhoeffer, and Tillich.

Early Lutheranism Through the Nineteenth Century

Andreae, Johann Valentin. *Christianopolis: An Ideal State of the Seventeenth Century*. Trans. from the Latin by Felix Emil Held. New York: Oxford University Press, 1916. First published in 1619.

Arndt, Johann. *True Christianity*. Trans. and with an Introduction by Peter Erb. New York: Paulist Press, 1979. 1606 book on the practice of the Christian life.

Blumhardt, Johann Christoph, and Christoph Blumhardt. *Thy Kingdom Come: A Blumhardt Reader*, ed. Vernard Eller. Grand Rapids, Mich.: Eerdmans, 1980. Sampling of thought of father (d. 1880) and son (d. 1919).

Chemnitz, Martin. *Loci Theologici*, II. Trans. from the German by J.A.O. Preus. St. Louis: Concordia Publishing House, 1989. Late sixteenth century systematic work with loci on the divine law, justification, good works, and the difference between mortal and venial sin.

Dorner, Isaak August. *System of Christian Ethics*. New York: Scribner & Welford, 1887.

Erb, Peter C., ed. *Pietists: Selected Writings*. New York: Paulist Press, 1983. Selections from Philipp Jakob Spener, August Hermann Francke, Gottfried Arnold, Johann Albrecht Bengel, and Friedrich Christoph Oetinger.

Grundtvig, N.F.S. *Selected Writings of N.F.S. Grundtvig*, ed. and with an Introduction by Johannes Knudsen, 49–82. Philadelphia: Fortress Press, 1976. Nineteenth century Danish theologian on the Christian life.

Harleß, Gottlieb Christoph Adolph von. *System of Christian Ethics*. 6th ed., 1868. Trans. from the German by A. W. Morrison and rev. by William Findlay. Edinburgh: T. & T. Clark, 1868.

Kierkegaard, Søren. *Either/Or*. 2 vols. Ed. and trans. from the Danish with an Introduction and notes by Howard V. Hong and Edna H. Hong. Princeton: Princeton University Press, 1987. Nineteenth century Danish theologian.

_____. *Fear and Trembling*. In *Fear and Trembling* and *Repetition*, ed. and trans. from the Danish with an Introduction and notes by Howard V. Hong and Edna H. Hong, 1–123. Princeton: Princeton University Press, 1983.

_____. *Practice in Christianity*. Ed. and trans. from the Danish with an Introduction and notes by Howard V. Hong and Edna H. Hong. Princeton: Princeton University Press, 1991.

_____. *Works of Love*. Ed. and trans. from the Danish with an Introduction and notes by Howard V. Hong and Edna H. Hong. Princeton: Princeton University Press, 1995.

Kolb, Robert. *Andreae and the Formula of Concord: Six Sermons on the Way to Lutheran Unity*, 61–120. St. Louis: Concordia Publishing House, 1977. Jakob Andreae's 1573 sermons, including ones on free will, good works, and the place of the law in the Christian life.

Luthardt, Christoph Ernst. *Apologetic Lectures on the Moral Truths of Christianity*. Trans. from the German by Sophia Taylor. 4th Ed. Edinburgh: T. & T. Clark, 1889.

_____. *History of Christian Ethics: Before the Reformation*, 1. Trans. from the German by W. Hastie. Edinburgh: T. & T. Clark, 1889.

Mann, W. J. *General Principles of Christian Ethics: The First Part of the System of Christian Ethics by Chr. Fr. Schmid*. Abridged by Mann. Philadelphia: The Lutheran Bookstore, 1872.

Martensen, Hans Lassen. *Christian Ethics*. 3 vols. First volume trans. from the Danish by C. Spence. Second volume trans. from the author's German by William Affleck. Third volume trans. from the author's German by Sophia Taylor. Edinburgh: T. & T. Clark, 1873–1899. Volume one is called "General" (the highest good, virtue, and law), two "Individual Ethics," and three "Social Ethics."

Ritschl, Albrecht. *Instruction in the Christian Religion*. In *The Theology of Albrecht Ritschl*, by Albert Temple Swing, 169–286. Trans. from the German by Swing. New York: Longmans, Green & Co., 1901. First published in 1875.

Sartorius, Ernst Wilhelm Christian. *The Doctrine of Divine Love, or, Outlines of the Moral Theology of the Evangelical Church*. Trans. from the German by Sophia Taylor. Edinburgh: T. & T. Clark, 1884. First published in 1846–50.

Schmucker, S. S. *Elements of Popular Theology*, 164–82, 271–87. New York: Leavitt, Lord & Co., 1834. On "the great moral change" and "civil governments." Schmucker continued to revise the book through several editions.

Spener, Philip Jacob. *Pia Desideria*. Trans. from the German, ed., and with an Introduction by Theodore Tappert. Philadelphia: Fortress Press, 1964. Abridged version of 1675 book calling for spiritual and moral reform in the church.

Stuckenberg, John H. W. *The Age and the Church: Being a Study of the Age, and of the Adaptation of the Church to Its Needs*. Hartford, Conn.: Student Publishing, 1893.

_____. *Christian Sociology*. New York: I.K. Funk, 1880.

_____. *The Social Problem*. York, Pa: Social Problems Publishing, 1897.

Weidner, Revere Franklin. *A System of Christian Ethics: Based on Martensen and Harless*. New York: Fleming H. Revell, 1891.

Wuttke, Adolf. *Christian Ethics*. 2 vols. Trans. from the 1864–1865 German ed. by John P. Lacroix. New York: Nelson & Phillips, 1874. The first volume is a history of ethics and the second a constructive statement of "pure ethics."

Twentieth Century

1900–1949

Aulen, Gustaf. *Church, Law and Society*. New York: Scribner's Sons, 1948.

_____. "The Church and Social Justice." *This is the Church*, ed. Anders Nygren, 307–21. Philadelphia: Muhlenberg Press, 1952. First published in Sweden in 1943.

Barth, Karl. *Community, State and Church*. With an Introduction by Will Herberg. Garden City, N.Y.: Doubleday, 1960. Three essays, from 1935, 1938, and 1946, on the relation of gospel and law and on the Lordship of Jesus Christ.

_____. "First Letter to the French Protestants." In *A Letter to Great Britain from Switzerland*, 30–41. London: Sheldon Press, 1941. 1940 letter claims Germany suffers from Luther's error on the relation of law and gospel.

Bergendoff, Conrad, "The Lutheran Christian in Church and State." *Lutheran Quarterly* I, 4 (November 1949): 411–24.

_____. "Lutheran Ethics and Scandinavian Lutheranism." *Christendom* VI, 1 (Winter 1941): 57–69.

Berggrav, Eivind. *Man and State*. Trans. from the Norwegian by George Aus. Philadelphia: Muhlenberg Press, 1951. Written from 1942–44 while Bishop Berggrav was under house arrest by the Nazi occupation government.

Billing, Einar. *Our Calling*. Ed. Franklin Sherman. Trans. from the Swedish by Conrad
Bergendoff. Philadelphia: Fortress Press, 1964. First published in 1909.

Bonhoeffer, Dietrich. *The Cost of Discipleship*. Trans. from the German by R. H. Fuller, rev. by
Irmgard Booth. New York: Macmillan, 1963. First published in 1937.

_____. *Ethics*. Ed. Eberhard Bethge. Trans. from the German by Neville Horton Smith. New
York: Macmillan, 1962. Compilation of unfinished manuscripts from 1940–1943.

_____. *Letters and Papers from Prison*. Enlarged ed. Ed. Eberhard Bethge. Trans. from the
German by R. H. Fuller, John Bowden et al. New York: Macmillan, 1972. Written in
1943–45 in a Nazi prison before his execution on April 9, 1945.

Brunner, Emil. *The Divine Imperative*. Trans. from the German by Olive Wyon. Philadelphia:
Westminster Press, 1957. Reformed theologian draws on Luther as well as Calvin in this
1932 book on Protestant ethics.

Elert, Werner. *The Christian Ethos*. Trans. from the German by Carl J. Schindler. Philadelphia:
Muhlenberg Press, 1957. First published in 1949.

_____. *Law and Gospel*. Ed. Franklin Sherman. Trans. from the German by Edward H.
Schroeder. Philadelphia: Fortress Press, 1966. First published in 1948.

Fischer, Emil E. *Social Problems: The Christian Solution*. Philadelphia: United Lutheran Publishing
House, 1927.

Forell, George. "Luther's Conception of Natural Orders." *Lutheran Church Quarterly* XVIII, 2
(April 1945): 160–77.

Haas, John A. W. *The Christian Way of Liberty*. Philadelphia: United Lutheran Publishing House,
1930.

_____. "Ethics, Lutheran." *The Lutheran Cyclopedia*, eds. Henry Eyster Jacobs and Haas,
171–73. New York: Charles Scribner's Sons, 1905.

_____. *Freedom and Christian Conduct: An Ethic*. New York: Macmillan, 1923.

_____. *What Ought I to Believe: A Moral Test*. Philadelphia: United Lutheran Publishing House,
1929.

Haering, Theodor von. *The Ethics of the Christian Life*. With an Introduction by W. R. Morrison.
Trans. from the German by James S. Hill. New York: G. P. Putnam's Sons, 1909.

Harnack, Adolf. *What Is Christianity?* Trans. from the German by Thomas Bailey Saunders. New
York: Harper & Row, 1957. First published in 1900.

Herrmann, Wilhelm. *The Communion of the Christian With God: Described on the Basis of Luther's
Statements*. Ed. and with an Introduction by Robert T. Voelkel. Trans. from the 4th German
ed. of 1903 by R. W. Stewart. Philadelphia: Fortress Press, 1971.

Kantonen, T. A. *The Message of the Church to the World of Today*. Minneapolis: Augsburg, 1941.

Keyser, Leander S. *A System of Christian Ethics*. Philadelphia: Lutheran Publication Society, 1913.
Textbook for Christian colleges.

Koeberle, Adolf. "The Social Problem in the Light of the Augsburg Confession." *Lutheran Church
Quarterly* XVIII, 3 (July 1945): 258–75.

_____. *The Quest for Holiness: A Biblical, Historical, and Systematic Investigation*. Trans. from the 3rd
German ed. by John C. Mattes. Minneapolis: Augsburg Publishing House, 1938.

Lee, G. T. *Church and State: Can We Save the Country by Legislation?* Minneapolis: Augsburg, 1927.

Mattson, A, D. *Christian Ethics: The Basis and Content of the Christian Life*. Rock Island, Ill.: Augustana
Book Concern, 1938.

_____. "The Church and Society." In *What Lutherans Are Thinking: A Symposium on Lutheran Faith
and Life*, ed. E. C. Fendt, 455–70. Columbus, Ohio: Wartburg Press, 1947.

Niebuhr, Reinhold. *The Nature and Destiny of Man. I: Human Nature. II: Human Destiny*. New York:
Scribner's, 1964. First published in 1941 and 1943, Niebuhr's major work shows his interpretation of, reliance on, and criticism of Luther.

Nolde, O. Frederick. "Christian Community and World Order." In *Toward World-wide Christianity*,
ed. Nolde, 126–68. New York: Harper, 1946.

Nygren, Anders. *Agape and Eros Part I: A Study of the Christian Idea of Love. Part II: The History of the
Christian Idea of Love*. Trans. from the Swedish by Philip S. Watson. Philadelphia: Westminster
Press, 1953. First published in the 1930s.

_____. "The State and the Church." In *This is the Church*, ed. Nygren, 294–306. Philadelphia:
Muhlenberg Press, 1952. First published in Swedish in 1943.

Pfatteicher, E. P. *Christian Social Service*. New York: Falcon Press, 1933.

Pieper, Franz. *Christian Dogmatics*, III, 3–88. St. Louis: Concordia Publishing House, 1953. On "The Christian Life, or Sanctification and Good Works." First published in German in 1920.

Rasmussen, Carl C. "The Lutheran View of Christian Ethics." In *What Lutherans Are Thinking: A Symposium on Lutheran Faith and Life*, ed. E. C. Fendt, 443–54. Columbus, Ohio: Wartburg Press, 1947.

Reu, Johann Michael. *Anthology of the Theological Writings of J. Michael Reu*, ed. and with an Introduction by Paul I. Johnson, 101–20. Lewiston, N. Y: Edwin Mellen, 1997. A 1931 article on the kingdom of God.

————, in conjunction with Paul H. Buehring. *Christian Ethics*. Columbus, Ohio: Lutheran Book Concern, 1935.

Stump, Joseph. *The Christian Life: A Handbook of Christian Ethics*. New York: Macmillan, 1930.

Tillich, Paul. *Political Expectation*. Ed. with an Introduction by James L. Adams. New York: Harper & Row, 1971. Seven essays on social ethical themes from 1923 to 1965.

————. *The Protestant Era*, 115–81. Trans. from the German and with a Concluding Essay by James Luther Adams. Chicago: University of Chicago Press, 1948. Section on "religion and ethics" contains essays on personality, conscience, ethics in a changing world, and the Protestant principle, most from the 1920s.

————. *The Socialist Decision*. Introduction by John R. Stumme. Trans. from the German by Franklin Sherman. New York: Harper & Row, 1977. First published in 1933.

Wingren, Gustaf. "The Church and Christian Vocation." In *This is the Church*, ed. Anders Nygren, 281–93. Philadelphia: Muhlenberg Press, 1952. First published in Swedish in 1943.

1950–1974

Alpers, Kenneth P. "Bases for Lutheran Social Action." Minneapolis: Commission on Research and Social Action, The American Lutheran Church, 1965.

Althaus, Paul. *The Divine Command*. Introduction by William H. Lazareth. Trans. from the German by Franklin Sherman. Philadelphia: Fortress Press, 1966. First published in 1952.

Asheim, Ivar, ed. *Christ and Humanity: A Workshop in Christian Social Ethics*. Philadelphia: Fortress Press, 1970. Essays by Asheim, John Reumann, Ragnar Holte, and James Scherer, and a study from the German Democratic Republic.

Becker, Arthur H. "Making Ethical Judgments in a Changing World." Minneapolis: Commission on Research and Social Action, The American Lutheran Church, 1966.

Benne, Robert, and Philip J. Hefner. *Defining America: A Christian Critique of the American Dream*. Philadelphia: Fortress Press, 1974.

Bergendoff, Conrad. "Justification and Sanctification: Liturgy and Ethics." In *A Reexamination of Lutheran and Reformed Traditions-III*, 19–28. New York: National Lutheran Council, 1965.

Berger, Peter L., and Richard John Neuhaus. *Movement and Revolution*. Garden City, N.Y.: Doubleday, 1970.

Berggrav, Eivind. "State and Church—The Lutheran View." *Lutheran Quarterly* IV, 4 (November 1952): 363–76.

Braaten, Carl E. *Eschatology and Ethics: Essays on the Theology and Ethics of the Kingdom of God*. Minneapolis: Augsburg Publishing House, 1974.

————. "Reflections on the Lutheran Doctrine of the Law." *Lutheran Quarterly* XVIII, 1 (February 1966): 72–84.

Brauer, Jerald C. "His Church and His World." In *The Scope of Grace*, ed. Philip J. Hefner, 257–78. Philadelphia: Fortress Press, 1964.

Brunner, Peter. "The Christian in a Responsible Society." *Lutheran World* V, 3 (1958): 234–48.

Burtness, James H. "The New Morality: Some Bibliographical Comment." *Dialog* 5, 1 (Winter 1966): 10–7.

————. *Whatever You Do: An Essay on the Christian Life*. Minneapolis: Augsburg Publishing House, 1967. For lay audience.

Buthelezi, Manas. "Theological Grounds for an Ethic of Hope." *The Challenge of Black Theology in South Africa*, ed. Basil Moore, 147–56. Atlanta: John Knox Press, 1973.

_____. "The Theological Meaning of True Humanity." *The Challenge of Black Theology in South Africa*, ed. Basil Moore, 93–103. Atlanta: John Knox Press, 1973.

Carlson, Edgar. *The Church and the Public Conscience*. Philadelphia: Muhlenberg Press, 1956.

_____. "The Two Realms and the Modern World." *Lutheran World* XII, 4 (1965): 373–83.

Ditmanson, Harold H. "New Themes in Christian Social Ethics." *Lutheran World* XV, 1 (1968): 25–40.

Ebeling, Gerhard. *Word and Faith*, 62–78, 247–82, and 387–406. Trans. from the German by James W. Leitch. Philadelphia: Fortress Press, 1963. Essays on the third use of the law, the doctrine of the law, and the two kingdoms.

Forde, Gerhard O. *"Lex Semper Accusat?* Nineteenth Century Roots of our Current Dilemma." *Dialog* 9, 4 (Autumn 1970): 265–74.

_____. "Sense and Nonsense About Luther." *Dialog* 10, 1 (Winter 1971): 65–67. On Luther's "The Freedom of the Christian."

Forell, George W. *Ethics of Decision: An Introduction to Christian Ethics*. Philadelphia: Muhlenberg Press, 1955.

_____, Herman A. Preus, and Jaroslav Pelikan. "Toward a Lutheran View of Church and State." *Lutheran Quarterly* V, 3 (August 1953): 280–9.

Gollwitzer, Helmut. *The Rich Christians and Poor Lazarus*. Trans. from the German by David Cairns. New York: Macmillan, 1970.

Hefner, Philip. "Theological Perspectives on Social Ministry." New York: Board of Social Ministry, Lutheran Church in America, 1968.

_____. "Theological Reflections: Passion for the Things of the Earth." *Una Sancta* XXIV, 2 (Pentecost, 1967): 41–51.

Heiges, Donald R. *The Christian's Calling*. Philadelphia: Fortress Press, 1958. A rev. ed. was published in 1984.

Hertz, Karl H. *Christian Behavior*. Ed. Philip R. Hoh. Philadelphia: Lutheran Church Press, 1964.

_____. "The Church and Social Action." In *Theology in the Life of the Church*, ed. Robert W. Bertram, 153–71. Philadelphia: Fortress Press, 1963.

_____. *Everyman a Priest*. Philadelphia: Muhlenberg Press, 1960.

_____. *Politics Is a Way of Helping People*. Minneapolis: Augsburg Publishing House, 1974.

_____. "The Social Role of the Man of God." In *The Scope of Grace*, ed. Philip J. Hefner, 215–30. Philadelphia: Fortress Press, 1964.

Hillerdal, Gunner. "Church and Politics: A Critical Discussion of Recent Research in Political Ethics." *Lutheran World* II, 2 (Summer 1955): 147–59.

Hong, Howard. *This World and the Church*. Augsburg Publishing House, 1955.

Hulme, William E. *The Dynamics of Sanctification*. Minneapolis: Augsburg Publishing House, 1966.

Jersild, Paul T. "Situationalism and Law in Christian Ethics." *Concordia Theological Monthly* XL, 10 (November 1969): 692–701.

Kersten, Lawrence K. *The Lutheran Ethic: The Impact of Religion on Laymen and Clergy*. Detroit: Wayne State University Press, 1970.

Kitamori, Kazoh. *Theology of the Pain of God*, 85–97, 117–28. Richmond, Virginia: John Knox Press, 1965. On ethics and love.

Koenker, Ernest B. "Man: *Simul Justus et Peccator.*" In *Accents in Luther's Theology*, ed. Heino O. Kadai, 199–229. St. Louis: Concordia Publishing House, 1968.

Lau, Franz. "The Lutheran Doctrine of the Two Kingdoms." *Lutheran World* XII, 4 (1965): 355–72.

Lazareth, William H. "The Church as Advocate of Social Justice." *Lutheran World* XVIII, 3 (1971): 245–67.

_____. "Luther on Civil Righteousness and Natural Law." In *The Church, Mysticism, Sanctification and the Natural in Luther's Thought*, ed. Ivar Asheim, 180–88. Philadelphia: Fortress Press, 1967.

_____. "Luther's 'Two Kingdoms' Ethic Reconsidered." In *Christian Social Ethics in a Changing World*, ed. John C. Bennett, 119–31. New York: Association Press, 1966.

_____. "Political Responsibility as the Obedience of Faith." In *The Gospel and Human Destiny*, ed. Vilmos Vajta, 218–70. Minneapolis: Augsburg Publishing House, 1971.

_____. "Social Ministry: Biblical and Theological Perspectives." New York: Board of Social Ministry, Lutheran Church in America, 1968.

_____. A Theology of Politics. New York: Board of Social Missions, Lutheran Church in America, 1960.

_____. "The Twentieth Century Recovery of Lutheran Political Responsibility." In The Ethics of Power: The Interplay of Religion, Philosophy, and Politics, eds. Harold Lasswell and Harlan Cleveland, 119–39. New York: Harper and Brothers, 1962.

_____. "The 'Two Kingdom' Ethic Reconsidered." Dialog 1, 4 (Autumn 1962): 30–35.

Letts, Harold C., ed. Existence Today. Vol. One. Christian Social Responsibility. Philadelphia: Muhlenberg Press, 1957. Chapters by Karl H. Hertz, Charles A. Kegley, Franklin Sherman, and Martin J. Heinecken.

_____, ed. Life in Community. Vol. Three. Christian Social Responsibility. Philadelphia: Muhlenberg Press, 1957. Joseph Sittler and William H. Lazareth present two approaches to Lutheran ethics. Rufus Cornelsen writes on economic life, Taito Almar Kantonen on the political order, Harold Haas on family life, and Letts on the church.

Løgstrup, Knud E. The Ethical Demand. Trans. from the Swedish by Theodor I. Jensen. Philadelphia: Fortress Press, 1971. Rev. and expanded ed. Ed. Hans Fink and Alasdair MacIntyre. Notre Dame. University of Notre Dame Press, 1997.

Luecke, Richard. New Meanings for New Beings, 114–46. Philadelphia: Fortress Press, 1964. On "law and love."

_____. "The Prophetic Word for Today." Dialog 1, 1 (Winter 1962): 49–58.

_____. "The Secular City Revisited." Lutheran Quarterly XVIII, 1 (February 1966): 5–17.

_____. Violent Sleep Notes Toward the Development of Sermons for the Modern City. Philadelphia: Fortress Press, 1969.

Lutz, Charles P. You Mean I Have a Choice? Minneapolis: Augsburg Publishing House, 1971.

Marty, Martin E. "The Church in the World." In The Lively Function of the Gospel, ed. Robert Bertram, 133–50. St. Louis: Concordia Publishing House, 1966.

_____. The Hidden Discipline. St. Louis: Concordia Publishing House, 1962. "A commentary on the Christian life of forgiveness in the light of Luther's Large Catechism."

_____. "Luther on Ethics: Man Free and Slave." In Accents in Luther's Theology, ed. Heino O. Kadai, 199–229. St. Louis: Concordia Publishing House, 1968.

Mattson, A. D. Christian Social Consciousness: An Introduction to Christian Sociology. Rock Island, Ill.: Augustana Book Concern, 1953.

_____. The Social Responsibility of Christians. Philadelphia: Board of Publication of the United Lutheran Church in America, 1960.

Nagy, Gyula. "Man as Responsible Co-worker with God in a Dynamic World." In The Gospel and Human Destiny, ed. Vilmos Vajta, 178–217. Minneapolis: Augsburg Publishing House, 1971.

Neuhaus, Richard John. In Defense of People: Ecology and the Seduction of Radicalism. New York: Macmillian Company, 1971.

Niebuhr, H. Richard. "Evangelical and Protestant Ethics." In The Heritage of the Reformation, ed. Elmer J. F. Arndt, 211–29. New York: Richard R. Smith, 1950.

Niebuhr, Reinhard. "The Relevance of Reformation Doctrine in Our Day." In The Heritage of the Reformation, ed. Elmer J. F. Arndt, 249–64. New York: Richard R. Smith, 1950. On justification.

Nolde, O. Frederick. The Churches and the Nations. Philadelphia: Fortress Press, 1970.

Nygren, Anders. "Christianity and Law." Dialog 1, 4 (Autumn 1962): 36–45.

Outka, Gene. Agape: An Ethical Analysis. New Haven: Yale University Press, 1972.

_____. "Character, Conduct, and the Love Commandment." In Norm and Context in Christian Ethics, ed. Outka and Paul Ramsey, 37–66. New York: Charles Scribner's Sons, 1968. Examines how Luther in the "Large Catechism" connects character and conduct.

Pannenberg, Wolfhart. "Facts of History and Christian Ethics." Dialog 8, 4 (Autumn 1969): 287–96.

_____. "The Kingdom of God and the Foundation of Ethics." In Theology and the Kingdom of God, ed. Richard John Neuhaus, 102–26. Philadelphia: Westminster Press, 1969.

Pelikan, Jaroslav. "Justitia as Justice and Justitia as Righteousness." In Law and Theology, ed. Andrew J. Buehner, 87–98. St. Louis: Concordia Publishing House, 1965.

_____. "Luther Comes to the New World." In *Luther and the Dawn of the Modern Era*, ed. H. A. Oberman,1–10. Leiden: E.J. Brill, 1974.

_____. "A Protestant View." In *Religious Responsibility for the Social Order: A Symposium by Three Theologians*, 5–8. Pelikan, Gustave Weigel, and Emil L. Fackenheim. Washington, D.C.: National Conference of Christians and Jews, 1962.

Piepkorn, Arthur Carl. "Christ and Culture: A Lutheran Approach." *Response* II, 1 (1960): 3–16.

Pinomaa, Lennart. "The Meaning of Luther for Our Times." *Lutheran Quarterly* XIX, 2 (August 1967): 274–82.

Quanbeck, Warren A., ed. *God and Caesar: A Christian Approach to Social Ethics*. Minneapolis: Augsburg Publishing House, 1959. Includes chapters by George W. Forell on "The State as Order of Creation" and by Otto A. Piper on "Justification and Christian Ethics" and "Faith and Daily Life."

Rasmussen, Larry L. "Law and Morality/Morality and Law." *Dialog* 9, 4 (Autumn 1970): 249–56.

Rendtorff, Trutz. "Institutions as a Socio-Ethical Problem." In *Faith and Society: Toward a Contemporary Social Ethics. Supplement to the Lutheran World* 2 (1966): 34–47.

Reumann, John, and William Lazareth. *Righteousness and Society: Ecumenical Dialog in a Revolutionary Age*. Philadelphia: Fortress Press, 1967.

Reuss, Carl F. "The Role of the Church in Contemporary Society." In *Faith and Society: Toward a Contemporary Social Ethics. Supplement to the Lutheran World* 2 (1966): 66–76.

Ruff, G. Elson. *The Dilemma of Church and State*. Philadelphia: Board of Publication of the United Lutheran Church in America, 1954.

Santmire, H. Paul. *Brother Earth: Nature, God, and Ecology in Time of Crisis*. New York: Thomas Nelson, 1970. A theology of nature influenced by Luther.

Scharlemann, Martin H. *The Church's Social Responsibilities*. Saint Louis: Concordia Publishing House, 1971.

Schmidt, Karl T. Theodore. *Rediscovering the Natural in Protestant Theology*. Minneapolis: Augsburg Publishing House, 1962.

Schroeder, Edward. "The Orders of Creation: Some Reflections on the History and Place of the Term in Systematic Theology." *Concordia Theological Monthly* XLIII, 3 (March 1972): 165–78.

Schulze, Hans. "Man and Institution: Their Relationship as a Theme of Social Ethics." *Lutheran World* XVI, 1 (1969): 237–48.

Schuurman, Lambert. "Some Observations on the Relevance of Luther's Theory of the Two Realms for the Theological Task in Latin America." *Lutheran Quarterly* XXII, 1 (1970): 77–91. View of a Dutch Reformed theologian.

Sherman, Franklin. "The Christian in Secular Society: Insights from the Reformation." *Una Sancta* 25, 2 (Summer 1963): 208–13.

_____. "Christian Love and Public Policy Today." *Lutheran Quarterly* XIII, 3 (August 1961): 229–38.

_____. "Christology, Politics, and the Flacian Heresy." *Dialog* 2, 3 (Summer 1963): 208–13.

_____. "The Church and the Proximate Goals of History." In *Christian Hope and the Future of Humanity*, ed. Sherman, 68–90. Minneapolis: Augsburg Publishing House, 1969.

_____. *The Courage to Care: A Study in Christian Social Responsibility*, ed. Arthur H. Getz. Philadelphia: Muhlenberg Press, 1959.

_____. "Needed: Prophets, Priests, and Pragmatists—Some Comments on Recent Trends in Christian Ethics." *Lutheran Quarterly* XXIV, 4 (November 1972): 351–65.

_____. "The Vital Center: Toward a Chalcedonian Social Ethic." In *The Scope of Grace*, ed. Philip J. Hefner, 231–56. Philadelphia: Fortress Press, 1964.

Sittler, Joseph. "Ethics and New Testament Style." *Union Seminary Quarterly Review* 13 (May 1958): 29–36.

_____. "Secularization as an Ethical Problem." In *Faith and Society: Toward a Contemporary Social Ethics. Supplement to the Lutheran World* 2 (1966):15–20.

_____. *The Structure of Christian Ethics*. Introduction by Franklin Sherman. Louisville, Ky.: Westminster John Knox Press, 1998. Incorporates much of his essay in Letts, *Life in Community*. First published in 1958.

_____. "Urban Fact and the Human Situation." In *Challenge and Response in the City: A Theological Consultation on the Urban Church*, ed. Walter Kloetzli, 9–20. Rock Island, Ill.: Augustana Press, 1962.

Söe, Niels Hansen. "Ethics: As Theological Science." In *The Encyclopedia of the Lutheran Church*, I, ed. Julius Bodensieck, 810–13. Minneapolis: Augsburg Publishing House, 1965.

————. "Natural Law and Social Ethics." In *Christian Social Ethics in a Changing World*, ed. John C. Bennett, 289–309. New York: Association Press, 1966.

————. "The Three 'Uses' of the Law." In *Norm and Context in Christian Ethics*, ed. Gene Outka and Paul Ramsey, 297–322. New York: Charles Scribner's Sons, 1968.

Strommen, Merton P., and others. *A Study of Generations: Report of a Two-year Study of 5000 Lutherans between the Ages of 15 and 65, Their Beliefs, Values, Attitudes, Behavior*. Minneapolis: Augsburg Publishing House, 1972.

Stuhr, Walter M. *The Public Style: A Study of the Community Participation of Protestant Ministers*. Chicago: Center for the Scientific Study of Religion, 1972.

Thielicke, Helmut. *Theological Ethics*, ed. William H. Lazareth. 2 vols. Trans. and abridged from the German. Philadelphia: Fortress Press, 1966, 1969. The first volume is on "foundations" and the second on "politics."

Tillich, Paul. *Love, Power and Justice: Ontological Analysis and Ethical Applications*. New York: Oxford University Press, 1960.

————. *Morality and Beyond*. New York: Harper & Row, Publishers, 1963. The religious element in morality.

————. *Systematic Theology*, III. Chicago: University of Chicago, 1963. Treats morality under "Life and the Spirit" and society under "History and the Kingdom of God."

Trillhaas, Wolfgang. "The Contribution of Lutheranism to Social Ethics Today—A Critique and a Program." In *Faith and Society: Toward a Contemporary Social Ethics. Supplement to the Lutheran World* 2 (1966): 48–65.

Wendland, H. D. "The Theology of the Responsible Society." In *Christian Social Ethics in a Changing World*, ed. John C. Bennett, 135–52. New York: Association Press, 1966.

Wingren, Gustaf. "Creation and Ethics: From *Ordnungstheologie* to the Theology of Revolution." In *The Flight from Creation*, 33–56. Minneapolis: Augsburg Publishing House, 1971.

————. *Creation and Law*. Trans. from the Swedish by Ross Mackenzie. Philadelphia: Muhlenberg Press, 1961.

————. *Gospel and Church*. Trans. from the Swedish by Ross Mackenzie. Philadelphia: Fortress Press, 1964.

1975—1997

Altmann, Walter. "Interpreting the Doctrine of the Two Kingdoms: God's Kingship in the Church and in Politics." *Word & World* VII, 1 (Winter 1987): 43–58.

————. "A Latin American Perspective on the Cross and Suffering." In *The Scandal of a Crucified World*, ed. Yacob Tesfai, 75–86. Maryknoll, N. Y.: Orbis, 1994.

————. *Luther and Liberation: A Latin American Perspective*. Trans. from the Spanish by Mary M. Solberg. Minneapolis: Fortress Press, 1992.

————. "Luther's Theology and Liberation Theology." In *Lutherans in Brazil, 1990: History, Theology, Perspectives*, eds. Gottfried Brakemeier and Altmann, 67–80. Sao Leopoldo: Post-Graduate Institute of the IECLB, 1989.

————. "Methodology of Latin American Liberation Theology and a Contextual Re-Reading of Luther." In *Prejudice: Issues in Third World Theologies*, ed. Andreas Nehring, 102–19. Madras, India: Gurukul Summer Institute, 1996.

————. "The Reception of Luther's Concept of Freedom in Latin America." *Lutherjahrbuch, 1995*, ed. Helmar Junghaus, 167–88.

————. "Theology in Latin America." In *Lutherans in Brazil, 1990: History, Theology, Perspectives*, eds. Gottfried Brakemeier and Altmann, 39–54. Sao Leopoldo: Post-Graduate Institute of the IECLB, 1989.

Anderson, Per. "Reading Luther on Plague in a Technological Age." *Word & World* XIII, 4 (Summer 1993): 277–83.

Bakken, Peter W., Joan Gibb Engel, and J. Ronald Engel. *Ecology, Justice, and Christian Faith: A Critical Guide to the Literature*. Westport, Conn.: Greenwood Press, 1995.

Bayer, Oswald. "Does Evil Persist?" *Lutheran Quarterly* XI, 2 (Summer 1997): 143–50.

_____. "Nature and Institution." *Lutheran Quarterly* (forthcoming).

_____. "Social Ethics as an Ethics of Responsibility." In *Worship and Ethics: Lutherans and Anglicans in Dialogue*, eds. Bayer and Alan Suggate, 187–201. New York: Walter de Gruyter, 1996.

_____. "Worship and Theology." In *Worship and Ethics: Lutherans and Anglicans in Dialogue*, eds. Bayer and Alan Suggate, 148–61. New York: Walter de Gruyter, 1996.

Beckmann, David. *Where Faith and Economics Meet*. Minneapolis: Augsburg Press, 1981.

Benne, Robert. "The Calling of the Church in Economic Life." In *The Two Cities of God: The Church's Responsibilities for the Earthly City*, eds. Carl E. Braaten and Robert W. Jenson, 95–116. Grand Rapids, Mich.: Eerdmans, 1997.

_____. "The Church and Politics: Four Possible Connections." *This World* 25 (Spring 1989): 26–37.

_____. *The Ethic of Democratic Capitalism: A Moral Reassessment*. Philadelphia: Fortress Press, 1981.

_____. "The Lutheran Tradition and Public Theology." *Lutheran Theological Seminary Bulletin* 76, 4 (Fall 1995): 15–26.

_____. *Ordinary Saints: An Introduction to the Christian Life*. Philadelphia: Fortress Press, 1988.

_____. "The Paradoxical Vision: A Lutheran Nudge for Public Theology." *Pro Ecclesia* IV, 2 (Spring 1994): 212–25.

_____. *The Paradoxical Vision: A Public Theology for the Twenty-first Century*. Minneapolis: Fortress Press, 1995.

_____. "The Preferential Option for the Poor and American Public Policy." In *The Preferential Option for the Poor*, ed. and with an Introduction by Richard John Neuhaus, 53–71. Grand Rapids, Mich.: Eerdmans, 1988.

Berger, Peter L., and Richard John Neuhaus, eds. *Against the World for the World: The Hartford Appeal and the Future of American Religion*. New York: Seabury, 1976. Includes chapters by Berger, Neuhaus, George Lindbeck, and George Forell.

_____. "Lutheran Ethics and the Ambiguities of Power." In *Piety, Politics, and Ethics: Reformation Studies in Honor of George Wolfgang Forell*, ed. Carter Lindberg, 75–84. Kirksville, Mo.: Sixteenth Century Journal Publishers, 1984.

_____, and Richard John Neuhaus. *To Empower People: The Role of Mediating Structures in Public Policy*. Washington, D.C.: American Enterprise Institute for Public Policy Research, 1977.

_____. "Worldly Wisdom, Christian Foolishness." *First Things* 5 (August/September 1990): 16–22.

Bertram, Robert. "Political Preaching, 39 Propositions for Addressing Controversial Issues." *The Cresset* 38 (December 1984): 4–6.

_____. "Recent Lutheran Theologies on Justification by Faith: A Sampling." In *Justification by Faith: Lutherans and Catholics in Dialogue VII*, eds. H. George Anderson, T. Austin Murphy, and Joseph A. Burgess, 241–55. Minneapolis: Augsburg Publishing House, 1985.

Bettenhausen, Elizabeth. "The Concept of Justice and a Feminist Lutheran Social Ethic." In *Annual of the Society of Christian Ethics, 1986*, ed. Alan B. Anderson, 163–82. Washington, D.C.: Georgetown University Press, 1987.

_____. "Dependence, Liberation, and Justification." *Word & World* VII, 1 (Winter 1987): 59–69.

_____. "Faith is a Matter of Experience." *Word & World* I, 3 (Summer 1981): 262–71.

Birch, Bruce C., and Larry L. Rasmussen. *Bible and Ethics in the Christian Life*. Rev. and expanded ed. Minneapolis: Augsburg Fortress, 1989.

Bloomquist, Karen L. *The Dream Betrayed: Religious Challenges of the Working-Class*. Minneapolis: Fortress Press, 1990.

_____. "Given Feminism, Does Theology Need a New Starting Point?" *Word & World* VIII, 4 (Fall 1988): 374, 376.

Boff, Leonardo. "Luther, the Reformation, and Liberation." In *Faith Born in the Struggle for Life: A Rereading of Protestant Faith in Latin America Today*, ed. Dow Kirkpatrick, 195–212. Grand Rapids, Mich.: Eerdmans, 1988.

Bouman, Walter R. "The Concept of the 'Law' in the Lutheran Tradition." *Word & World* III, 4 (Fall 1983): 413–22.

Braaten, Carl E. *The Flaming Center*, 57–63. Philadelphia: Fortress Press, 1977. For and against the two kingdoms.

_____. "God in Public Life: Rehabilitating the 'Orders of Creation'." *First Things* 8 (December 1990): 32–38.

_____. *Justification: The Article by Which the Church Stands or Falls*. Minneapolis: Fortress Press, 1990.

_____. "Natural Law in Theology and Politics." In *The Two Cities of God: The Church's Responsibilities for the Earthly City*, eds. Braaten and Robert W. Jenson, 42–58. Grand Rapids, Mich.: Eerdmans, 1997.

_____. *Principles of Lutheran Theology*, 123–39. Philadelphia: Fortress Press, 1983. On the two-kingdoms principle.

_____, with Robert Benne et al. "'Two Kingdoms' as Social Doctrine." *Dialog* XXIII, 3 (Summer 1984): 207–12.

Brakemeier, Gottfried. "Justification by Grace and Liberation Theology: A Comparison." *Ecumenical Review* 40, 2 (April 1988): 215–22.

Brakenhielm, Carl Reinhold. *Forgiveness*. Trans. from the Swedish by Thor Hall. Minneapolis: Fortress Press, 1993. Relates forgiveness to ethics and politics.

Burtness, James H. "Doing What Comes Naturally: Christian Ethics and the Is/Ought Question." *Dialog* 25, 3 (Summer 1986): 186–92.

_____. "Law and Life: A New Invitation to an Old Problem." In *All Things New: Essays in Honor of Roy A. Harrisville*, eds. Arland J. Hultgren, Donald H. Juel, and Jack D. Kingsbury, 155–64. St. Paul: Word & World, Luther Seminary, 1992.

_____. "Life-Style and Law: Some Reflections on Matthew 5:17." *Dialog* 14, 1 (Winter 1975): 13–20.

Campbell, Charles L. "Living Faith: Luther, Preaching, and Ethics." *Word & World* VIII, 4 (Fall 1988): 374–79.

Childs, James M. *Christian Anthropology and Ethics*. Philadelphia: Fortress Press, 1978.

_____. "The Church and Human Rights: Reflections on Morality and Mission." *Currents in Theology and Mission* 7, 1 (February 1980): 15–23.

_____. *Ethics in Business: Faith at Work*. Minneapolis: Fortress Press, 1995.

_____. *Faith, Formation and Decision: Ethics in the Community of Promise*. Minneapolis: Fortress Press, 1992.

_____. "On Seeing Ourselves: Anthropology and Social Ethics." *Word & World* II, 3 (Summer 1982): 225–33.

_____. "A Theology for Lutheran Social Services." *Trinity Seminary Review* 1, 1 (Spring 1979): 9–15.

_____. "Third Use of the Law and Constructive Ethics." *Currents in Theology and Mission* 2, 1 (February 1975): 35–40.

Dawn, Marva J. *The Hilarity of Community: Romans 12 and How To Be the Church*. Grand Rapids, Mich.: Eerdmans, 1992.

_____. "Worship and Ethics." *Dialog* 32, 4 (Fall 1993): 297–302.

DeBerg, Betty A. with Elizabeth Sherman, compilers. *Women and Women's Issues in North American Lutheranism: A Bibliography*. Minneapolis: Augsburg Fortress Publishing House, 1992.

Deifelt, Wanda. "Toward a Latin American Feminist Hermeneutics: A Dialogue with the Biblical Methodologies of Elisabeth Schuessler Fiorenza, Phyllis Trible, Carlos Mesters, and Pablo Richard." Unpublished Ph.D. diss., Northwestern University/Garrett-Evangelical Theological Seminary, 1990.

Diehl, William E. *The Monday Connection: A Spirituality of Competence, Affirmation, and Support in the Workplace*. San Francisco: Harper, 1991.

_____. *In Search of Faithfulness: Lessons from the Christian Community*. Philadelphia: Fortress Press, 1987.

Ditmanson, Harold. "Christian Faith and Public Morality." *Dialog* 26, 2 (Spring 1987): 87–97.

Duchrow, Ulrich, ed. *Lutheran Churches—Salt or Mirror of Society? Case Studies on the Theory and Practice of the Two Kingdoms Doctrine*. Geneva: Lutheran World Federation, 1977.

_____. *Two Kingdoms—The Use and Misuse of a Lutheran Theological Concept*. Geneva: Lutheran World Federation, 1977.

Echols, James K. "White Theology: A Contrast to Black Theology." *Dialog* 23, 1 (Winter 1984): 27–31.

Ellingsen, Mark. "Niebuhr for the '90s." *Lutheran Forum* 27, 2 (Pentecost 1993): 40–43.

Elshtain, Jean Bethke. *Augustine and the Limits of Politics.* Notre Dame: University of Notre Dame Press, 1995.

————. "Caesar, Sovereignty, and Bonhoeffer." In *Caesar's Coin Revisited: Christians and the Limits of Government*, ed. Michael Cromartie, 45–58. Grand Rapids, Mich.: Eerdmans, 1996.

————. "Judge Not?" *First Things* 46 (October 1994): 36–40.

————. "Luther 'sic'—Luther 'non'." *Theology Today* XLIII, 2 (July 1986): 155–68.

————. "Shame and Public Life." *Dialog* 34, 1 (Winter 1995): 18–22.

Enquist, Roy J. *Namibia: Land of Tears, Land of Promise*, 76–146. Selinsgrove, Pa.: Susquehanna University Press, 1990. Under "An African Vision" discusses "the Africanization of the two kingdoms."

————. "A Paraclete in the Public Square." *Theology & Public Policy* II, 2 (Fall 1990): 17–33.

————. "Two Kingdoms and the American Future." *Dialog* 26, 2 (Spring 1987): 111–14.

Falcke, Heino. "The Challenge of the 'New Thinking' in Eastern Europe." *Ecumenical Review* 40, 2 (April 1988): 204–14.

————. "The Place of the Two Kingdom Doctrine in the Life of the Evangelical Churches in the German Democratic Republic." *Lutheran World* 24, 1 (1977): 22–30.

Fisher, Wallace E. *Stand Fast in Faith: Finding Freedom through Discipline in the Ten Commandments.* Nashville: Abingdon, 1978.

Folk, Jerry. *Doing Theology, Doing Justice.* Minneapolis: Fortress Press, 1991.

————. *Worldly Christians: A Call to Faith, Prayer, and Action.* Minneapolis: Augsburg Publishing House, 1983.

Forde, Gerhard O. "Called to Freedom." *Lutherjahrbuch, 1995*, ed. Helmar Junghaus, 13–27.

————. "Christian Life." In *Christian Dogmatics*, II, eds. Carl E. Braaten and Robert W. Jenson, 391–469. Philadelphia: Fortress Press, 1984.

————. *Justification by Faith—A Matter of Life and Death.* Philadelphia: Fortress Press, 1982.

————. *On Being a Theologian of the Cross: Reflections on Luther's Heidelberg Disputation, 1518.* Grand Rapids, Mich.: Eerdmans, 1997.

Forell, George W. "A Christian Rationale for Political Engagement Today." *Lutheran Theological Seminary Bulletin* 68, 3 (Summer 1988): 7–16.

————. "Is There Lutheran Ethical Discourse?" *Word & World* XV, 1 (Winter 1995): 5–13.

————. *Martin Luther, Theologian of the Church: Collected Essays*, ed. William R. Russell. St. Paul, Minnesota: *Word & World*, Luther Seminary, 1994. Constructive as well as historical essays.

Gaebler, Mary D. "Retrieving Luther's Ethic: Christian Identity and Action in a Post-Foundationist Age." Unpublished Ph.D. diss, Yale University. Forthcoming.

Glennon, Fred. "Ethical Challenges for Social Ministry Today: Some Theological and Ethical Considerations." *Currents in Theology and Mission* 23, 4 (August 1996): 279–86.

Gomez, Medardo Ernesto. *And the Word Became History: Messages Forged in the Fires of Central American Conflict.* Trans. from the Spanish by Robert F. Gussick. Minneapolis: Augsburg, 1992.

————. *Fire Against Fire: Christian Ministry Face-to-face with Persecution.* Trans. from the Spanish by Mary M. Solberg. Minneapolis: Augsburg, 1990.

Grenholm, Carl-Henric. *Protestant Work Ethics: A Study of Work Ethical Theories in Contemporary Protestant Theology.* Trans. from the Swedish by Craig Graham McKay. Uppsala: Uppsala Studies in Social Ethics 15, 1993.

Gritsch, Eric W. "Bold Sinning: The Lutheran Option." *Dialog* 14, 1 (Winter 1975): 26–32.

————, and Robert W. Jenson. *Lutheranism: The Theological Movement and Its Confessional Writings*, 137–52, 179–90. Philadelphia: Fortress Press, 1976. An historian and a systematic theologian discuss "Christian Life—Brave Sinning" and "Politics—Two Kingdoms?"

Gustafson, James M. *Protestant and Roman Catholic Ethics: Prospects for Rapprochement.* Chicago: University of Chicago Press, 1978.

Hall, Douglas John. "The Diversity of Christian Witnessing in the Tension Between Subjection to the Word and Relation to the Context." In *Luther's Ecumenical Significance*, eds. Peter Manns and Harding Meyer, 247–68. Philadelphia: Fortress Press, 1984.

_____. *Lighten Our Darkness: Toward an Indigenous Theology of the Cross*. Philadelphia: Westminster Press, 1976. Draws on Luther's theology of the cross.

Hampson, Daphne. "Luther on the Self: A Feminist Critique." *Word & World* VIII, 4 (Fall 1988): 334–42.

Hansen, Guillermo C. "The Doctrine of the Trinity and Liberation Theology: A Study of the Trinitarian Doctrine and Its Place in Latin American Liberation Theology." Unpublished Th.D. diss., Lutheran School of Theology at Chicago, 1994.

Hefner, Philip. "Determinism, Freedom, and Moral Failure." *Dialog* 33, 1 (Winter 1994): 23–29.

Heinecken, Martin J. "Justification by Faith." In *The Westminster Dictionary of Christian Ethics*, eds. James F. Childress and John Macquarrie, 333–34. Philadelphia: Westminster Press, 1986.

_____. "Law and Gospel." In *The Westminster Dictionary of Christian Ethics*, eds. James F. Childress and John Macquarrie, 344–47. Philadelphia: Westminster Press, 1986.

Herman, Stewart W. "The Ethics of Business Corporations: A Possible Lutheran Contribution." *Word & World* X, 4 (Fall 1990): 356 67.

_____. "Luther, Law and Social Covenants: Cooperative Self-Obligation in the Reconstruction of Lutheran Social Ethics." *Journal of Religious Ethics* 25, 2 (Fall 1997): 257–75.

Hertz, Karl H. "Lutheran Theology and Normative Social Theory." *Lutheran World* 23, 1 (1976): 4 10.

Hinlicky, Paul R. "Breaking Free of the Liberal Hegemony." *Lutheran Forum* 27, 2 (Pentecost 1993): 44–52.

_____. "The Human Predicament in Emergent Post-Modernity." *Dialog* 23, 3 (Summer 1984): 167–73.

_____. "The Task of Lutheran Political Thought Today." *Word & World* VIII, 3 (Summer 1988): 271–81.

Hoehn, Richard A. *Up from Apathy: A Study of Moral Awareness & Social Involvement*. Nashville: Abingdon Press, 1983.

Hordern, William. "Liberation Theology in a Canadian Context." In *Hinterland Theology in an Ecumenical Context: Essays in Honor of Benjamin Smillie and Charles F. Johnston*, ed. Michael Bourgeois, 17–26. Saskatoon, Sask.: St. Andrew's College, 1995.

_____. *Living by Grace*. Philadelphia: Westminster Press, 1975.

Hoy, Michael. *The Faith That Works: The Relationship of Faith and Works in the Theology of Juan Luis Segundo, S.J.* Lanham, Md.: University Press of America, 1995.

Huber, Wolfgang. "The Barmen Theological Declaration and the Two Kingdoms Doctrine." *Lutheran World* 24, 1 (1977): 31–44.

Huovinen, Eero. "Diakonia—A Basic Task of the Church." *Pro Ecclesia* III, 2 (Spring 1994): 206–14.

Hütter, Reinhard. "The Church as Public: Dogma, Practice, and the Holy Spirit." *Pro Ecclesia* III, 3 (Summer 1994): 334–61.

_____. "The Church: Midwife of History or Witness of the Eschaton?" *Journal of Religious Ethics* 19,1 (1990): 27–54.

_____. "The Church's Public Ministry in Her Babylonian Captivity." *Pro Ecclesia* II, 1 (Winter 1993): 18–20.

_____. "Considering *Veritatis Splendor*: A Book Worth Discussing." *Currents in Theology and Mission* 23, 3 (June 1996): 200–209.

_____. "Ecclesial Ethics, The Church's Vocation and Paraclesis." *Pro Ecclesia* II, 4 (Fall 1993): 433–50.

_____. "The Ecclesial Ethics of Stanley Hauerwas." *Dialog* 30, 2 (Summer 1991):231–41.

_____, and Theodor Dieter, eds. *Ecumenical Ventures in Ethics: Protestants Engage Pope John Paul II's Moral Encyclicals*. Grand Rapids, Mich.: Eerdmans, 1998. Includes articles by Dieter, Karl P. Donfried, Jean Bethke Elshtain, Hütter, Lois Malcolm, Gilbert Meilaender, Risto Saarinen, and Bernd Wannenwetsch.

_____. "On *John Milbank's* Theology and Social Theory: Beyond Secular Reason." *Pro Ecclesia* II, 1 (Winter 1993): 106–16.

Ickert, Scott. "The Uses of the Law." *Lutheran Forum* 25, 1 (Lent 1991): 20–23.

Jensen, Robert W. "The Church's Responsibility for the World." In *The Two Cities of God: The Church's Responsibilities for the Earthly City*, eds. Carl E. Braaten and Jenson, 1–11. Grand Rapids, Mich.: Eerdmans, 1997.

_____. "The Division of the Moral Person." In *Encounter with Luther*, 1, ed. Eric W. Gritsch, 259–70. Gettysburg, Pa.: Institute for Luther Studies, 1980.

_____. *Essays in Theology of Culture*. Grand Rapids, Mich.: Eerdmans, 1995.

_____. "Faithfulness." *Dialog* 14, 1 (Winter 1975): 38–41.

_____. "The Return to Baptism." In *Encounter with Luther*, 2, ed. Eric W. Gritsch, 217–29. Gettysburg, Pa.: Institute for Luther Studies, 1982.

_____. "Spiritual Formation and the Foundations of Ethics." *Lutheran Theological Seminary Bulletin* 58, 4 (November 1978): 22–27.

Jersild, Paul T. *Making Moral Decisions: A Christian Approach to Personal and Social Ethics*. Minneapolis: Fortress Press, 1990. An introduction for serious lay audience.

_____. "Reinhold Niebuhr: Continuing the Assessment." *Dialog* 22, 4 (Fall 1983): 284–93.

_____. "Understanding the Law When 'Everything is Relative'." *Currents in Theology and Mission* 11, 4 (August 1984): 204–12.

Jüngel, Eberhard. *Christ, Justice and Peace: Toward a Theology of the State*. Trans. by D. Bruce Hamill and Alan J. Torrance. Edinburgh: T. & T. Clark, 1992.

_____. *The Freedom of a Christian: Luther's Significance for Contemporary Theology*. Trans. by Roy A. Harrisville. Minneapolis: Augsburg Publishing House, 1988. Commentary on Luther's essay.

_____. *Theological Essays II*, 163–263. Ed. with an Introduction by J.B. Webster. Trans. by Arnold Neufeldt-Fast and J.B. Webster. Edinburgh: T. & T. Clark, 1995. Four essays on ethical topics.

Justification and Justice: A Meeting of Lutheran Theologians of the Americas. Minneapolis: America Lutheran Church, 1985. Typescript. Collection of papers from a consultation in Mexico City.

Kanyoro, Musimbi. "Cultural Hermeneutics: An African Contribution." In *Women's Visions: Theological Reflection, Celebration, Action*, ed. Ofelia Ortega, 18–28. Geneva: WCC Publications, 1995.

_____, and Wendy S. Robins, eds. *The Power We Celebrate: Women's Stories of Faith and Power*. Geneva: WCC Publications, Lutheran World Federation, 1992. Articles by Wanda Deifelt, Kanyoro, Jean Sindab, Ranjini Rebera, Raquel Rodriguez, Violet Cucciniello Little, Constance F. Parvey, Barbel von Wartenberg-Potter, Christa Berger, Lynda Katsuno-Ishii, and Robins.

Keifert, Patrick R. "The Bible, Congregational Leaders, and Moral Conversation." *Word & World* XIII, 4 (Fall 1993): 392–97.

Kelly, Robert. "The Liberatory Possibilities of the Doctrine of Justification." *Consensus* 19, 2 (1993): 53–70.

Kennedy, Thomas D. "Introduction." In *From Christ to the World: Introductory Readings in Christian Ethics*, eds. Wayne G. Boulton, Kennedy, and Allen Verhey, 1–11. Grand Rapids, Mich.: Eerdmans, 1995.

Kirst, Nelson, ed. *Rethinking Luther's Theology in the Contexts of the Third World*. Geneva: Lutheran World Federation, 1988. Major essays by Alberico Baeske, Ricardo Pietrantonio, Devasahayam W. Jesudoss, and M. Philip Moila.

Kittelson, James M. "Contemporary Spirituality's Challenge to *Sola Gratia*." *Lutheran Quarterly* IX, 4 (Winter 1995): 367–90.

Klein, Christa Ressmeyer. "The Lay Vocation: At the Altar in the World." In *Being Christian Today: An American Conversation*, eds. Richard John Neuhaus and George Weigel, 197–210. Lanham, Md.: Ethics and Public Policy Center, 1992.

_____. "Our Quest for a Public Theology." *Lutheran Forum* 27, 2 (Pentecost 1993): 28–32.

Knutsen, Mary M. "Given Feminism, Does Theology Need a New Starting Point?" *Word & World* VIII, 4 (Fall 1988): 375, 377.

Kolden, Marc. *Called by the Gospel: An Introduction to the Christian Faith*. Minneapolis: Fortress Press, 1983.

_____. "Christian Vocation in Light of Feminist Critiques." *Lutheran Quarterly* X, 1 (Spring 1996): 71–85.

Krueger, David A. *Keeping Faith at Work: The Christian in the Workplace*. Nashville: Abingdon Press, 1994.

Krusche, Günter. "Lutheran Identity and Responsibility in and for the World." In *Studies on the Identity of the Church*, 51–78. Geneva: Lutheran World Federation, 1979.

Kuhl, Steven. "Christ and Agriculture: Toward a Theologically Useful Understanding of the Crisis of American Agriculture Utilizing the Theologies of Culture of H. Richard Niebuhr, Martin Luther and Paul." Unpublished Th.D. diss., Lutheran School of Theology at Chicago, 1993.

_____. "To Speak or Not to Speak? Critical Reflections on the Relation of Church and Society." *Dialog* 30, 2 (Spring 1991): 166–71.

Kuitert, H. M. *Everything Is Politics but Politics Is Not Everything: A Theological Perspective on Faith and Politics*. Trans. by John Bowden. Grand Rapids, Mich.: Eerdmans, 1986. Dutch Reformed theologian takes a two-kingdom approach.

Kvam, Kristen E. "'Honoring God's Handiwork': Challenges of Luther's Doctrine of Creation." In *A Reforming Church—Gift and Task: Essays from a Free Conference*, ed. Charles P. Lutz, 173–86. Minneapolis: Kirk House, 1995.

Lambert, Lake. "Called to Business. Management as Profession of Faith." Unpublished Ph.D. diss., Princeton Theological Seminary, 1997.

Lazareth, William H. "God's Call to Public Responsibility." In *God's Call to Public Responsibility*, 36–44 Philadelphia: Fortress Press, 1978

_____. "Love and Law in Christian Life." In *Piety, Politics, and Ethics: Reformation Studies in Honor of George Wolfgang Forell*, ed. Carter Lindberg, 103–18. Kirksville, Mo.: Sixteenth Century Journal Publishers, 1984.

_____. "Lutheran Ethics." In *The Westminster Dictionary of Christian Ethics*, eds. James F. Childress and John Macquarrie, 360–63. Philadelphia: Westminster Press, 1986.

_____. "Orders." In *The Westminster Dictionary of Christian Ethics*, eds. James F. Childress and John Macquarrie, 440–41. Philadelphia: Westminster Press, 1986.

_____. "Sentinels for the Tricentennial." In *The Left Hand of God*, ed. Lazareth, 113–68. Philadelphia: Fortress Press, 1976. A Lutheran approach to justice.

_____. "Two Realms." In *The Westminster Dictionary of Christian Ethics*, eds. James F. Childress and John Macquarrie, 633–34. Philadelphia: Westminster Press, 1986.

Lee, Daniel E. *Generations and the Challenge of Justice*. Lanham, Md.: University Press of America, 1996.

_____. *Hope Is Where We Least Expect to Find It*. Lanham, Md.: University Press of America, 1993.

Lehmann, Paul L. *The Decalogue and a Human Future: The Meaning of the Commandments for Making and Keeping Human Life Human*. Grand Rapids, Mich.: Eerdmans, 1995. Draws on Luther's "Large Catechism."

Lindbeck, George. "Modernity and Luther's Understanding of the Freedom of the Christian." In *Martin Luther and the Modern Mind: Freedom, Conscience, Toleration, Rights*, ed. Manfred Hoffmann, 1–22. Lewiston, N. Y.: Edwin Mellen, 1985.

Lissner, Jørgen, and Arne Sovik, eds. *A Lutheran Reader on Human Rights*. Geneva: Lutheran World Federation, 1978. Statements from Lutheran churches and individual articles, including ones by Marc Lienhard, Wolfgang Huber and Heinz Eduard Tödt, Helmut Frenz, and Richard J. Niebanck.

Lønning, Per. *Creation—An Ecumenical Challenge?: Reflections Issuing from a Study by the Institute for Ecumenical Research, Strasbourg, France*. Macon, Georgia: Mercer University Press, 1989.

Lorenz, Eckehart, ed. *How Christian Are Human Rights?* Geneva: Lutheran World Federation, 1980. Includes essays by Carl E. Braaten, Trutz Rendtorff, and Günter Krusche. Bibliography.

Luecke, Richard H. "Lutheran Urban Ministry, 1945–1990." *Currents in Theology and Mission* 23, 1 (February 1996): 5–28.

Lull, Timothy F. "The (Normative) Sexual Hole." *Dialog* 32, 1 (Winter 1993): 65–68.

Madsen, Meg. "Feminism Come of Age." *Dialog* 27, 2 (Spring 1988): 125–30.

Maimela, Simon S. *God's Creative Activity Through the Law: A Constructive Statement Toward a Theology of Social Transformation*. Pretoria: University of South Africa, 1984.

_____. "Jesus Christ: The Liberator and Hope of Oppressed People." In *Exploring Afro-Christology*, ed. John Pobee, 31–42. New York: Peter Lang, 1992.

_____. *Proclaim Freedom to My People: Essays on Religion and Politics*. Johannesburg: Skotaville Publishers, 1987.

_____. "The Suffering of Human Divisions and the Cross." In *The Scandal of a Crucified World*, ed. Yacob Tesfai, 35–47. Maryknoll, N. Y.: Orbis, 1994.

_____. "The Task of Theology in South Africa Today." *Dialog* 25, 4 (Fall 1986): 281–85.

Malcolm, Lois. "The Gospel and Feminism: A Proposal for Lutheran Dogmatics." *Word & World* XV, 3 (Summer 1995): 290–98.

Martin-Schramm, James B. "Justification and the Center of Paul's Ethics." *Dialog* 33, 2 (Spring 1994): 106–10.

_____. *Population Perils and the Churches' Response*. Geneva: WCC Publications, 1997.

Marty, Martin E. *Being Good and Doing Good*. Philadelphia: Fortress Press, 1984. An introduction to Lutheran ethics for a general audience.

_____. *The One and the Many: America's Struggle for the Common Good*. Cambridge: Harvard University Press, 1997.

_____. *The Public Church: Mainline-Evangelical-Catholic*. New York: Crossroad, 1981.

Meilander, Gilbert. *Bioethics: A Primer for Christians*. Grand Rapids, Mich.: Eerdmans, 1996.

_____. "*Eritus Sicut Deus*: Moral Theory and the Sin of Pride." *Faith and Philosophy* 3, 4 (October 1986): 397–415.

_____. *Faith and Faithfulness: Basic Themes in Christian Ethics*. Notre Dame: University of Notre Dame Press, 1991.

_____. *Friendship: A Study in Theological Ethics*. Notre Dame: University of Notre Dame Press, 1981.

_____. "The First of Institutions." *Pro Ecclesia* VI, 4 (Fall 1997): 444–55.

_____. "Is What Is Right for Me Right for All Persons Similarly Situated?" *Journal of Religious Ethics* 8, 1 (Spring 1980): 125–34.

_____. *Letters to Ellen*. Grand Rapids, Mich.: Eerdmans, 1996.

_____. *The Limits of Love: Some Theological Explorations*. University Park, Pa.: The Pennsylvania State University Press, 1987.

_____. "The Singularity of Christian Ethics." *Journal of Religious Ethics* 17, 2 (Fall 1989): 95–120.

_____. *The Theory and Practice of Virtue*. Notre Dame: University of Notre Dame Press, 1984.

_____. "To Throw Oneself into the Wave: The Problem of Possessions." In *The Preferential Option for the Poor*, ed. and with an Introduction by Richard John Neuhaus, 72–86. Grand Rapids, Mich.: Eerdmans, 1988.

_____. "The Venture of Marriage." In *The Two Cities of God: The Church's Responsibilities for the Earthly City*, eds. Carl E. Braaten and Robert W. Jenson, 117–32. Grand Rapids, Mich.: Eerdmans, 1997.

_____. "*Veritatis Splendor*: Reopening Some Questions of the Reformation." *Journal of Religious Ethics* 23, 2 (Fall 1995): 225–38.

_____. "Virtue in Contemporary Religious Thought." In *Virtue—Public and Private*, ed. and with an Introduction by Richard John Neuhaus, 7–29. Grand Rapids, Mich.: Eerdmans, 1986.

Moltmann, Jürgen. *The Crucified God: The Cross of Christ as the Foundation and Criticism of Christian Theology*. Trans. from the German by R. A. Wilson and John Bowden. New York: Harper & Row, 1973.

_____. *On Human Dignity*, 61–77. Trans. from the German and with an Introduction by M. Douglas Meeks. Philadelphia: Fortress Press, 1984. On the two kingdoms.

Mortensen, Viggo, ed. *Concern for Creation: Voices on the Theology of Creation*. Sweden: Svenska kyrkan. Forskningsrad, 1995. Essays from a Lutheran World Federation Consultation, May 1994. Includes contributions from Per Lønning, Heinrich Holze, Ricardo Pietrantonio, Won Jong Ji, Elizabeth Bettenhausen, Grace N. Ndyabahika, Kjetil Hafsted, Philip Hefner, and Vitor Westhelle.

_____, ed. *Justification and Justice*. Geneva: Lutheran World Federation, 1992. Articles by Mortensen, Juhani Forsberg, Vitor Westhelle, and Mercedes Garcia Bachmann.

Nelson, Paul. *Narrative and Morality: A Theological Inquiry*. University Park, Pa.: Pennsylvania State University Press, 1987.

Nelson, Randolph A. "Theological Foundations for Social Ethics." *Word & World* IV, 3 (Summer 1984): 248–59.

Nessan, Craig L. "How Social Is the Gospel? Some Twentieth Century Answers." *Currents in Theology and Mission* 18, 3 (June 1991): 166–75.

_____. "Liberation Theology's Critique of Luther's Two Kingdoms Doctrine." *Currents in Theology and Mission* 16, 4 (August 1989): 257–66.

_____. *Orthopraxis or Heresy: The North American Theological Response to Latin America Liberation Theology*. Atlanta: Scholars Press, 1989.

Neuhaus, Richard John. *Freedom for Ministry: A Critical Affirmation of the Church and Its Mission*. New York: Harper & Row, 1979.

_____. *The Naked Public Square: Religion and Democracy in America*. Grand Rapids, Mich.: Eerdmans, 1984.

_____. *Time Toward Home: The American Experiment as Revelation*. New York: Seabury Press, 1975.

_____. "To Serve the Lord of All: Law, Gospel, and Social Responsibility." *Dialog* 30, 2 (Spring 1991): 140–49.

Nevile, Don. "The Two Kingdoms' Today." *Consensus* 21, 2 (1995): 39–58.

Niebanck, Richard J. "Grace and Public Theology." *Lutheran Forum* 23, 1 (Lent 1989): 8–11.

Østnor, Lars, Jaana Hallamaa et al., "The Lutheran Approach to Bioethics." In *Life and Death: Moral Implications of Biotechnology*, ed. Viggo Mortensen, 9–34. Geneva: WCC Publications, 1995. Introductory essay of a study book from the Lutheran World Federation sketches a Lutheran approach to ethics.

Outka, Gene. "Augustinianism and Common Morality." In *Prospects for a Common Morality*, eds. Outka and John P. Reeder, Jr., 114–48. Princeton, N. J.: Princeton University Press, 1993.

_____. "Love. II. Contemporary Discussion." In *The Westminster Dictionary of Christian Ethics*, eds. James F. Childress and John Macquarrie, 357–59. Philadelphia: Westminster Press, 1986.

_____. "On Harming Others." *Interpretation* XXXIV, 4 (October 1980). 381–93.

_____. "The Particularist Turn in Theological and Philosophical Ethics." In *Christian Ethics: Problems and Prospects*, eds. Lisa Sowle Cahill and James F. Childress, 93–118. Cleveland: Pilgrim Press, 1996.

_____. "The Protestant Tradition and Exceptionless Moral Norms." In *Moral Theology Today: Certitudes and Doubts*, 136–64. St. Louis. The Pope John Center, 1984.

_____. "Respect for Persons." In *The Westminster Dictionary of Christian Ethics*, eds. James F. Childress and John Macquarrie, 541–45. Philadelphia: Westminster Press, 1986.

_____. "Universal Love and Impartiality." In *The Love Commandments: Essays in Christian Ethics and Moral Philosophy*, ed. Outka, 1–103. Washington, D. C.: Georgetown University Press, 1992.

Pannenberg, Wolfhart. *Anthropology in Theological Perspective*. Trans. from the German by Matthew J. O'Connell. Philadelphia: Westminster Press, 1985. Bibliography.

_____. *Christian Spirituality*. Philadelphia: Westminster Press, 1983.

_____. *Ethics*. Trans. from the German by Keith Crim. Philadelphia: Westminster Press, 1981.

_____. "Freedom and the Lutheran Reformation." *Theology Today* XXXVIII, 3 (October 1981): 287–97.

Pasewark, Kyle A. "The Body in Ecstasy: Love, Difference, and the Social Organism in Luther's Theology of the Lord's Supper." *Journal of Religion* 77, 4 (October 1997): 511–40.

_____. *A Theology of Power: Being Beyond Domination*. Minneapolis: Fortress Press, 1993. Takes principal clues from Luther in redefining power.

Pellauer, Mary D., with Susan Brooks Thistlethwaite. "Conversations on Grace and Healing: Perspectives from the Movement to End Violence Against Women." In *Lift Every Voice: Constructing Christian Theologies from the Underside*, eds. Thistlethwaite and Mary Potter Engel, 168–85. San Francisco: Harper & Row, 1990.

_____. "Feminist Theology: Challenges and Consolations for Lutherans." *Dialog* 24, 1 (Winter 1985): 19–24.

_____. *Towards a Tradition of Feminist Theology: The Religious Social Thought of Elizabeth Cady Stanton, Susan B. Anthony, and Anna Howard Shaw*. Brooklyn, N.Y.: Carlson, 1991.

Pero, Albert, and Ambrose Moyo, eds. *Theology and the Black Experience: The Lutheran Heritage Interpreted by African and African-American Theologians*. Minneapolis: Augsburg Publishing House, 1988. Essays by Richard J. Perry, Simon S. Maimela, Rudolph R. Featherstone, Judah Kiwovele, Moyo, James Kenneth Echols, John S. Pobee, Sibusiso M. Bengu, Pero, Cheryl A. Stewart, Vivian V. Msomi, and Craig J. Lewis.

Perry, Richard J. Jr. "Which Way Should We Go? The Ethical Dilemma of African American Lutheranism." *Currents in Theology and Mission* 24, 3 (June 1997): 252–59.

Persaud, Winston D. "The Article of Justification and the Theology of Liberation." *Currents in Theology and Mission* 16, 5 (October 1989): 361–71.

_____. "The Cross of Jesus Christ, the Unity of the Church, and Human Suffering." In *The Scandal of a Crucified World*, ed. Yacob Tesfai, 111–29. Maryknoll, N. Y.: Orbis, 1994.

_____. "Luther's *Theologia Crucis*: A Theology of 'Radical Reversal' in Response to the Challenge of Marx's *Weltanschauung*." *Dialog* 29, 4 (Autumn 1990): 264–73.

_____. "Towards a Trinitarian Theology of Justification and Vision of Eco-Justice." *Dialog* 31, 4 (Autumn 1992): 294–302.

Peters, Ted. *God—the World's Future: Systematic Theology for a Postmodern Era*, 357–77. Minneapolis: Fortress Press, 1992. Proleptic Ethics.

_____. *Sin: Radical Evil in Soul and Society*. Grand Rapids, Mich.: Eerdmans, 1994.

Petty, John. "The Doctrine of the Two Kingdoms and the Church Today." *Dialog* 31, 4 (Autumn 1992): 313–19.

Rasmussen, Larry L. "A Community of the Cross." *Dialog* 30, 2 (Spring 1991): 150–62.

_____, with Renate Bethge. *Dietrich Bonhoeffer: His Significance for North Americans*. Minneapolis: Fortress Press, 1990. An ethic of the cross.

_____. *Earth Community, Earth Ethics*. Maryknoll: Orbis Books, 1996.

_____. "The Future Isn't What It Used to Be: Limits to Growth and Christian Ethics." *Lutheran Quarterly* XXVII, 2 (May 1975): 101–11.

_____. "Going Public: The Church's Roles." In *God, Goods, and the Common Good: Eleven Perspectives on Economic Justice in Dialog with the Roman Catholic Bishops' Pastoral Letter*, ed. Charles P. Lutz, 29–44. Minneapolis: Augsburg Publishing House, 1987.

_____. "Moral Community and Moral Formation." In *Ecclesiology and Ethics: Costly Commitment*, eds. Thomas F. Best and Martin Robra, 54–60. Geneva: World Council of Churches, 1995.

_____. *Moral Fragments and Moral Community: A Proposal for Church in Society*. Minneapolis: Fortress Press, 1993.

_____. "Niebuhr on Power." In *Reinhold Niebuhr (1892–1971): A Centenary Appraisal*, eds. Gary A. Gaudin and Douglas John Hall, 145–86. Atlanta: Scholars Press, 1994.

_____. "The Obsolescence of Conventional Deciding." *Dialog* 14, 1 (Winter 1975): 42–47.

_____. "Power Analysis: A Neglected Agenda in Christian Ethics." In *Annual of the Society of Christian Ethics*, 1991, ed. D. M. Yeager, 3–17. Washington, D.C.: Georgetown University Press, 1991.

_____. "The Public Vocation of an Eschatological Community." *Union Seminary Quarterly Review* 42, 4 (1988): 25–36.

_____. "Shaping Communities." In *Practicing Our Faith: A Way of Life for a Searching People*, ed. Dorothy Bass, 119–32. San Francisco: Jossey-Bass Publishers, 1997.

Raunio, Antti. "Natural Law and Faith: The Forgotten Foundations of Ethics in Luther's Theology." In *Union with Christ: The New Finnish Interpretation of Luther*, eds. Carl E. Braaten and Robert W. Jenson. Grand Rapids, Mich.: Eerdmans, 1998. Response by William H. Lazareth.

Reavis, Ralph. *The Meaning of Martin Luther for the Black Experience*. New York: Vantage Press, 1976.

Rendtorff, Trutz. *Ethics 1: Basic Elements and Methodology in an Ethical Theology. 2: Applications of an Ethical Theology*. Trans. from the German by Keith Crim. Philadelphia: Fortress Press, 1986, 89.

Riegert, Eduard. "Preaching on Social-Ethical Issues." *Consensus* 18, 2 (1992): 9–34.

Rodriguez, José David. "Confessing Our Faith in Spanish: Challenge or Promise?" In *Hispanic/Latino Theology: Challenge and Promise*, eds. Isasi-Diaz, Ada Maria, and Fernando F. Segovia, 351–66. Minneapolis: Fortress Press, 1996.

_____. "Fellowship of the Poor: A New Point of Departure for a Lutheran Ecclesiology Taking the Poor as a Theological Locus." Unpublished Th.D. diss., Lutheran School of Theology at Chicago, 1987.

_____. "Theology from the Underside of History: The Perspective of Liberation Theology." *Lutheran Theological Seminary Bulletin* 68, 1 (Winter 1988): 16–30.

Santmire, H. Paul. *The Travail of Nature: The Ambiguous Ecological Promise of Christian Theology.* Philadelphia: Fortress Press, 1985. Discusses Luther (121–33) in presenting an ecological reading of theology.

Sauter, Gerhard. "God Creating Faith: The Doctrine of Justification from the Reformation to the Present." *Lutheran Quarterly* XI, 1 (Spring 1997): 17–102.

_____. "Theological Reflections on the Political Changes in Europe." *Lutheran Quarterly* VIII, 1 (Spring 1994): 15–28.

Schild, Maurice E. "Being a Christ to the Neighbour: Luther and the Development of Human Rights." *Lutheran Theological Journal* 24 (May 1990): 11–17.

Schlichting, Wolfhart. "Justification and Responsibility for the World." *Lutheran Quarterly* VII, 1 (Spring 1993): 19–44.

Schneider, Edward D. "Lutheran Theological Foundations for Social Ethics." *LWF Documentation* 29 (December 1990): 15–24.

Schuurman, Douglas J. "Protestant Vocation Under Assault: Can It Be Salvaged?" In *Annual of the Society of Christian Ethics, 1994*, ed. Harlan Beckley, 23–52. Washington, D.C.: Georgetown University, 1994.

Sherman, Franklin. "The Lutheran Ethos and Biomedical Ethics Today." *Currents in Theology and Mission* 15, 6 (December 1988): 565–73.

_____. "Lutheran Theology and American Democracy." In *Religion and the Dilemmas of Nationhood*, ed. Sydney Ahlstrom, 29–35. Philadelphia: Lutheran Church in America, 1976.

_____. "Messianism, Mysticism, and the Mitzvot." In *American Society of Christian Ethics, 1979: Selected Papers from the Twentieth Annual Meeting*, ed. Max L. Stackhouse, 167–78. Newton Center, Mass.: American Society of Christian Ethics, 1979.

_____. "A New Ethic for a New Age?" *Dialog* 14, 1 (Winter 1975): 33–37.

_____. "The Problem of Evil in the Public Sphere." *Dialog* 25, 2 (Spring 1986): 97–100.

_____. "Secular Calling and Social Ethical Thinking." In *The Lutheran Church Past and Present*, ed. Vilmos Vajta, 185–205. Minneapolis: Augsburg Books, 1977.

Siemon-Netto, Uwe. *The Acquittal of God.* New York: Pilgrim Press, 1990. Views the plight of Vietnam veterans in light of Bonhoeffer's theology of the cross.

Simon, Arthur. *Christian Faith and Public Policy: No Grounds for Divorce.* Grand Rapids, Mich.: Eerdmans, 1987.

Simpson, Gary. "Civil Society and Congregations as Public Moral Companions." *Word & World* XV, 4 (Fall 1995): 420–27.

_____. "Human Nature and Communicative Ethics." *Dialog* 33, 4 (Fall 1994): 280–87.

_____. "*Theologia Crucis* and the Forensically Fraught World." *Journal of the American Academy of Religion* LVII, 3 (Fall 1989): 509–41.

Solberg, Mary M. *Compelling Knowledge: A Feminist Proposal for an Epistemology of the Cross.* New York: Suny Press, 1997.

Sorum, Jonathan. "A Political Theology." *Lutheran Forum* 25, 1 (Lent 1991): 28–33.

Sponheim, Paul. "How Do We Decide? With Reality!" *Dialog* 14, 1 (Winter 1975): 21–25.

Stortz, Martha Ellen. "Beyond Justice: Friendship in the City." *Word & World* XIV, 4 (Fall 1994): 409–18.

_____. "By the Laying on of Hands and by Prayer: An Analysis of Power in the Rite of Ordination." *Consensus* 20, 1 (1994): 9–28.

_____, and Larry L. Rasmussen. "A Coast-to-Coast Conversation on Sexuality." In *A Reforming Church—Gift and Task: Essays from a Free Conference*, ed. Charles P. Lutz, 151–72. Minneapolis: Kirk House, 1995.

_____. "Ethics, Conservation, and Theology in Ecological Perspective." In *Covenant for a New Creation*, eds. Carol S. Robb and Carl J. Casebolt, 196–211. Maryknoll, N.Y.: Orbis Books, 1991.

_____. "The Mother, the Son, and the Bullrushes." *Dialog* 23, 1 (Winter 1984): 21–26.

_____. *Pastorpower.* Nashville: Abingdon Press, 1993. Ethical reflection on power.

_____. "Pelagius Reconsidered." *Word & World* 8, 2 (Spring 1988): 133–40.

Strieter, Thomas. "Two Kingdoms and Governances Thinking for Today's World." *Dialog* 27, 3 (Summer 1988): 204–14.

Strohl, Jane E. "Lutheranism's Call to Action amidst Ambiguity." *Currents in Theology and Mission* 18, 1 (February 1991): 27–33. Jeannie E. Olson responds to Strohl on the "third use" of the law.

Stumme, John R. "Democracy in Argentina." In *The Public Vocation of Christian Ethics,* eds. Beverly W. Harrison, Robert L. Stivers, and Ronald H. Stone, 69–94. New York: Pilgrim Press, 1986.

_____. "Interpreting the Doctrine of the Two Kingdoms." *Dialog* 27, 4 (Fall 1988): 277–84.

_____. "Luther's Concept of the Two Kingdoms in the Context of Liberation Theology." *Word & World* III, 4 (Fall 1983): 423–34.

Stumme, Wayne, ed. *Christians and the Many Faces of Marxism.* Minneapolis: Augsburg Publishing House, 1984. Essays by Stumme, Ronald F. Thiemann, Russell B. Norris, Paul V. Martinson, Paul T. Jersild, James M. Childs Jr., Marc Kolden, Will L. Herzfeld, and Faith E. Burgess.

_____, ed. *The Experience of Hope: Mission and Ministry in Changing Urban Communities.* Minneapolis: Augsburg, 1991.

Sundberg, Walter. "Religion and Politics in America." *Word & World* XII, 4 (Fall 1992): 376–83.

Sundermeier, Theo. "Contextualizing Luther's Theology of the Cross." In *The Scandal of a Crucified World,* ed. Yacob Tesfai, 99–110. Maryknoll, N. Y.: Orbis, 1994.

Tamez, Elsa. *The Amnesty of Grace: Justification by Faith from a Latin American Perspective.* Trans. from the Spanish by Sharon H. Ringe. Nashville: Abingdon Press, 1993.

Thiemann, Ronald F. "Challenges to the Common Good." In *The Church and American Civil Religion: A Report from the USA Lutheran World Federation Study Group,* ed. David G. Burke, 140–46. New York: Lutheran World Ministries, 1987.

_____. *Religion in Public Life: A Dilemma for Democracy.* Washington, D.C.: Georgetown University Press, 1996.

Tinder, Glenn. *The Political Meaning of Christianity: An Interpretation.* Baton Rouge: Louisiana State University Press, 1989. An Episcopalian and political scientist, Tinder identifies himself with the Reformation tradition, particularly Luther.

Tinker, George E. "Does 'All People' Include Native Peoples?" In *God, Goods, and the Common Good: Eleven Perspectives on Economic Justice in Dialog with the Roman Catholic Bishops' Pastoral Letter,* ed. Charles P. Lutz, 125–38. Minneapolis: Augsburg Publishing House, 1987.

Tödt, Heinz E. "Towards a Theory of Making Ethical Judgments." *Journal of Religious Ethics* 6, 1 (Spring 1978): 108–20.

Tokuzen, Yoshikazu. "Luther's Contribution to an Asian Understanding of Nature and the Natural." In *Piety, Politics, and Ethics: Reformation Studies in Honor of George Wolfgang Forell,* ed. Carter Lindberg, 57–64. Kirksville, Mo.: Sixteenth Century Journal Publishers, 1984.

Tsele, Molefe S. "The Dialectic of Salvation and Liberation: A Critical Analysis of the Correlation Models and a Construction of the Two Kingdoms Theology as a Theological Critical Model of Correlation." Unpublished Th.D. diss., Lutheran School of Theology at Chicago, 1995.

Tuttle, Robert William. "A Treason of the Clerks: Paul Ramsey on Christian Ethics and the Common Law." Unpublished Ph.D. diss., University of Virginia, 1997.

Ulrich, Hans G. "A Modern Understanding of Christian Ethics in the Perspective of Its Own Tradition." In *Worship and Ethics: Lutherans and Anglicans in Dialogue,* eds. Oswald Bayer and Alan Suggate, 26–58. New York: Walter de Gruyter, 1996.

_____. "Retrospect and Prospect." In *Worship and Ethics: Lutherans and Anglicans in Dialogue,* eds. Oswald Bayer and Alan Suggate, 285–93. New York: Walter de Gruyter, 1996.

Wainright, Geoffrey. "Eucharist and/as Ethics." *Worship* 62, 2 (March 1988): 123–38.

Wannenwetsch, Bernd. "The Political Worship of the Church: A Critical and Empowering Practice." *Modern Theology* 12, 3 (1966): 269–99.

Wee, Paul A. "Systemic Injustice and the Biblical Witness." Geneva: Lutheran World Federation, 1984.

Weiss, David. "Justification, Faith Development, and Ethics in a Lutheran Perspective." Unpublished Ph.D. diss., University of Notre Dame, 1998.

Westhelle, Vitor. "Creation Motifs in the Search for a Vital Space." In *Lift Every Voice: Constructing Christian Theologies from the Underside*, eds. Susan Brooks Thistlethwaite and Mary Potter Engel, 128–40. San Francisco: Harper & Row, 1990.

_____. "Labor: A Suggestion for Rethinking the Way of the Christian." *Word & World* III, 2 (Spring 1986): 194–206.

_____. "Luther and Liberation." *Dialog* 25, 1 (Winter 1986): 51–57.

_____. "Luther and Liberation." *Tugon* 8, 1 (1988): 54–71.

_____. "Thinking about Luther in a Submersed Reality (Latin America)." *Lutherjahrbuch*, 1990, ed. Helmar Junghaus, 163–73.

Wilken, Robert L. "The Image of God: A Neglected Doctrine." *Dialog* 28, 4 (Autumn 1989): 292–96.

Wingren, Gustaf. "God's World and the Individual." In *The Gospel as History*, ed. Vilmos Vajta, 43–75. Philadelphia: Fortress Press, 1975.

Wisnefske, Ned. "Living and Dying with Christ: Do We Mean What We Say?" *Word & World* X, 3 (Summer 1990): 254–59.

Yeago, David S. "Gnosticism, Antinomianism and Reformation Theology: Reflections on the Costs of a Construal." *Pro Ecclesia* II, 1 (Winter 1993): 37–49.

_____. "The Promise of God and the Desires of our Hearts." *Lutheran Forum* 30, 2 (May 1996): 21–30.

Church Documents and Studies about Them

Anderson, Per. "In Defense of Unruly Discernment: Moral Deliberation in the ELCA." *Currents in Theology and Mission* 23, 2 (April 1996): 104–18.

Bachmann, E. Theodore, ed. *The Activating Concern: Historical and Theological Basis, 1 Churches and Social Welfare*, 51–62. With an Introduction by Roswell P. Barnes. New York: National Council of the Churches of Christ in the U.S.A., 1955. A statement from "The Lutheran Churches."

Black, Roger H. "The Word of God and Social Responsibility in the Lutheran Church in the United States of America." Unpublished Ph.D. diss., Marquette University, 1996.

Bloomquist, Karen. "Our Church and Social Issues." Chicago: Commission for Church in Society, Evangelical Lutheran Church in America, 1989.

_____. "Moral Deliberation as a Public Witness of the Church." *Theology & Public Policy* III, 1 (Summer 1991): 26–36.

_____. "The Postmodern Challenge of Moral Deliberation in the Evangelical Lutheran Church in America." In *The Church as Communion: Lutheran Contributions to Ecclesiology*, ed. Heinrich Holze, 391–98. Geneva: Lutheran World Federation, 1997.

Childs, James. "The Confession's Impact on Recent Social Ethics." *Lutheran Forum* 14, 2 (Pentecost 1980): 16–22.

A Collection of Responses from ELCA Academicians and Synodical Bishops to: The Church and Human Sexuality: A Lutheran Perspective. First Draft of an ELCA Social Statement. Chicago: Division for Church in Society, Evangelical Lutheran Church in America, 1994. Typescript. Fifty contributions illustrate various approaches to Lutheran ethics.

Cornelsen, Rufus, ed. *Social Statements of the United Lutheran Church in America, 1918–1962*. New York: Board of Social Missions, United Lutheran Church in America, 1962.

Dehsen, Christian D. von. "The Church in Society: Review Essay." *Lutheran Quarterly* IV, 3 (Autumn 1990): 355–65.

Dietz, Reginald. "Eastern Lutheranism in American Society and American Christianity 1870–1914." Unpublished Ph.D. diss., University of Pennsylvania, 1958.

Ellingsen, Mark. *The Cutting Edge: How Churches Speak on Social Issues.* Grand Rapids, Mich.: Eerdmans, 1993. Studies social statements from churches throughout the world written between 1964 and 1985.

Enquist, Roy J., ed. *The Evangelical Lutheran Church in America and Public Policy Advocacy: Papers from a Consultation.* Chicago: Commission for Church in Society, ELCA, 1990. Includes papers on the history of Lutheran advocacy, what advocates do, critiques and analyses, and theological perspectives.

Evangelical Lutheran Church in America Messages:
"Aids and the Church's Ministry of Caring," 1988.
"The Israeli/Palestinian Conflict," 1989.
"A Changing Europe: Peace and the Churches," 1990.
"Homelessness: A Renewal of Commitment," 1990.
"End-of-Life Decisions," 1992.
"Community Violence," 1994.
"Sexuality: Some Common Convictions," 1996.

Evangelical Lutheran Church in America Social Statements:
"Social Statements in the Evangelical Lutheran Church in America: Policies and Procedures,"
    1989 (in effect until 1997).
"Policies and Procedures of the Evangelical Lutheran Church in America for Addressing Social
    Concerns," 1997.
"The Church in Society: A Lutheran Perspective," 1991.
"Abortion," 1991.
"The Death Penalty," 1991.
"Caring for Creation: Vision, Hope, and Justice," 1993.
"Freed in Christ: Race, Ethnicity, and Culture," 1993.
"For Peace in God's World," 1995.

Evangelical Lutheran Church in Canada Social Statements:
"The Public Witness of the Evangelical Lutheran Church in Canada: A Policy on How the
    Church Addresses Social Issues," 1991.
"Horizons of the Reign of God: Discerning the Path of Sustainable Social Economics," 1997.

Geisler, Albert. "Official Pronouncements of the United Lutheran Church in America Relating
    to Certain Moral and Social Problems." Unpublished Ph.D. diss., University of Pittsburgh,
    1941.
Haas, Harold. "The Social Thinking of the United Lutheran Church in America, 1918–1948."
    Unpublished Ph.D. diss., Drew University, 1953. Bibliography.
Inskeep, Kenneth W. "Views on Social Responsibility: The Investment of Pension Funds in the
    Evangelical Lutheran Church in America." *Review of Religious Research* 33, 3 (1992): 270–82.
Johnson, Kent L. "The Church in an Era of Crisis (1933–41)." *Word & World* VIII, 3 (Summer
    1988): 241–51. A study of Sunday school material.
Klein, Christa, with Christian D. Von Dehsen. *Politics and Policy: The Genesis and Theology of Social
    Statements in the Lutheran Church in America.* Philadelphia: Fortress Press, 1989. Includes all the
    social statements from the LCA.
Lentz, Harold H. "History of the Social Gospel in the General Synod of the Lutheran Church
    in America, 1867–1918." Unpublished Ph.D. diss., Yale University, 1943.
Lewis-Small, Elaine Louise. "Church Investments and South Africa: Policy Formulation in the
    Lutheran Church in America, the Southern Baptist Convention, and the United Church of
    Christ (Divestment)." Unpublished Ph.D. diss., Drew University, 1993.
Lorenz, Eckehart, ed. *The Debate on Status Confessionis: Studies in Christian Political Theology.* Geneva:
    Lutheran World Federation, 1983.
Lull, Timothy. "Those 'Conservative' Lutherans." In *Views from the Pews: Christian Beliefs and
    Attitudes,* ed. Roger A. Johnson, 123–42. Philadelphia: Fortress Press, 1983.
Lutz, Charles P. *Public Voice: Social Policy Development in The American Lutheran Church.* Minneapolis:
    ALC, 1987. A description and an appraisal. Lists all the social statements and resolutions
    from the ALC.
Mansbach, Robert Earl. "Church and State: A Critical Evaluation of the Official Social
    Statements and Study Reports (1962–72) of the Lutheran Church in America, in the Light
    of the Augsburg Confession and Luther's Thought." Unpublished Ph.D. diss., University of
    Iowa, 1977.

Manske, Charles Louis. "Luther's Ethics of Social Responsibility as the Criterion for Evaluating the Social-Ethical Statements of the Lutheran Church-Missouri Synod (1959–1971)." Unpublished Ph.D. diss., University of Southern California, 1978. Lists LC-MS statements of these years. Bibliography.

McClure, Kevin Robert. "The Denominational Ministry Strategy: A Rhetorical Study of the Public Sphere." Unpublished Ph.D. diss., Pennsylvania State University, 1992.

McCurley, Foster R. *The Social Ministry of the Church*. Chicago: Evangelical Lutheran Church in America, Division for Social Ministry Organizations, 1989.

Moellering, Ralph Luther. "The Missouri Synod and Social Problems: A Theological and Sociological Analysis of the Reaction to Industrial Tensions, War, and Race Relations from 1917–1941." Unpublished Ph.D. diss., Harvard University, 1964.

Mortensen, Viggo; Jens Holger Schjorring, Prasanna Kumari, and Norman Hjelm, eds. "Responsibility for the World: The Public Role of the LWF." In *From Federation to Communion: The History of the Lutheran World Federation*, 323–44. Minneapolis: Fortress Press, 1997.

Nelson, Paul. "Bioethics and the Lutheran Communion." In *Bioethics Yearbook, V: Theological Developments 1992–1994*, eds. Baruch Brody, Andrew Lustig, and Tristram Engelhardt, Jr., 143–69. Boston: Kluwer Academic Publishers, 1997.

————. "Bioethics in the Lutheran Tradition." In *Bioethics Yearbook, I: Theological Developments 1988–1990*, eds. Baruch Brody, Andrew Lustig, and Tristram Engelhardt, Jr., 119–43. Boston: Kluwer Academic Publishers, 1991.

————. "Lutheran Perspectives on Bioethics." In *Bioethics Yearbook, III: Theological Developments 1990–1992*, eds. Baruch Brody, Andrew Lustig, and Tristram Engelhardt, Jr., 149–84. Boston: Kluwer Academic Publishers, 1993.

————. "Moral Discourse in the Church. A Process Politicized. How Do and Should Lutherans Address Social Ethics?" *Lutheran Forum* 20, 1 (Lent 1986): 19–21.

Neuhaus, Richard John. *Christian Faith and Public Policy: Thinking and Acting in the Courage of Uncertainty*. Minneapolis: Augsburg, 1977.

Niebanck, Richard J. *By What Authority? The Making and Use of Social Statements*. New York: Division for Mission in North America, Lutheran Church in America, 1977.

Pettenger, Roger Wesley. "The Peace Movement of the Augustana Lutheran Church as a Catalyst in the Americanization Process." Unpublished Ph.D. diss., Washington State University, 1987.

Reuss, Carl F., ed. *The Christian in His Social Living*. Minneapolis: Board for Christian Social Action, American Lutheran Church, 1960. A compilation of study and discussion statements from 1948 to 1960.

————. ed. *Conscience and Action: Social Statements of the American Lutheran Church 1961–1970*. Minneapolis: Augsburg Press, 1971.

Scherer, Ross P. "Faith and Social Ministry in American Lutheranism." In *Faith and Social Ministry: Ten Christian Perspectives*, eds. James D. Davidson, C. Lincoln Johnson, and Alan K. Mock, 97–122. Chicago: Loyola University Press, 1990.

Schmid, Byron Lee. "The American Lutheran Church and Public Policy." Unpublished Ph.D. diss., Duke University, 1970.

————, ed. "The Lutheran Churches Speak, 1960–1974: A Bibliography of Social Statements, Study Reports and Testimony by the American Lutheran Church, Lutheran Church in America, Lutheran Church-Missouri Synod, and Lutheran Council in the USA." New York: Lutheran Council in the USA, 1975.

Schneider, Edward. "An Examination of the Social Statements of the American Lutheran Church from 1961 to 1972 from the Perspective of Luther and the Augsburg Confession." Unpublished Ph.D. diss., University of Iowa, 1978.

Sherman, Franklin. "Church Social Pronouncements—Open Questions." In *To Speak or Not to Speak? Proposed Criteria for Public Statements on Violations of Human Rights*, ed. Eckehart Lorenz, 33–40. Geneva: Lutheran World Federation, 1984.

Sleeper, C. Freeman. "The Use of Scripture in Church Social Policy Statements." *Theology & Public Policy* II, 2 (Fall 1990): 47–60.

Social Pronouncements of the Augustana Lutheran Church, 1937–1962. New York: Board of Social Ministry, Lutheran Church in America, 1968.

Stange, Douglas C. "The One Hundred and Twenty-fifth Anniversary of a Fraternal Appeal."
    Concordia Historical Institute Quarterly XL, 1 (April 1967): 43–47. Text of 1842 abolitionist
    appeal from the Franckean Synod.
Svendsbye, Lloyd. "The History of a Developing Social Responsibility Among Lutherans in
    America from 1930 to 1960, with Reference to the American Lutheran Church, the
    Augustana Lutheran Church, the Evangelical Lutheran Church, and the United Lutheran
    Church." Unpublished Th.D. diss., Union Theological Seminary, New York, 1966.

Studies of the Lutheran Ethical Tradition

On the Reformation and the Tradition as a Whole

Allen, J. W. *History of Political Thought in the Sixteenth Century*, 15–34. New York: Barnes & Noble,
    1928. On Luther and Melanchthon.
Althaus, Paul. *The Ethics of Martin Luther*. Trans. from the German and with a Foreword by Robert
    C. Schultz. Philadelphia: Fortress Press, 1972.
Arand, Charles P. "Luther on God Behind the First Commandment." *Lutheran Quarterly* VIII, 4
    (Winter 1994): 397–424.
Atkinson, James. "Lutheranism." In *Dictionary of Ethics, Theology and Society*, eds. Paul Barry Clarke
    and Andrew Linzey, 536–41. New York: Routledge, 1996.
Avis, P. D. L. "Moses and the Magistrate: A Study in the Rise of Protestant Legalism." *Journal of
    Ecclesiastical History* XXVI, 2 (April 1975): 149–72.
Bainton, Roland Herbert. "The Development and Consistency of Luther's Attitude to Religious
    Liberty." *Harvard Theological Review* XXII, 2 (April 1929): 107–50.
Bayer, Oswald. "Luther's Ethics as Pastoral Care." *Lutheran Quarterly* IV, 2 (Summer 1990):
    125–42.
Baylor, Michael J. *Action and Person: Conscience in Late Scholasticism and the Young Luther*. Leiden: E. J.
    Brill, 1977.
Benne, Robert. "Luther, Martin (1483–1546)." In *Encyclopedia of Ethics*, eds. Lawrence Becker and
    Charlotte B. Becker, 755–56. New York: Garland, 1992.
Bergendoff, Conrad. "Christian Love and Public Policy in Luther." *Lutheran Quarterly* XIII, 3
    (August 1961): 218–28.
Berman, Harold. "Conscience and Law: The Lutheran Reformation and the Western Legal
    Tradition." *Journal of Law and Religion* 5:1 (1987): 177–202.
_____, and John Witte Jr. "The Transformation of Western Legal Philosophy in Lutheran
    Germany." *Southern California Law Review* 62, 6 (September 1989): 1575–659.
Bertram, Robert. "The Radical Dialectic Between Faith and Works in Luther's Lectures on
    Galatians (1535)." In *Luther for an Ecumenical Age: Essays in Commemoration of the 450th Anniversary
    of the Reformation*, ed. Carl S. Meyer, 219–41. St. Louis: Concordia Publishing House, 1967.
Bielfeldt, Dennis. "Freedom, Love, and Righteousness in Luther's Sermo de Duplici Iustitia." In
    Freedom as Love in Martin Luther, eds. Bielfeldt and Klaus Schwarzwaller, 19–34. New York:
    Peter Lang, 1995.
Bornkamm, Heinrich. *Luther in Mid-Career, 1521–1530*. Ed. and with a Foreword by Karin
    Bornkamm. Trans. from the German by E. Theodore Bachmann. Philadelphia: Fortress Press,
    1983.
_____. *Luther's World of Thought*. Trans. from the German by Martin H. Bertram. St. Louis:
    Concordia Publishing House, 1958.
_____. *Luther's Doctrine of the Two Kingdoms in the Context of His Theology*. Trans. from the German
    by Karl H. Hertz. Philadelphia: Fortress Press, 1966.
Brady, Thomas A., Jr. "Luther's Social Teaching and the Social Order of His Age." In *The Martin
    Luther Quincentennial*, ed. Gerhard Dunnhaupt, 270–90. Detroit: Wayne State University
    Press, 1985.
Brecht, Martin. "Divine Right and Human Rights in Luther." In *Martin Luther and the Modern Mind:
    Freedom, Conscience, Toleration, Rights*, ed. Manfred Hoffmann, 61–84. Lewiston, N.Y.: Edwin
    Mellen, 1985.
_____. *Martin Luther*. I. *His Road to Reformation, 1483–1521*. II. *Shaping and Defining the Reformation,
    1521–1532*. III. *The Preservation of the Church, 1532–1546*. Trans. from the German by James L.
    Schaaf. Minneapolis: Fortress Press, 1985–1993.

_____. "Luther, Martin." In *The Oxford Encyclopedia of the Reformation*, 2, ed. Hans J. Hillerbrand, 461–67. New York: Oxford University Press, 1996. Bibliography.

Cargill Thompson, W.D.J. *The Political Thought of Martin Luther*, ed. Philip Broadhead. Totowa, N. J.: Barnes & Noble, 1984. Bibliography.

_____. *Studies in the Reformation: Luther to Hooker*, ed. C. W. Dugmore, 3–59. London: The Athlone Press, 1980. "Luther and the Right of Resistance to the Emperor" and "The 'Two Kingdoms' and the 'Two Regiments': Some Problems of Luther's 'Zwei-Reiche-Lehre'."

Carlson, Edgar. "Luther's Conception of Government." *Church History* XV, 4 (December 1946): 257–70.

_____. *The Reinterpretation of Luther*. Philadelphia: Muhlenberg Press, 1958.

Cranz, F. Edward. *An Essay on the Development of Luther's Thought on Justice, Law, and Society*. Eds. Gerald Christianson and Thomas M. Izbicki with a new Introduction by Scott Hendrix. Mifflintown, Pa.: Sigler Press, 1997. Originally published in 1959.

Douglass, Jane Dempsey. "The Image of God in Women as Seen by Luther and Calvin." In *The Image of God: Gender Models in Judaeo-Christian Tradition*, ed. Kari Elisabeth Borresen, 236–66. Minneapolis: Fortress Press, 1995.

Dowey, Edward A. "Law in Luther and Calvin." *Theology Today* XLI, 2 (July 1984): 146–53.

Ebeling, Gerhard. *Luther: An Introduction to His Thought*, 110–209. Trans. from the German by R. A. Wilson. Philadelphia: Fortress Press, 1972.

Edwards, Mark U. "The Reception of Luther's Understanding of Freedom in the Early Modern Period." *Lutherjahrbuch, 1995*, ed. Helmar Junghans, 104–20.

Erling, Bernhard. "The Role of Law in How a Christian Becomes What He/She Is." In *Freedom as Love in Martin Luther*, eds. Dennis D. Bielfeldt and Klaus Schwarzwaller, 63–77. New York: Peter Lang, 1995.

Figgis, John Neville. "Luther and Machiavelli." In *Studies of Political Thought from Gerson to Grotius, 1414–1625*, 55–93. Lecture delivered in 1900. Cambridge: University Press, 1956.

Fischer, Robert H. "The Reasonable Luther." In *Reformation Studies: Essays in Honor of Roland H. Bainton*, ed. Franklin Littell, 30–45. Richmond, Va.: John Knox Press, 1962.

Forell, George W. *The Augsburg Confession: A Contemporary Commentary*. Minneapolis: Augsburg Publishing House, 1968. For general audience.

_____. *Faith Active in Love: An Investigation of the Principles Underlying Luther's Social Ethics*. Minneapolis: Augsburg Publishing House, 1954. Critique of dualistic interpretations of Luther.

_____. "Freedom as Love: Luther's Treatise on Good Works." In *Freedom as Love in Martin Luther*, eds. Dennis D. Bielfeldt and Klaus Schwarzwaller, 79–84. New York: Peter Lang, 1995.

_____. *History of Christian Ethics, 1: From the New Testament to Augustine*. Minneapolis: Augsburg Publishing House, 1979.

_____. "Luther's Conception of Natural Orders." *Lutheran Church Quarterly* XLIII, 2 (July 1945): 160–77.

_____, and James F. McCue. "Political Order and Vocation in the Augsburg Confession." In *Confessing One Faith*, ed. Forell and McCue, 322–33. Minneapolis: Augsburg Press, 1982. By a Lutheran and a Roman Catholic.

Gerrish, B. A. *Grace and Reason: A Study in the Theology of Luther*. 1962. Reprint. Chicago: University of Chicago Press, 1979.

_____. "Martin Luther." In *The Encyclopedia of Philosophy*, V, ed. Paul Edwards, 109–13. New York: Macmillan, 1967.

Grislis, Egil. "The Foundation of Creative Freedom in Martin Luther's 'Von den Guten Werken' (1520)." In *Freedom as Love in Martin Luther*, eds. Dennis D. Bielfeldt and Klaus Schwarzwaller, 85–103. New York: Peter Lang, 1995.

_____. "The Meaning of Good Works: Luther and the Anabaptists." *Word & World* III, 2 (Spring 1986): 170–80.

Gritsch, Eric W. *Fortress Introduction to Lutheranism*. Minneapolis: Fortress Press, 1994.

_____. "Martin Luther's Commentary on Gal 5,2–24, 1519 (WA 2, 574–97) and Sermon on Gal 4, 1–7, 1522 (WA 10 I 1, 325–78)." In *Freedom as Love in Martin Luther*, eds. Dennis D. Bielfeldt and Klaus Schwarzwaller, 105–11. New York: Peter Lang, 1995.

Gualtieri, Antonio R. "Soteriology and Ethics in Martin Luther." In *Encounters with Luther: Papers from the McGill Luther Symposium, 1983*, ed. Edward J. Furcha, 67–84. Montreal, 1984.

Gustafson, James M. *Christ and the Moral Life*, 116–49. New York: Harper & Row, 1968. Discusses Luther under "Jesus Christ, the Justifier."

Hall, Thomas Cuming. *History of Ethics within Organized Christianity*, 468–504. New York: Scribner, 1910. On Luther and Melanchthon.

Harran, Marilyn J. "Luther and Freedom of Thought." In *Martin Luther and the Modern Mind: Freedom, Conscience, Toleration, Rights*, ed. Manfred Hoffmann, 191–236. Lewiston, N.Y.: Edwin Mellen, 1985.

Headley, John M. "Luther and the Problem of Secularization." *Journal of the American Academy of Religion* LV, 1 (Spring 1987): 21–37.

Hendrix, Scott. "Christianizing Domestic Relations: Women and Marriage in Johann Freder's Dialogus dem Ehestand zu Ehren (1545)." *Sixteenth Century Journal* 23, 2 (1992): 251–66.

_____. "Masculinity and Patriarchy in Reformation Germany." *Journal of the History of Ideas* 56, 2 (1995): 177–93.

Heinecken, Martin J. "Luther and the 'Orders of Creation' in Relation to a Doctrine of Work and Vocation." *Lutheran Quarterly* IV, 4 (November 1952): 393–414.

Hinlicky, Paul R. "Luther Against the Contempt of Women." *Lutheran Quarterly* II, 4 (Winter 1988): 515–30.

Hoffman, Bengt R. "Lutheran Spirituality." In *Spiritual Traditions for the Contemporary Church*, eds. Robin Maas and Gabriel O'Donnell, 145–61. Nashville: Abingdon Press, 1990.

_____. "On the Relationship Between Mystical Faith and Moral Life in Luther's Thought." In *Encounter with Luther*, 1, ed. Eric W. Gritsch, 236–58. Gettysburg, Pa.: Institute for Luther Studies, 1980.

Hoffman, Manfred. "Reformation and Toleration." In *Martin Luther and the Modern Mind: Freedom, Conscience, Toleration, Rights*, ed. Manfred Hoffmann, 85–124. Lewiston, N.Y.: Edwin Mellen, 1985.

Holl, Karl. *The Cultural Significance of the Reformation*. Trans. by Karl and Barbara Hertz and John H. Lichtblau. New York: Meridian Books, 1959.

_____. *The Reconstruction of Morality*, eds. James Luther Adams & Walter F. Bense. Trans. from the German by Fred W. Meuser and Walter R. Wietzke. Minneapolis: Augsburg Publishing House, 1979.

Hopfl, Harro. "Luther, Martin." In *The Blackwell Encyclopaedia of Political Thought*, eds. David Miller, Janet Coleman, William Connolly, and Alan Ryan, 297–99. New York: Basil Blackwell, 1987.

Huegli, Albert G., ed. *Church and State Under God*. St. Louis: Concordia Publishing House, 1964. Includes Lewis W. Spitz on the Reformation, H. Richard Klann and William H. Lehmann on developments since the Reformation, and Martin E. Marty on contemporary alternative approaches.

Hütter, Reinhard. "Martin Luther and Johannes Dietenberger on 'Good Works'." *Lutheran Quarterly* VI, 2 (Summer 1992): 127–52.

Jacobsen, H. K. "Lutheran Ethics." In *New Dictionary of Christian Ethics & Pastoral Theology*, eds. David J. Atkinson and David H. Field, 560–61. Downers Grove, Ill.: InterVarsity Press, 1995.

Jenson, Robert W. "An Ontology of Freedom in the 'De Servo Arbitrio' of Luther." In *Freedom as Love in Martin Luther*, eds. Dennis D. Bielfeldt and Klaus Schwarzwaller, 113–18. New York: Peter Lang, 1995.

Keen, Ralph. *Divine and Human Authority in Reformation Thought: German Theologians on Political Order, 1520–1555*. Nieuwkoop: B. De Graaf, 1997.

_____. "The Moral World of Philip Melanchthon." Unpublished Ph.D. diss., University of Chicago, 1990.

_____. "Political Authority and Ecclesiology in Melanchthon's 'De Ecclesiae Autoritate'." *Church History* 65, 1 (March 1996): 1–14.

Kinder, Ernst. "Agape in Luther." In *The Philosophy and Theology of Anders Nygren*, ed. Charles W. Kegley, 203–19. Carbondale, Ill.: Southern Illinois University Press, 1970.

Klann, Richard. "Lutheran Ethics." In *Baker's Dictionary of Christian Ethics*, ed. Carl F. H. Henry, 399–400. Grand Rapids, Mich.: Baker, 1973.

_____. "Luther's Political Ethics: An Investigation of His Principles." Unpublished Ph.D. diss., Columbia University, 1951.

Kolb, Robert. *Nikolaus von Amsdorf (1483–1565): Popular Polemics in the Preservation of Luther's Legacy*, 123–80. Nieuwkoop: B. De Graaf, 1978. Controversy on the meaning of good works.

———. "Niebuhr's 'Christ and Culture in Paradox' Revisited." *Lutheran Quarterly* X, 3 (Autumn 1996): 259–80.

Kolden, Marc. "Luther on Vocation." *Word & World* III, 4 (Fall 1983): 382–91.

Kvam, Kristen E. "Luther, Eve, and Theological Anthropology: Reassessing the Reformer's Response to the *Frauenfrage*." Unpublished Ph.D. diss., Emory University, 1992. Bibliography.

Lage, Dietmar. *Martin Luther's Christology and Ethics*. Lewiston, N.Y.: Edwin Mellen Press, 1990.

Lazareth, William H. *Luther on the Christian Home: An Application of the Social Ethics of the Reformation*. Philadelphia: Muhlenberg Press, 1960.

Letts, Harold C., ed. *The Lutheran Heritage*. Vol. Two. *Christian Social Responsibility*. Philadelphia: Muhlenberg Press, 1957. Jerald C. Brauer writes on the Reformation; Theodore G. Tappert on orthodoxism, pietism, and rationalism; E. Theodore Bachmann on the rise of modern society; and Howard Hong on liberalism.

Lienhard, Marc. "Luther and Beginnings of the Reformation." In *Christian Spirituality: High Middle Ages and Reformation*, ed. Jill Raitt in collaboration with Bernard McGinn and John Meyendorff, 268–99. New York: Crossroad, 1987.

Lindbeck, George. "Luther on Law in an Ecumenical Context." *Dialog* 22, 4 (Fall 1983). 270–74.

———. "Martin Luther and the Rabbinic Mind." In *Understanding the Rabbinic Mind: Essays on the Hermeneutic of Max Kadushin*, ed. Peter Ochs, 141–64. Atlanta: Scholars Press, 1990.

Lindberg, Carter. *Beyond Charity: Reformation Initiatives for the Poor*. Minneapolis: Fortress Press, 1993. Bibliography.

———. "Justice and Injustice in Luther's Judgment of 'Holiness Movements.' " In *Luther's Ecumenical Significance*, eds. Peter Manns and Harding Meyer, 161–82. Philadelphia: Fortress Press, 1984. On Luther's *simul*.

———. "Martin Luther: Copernican Revolution or Ecumenical Bridge." *Una Sancta* 24, 1 (1967): 31–38. On agape in Luther.

———. "The Ministry and Vocation of the Baptized." *Lutheran Quarterly* VI, 4 (Winter 1992): 385–402.

———. "Reformation Initiatives for Social Welfare: Luther's Influence at Leisnig." In *The Annual of the Society of Christian Ethics 1987*, ed. D. M. Yeager, 79–99. Washington, D. C.: Georgetown University Press, 1987.

———. "Theology and Politics: Luther the Radical and Munster the Reactionary." *Encounter* 37, 4 (Autumn 1976): 356–71.

Loewenich, Walter von. *Luther's Theology of the Cross*. Trans. from the German by Herbert J. A. Bouman. Minneapolis: Augsburg Publishing House, 1976.

Lohse, Bernhard. "Conscience and Authority in Luther." In *Luther and the Dawn of the Modern Era*, ed. H. A. Oberman, 158–83. Leiden: E. J. Brill, 1974.

———. *Martin Luther: An Introduction to His Life and Work*. Philadelphia: Fortress Press, 1980. An overview of issues in Luther research, including the two kingdoms (186–92). Bibliography.

Lotz, David W. "*Sola Scriptura*: Luther on Biblical Authority." *Interpretation* XXXV, 3 (July 1981): 258–73.

Ludolphy, Ingetraut. "Luther's Attitude Toward Women." In *Encounters with Luther: Papers from the McGill Luther Symposium, 1983*, ed. Edward J. Furcha, 67–84. Montreal, 1984.

Lund, N. J. "Lutheran Ethics." In *Encyclopedia of Biblical and Christian Ethics*, rev. ed., ed. R. K. Harrison, 241–42. Nashville: Thomas Nelson, 1992.

MacIntyre, Alasdair. *A Short History of Ethics: A History of Moral Philosophy from the Homeric Age to the Twentieth Century*, 121–27. New York: Macmillian, 1966. On Luther.

Mannermaa, Tuomo. "*Theosis* as a Subject of Finnish Luther Research." *Pro Ecclesia* IV, 4 (Winter 1994): 37–48.

Maurer, Wilhelm. *Historical Commentary on the Augsburg Confession*. Trans. from the German by H. George Anderson. Philadelphia: Fortress Press, 1986.

McNeill, John T. "Natural Law in the Teaching of the Reformers." *Journal of Religion* XXVI, 3 (July 1946): 168–82.

_____. "Natural Law in the Thought of Luther." *Church History* X, 3 (1941): 211–27.

Mehl, Roger. *Catholic Ethics and Protestant Ethics*, 19–31. Trans. from the French by James H. Farley. Philadelphia: Westminster Press, 1971. On Luther.

Mildenberger, Friedrich. *Theology of the Lutheran Confessions*, ed. Robert C. Schultz, 83–94, 121–31, 142–47, 162–73, 221–30. Trans. from the German by Erwin L. Lueker. Philadelphia: Fortress Press, 1986.

Mitchell, Joshua. "The Equality of All under the One in Luther and Rousseau: Thoughts on Christianity and Political Theory." *Journal of Religion* 72, 3 (July 1992): 351–65.

_____. "Luther and Hobbes on the Question: Who Was Moses, Who Was Christ?" *Journal of Politics* 53, 3 (August 1991): 676–700.

Mueller, William A. *Church and State in Luther and Calvin: A Comparative Study*, 3–69. Nashville: Broadman, 1954.

Mühlen, Karl-Heinz zur. "Law: Theological Understanding of Law." In *The Oxford Encyclopedia of the Reformation*, 2, ed. Hans J. Hillerbrand, 404–8. New York: Oxford University Press, 1996. Bibliography.

_____. "Two Kingdoms." In *The Oxford Encyclopedia of the Reformation*, 4, ed. Hans J. Hillerbrand, 184–88. New York: Oxford University Press, 1996.

Nestingen, James Arne. "*The Catechism's* Simul." *Word & World* III, 4 (Fall 1983): 364–72.

_____. "Luther: The Death and Resurrection of Moses." *Dialog* 22, 4 (Fall 1983): 275–79.

Niebuhr, H. Richard. *Christ and Culture*, 116–48. New York: Harper & Brothers, 1951. Views Luther in terms of "Christ and Culture in Paradox."

Nygren, Anders. "Luther's Doctrine of the Two Kingdoms." *Ecumenical Review* I, 3 (Spring 1949): 301–10.

Oberman, Heiko A. *Luther: Man Between God and the Devil*. Trans. from the German by Eileen Walliser-Schwarzbart. New Haven: Yale University Press, 1989.

Olson, Jeannine E. *One Ministry, Many Roles: Deacons and Deaconesses Through the Centuries*. St. Louis: Concordia Publishing House, 1992.

Ozment, Steven. "Luther's Political Legacy." In *Protestants: The Birth of a Revolution*, 118–48. New York: Doubleday, 1992.

Pauck, Wilhelm. "Luther and Butzer." In *The Heritage of the Reformation*, 73–84. New York: Oxford University Press, 1961.

_____. "Luther and Melanchthon." In *Luther and Melanchthon in the History and Theology of the Reformation*, ed. Vilmos Vajta, 13–31. Philadelphia: Muhlenberg Press, 1961.

Persaud, Winston. "Globalization and Fragmentation: Las Casas and Luther in Context." *Dialog* 36, 1 (Winter 1997): 25–31.

Pesch, Otto Hermann. "Free by Faith: Luther's Contribution to a Theological Anthropology." In *Martin Luther and the Modern Mind: Freedom, Conscience, Toleration, Rights*, ed. Manfred Hoffmann, 23–60. Lewiston, N.Y.: Edwin Mellen, 1985.

Pinomaa, Lennart. *Faith Victorious: An Introduction to Luther's Theology*. Trans. from the Finnish by Walter J. Kukkonen. Philadelphia: Fortress Press, 1963. Includes chapters on justification and sanctification, the foundation of social ethics, and vocation.

Raines, John C. "Luther's Two Kingdoms and the Desacralization of Ethics." *Encounter* 31, 2 (Spring 1970): 121–48.

Reed, Stephen D. "The Decalogue in Luther's Large Catechism." *Dialog* 22, 4 (Fall 1983): 264–69.

Rupp, E. Gordon. *Martin Luther: Hitler's Cause or Cure?: In Reply to Peter F. Wiener*. London: Lutterworth Press, 1945.

Sanders, Thomas G. *Protestant Concepts of Church and State: Historical Backgrounds and Approaches for the Future*, 23–74. New York: Holt, Rinehart and Winston, 1964. On Luther and Lutheranism.

Schlink, Edmund. *Theology of the Lutheran Confessions*, 67–140, 226–69. Trans. from the German by Paul F. Koehneke and Herbert J. A. Bouman. Philadelphia: Fortress Press, 1961. On "Law and Gospel" and "Civil and Ecclesiastical Government."

Schwarz, Hans. *Truth Faith in the True God: An Introduction to Luther's Life and Thought*. Trans. from the German by Mark William Worthing. Minneapolis: Augsburg Fortress, 1996.

Senn, Frank C. "Lutheran Spirituality." In *Protestant Spiritual Traditions*, ed. Frank C. Senn, 9–54. New York: Paulist Press, 1986.

Skinner, Quentin. "Absolutism and the Lutheran Reformation." In *The Foundations of Modern Political Thought*, 2: *The Age of the Reformation*, 3–108. Cambridge: Cambridge University Press, 1978.

Sockness, Brent W. "Luther's Two Kingdoms Revisited: A Response to Reinhold Niebuhr's Criticism of Luther." *Journal of Religious Ethics* 20, 1 (Spring 1992): 93–110.

Stephenson, John R. "The Two Governments and the Two Kingdoms in Luther's Thought." *Scottish Journal of Theology* 34, 4 (1981): 321–37.

Spitz, Lewis W. "The Christian in Church and State." In *Martin Luther and the Modern Mind: Freedom, Conscience, Toleration, Rights*, ed. Manfred Hoffmann, 125–62. Lewiston, N.Y.: Edwin Mellen, 1985.

Steinmetz, David. *Luther in Context*, 112–25. Bloomington: Indiana University Press, 1986. On the two kingdoms.

Strauss, Gerald. "Three Kinds of 'Christian Freedom': Law, Liberty, and License." In *The Martin Luther Quincentennial*, ed. Gerhard Dunnhaupt, 291–306. Detroit: Wayne State University Press, 1985.

Strohl, Jane E. "Luther's Invocavit Sermons." In *Freedom as Love in Martin Luther*, eds. Dennis D. Bielfeldt and Klaus Schwarzwaller, 159–66. New York: Peter Lang, 1995.

Tiefel, Hans O. "The Ethics of Gospel and Law: Aspects of the Barth-Luther Debate." Unpublished Ph.D. diss., Yale University, 1968.

———. "The Relationship between Salvation and Ethics in Luther's Theology." *Lutheran Quarterly* XXV, 3 (August 1973): 284–94.

Toulin, John. "Reformation Studies." In *The Oxford Encyclopedia of the Reformation*, 3, ed. Hans J. Hillerbrand, 398–410. New York: Oxford University Press, 1996. Bibliography.

Tracy, James D., ed. *Luther and the Modern State in Germany*. Kirksville, Mo.: Sixteenth Century Journal Publishers, 1986. Essays by Tracy, Heinz Schilling, Thomas A. Brady, Jr., Eric W. Gritsch, Karlheinz Blaschke, and Brent O. Peterson.

Trigg, Jonathan D. *Baptism in the Theology of Martin Luther*, 151–73. New York: E. J. Brill, 1994. On baptism and the Christian life.

Troeltsch, Ernst. *The Social Teaching of the Christian Churches*, II, 465–576. Trans. from the German by Olive Wyon. New York: Harper & Row, 1960. On Luther and the Lutheran tradition.

Wagner, Walter H. "Luther and the Positive Use of the Law." *Journal of Religious History* 11, 1 (1980): 45–63.

Waring, Luther H. *The Political Theories of Martin Luther*. New York: G. P. Putnam's Sons, 1910.

Watson, Philip S. "Luther's Doctrine of Vocation." *Scottish Journal of Theology* II, 4 (December 1949): 364–77.

Wengert, Timothy J. *Human Freedom, Christian Righteousness: Philip Melanchthon's Exegetical Dispute with Erasmus of Rotterdam*. New York: Oxford University, 1997.

Williams, George Huntston. "German Mysticism in the Polarization of Ethical Behavior in Luther and the Anabaptists." *The Mennonite Quarterly Review* XLVIII, 3 (July 1974): 275–304.

Wingren, Gustaf. *Luther on Vocation*. Trans. from the Swedish by Carl C. Rasmussen. Philadelphia: Muhlenberg Press, 1957. Thorough study of Luther's concept.

Wolin, Sheldon S. *Politics and Vision: Continuity and Innovation in Western Political Thought*, 141–64. Boston: Little, Brown and Company, 1960. On Luther.

Ziemke, Donald C. *Love for the Neighbor in Luther's Theology: The Development of His Thought 1512–1529*. Minneapolis: Augsburg Press, 1963.

On Later Persons and Developments

Addison, Duane LeRoy. "The Changing Understanding of the Role of the Church in Ecumenical Social Thought, 1925–1937." Unpublished Ph.D. diss., Yale University, 1966.

Bakken, Peter W. "The Ecology of Grace: Ultimacy and Environmental Ethics in Aldo Leopold and Joseph Sittler." Unpublished Ph.D. diss, University of Chicago, 1991.

———, compiler. *Joseph A. Sittler: A Bibliography*. Madison, Wis.: [The author], 1994.

Barker, H. Gaylon. "Bonhoeffer, Luther, and *Theologia Crucis*." *Dialog* 34, 1 (Winter 1995): 10–17.

Baum, Gregory. *The Church for Others: Protestant Theology in Communist East Germany*. Grand Rapids, Mich.: Eerdmans, 1996.

Bergendoff, Conrad. "The Ethical Thought of Einar Billing." In *The Scope of Grace*, ed. Philip J. Hefner, 279–306. Philadelphia: Fortress, 1964.

Burgess, John P. *The East German Church and the End of Communism*. New York: Oxford University Press, 1997.

Burtness, James H. *Shaping the Future: The Ethics of Dietrich Bonhoeffer*. Philadelphia: Fortress Press, 1985. Bibliographical essay.

Childs, James M. "The Significance of Wolfhart Pannenberg for Contemporary Theology." *Trinity Seminary Review* 13, 2 (Fall 1991): 61–68.

Christianson, Gerald. "J.H. Wichern and the Rise of the Lutheran Social Institution." *Lutheran Quarterly* XIX, 4 (November 1967): 357–70.

Ericksen, Robert P. *Theologians Under Hitler: Gerhard Kittel, Paul Althaus and Emanuel Hirsch*. New Haven: Yale University Press, 1985. A critical study of three Lutheran theologians.

Evjen, John O. *The Life of J. H. W. Stuckenberg*. Minneapolis: Lutheran Free Church Publishing, 1938.

Fischer, Robert H. "Passavant: Pioneer in the Church's Ministry of Mercy." *Lutheran Forum* 28, 2 (May 1994): 42–44.

Forde, Gerhard O. *The Law-Gospel Debate: An Interpretation of Its Historical Development*. Minneapolis: Augsburg Publishing House, 1969. On nineteenth and twentieth century developments.

Forstman, Jack. *Christian Faith in Dark Times: Theological Conflicts in the Shadow of Hitler*. Louisville, Ky.: Westminster/John Knox Press, 1992. Studies controversies among six theologians (five Lutheran), three of whom opposed Hitler and three of whom welcomed him in 1933.

Gerberding, G. H. *Life and Letters of W. A. Passavant, D. D.* Greenville, Pa.: Young Lutheran, 1906.

Gluchman, Vasil. *Slovak Lutheran Social Ethics*. Lewiston, N.Y.: Edwin Mellen, 1997. Focuses on writings from the twentieth century, particularly since 1948.

Graebner, Alan. "Immigrant Acculturation in the Missouri Synod, 1917–1929." Unpublished Ph.D. diss., Columbia University, 1964. Bibliography.

Grenholm, Carl-Henric. *Christian Social Ethics in a Revolutionary Age: An Analysis of the Social Ethics of John C. Bennett, Heinz-Dietrich Wendland and Richard Shaull*. Uppsala: Verbum, 1973.

Hall, Thor. "Nygren's Ethics." In *The Philosophy and Theology of Anders Nygren*, ed. Charles W. Kegley, 263–81. Carbondale, Ill.: Southern Illinois University Press, 1970.

Heinecken, Martin J. "Pietism, Ethics of." In *The Westminster Dictionary of Christian Ethics*, eds. James F. Childress and John Macquarrie, 475–76. Philadelphia: Westminster Press, 1986.

Hoehn, Richard A. "J. H. W. Stuckenberg: American Lutheranism's First Social Ethicist." *Dialog* 22, 1 (Winter 1983): 15–20.

Hoffman, Bengt R. *Christian Social Thought in India, 1947–1962: An Evaluation*. Bangalore: Christian Institute for the Study of Religion and Society, 1967.

Jackson, Gregory Lee. *Prophetic Voice for the Kingdom: The Impact of Alvin Daniel Mattson upon the Social Consciousness of the Augustana Synod*. Rock Island, Ill.: Augustana Historical Society, 1986.

Johnson, Jeff G. *Black Christians: The Untold Lutheran Story*. St. Louis: Concordia Publishing House, 1991.

Johnson, Karl E., Jr., and Joseph A Romeo. "Jehu Jones (1786–1852), The First African American Lutheran Minister." *Lutheran Quarterly* X, 4 (Winter 1996): 425–44.

Kegel, James David. "A Church Come of Age: American Lutheranism and National Socialism, The German Church Conflict, and the Reconstitution of the Church: 1933–1948." Unpublished Th.D. diss., Lutheran School of Theology at Chicago, 1988.

Klemperer, Klemens von. "Beyond Luther? Dietrich Bonhoeffer and Resistance Against National Socialism." *Pro Ecclesia* VI, 2 (Spring 1994): 184–98.

Kohlhoff, Dean. "Lutherans and the New Deal: The Missouri Synod as a Case Study." *Essays and Reports*, X, 1982, 99–115. St. Louis: The Lutheran Historical Conference, 1984.

Kruger, Günter. "Johann Christoph Blumhardt (1805–1880): A Man for the Kingdom." *Currents in Theology and Mission* 23, 6 (December 1996): 427–41.

Krusche, Günter. "The Church Between Accommodation and Refusal: The Significance of the Lutheran Doctrine of the 'Two Kingdoms' for the Churches of the German Democratic Republic." *Religion, State, and Society* 22, 2 (1994): 323–32.

Kuenning, Paul P. *The Rise and Fall of American Lutheran Pietism: The Rejection of an Activist Heritage*. Macon, Ga.: Mercer, 1988. Bibliography.

Lambert, Lake. "Ethics and Ecclesiology in Pittsburgh." *Lutheran Quarterly* VI, 2 (Summer 1992): 153–74.

Lebacqz, Karen. "Alien Dignity: The Legacy of Helmut Thielicke." In *Religion and Medical Ethics: Looking Back, Looking Forward*, ed. Allen Verhey, 44–60. Grand Rapids, Mich.: Eerdmans, 1996.

Lehmann, Hartmut. *Martin Luther in the American Imagination*. Munchen: W. Fink, 1988.

Lotz, David W. *Ritschl & Luther: A Fresh Perspective on Albrecht Ritschl's Theology in the Light of His Luther Study*, 127–38. Nashville: Abingdon Press, 1974. The relation of faith to ethics in Ritschl and Luther.

Lovin, Robin W. *Christian Faith and Public Choices: The Social Ethics of Barth, Brunner and Bonhoeffer*. Philadelphia: Fortress Press, 1984.

Macquarrie, John. "Ritschlian Ethics." In *The Westminster Dictionary of Christian Ethics*, eds. James F. Childress and Macquarrie, 559–60. Philadelphia: Westminster Press, 1986.

Nielsen, Paul. "Vocation, Responsibility, and the Ethics of Dietrich Bonhoeffer." Unpublished Ph.D. diss., University of Chicago, 1998.

Noll, Mark A. "The Lutheran Difference." *First Things* 20 (February 1992): 31–40.

Outka, Gene. "Equality and Individuality: Thoughts on Two Themes in Kierkegaard." *Journal of Religious Ethics* 10, 2 (Fall 1982): 171–203.

_____. "Kierkegaardian Ethics." In *The Westminster Dictionary of Christian Ethics*, eds. James F. Childress and John Macquarrie, 337–39. Philadelphia: Westminster Press, 1986.

_____. "Religious and Moral Duty: Notes on *Fear and Trembling*." In *Religion and Morality: A Collection of Essays*, 204–54, eds. Outka and John P. Reeder Jr. Garden City, N. Y.: Doubleday, 1973.

Rasmussen, Larry L. *Dietrich Bonhoeffer: Reality and Resistance*. Nashville: Abingdon Press, 1972.

Reimer, James A. *The Emanuel Hirsch and Paul Tillich Debate: A Study in the Political Ramifications of Theology*. Lewiston, N.Y.: Edwin Mellen, 1989.

Rohrbough, Faith E. "The Political Maturation of Henry Melchior Muhlenberg." *Lutheran Quarterly* X, 4 (Winter 1996): 385–406.

Root, Michael John. "Creation and Redemption: A Study of Their Interrelation, with Special Reference to the Theology of Regin Prenter." Unpublished Ph.D. diss., Yale University, 1979. Includes discussion of Luther.

Scholder, Klaus. *The Churches and the Third Reich, One: 1918–1934; Two: 1934 Barmen and Rome*. Trans. from the German by John Bowden. Philadelphia: Fortress Press, 1988.

Scott, David. A. "The Trinity and Ethics: The Thought of Helmut Thielicke." *Lutheran Quarterly* XXIX, 1 (February 1977): 3–12.

Scott-Thomas, Elaine. "Lutherans and the Social Gospel in Canada in the First Quarter of the Twentieth Century." *Consensus* 22, 1 (1995): 9–27.

Sernett, Milton C. "Lutheran Abolitionism in New York State: A Problem in Historical Explication." In *Essays and Reports, X, 1982*, 1–15. St. Louis: The Lutheran Historical Conference, 1984.

Shanahan, William O. *German Protestants Face the Social Question, 1: The Conservative Phase, 1815–1871*. Notre Dame: University of Notre Dame Press, 1954.

Siemon-Netto, Uwe. *The Fabricated Luther: The Rise and Fall of the Shriver Myth*. St. Louis: Concordia Publishing House, 1993.

_____. "Luther and Hitler: Friends or Foes?" *Dialog* 35, 3 (Summer 1996): 188–92.

_____. "Luther Vilified—Luther Vindicated, 1." *Lutheran Forum* 27, 2 (Pentecost 1993): 33–39.

_____. "Luther Vilified—Luther Vindicated, 2." *Lutheran Forum* 27, 3 (Reformation 1993): 42–49.

Simpson, Gary. "Reciprocity and Political Theology: Wolfhart Pannenberg and Three Americans—John B. Cobb, Jr., Carl E. Braaten, and Richard John Neuhaus." Unpublished Ph.D. diss., Christ Seminary-Seminex, 1983.

Sittler, Joseph. "Social Gospel." In *The Encyclopedia of the Lutheran Church*, III, ed. Julius Bodensieck, 2197–98. Minneapolis: Augsburg Publishing House, 1965.

Sockness, Brent W. "Ethics as Fundamental Theology: The Function of Ethics in the Theology of Wilhelm Herrmann." In *Annual of the Society of Christian Ethics, 1992*, ed. Harlan Beckley, 75–96. Washington, D.C.: Georgetown University, 1992.

————. "Troeltsch's 'Practical Christian Ethics': the Heidelberg Lectures (1911/12)." In *Annual of the Society of Christian Ethics*, 1997, 17, eds. John Kelsay and Summer B. Twiss, 71–94. Washington, D.C.: Georgetown University Press, 1997.

Stange, Douglas C. *Radicalism for Humanity: A Study of Lutheran Abolitionism*. St. Louis: Oliver Slave, 1970.

Strieter, Thomas. "Contemporary Two-Kingdoms and Governances Thinking for Today's World: A Critical Assessment of Types of Interpretation of the Two-Kingdoms and Governances Model, Especially Within American Lutheranism." Unpublished Th.D. diss., Lutheran School of Theology at Chicago, 1986. Studies eight theologians. Bibliography.

Stumme, John R. *Socialism in Theological Perspective: A Study of Paul Tillich 1918–1933*. Missoula, Montana: Scholars Press, 1978.

Watt, Alan. "Two Approaches to Social Action in 19th Century Lutheranism." *Trinity Seminary Review* 4 (1982):32–43.

Weborg, John. "Pietism: 'The Fire of God Which . . . Flames in the Heart of Germany'." In *Protestant Spiritual Traditions*, ed. Frank Senn, 9–54. New York: Paulist Press, 1986.

Index